POLARIS

POLARIS

SUBMARINES, MISSILES, THE US NAVY AND THE ROYAL NAVY

JOHN BOYES

FONTHILL

First published in Great Britain in 2025 by
Fonthill
An imprint of
Pen & Sword Books Ltd
Yorkshire – Philadelphia
www.fonthill.media

ISBN 978-1-78155-931-4

A CIP catalogue record for this book
is available from the British Library.

Typeset in Sabon LT 10/13
Typeset by Fonthill
Printed and bound in the UK by CPI Group (UK) Ltd, Croydon, CR0 4YY

The Publisher's authorised representative in the EU for product
safety is Authorised Rep Compliance Ltd., Ground Floor,
71 Lower Baggot Street, Dublin D02 P593, Ireland.
www.arccompliance.com

For a complete list of Pen & Sword titles please contact
PEN & SWORD BOOKS LIMITED
47 Church Street, Barnsley, South Yorkshire, S70 2AS, England
E-mail: enquiries@pen-and-sword.co.uk
Website: www.pen-and-sword.co.uk

Or
PEN AND SWORD BOOKS
1950 Lawrence Rd, Havertown, PA 19083, USA
E-mail: Uspen-and-sword@casematepublishers.com
Website: www.penandswordbooks.com

Foreword

I am greatly honoured to have two senior naval officers who have contributed the Foreword to my book. Between them, they provide a valuable introduction to the role of the UK deterrent from both a management point of view and an operational one. Admiral Sir George Zambellas GCB, DSC, DL, in 2006, as a rear admiral, was appointed as chief of staff (transformation), leading the change programme to design and deliver the fleet's new approach to the generation of maritime capability. He was first sea lord and chief of naval staff from 2013 to 2016 during a period of much change within the Royal Navy. Commodore Toby Elliott served in Polaris submarines on three separate occasions, in 1968 first in HMS *Repulse* as the most junior officer in the port crew, standing by the boat during build and through to the first two operational patrols. Later, he served as the second-in-command HMS *Renown* (port crew), and then after promotion to commander, he served as the port crew commanding officer (1980–82). His first appointment as a captain was as the Captain SM Tenth Submarine Squadron then consisting of the four Polaris submarines with the first of the Trident-class submarines just starting to emerge from the builder's yard.

Writing a comprehensive book about the concept, components, and delivery of submarine-based nuclear deterrence is an unenviable task. At best, it is both complicated and subtle. At worst, it is a continuous and giddy mix of politics, people, and process, and it requires the unwavering management and commitment of all three elements. And, at every turn, there is the nagging doubt about the reliability of the systems, the certainty of the people, longevity in political support, and the risk of counter-detection.

Nevertheless, by dint of uninterrupted delivery over many decades, and no counter-detection, it is reasonable to claim that the concept is proven. Prime ministers, on their first hours in office, are required to understand the nuclear firing chain, and their direct and indirect responsibility. It is a deeply personal matter which they take very seriously indeed.

Meanwhile, the day-to-day management of the whole UK nuclear submarine fleet, attack and ballistic, remains an unending leadership challenge. Despite the relentless march of technology into weapons and sensors, and the promises of artificial intelligence, the dependency on human expertise and intuition dominates the management effort. That said, UK strategic nuclear deterrence, founded on principles that the UK government has deemed unchanged since the end of the Cold War, is an evolving responsibility and faces new challenges over scale and geography.

Then there is the absolute centrality of the transatlantic relationship. The United Kingdom and the United States have been bound together on a technical, nuclear, and intelligence journey for many, many decades. That relationship is of clear mutual benefit—a marriage of genuine strategic convenience rather than the suggestion of artificially imbalanced cooperation sometimes implied by the term 'special relationship'. Technical, nuclear, and intelligence matters, by their nature, invoke very significant security and secrecy. The 'need to know' has served both sides well but does not allow much light to be shone on the inner workings.

That transatlantic mutual benefit is complex. It affects every layer of the submarine-based nuclear deterrence concept—strategic, operational, and tactical. It builds on transferred technology, and the shared expertise and ambition built into the nuclear attack submarine partnership. The common strategic ambition is best described as 'the Cold War need'—the pursuance of an ambition to command the undersea, without which no maritime contribution to the joint and combined battlespace is complete. The common operational ambition is the optimised and coordinated capability delivery between two nations. The common tactical ambition is the sharing of standards, processes, and procedures that allow interoperable patterns, crew exchanges, and common technical support. And the end of the Cold War has done nothing to reduce the need to maintain authority in the undersea domain. The simple fact is that, for very many decades, major nations have independently concluded that a commitment to undersea maritime strategic nuclear forces is an essential arm of their national security.

The move from Polaris to Trident, from *Resolution* to *Vanguard* to *Dreadnought*, is further reinforcement of the nature of continuity in the UK–US strategic partnership. The fact that the Trident replacement plan set UK acceptance and testing of the Trident Common Missile Compartment in the new *Dreadnought* class before the US, says everything.

As the first sea lord between 2013 and 2016, though the period is otherwise noted for the naming of two new super carriers, the acquisition of their F-35B jets, new warships and support shipping, helicopters, and equipment for the Royal Marines, the dominant leadership and management challenge then, and now, was and is centred on nuclear submarines matters, and mostly their manning requirements and supply chain support.

In truth, navies without a long-range submarine capability are lesser navies. The AUKUS agreement is a case in point: if you want to influence the undersea warfare domain in the Pacific, then you need the equivalent of the UK partnership in the North Atlantic during the Cold War. But the process is long and expensive and requires the deep-seated and lasting commitments previously described.

In this book, John Boyes has not shied away from the 'unenviable task', as I put it. The Polaris journey was the formative submarine deterrence journey and captured most or all of the complex challenges, and John has dug deep to get the detail as right as he can. Submariners build professional authority by understanding the detail, applying it assiduously where necessary, but using creatively where possible. In the dangerous world of the deep, the room for error is almost none.

Admiral Sir George Zambellas GCB, DSC, DL

The nuclear age has its genesis in the Second World War. Post-1945, and in short order, the Soviet Union was going to go its own way, and so began the nuclear weapons arms race between the USA and subsequently Great Britain and France on the one hand and the Soviet Union on the other—the Cold War.

Taking the V2 as its model, early thinking suggested that a nuclear armed ballistic missile could be launched from surface ships and submarines as well as from the air and land-based launch systems, but it was some years before the USA brought this concept to reality. The author's account of how the nuclear submarine armed with the Polaris missile came into service, both in the USN and in the RN, is multifaceted and hugely complex; it is also fascinating both as Cold War thinking and as a monument to the many on both sides of the Atlantic involved in such an achievement, but above all to the goodwill which existed and still exists between the two great naval services involved.

Since 1969, the Royal Navy has been responsible for the maintenance of the UK national nuclear deterrent, with Polaris eventually giving way to Trident-class SSBNs, fitted with the strategic missile systems and launched from these nuclear-powered submarines. The submarines have carried out a continuous at-sea patrol cycle, with at least one SSBN on patrol and at the required readiness to launch at all times. The continuous UK at-sea independent nuclear deterrent (CASD) is allocated defence priority 1 status and requires a high level of support from the Cabinet Office downwards, as well as the most assiduously maintained operational standards not least by those responsible for the custody and control of the SSBNs and their nuclear weapons. In particular, SSBN crews and their families bear the brunt of lengthy deployments and all that this entails, but go about their business without complaint, as is the tradition of the Silent Service.

The days of Polaris are long past, while the UK Trident SSBNs are now coming up to the time when they too need to be replaced. Politically highly charged and important decisions have been or are about to be taken at the highest government level about the new build submarines and the weapons system. The USN has recently announced that the D5 missile system will be extended in service and fitted in its new SSBN fleet, and it must be that the RN goes the same way—actually there is no alternative.

Be in no doubt, replacing Trident will stretch the UK's industrial capacity and capability to the full. In the meantime, President Putin has uttered some pretty loose talk about the use of tactical nuclear weapons in Ukraine; this helps focus minds, and will also do much to help in the understanding of why there is a need to continue with the deterrent force.

Commodore Toby Elliott OBE

Acknowledgements

Thanks go to Anne Jensen (News Corp), John Coker, Hannah Morgan-Donovan and Jemma Byrne (West Wickham Library), Brian Burnell, Karl Rubis, the late Roy Dommett for his untiring assistance, the late Kate Pyne for being ever-patient, helpful, and encouraging, and the late John Harlow, Admiral Sir George Zambellas, and Cdre Toby Elliott for contributing the Foreword, Cdr Mike Jones and Lt Cdr Nick Wraith both of HMS *Renown*'s starboard crew, Lt Michael Dobson, Lt Stephen Upright (their naval ranks at the time I spoke to them)—the latter later to command the Trident submarine HMS *Vengeance*—Dr Richard Moore and the various contributions made over a number of years by participants at the BROHP and British Nuclear History meetings at Charterhouse, Janis Jorgensen of the USNI for great help with the oral history transcripts. The Castle Museum: Dunoon, Paul Jackman, Beatrice Okoro (National Maritime Museum), Jonathan Aylen, Wendy Gulley (US Navy Submarine Museum), Wayne Cocroft (English Heritage), James W. Draper, Randal Coppola and Rupert the Space Armadillo (Cape Canaveral Air Force Station), Katharine Thomson (Churchill Papers), Ed Allen (Westcott VP), John Chambers, Sgt Paul Marr (JSCSC), and Michael Lennon for photographs, Jeff Jefford whose remarkable knowledge of matters RAF always amazes me, Jamie Hardwick, Jay Slater, Jasper Hadman, and Joshua Greenland at Fonthill Media. The Scotland Shop (Polaris tartan). Also to my wife Sylvia for learning more about Polaris (as well as Thor and Blue Streak) than she ever thought necessary. For those whom I may have omitted, my apologies. And finally, but by no means least, Mark Burgess for his untiring work on the many excellent diagrams and profiles within the book which can be viewed in colour on my website. Thank you all.

Many years ago, when I worked for a major motor manufacturer, the sales director (who I have always believed was formerly in the SBS), regional manager, and myself shared an interest in military matters and this led to a periodic exchange of tricky questions to pose to the other two. One of my questions was: 'when was an arachnid cut in half to become a president of the United

States?' This, perhaps predictably, proved impossible to answer and led to the sales director later asking, I hope in jest, if I could be sectioned under the Mental Health Act! The answer lies within this book.

John Boyes
West Wickham
September 2024
Ukballisticmissiles.co.uk

Contents

Glossary

A1, 2, 3	Polaris Missile nomenclature generally used by the UK
AX	Polaris Development Missile
A1X, A2X, A3X	Preproduction Test Missiles
A-1, -2, -3	Polaris nomenclature generally used by the US
ABM	Anti-Ballistic Missile
ABMA	Army Ballistic Missile Agency
ADM	Admiral (US Navy)
AEC	Atomic Energy Commission
AERE	Atomic Energy Research Establishment
AICBM	Advanced Intercontinental Ballistic Missile
ARDC	Air Research and Development Command
BNDSG	British Nuclear Deterrent Study Group ('Benders')
BuAer	Bureau of Aeronautics
BuOrd	Bureau of Ordnance
BuShips	Bureau of Ships
C-3	Poseidon Missile
C-4	Trident I Missile
CAS	Chief of the Air Staff
CASD	Continuous at Sea Deterrent
CCP	Chinese Communist Party
CDS	Chief of the Defence Staff
CG	Centre of Gravity
CGWL	Controller Guided Weapons and Electronics
CIGS	Chief of the Imperial General Staff
CINCLANTFLT	Commander in Chief Atlantic Fleet
CINCPAC	Commander in Chief Pacific Command
CINC WF	Commander in Chief Western Fleet
CND	Campaign for Nuclear Disarmament
COMSUBPAC	Commander, Submarine Force, US Pacific Fleet

CPAE	Controller of Production (Atomic Energy)
D-5	Trident II Missile
DASO	Demonstration and Shakedown Operation
DDR&E	Director of Defense Research and Engineering
DoD	Department of Defense
DSRV	Deep Submergence Rescue Vehicle
DPT	Dreadnought Project Team/Director Polaris Technical
EB	Electric Boat (Division of General Electric)
ECCM	Electronic Counter-Countermeasure
EMP	Electromagnetic Pulse
ETR	Eastern Test Range (Cape Canaveral)
FADM	Fleet Admiral (US Navy)
FBM	Fleet Ballistic Missile
FOSNI	Flag Officer Scotland and Northern Ireland
GE	General Electric
GUPPY	Greater Underwater Propulsion Power Program
HAS	Hydrazine Actuation System
HEL	Hunting Engineering Limited
HTP	High Test Peroxide
ICBM	Intercontinental Ballistic Missile
IFE	Improved Front End (Chevaline)
IL	Instrumentation Laboratory (MIT)
IRBM	Intermediate Range Ballistic Missile
JANBMC	Joint Army Navy Ballistic Missile Committee
JCS	Joint Chiefs of Staff
JSTPS	Joint Strategic Targeting Planning Staff
LASL	Los Alamos Scientific Laboratory
LMSC	Lockheed Missiles and Space Corporation
LMSD	Lockheed Missile Systems Division
MARV	Manoeuvrable Re-entry Vehicle
MDA	Mutual Defence Agreement
MED	Manhattan Engineer District
MIRV	Multiple Independently Targeted Re-entry Vehicle
MIT	Massachusetts Institute of Technology
MOD/MoD	Ministry of Defence
MRV	Multiple Re-entry Vehicle
NOTU	Naval Ordnance Test Unit
NSC	National Security Council
NSTL	National Strategic Target List
NTS	Nevada Test Site
OSD	Office of the Secretary of Defense
OSD-BMC	Office of the Secretary of Defense Ballistic Missile Committee

PAC	Penetration Aid Carrier
PEM	Performance Evaluation Missile
PRESG	Polaris Re-entry Systems Group
PX	Penetration Aid (Penaid)
QRA	Quick Reaction Alert
RADM	Rear Admiral (US Navy). *cf*. Royal Navy's RAdm
RAF	Royal Air Force
RCNC	Royal Corps of Naval Constructors
ReB	Re-entry Body (*cf*. RV) (naval terminology)
REM	Rocket Engine Module
RNAD	Royal Naval Armaments Depot
RV	Re-entry Vehicle (*cf*. ReB) (air force terminology)
SAC	Strategic Air Command
SCB	Ship Characteristics Board
SEAC	South East Asia Command
SecDef	Secretary of Defense
SecNav	Secretary of the Navy
SFR	Submarine Fleet Reactor
SINS	Ship's Inertial Navigation System
SIOP	Single Integrated Operational Plan
SLBM	Submarine-Launched Ballistic Missile
SM	Submarine Squadron (Royal Navy)
SMS	Strategic Missile Squadron
SP/SPO	Special Projects Office (used interchangeably)
SSBN	Ship, Submersible, Ballistic, Nuclear (Ballistic Missile Submarine)
SSGN	Ship, Submersible, Guided Missile, Nuclear (Cruise Missile)
SSM	Surface-to-Surface Missile
SSN	Ship, Submersible, Nuclear (Attack/Fleet Submarine)
STAFF	Stellar Acquisition Flight Feasibility
STS	Strategic Target System
SUBRON	Submarine Squadron
SWTTEU	Special Weapons Tactical Test and Evaluation Unit
TCHD	Truck Cargo Heavy Duty
TCP	Technological Capabilities Panel
TCPU	Twin Chamber Propulsion Unit
UCRL	University of California Radiation Laboratory
ULMS	Undersea Long-range Missile System
USAAF	United States Army Air Force
USAF	United States Air Force
USAREUR	US Army Europe
VADM	Vice Admiral (US Navy)
WDD	Western Development Division

| WSMR | White Sands Missile Range |
| WVA | *Wasserbau Versuchsanstalte* |

Some of the terminology used by both nations was at times interchangeable and inconsistent. For example, I have standardised in this text the designation Polaris A3 referring to UK missiles and A-3 for the equivalent US missile. I have used RV for US re-entry vehicles and ReB for the equivalent UK re-entry body. For clarity, for US Navy ranks I have used capitalised abbreviations. This is based only on the most commonly used term by each nation and does not seek to be definitive. Where British and American spelling of a word differs, I have used the spelling appropriate to the nation concerned.

Introduction

We have discovered the most terrible bomb in the history of the world.

President Truman's diary
25 July 1945

*For the stark reality of nuclear power, no man who lives with that
responsibility can speak or think lightly of the terrible forces that could be
unleashed on the World.*

Lyndon B. Johnson on becoming president following the assassination of
John F. Kennedy

At 7:28 a.m. on 8 September 1944, a German Army V2 ballistic missile was
launched from the sanctuary of a mobile site in the Ardennes Forest near to St
Vith.[1] Its target was Paris. Despite a successful launch, the missile never reached
its destination, apparently disintegrating on re-entering the atmosphere, a not
unknown problem which was never fully resolved during the war. However, a
second missile, launched some three hours later, landed on the Parisian suburb of
Maisons-Alfort, killing or injuring around thirty people. Without any warning,
the age of the strategic missile had arrived. That evening, the first V2 launched by
Flak Batterie 485 from Wassenar, north of The Hague, reached London, landing
on Staveley Road in Chiswick.

At 8:15 a.m. (local time) on 6 August 1945, the first atom bomb was dropped
on the unsuspecting and totally unprepared Japanese city of Hiroshima. The
bomb, a 9,700-lb uranium bomb called 'Little Boy', was released from a Boeing
B-29-45-MO Superfortress, commanded by Col. Paul W. Tibbets and named
Enola Gay after his mother.[2] The bomb was released from an altitude of 32,000
feet, and forty-three seconds later it detonated at a height of 1,900 feet above the
city. The yield was estimated to be around 15 Kt.[3] This represented, at a stroke,

a 2,000-fold increase in the lethality of a single bomb. Ninety per cent of the buildings in Hiroshima were damaged or destroyed. Some 70,000 people are thought to have died immediately from the explosion, with an eventual toll of up to 200,000 taking into account the longer-term effects of the radiation.

At 11:00 a.m. (EST) on 17 January 1955, the submarine USS *Nautilus* (SSN-571), under the command of CDR Eugene P. (Dennis) Wilkinson, slipped her berth at the Groton Connecticut shipyard of the Electric Boat (EB) Division of the General Dynamics Corporation to start her maiden voyage. She transmitted the now historic message which included the phrase 'under way on nuclear power...'

Signal from USS *Nautilus* 'Underway on Nuclear Power'.

* * * * *

Three different technologies: two of them forged in the crucible of the Second World War and the third a less explosive by-product of the very technology released over Hiroshima. In combination, they were to create a weapon of deterrence for the US and thereafter also for the UK, France, the Soviet Union, and later China and India—almost silent, essentially undetectable, generally invisible, and with an immense destructive capability far exceeding all the bombs dropped in the Second World War. This was to be the SSBN—Ship Submersible Ballistic Nuclear.[4] The weapon system on board the first US Navy SSBN, USS *George Washington* (SSBN-598), when she sailed from Charleston, South Carolina, on 15 November 1960 on her first deterrent patrol, was called Polaris. A fitting name reflecting the star, fixed in the heavens, that had guided navigators for centuries.

* * * * *

In 1945, the Allied armies advanced into Germany from east and west as the enemy's infrastructure disintegrated. Only the still greatly feared SS seemed able to impose some discipline, which still made unauthorised travel potentially dangerous. Many sought to surrender to the western Allies as their fate under the Soviets was at the very least considered uncertain and rumours of the ruthlessness of the advancing Soviet armies inspired little comfort. Among those who sought sanctuary with the western Allies as Germany capitulated was a team of scientists and engineers who had been responsible for the development of one of Germany's so-called 'revenge weapons' (*Vergeltungswaffen*), the V2 ballistic missile.

Alone among the warring nations, Germany had made considerable progress in developing two unmanned missiles. The first of the revenge weapons to achieve operational capability was the Fieseler Fi 103 cruise missile, better known as the V1. Powered by an Argus As-014 pulsejet and relatively simple to put into mass production, these flying bombs, being unmanned, outflanked defensive planning which assumed that intruders would take evasive action against anti-aircraft measures. Despite a concentrated bombing offensive against the launch sites in northern France, of 10,492 V1s launched, around a third escaped the defences and just under 2,500 hit the London Civil Defence Area—a far better ratio than had been achieved in conventional bombing tactics in the early war years. The genesis of the second weapon, the A-4/V2 ballistic missile can be traced to amateur rocket experiments that had taken place in Germany in the 1930s. Robert Goddard in America and Konstantin Tsiolkovsky in Russia had seen the advantages of liquid fuels, but it was the German Army that took the technology and developed an operational missile, thereby setting a course for a revolution in post-war weaponry.

Also disintegrating was the common cause that had cemented the Allies together. A terminally ill President Franklin D. Roosevelt, Prime Minister Winston Churchill, and *Vozhd* (Вождь: Leader) Joseph Stalin met at Yalta in early February 1945. Though tolerating Churchill's eloquent verbosity, Roosevelt sought to deal mainly with Stalin to seek a lasting, if utopian, peace. Many Americans were not unwilling to support this idea as they disliked Britain's overseas possessions and, seeing that Britain was nearing bankruptcy, sought to create a supremacy over British post-war ambitions.

1

The Nuclear Age

When there is mutual fear, men think twice before they make aggression upon one another.

Hermocrates of Syracuse to the Sicilian Envoys at Gela, 424 BC

The manufacture of a British atomic bomb was ... essential for our defence.

Prime Minister Clement Attlee

It was in the 1930s that the first possibilities of harnessing the power of the atom were being mooted. In 1939, the concept of a nuclear ship power plant was fully discussed between the nuclear scientist Dr Enrico Fermi and the US Navy to the extent that the Naval Research Laboratory (NRL) initiated preliminary work on a reactor design, which might ultimately be used as the power plant in a submarine. By the time that the United States joined the war, however, the increasing concern of the navy was the production of conventional ships, not toying with advanced theoretical ideas. Research did continue, spurred on by the belief that Germany could also be developing an atomic weapon. Meanwhile, the American atom bomb project was set up in great secrecy in June 1942 with the code name 'Development of Substitute Materials Project' at the Syracuse Engineer District, commanded by Col. James C. Marshall. As the project grew, Marshall moved it to the Manhattan Engineer District (MED) and changed the name to the Manhattan Project. Marshall in due course was replaced by Col. Leslie R. 'Dick' Groves, who was known for getting jobs done, although he had personally hoped for command of a combat engineer unit. Wartime circumstances mitigated against full-scale research into anything other than a weapon of immense destructive power. The successful Allied D-Day landings in Normandy in June 1944 promoted a confidence that hostilities in Europe would soon be over, and this shifted the emphasis to the wider possibilities of atomic research and the resulting range of benefits. The US government therefore formed the Tolman Committee, whose brief was to identify and recommend the path for future development of atomic energy in the US.

The NRL in Washington had been one of the participants in the Manhattan Project and was fortunate in having on its staff two eminent physicists, Drs Philip Abelson and Ross Gunn. Although not directly involved with the bomb project, they had already co-operated in the development of an isotope separation process, and both believed in the viability of the principle of a nuclear submarine. As part of their investigations, the Tolman Committee members had a meeting with staff from the NRL. Both Abelson and Gunn in their evidence spoke strongly in favour of a nuclear submarine programme, actively endorsed by the laboratory's director, Rear Admiral Alexander H. Van Keuren. The representations made by the three obviously bore some fruit as, in the committee's final report, a recommendation was made to promote research and development into a nuclear power plant suitable for the propulsion of naval vessels in general, although it fell short of actually identifying the submarine as a possible priority vessel for such use.

* * * * *

Of all the Air Force's faults, its greatest has always been the fact that it made its work seem too easy.

General Henry H. 'Hap' Arnold, Commanding General, USAAF

Regrettably, however, the navy was lethargic in its commitment to nuclear propulsion, perhaps understandable in a post-war environment when the number of ships was being substantially cut back and the prospects of forthcoming years of peace reduced the apparent need for a show of force. The Cold War was yet to come. This was despite the fact that the USAF—which in 1947 had gained its independence from the army under whose wing it had operated in the Second World War—had, with the development of Strategic Air Command (SAC), willingly adopted the nuclear role under its charismatic commander-in-chief, General Curtis E. LeMay, considered by many to be the pre-eminent combat commander in the Second World War.[1,2] It was an independence long awaited by airmen who had jealously eyed the autonomy enjoyed by Britain's Royal Air Force (RAF). The air force believed that it had won the war by dropping the two atom bombs and this led to the doctrine of air-centric war, which was to antagonise the navy and reopen wounds that had been inflicted in the 1930s. In President Roosevelt, the navy had a sympathetic supporter born of his time as assistant secretary to the navy during the First World War. In President Harry Truman, things were somewhat different. At his 1949 inauguration, 'a giant air armada like none ever seen over Washington roared across the sky, some seven hundred planes, including transports like those supplying Berlin and five gigantic B-36 bombers that had flown, nonstop, 2,000 miles from Texas'.[3] In the White House, Roosevelt's pictures of naval scenes were replaced with a series of prints of early airplanes.[4]

Although receiving US Navy Distinguished Civilian Service Awards in 1945 for the parts that they played in the Manhattan Project, Abelson and Gunn found the navy's attitude to nuclear development to be increasingly obstructive and both scientists left the laboratory in 1947. The navy's nuclear propulsion programme was therefore left leaderless until, almost by chance, it found a supporter without whose help and forceful persuasion the first nuclear submarine, USS *Nautilus*, would never have sailed by 1955. The man in question, the 'father' of the nuclear submarine, was Captain Hyman G. Rickover.

In 1906, weary of anti-Jewish sentiment in the town of Maków in Russian-controlled Poland, Rickover's parents emigrated to the US when their son, Hyman, was only six. Deciding to make the navy his career, he was nominated for the US Naval Academy by his senator, Adolph J. Sabath, and was duly commissioned in June 1922. Despite a relatively unremarkable operational wartime career, during which he had failed to achieve the two benchmarks of naval success— command at sea and performance under fire—it was not until the latter half of the war that he came to prominence as the chief of the Bureau of Ships' (BuShips) electrical section. In this role, Rickover had shown an abrasive determination to achieve his objective almost at any cost, a characteristic that he maintained for the rest of his life. However, this was not an approach that was guaranteed to have the universal backing of his superior officers, and even after the unqualified success of the nuclear submarine programme, it was an attitude that nearly cost him his promotion to the rank of rear admiral and his retention in the navy. To say that Rickover was unconventional is somewhat of an understatement. The British government's chief scientific adviser, Sir Solly Zuckerman, who along with fellow military scientist Dr Frank Panton were the only British citizens Rickover allowed into his office, described him as 'one of the most outstanding military technologists of his age', but he was also one of the most disliked officers in the US Navy, and in due course by some of those in the Royal Navy as well, seeing his superiors wedded to worn out traditions which inhibited progress.[5] He was parsimonious when it came to personal items. Brown lino covered his office floor, patched and re-patched as necessary.

On the cessation of hostilities, the large US fleet was no longer needed, and by 1946, the number of its personnel had halved, a traditional post-war policy born of American suspicions of retaining a standing military force. Thus, Rickover found himself in the somewhat unrewarding occupation of mothballing a large part of the US fleet in a variety of naval facilities on the United States' western seaboard. It was a job that required meticulous administration to ensure that the warships could be brought back to readiness in a short time should the need arise—as was proved when a number of the ships were reactivated for the Korean War. However, it was almost by chance that during a visit to Washington, Rickover heard of the planned navy involvement in a prototype nuclear reactor to be built at Oak Ridge, an atomic research facility in Clinch River Valley, Tennessee. The Manhattan Project team, some already harbouring doubts about the moral ethics of further development of the bomb, nevertheless showed no firm commitment to a full-scale reactor either. The modest interest showed by the navy was purely for an experimental power plant for an unspecified surface vessel—an operational vessel was not a serious consideration. For the Oak Ridge project, the navy had agreed to the secondment of four officers under the leadership of Capt. Henry 'Harry' Burris. Rickover sought a meeting with BuShips to request consideration for his own involvement in the programme. It does not seem that he had devoted any particular thought prior to this to the question of nuclear propulsion. He may just have seen it as the type of venture at which he could excel and would also enjoy. Nevertheless, he immediately set out to study the various reports prepared by the navy and paid particular attention to the Abelson proposals for a nuclear submarine. This report included an assessment of the wartime German Walter Type XXVI U-boat with its innovative perhydrol equipment removed and theoretically replaced with a nuclear power plant. He also came across a proposal of December 1945 made by Commodore Henry A. Schade, then director of the NRL, in which, based on studies undertaken by Gunn, he outlined a complete nuclear research and development programme.

Rickover's lack of practical knowledge, however, caused BuShips, while being sympathetic to his request for involvement, to decide that first of all he should attend the Massachusetts Institute of Technology (MIT) for a three-year course on nuclear physics. Fortunately for Rickover, and also ultimately for the nuclear submarine itself, the assistant chief at BuShips was Vice Admiral Earle Watkins Mills, under whom Rickover had served during his Second World War time at the bureau. Mills respected Rickover's abilities and, sensing that Oak Ridge would not be an easy posting because of the expected opposition to the project, he replaced Burris with Rickover. The four officers who were to form the Naval Group at Oak Ridge were Lt Cdr James M. Dunford, Lt Cdr Miles A. Libbey, Lt Cdr Louis H. Roddis Jr, and Lt Raymond 'Ray' Dick, the latter a brilliant US Navy Reserve officer who had volunteered for frogman duty during the war. Roddis had already come face to face with the power of the atom as, when the call came to report to Oak Ridge, he was at Bikini Atoll as part of the US Navy team taking part in the post-war atom bomb tests.

The war had seen considerable advances in anti-submarine technology. Destroyers equipped with ASDIC and sonar escorted the convoys. Long-range maritime patrol aircraft such as the Liberator, Sunderland, and Catalina provided much-needed air cover and exploited the submarines' significant remaining shortcoming, the need to surface on a regular basis to run the diesel engines to recharge the batteries which powered the electric motors used to provide drive when submerged. Contrary to popular opinion, submarines were really submersibles spending most of their time on the surface, a factor which determined their shape: optimised for surface running. While on the surface, a submarine was particularly vulnerable, subject to visual sighting and also detection by radar. The challenge to develop a true submarine was one that had proved difficult to solve as there was no realistic way of charging the batteries other than by an air-breathing engine. However, the simple extension of a pipe above the water so as to expose only it and not the whole vessel seems in retrospect an idea so obvious that it was surprising that it was not adopted earlier. It was a Dutch naval officer, *Kaptein-Luitenant* Jan Wichers, who first proposed the idea in the 1930s. His 'air mast' design was used in the Dutch O21 class first built in 1937. When, along with other units of the Dutch Navy, four of these submarines escaped to Britain in 1940, the Royal Navy, puzzlingly, removed the air mast equipment. Although these Dutch vessels had eluded capture, three others were incomplete but were subsequently commissioned into the *Kriegsmarine*. Much of their support was left behind, including spare parts for the air masts. Fortunately, it was not until 1943 that the Germans understood the significance of the pipes they had discovered in Rotterdam, but it did provide a form of solution to the regular need to surface.

Despite not commanding a submarine, Rickover's early service in submarines *S-9* and *S-48*, when as engineering officer in the latter, his swift actions averted what could have been a fatal battery explosion, stood him in good stead. He was acutely aware of the practical and operational problems faced by the frequent necessity to surface, and this caused him to think more and more of the Abelson report and its implications for the development of the true submarine limited only by the physical duration of its crew.

In May 1946, Rickover went to Washington to the headquarters of the Manhattan Project knowing that since the army controlled the project, his dream of a nuclear submarine would have to be played tactfully—not one of his greatest attributes—alongside the specific reason for the Oak Ridge programme: the mere research into nuclear reactors in much more non-specific terms. He and his four officers formed the 'Naval Group' at the Manhattan Engineer District and despite instructions to them that they should make individual reports to Washington, Rickover sensed that only as an integrated team would any hope of a positive result emerge from the group. The navy itself seemed divided and confused in its perception of its nuclear needs. Even as the Naval Group was being formed, its main interest seemed to lie in the remote Pacific Bikini Atoll site where development tests of the atomic bomb were taking place. As the bomb became more compact in size, the ability of carrier-borne aircraft to deliver it meant that the navy wanted to keep its toe in the door to ensure that SAC did not have the monopoly of carrying this awesome and prestigious weapon.

Unencumbered by such lofty considerations of service prestige, private enterprise was slowly becoming aware of the potentially lucrative profits to be made from this new energy source. Clearly there was no prospect of making such profits from atomic weapons, so the obvious commercial path to follow was the development of nuclear reactors. GE therefore decided to take the lead that the navy seemed unable to initiate when they approached the service with a proposal to formulate studies for a 'propulsion plant suitable for a naval vessel'. The vessel in question was interpreted as a destroyer type. Mills and Rickover were impressed with the proposals and requested the Manhattan District, still the overseer of all atomic research, to authorise the contract. The district agreed, and in planning the contract with GE, also allowed them to participate in the operation of the Knolls Atomic Power Laboratory, which was at that time being set up at Schenectady. The navy saw the contract as divorced from the operation of the Naval Group and so set up, under BuShips, its own nuclear power branch. Capt. Albert G. Mumma led this group and the original Oak Ridge nominee, Burris, was appointed to liaise with GE (Mumma had not endorsed Mills's appointment of Rickover over Burris to the Naval Group). Rickover expressed concern over these developments which he saw as a division of an already limited operation into two groups that were bound to find it difficult to co-operate with each other. Furthermore, the nuclear power branch did not possess the necessary security clearance to allow access to many of the Manhattan District's files. Being an overall army-administered operation, inter-service rivalry too was bound to ensure that the army's virtual monopoly of advanced atomic information was restricted to a minority of the other services' interests.

Rickover skilfully used the army's involvement in the district to his advantage by observing, in response to criticism of his activities by the nuclear power branch, that his secondment to Oak Ridge placed him and the other members of the Naval Group under army control. The Naval Group was, however, in no doubt as to whom their ultimate benefactors were and sent weekly progress reports to Mills. They viewed the operation of the Oak Ridge project with mixed feelings. On the one hand, they saw that the production of what they wanted, a naval nuclear reactor, was entirely feasible—indeed, there seemed no reason to suppose that a reactor small enough to fit into the hull of a submarine could not be developed very quickly given the will to do so and the required funds. On the other hand, the overall interest of those at Oak Ridge still seemed to be directed towards theoretical rather than practical results.

An even more confusing situation arose with the reorganisation of the existing US atomic industry and the creation, on 1 January 1947, of the Atomic Energy Commission (AEC). The Manhattan District was terminated, and the AEC assumed management of Oak Ridge. Suddenly the Naval Group's days seemed to be numbered. The advent of atomic weapons had created new capabilities in managing conflict and had potentially placed enormous power in the hands of the newly created USAF, the only service at that time capable of delivering atomic weapons on the enemy. The passing of the National Security Act in July 1947 further strengthened civilian control of the armed forces, and this also extended to the control of atomic weapons. In a letter of 6 August to Secretary of the Navy (SecNav) James V. Forrestal, shortly before he was promoted to the newly defined post of secretary of defense, Truman advised, 'I do not feel justified to order the transfer of the [atomic weapons] stockpiles to the armed services.' As a result of this decision, 'efforts were concentrated within the [Department of Defense], with the assistance of the [AEC], to improve to the maximum, the plans for emergency transfer of weapons … using the complicated transfer machinery [to] ensure that weapons were made available to the armed forces and placed in usable position in the shortest possible time'. The civilian element could not be ignored.

Things were scarcely better for the Nuclear Power Branch. GE was directing its attention to the commercially more attractive development of a breeder reactor and found little difficulty in scaling down its involvement in the naval reactor programme. Rickover determined nonetheless to produce one final report from his Naval Group. He and his fellow officers embarked on a comprehensive series of visits to AEC laboratories including, on 15 August 1947, a visit to Los Alamos. Here Rickover met Dr Edward Teller. Teller had been closely involved in the development of the atomic bomb and was leading the team that went on to produce the 'Super'—the thermonuclear hydrogen bomb (H-bomb). He was therefore capable of exerting considerable influence within the commission. Teller, described by some as someone who would fervently promote his ideas regardless of their flaws, was intrigued by the proposals that Rickover outlined to him, and he undertook to assist in every way possible to advance the Naval Group's ideas within the AEC and also by direct approach to the DoD.

Mills received the group's final report along with a detailed summary of work undertaken to date. Two specific recommendations were made. Firstly, the commitment to a naval reactor of water-cooled design for submarine use— development for other naval uses would thereafter not be so difficult. Secondly, and here he was clearly referring to his difficulties with the Nuclear Power Branch, that future development be handled by one specific team of officers representing the navy within the AEC and responsible for all naval nuclear matters. BuShips, which had a wide-ranging portfolio covering ship design construction and maintenance, however, rejected the report, despite the strong representation made by Teller. The Naval Group now had no further duties, and it was therefore disbanded. While it was not difficult to assign the four officers to other duties, Rickover presented more of a problem. By then, he almost certainly knew more about nuclear energy and its potential naval application than anyone else in the navy and yet a position for him within the Nuclear Power Branch could hardly be seen as a workable possibility. Initially it was agreed to retain him at Oak Ridge to work on the declassification of project documentation. Mills, still sympathetic to the captain's cause and recognising the degree of knowledge that he possessed, created a new post of 'special assistant for nuclear matter to the chief of BuShips' and thus he effectively appointed Rickover to be special assistant to himself. Almost certainly unwittingly, he had created the necessary infrastructure that would lead to the nuclear submarine.

Rickover lost little time in using the somewhat nebulous definition of his official duties to reassess the state of current reactor work. He quickly ascertained that there was almost total stagnation in all aspects of naval reactor research. Discreet approaches to certain staff at Oak Ridge revealed that they too were concerned for the future of their work, which was receiving little support from the senior ranks of the AEC. These scientists had been Rickover's colleagues when he was in the Naval Group, and they had already discussed in principle the basic design for the required submarine reactor. This design was fundamental to any reactor and so if serious work was to be started on a reactor it could, at least initially, be discussed as general reactor research work. The Oak Ridge staff, sensing a more secure future for themselves with the attractive possibility of an 'end product', accepted Rickover's proposals with enthusiasm.

Now sensing some realistic hope of obtaining a suitable reactor, Rickover knew that he had next to persuade the navy to commit itself to a nuclear submarine programme. But his optimism was tempered by knowing it was impossible to keep from the AEC the nature of the change in the Oak Ridge project. While initially they expressed concern at what had taken place, after further consideration, they informed BuShips that they would agree to a limited continuation of work. Otherwise, it would be their intention to order the termination of the Oak Ridge project. The AEC's now unequivocal preference for improved atomic weapons meant that few of the funds available would find their way to a naval reactor programme which many saw as a mere, perhaps even an annoying, distraction. They therefore determined that Oak Ridge would be closed by the end of 1947 and in future the Argonne Laboratory, situated west of Chicago, would undertake all reactor research. This fact in itself would cause an inevitable interruption in what was already a somewhat tenuous project.

Undaunted by what was now potentially a major setback, Rickover directed his attention towards the navy itself. If they could identify the need for nuclear submarines and indicated an intention to order them, the AEC would be forced into developing a suitable reactor because, legally, no other agency could undertake the work. Fortunately aware that his single-mindedness often caused him to overlook the question of diplomatic niceties, Rickover requested the assistance of his former colleague at the Naval Group, LCDR Ray Dick. Mills easily acceded to this request. Both Rickover and Dick were only too well aware that any mistake they might make politically could jeopardise the whole project, perhaps irrevocably. The proposal that the two drew up was to frame a memorandum to be sent Forrestal's successor as SecNav, the Hon. John L.

Sullivan, under the signature of Fleet Admiral Chester W. Nimitz, chief of naval operations (CNO). Nimitz had been wartime commander-in-chief, Pacific Fleet and Pacific Ocean Areas, controlling all Allied land, sea, and air forces in the Pacific—except General MacArthur's Southwest Pacific. Commanding great respect, he had also been a submariner and was known to be sympathetic to the needs of the submarine service.[6] It was therefore anticipated that, with this endorsement, Sullivan would be unlikely to reject the proposal. However, as the memorandum would in effect be a statement of US naval policy, there were a variety of other parties within the navy who would at least be able to express their own opinions—not all necessarily supportive—and these reactions would have to be both anticipated and provided for.

Between them, Rickover and Dick canvassed assistance from amongst their naval colleagues. They particularly sought support from serving submarine officers and they found it in CAPT. Elton W. 'Joe' Grenfell and LCDR Edward L. 'Ned' Beach Jr, both of whom were serving in the office of the CNO. These two officers provided the vital practical knowledge of contemporary trends in submarine warfare to add further authority to the memorandum. The four officers between them personally approached as many senior officers as possible whom they felt could influence the final decision. This took about eight weeks. Thereafter the whole memorandum was reviewed in the minutest detail to ensure that all important points were accounted for and explained. The content of the memorandum was in essence little different from the final report of the Naval Group which had been turned down only the previous August; nevertheless, on 5 December 1947, Nimitz enthusiastically signed it and forwarded it to Sullivan. Rickover on the one hand now had the navy committed to nuclear submarines, but he still did not have the AEC's commitment to building a suitable reactor.

BuShips was appointed to oversee the nuclear submarine design programme. Mills therefore wrote officially to the AEC on 20 January 1948 informing them that the navy was fully committed to the submarine programme. Again, echoing the Naval Group's final report, Mills suggested that the AEC and the bureau jointly manage the design. The latter would bear the major cost of training since it was hoped that this might alleviate the problem of the AEC's restricted funding. Perhaps trying to call their bluff, the AEC failed to make any response. Rickover, realising with utmost clarity that failure to move the AEC could still mean the failure of the whole project, embarked on a programme of media awareness of the navy's documented wish to base its future submarine fleet on nuclear-powered vessels. This, in turn, resulted in considerable public exposure of the whole question of the navy's need for nuclear submarines. Fortunately, the American public were generally responsive to new military technology and thereby, the navy's proposals. They were troubled by the rise of international communism, the build-up of armaments in the Soviet empire and wanted to see how the new world of atomic energy could be put to good use to defend them. It was decided that the government too should be made fully aware of the intransigence of the AEC. By great good fortune, the US Department of the Interior was holding a conference on 'Undersea Warfare'. Rickover was invited to attend with a team of fellow officers, it being made clear that the department was expecting a number of different papers to be presented. Rickover thought differently. He realised that this would be an ideal opportunity to present one single paper justifying the policy decision taken by the navy. He shrewdly invited Mills to make the presentation. The admiral agreed. While the paper itself covered in considerable depth the whole question of nuclear-powered submarines, it was a thinly disguised attack on the AEC's unwillingness to develop any reactor, let alone one suitable for submarine use. Again, the AEC failed to respond, so Rickover played his trump card when, through the AEC's Military Liaison Committee, the commission was informed in a letter from committee member Rear Admiral Thorvald A. Solberg that the project would go ahead regardless. If necessary, the navy would develop its own reactor. Unable to accept such a proposal, the AEC at last agreed to proceed with the development of a naval reactor.

The programme was in two principal sections. The reactor itself would be developed at the Argonne Laboratory using the staff transferred from the Oak Ridge project. Development of a system to transfer the reactor's energy to power a conventional turbine would be the subject of Project Wizard, a separate contract between BuShips and Westinghouse Electric Corporation. It required the design of suitable heat exchangers to generate steam for the turbines which would power the submarine.

In continued pursuance of his original aims, Rickover successfully argued that the Nuclear Power Branch was now superfluous. On 4 August 1948, it closed down and, in its place, BuShips created its own Nuclear Power Division under Rickover, who hoped to appoint the four officers from the Naval Group to serve yet again with him. However, only Roddis and Dick were immediately available. Dunford joined them in January 1949, but Libbey elected to remain with the AEC. Having thus secured leadership of all nuclear interests, Rickover only required authority within the AEC to create a union of interests that would still lead to an atomic powered submarine by the mid-1950s, as he had always predicted.

The AEC knew when it was beaten. The pro-bomb faction was forced to recognise the parallel need to develop reactors and so the AEC's Division of Reactor Development was created, headed by Dr Lawrence R. Hafstad. He hailed from the DoD where he had held the post of secretary to the Research and Development Committee. He was well liked by scientists and, importantly, enjoyed the support of Mills. Hafstad was already well aware of Teller's support for the project and was himself sympathetic towards it. On his appointment to the AEC post, he created a special Naval Reactor Branch, appointing Rickover as director (a position he was to hold until 31 January 1982). Although the Division of Reactor Development did not officially exist until February 1949, Rickover set to work at once to use his joint positions of command to make up for the time so far lost in the project. On his first meeting with Teller, Rickover famously introduced himself, 'I am Captain Rickover—I am stupid.' Rickover had no problem in bowing to the skills and knowledge of the scientists and engineers who would help him in fulfilling his goal of a US nuclear navy.

The apathy towards nuclear reactors displayed by the AEC was not mirrored by private industry. GE's interest in commercial applications was gathering momentum and Westinghouse, sensing that it had now got some lead time over its competitor, suggested that they became responsible for the design of the complete reactor along with the already confirmed heat exchangers. The AEC agreed and gave Westinghouse responsibility for the complete design of the submarine reactor that Rickover needed. The reactor itself would be constructed at a specially built laboratory at Pittsburgh's Bettis Airport. The cost of construction would be met by the AEC and they would also provide assistance from the Argonne Laboratory. Westinghouse would have been commercially unwise not to have taken advantage of this attractive offer and the company's forward-thinking president and CEO, Gwilym A. Price, ordered that the project receive maximum priority.

What Westinghouse had not considered, however, was Rickover's somewhat unconventional ways. The company had already determined to construct the prototype reactor spread out within a large building, so that every component was separate and could therefore be easily examined or inspected. Thereafter the reactor would be dismantled and rebuilt into a smaller space, imitating a complete submarine installation. This proposal proved totally unacceptable to Rickover who estimated that such a plan could add years to the development programme. His proposal was for two reactors, the first to be built with a few months' lead time over the second. The first reactor would still be the sole prototype, but it would be built inside a section of submarine hull on land to determine the installation details. The second reactor would incorporate necessary modifications as a result of experience from the first and would be installed in the world's first nuclear submarine. In overall control of the project, Rickover's view was bound to prevail.

The fundamental design of the submarine reactor was now complete. With the original Bettis site proposal now rejected by Rickover, a new site had to be found. The location chosen for the prototype was Arco in Idaho, a remote desert area ideally suited to the project. As this was a totally new concept in naval propulsion, in February 1950, Rickover approached the Portsmouth Naval Shipyard at New Hampshire to seek their assistance. This yard undoubtedly had the greatest experience in the navy in building submarines. However, Rickover's insistence that he must be in overall charge of both the construction of the hull section and the submarine itself proved unacceptable to the yard management, and the yard's CO, Captain Ralph E. McShane, refused to accept the contract. Undeterred by this lack of co-operation from a fellow officer, something not unknown to the maverick Rickover, he turned his attention to the Electric Boat Company (EB) at Groton in Connecticut. This company, formed in 1899, had been involved in the construction of submarines right from the building of the first US Navy *Holland* boats and thus had knowledge and a reputation that could at the very least match, and almost certainly exceed, that of any of the competition. More prescient than the Portsmouth Yard, EB willingly accepted both contracts and appointed the AEC's deputy general manager, Carleton Shugg, as general manager of the project. Shugg was a former naval officer with a background in submarine construction, salvage, and safety. Leaving the navy and after a period in civilian electronics, he had joined the AEC at its formation and was initially the manager of the Hanford Plant which produced plutonium. He was later appointed deputy general manager and transferred to Washington. Although he had no knowledge of atomic energy, like Rickover, he was attracted by the challenge of the unknown that this new science offered. The two postgraduate years that he had spent at the Naval Academy where he had chosen to work on submarine design now stood him in good stead when tasked with bringing the nuclear submarine project to completion.

There was now an ever-increasing urgency to construct the Arco reactor. The design chosen was a pressurised water reactor. Designated 'Submarine Thermal Reactor 1', or STR-1, it was in all respects a fully operational reactor although it would be permanently land-based. STR-2 would be the first operational power plant in the first operational nuclear submarine. In August 1950, President Truman signed the official order for this revolutionary submarine.

From then onwards, the whole project, slowed for so long by the foregoing delays, gathered increasing momentum. Along with STR-1, construction of which was now well advanced, GE had started a prototype liquid sodium-cooled reactor, which was being built at West Milton, New York. This reactor was designated Submarine Intermediate Reactor A (SIR-A). The second reactor, SIR-B, would be used for a second nuclear submarine. This would allow for critical analysis of the two types of reactor in operational conditions. Rickover's instinct for the pressurised water reactor design was to prove hugely beneficial when the sodium-cooled reactor design proved unsatisfactory in practice.

On 30 March 1953, STR-1 went critical. With a heat source equivalent to the ordinary ship's boiler, it was now possible to link up the reactor with the power plant steam turbine—achieved on 31 May. Initially a series of eight monitoring circuits surrounded the entire unit, ready to shut down the reactor in an emergency. Power was built up in stages until the full output was reached on 25 June. The team now had a working power plant built within the confines of a submarine hull, but would it have the required endurance characteristics to qualify it fully for operational use?

Annapolis graduate LCDR Edwin E. Kintner had been selected by Rickover to take charge of STR-1 and he ordered the next stage of the development programme, a forty-eight-hour test running of the plant at full power.[7] This was a strictly engineering test and after twenty-four hours of trouble-free running, and deciding that a further twenty-four-hour run was unnecessary, Kintner determined to close down the reactor. Rickover, however, countermanded the decision, and since the power plant was running without any apparent problems, he decided instead to keep it running at full power for a period of time sufficient to imitate a transatlantic crossing. Progress was plotted on a supposed route from Nova Scotia to Fastnet on the west coast of Ireland, and to simulate the voyage as accurately as possible, regular changes of 'crew' took place. Despite problems with a generator and one of the pumps that circulated the coolant in the reactor core, necessitating a reduction in power but never total shut down, after ninety-six hours the chart showed the arrival at the Irish coast. The team was jubilant. Performance such as this was far and away ahead of any previous submarine experience or expectation. Rickover commented: 'Nature seems to want to work for those who work hardest for themselves'.[8]

Rickover was also supervising progress with the submarine that was to use the first operational reactor, the design of which was a totally separate, though obviously related matter. The era of the true submarine was about to arrive, and future submarine design would incorporate hull forms giving maximum emphasis to underwater speed and efficiency. Possessing considerable numbers of submarines surplus to its post-war needs, the navy had embarked on an experimental programme to improve the performance of its existing fleet. Initiated under the Greater Underwater Power Propulsion Program (GUPPY), a variety of modifications were made to propulsion systems and also to hull forms based to a great extent on the advanced late-war designs of the captured U-boats. The effectiveness of the programme may be judged by the fact that around 100 conversions were undertaken. These enabled the navy to keep Second World War submarines in service until the final one, the *Tench*-class USS *Tigrone* (SS-419), was taken out of commission on 27 June 1975, some thirty years after the end of the war.

It is arguable that the nuclear submarine was not a mere advancement of existing submarine design but was a new type of war vessel. Whereas the diesel submarine would, typically, spend around 90 per cent of the time on the surface, the nuclear submarine would, apart from time spent negotiating shipping lanes, maybe less than 5 per cent, would remain totally submerged in distant waters. This also required them to be self-sufficient in the event of problems and this needed a rather different approach to crew expertise than the risk takers of the Pacific War where US submarine crews suffered the greatest attrition rate of any of the American armed forces.

Rickover originally approached the Portsmouth Naval Shipyard in Maine to take on the contract for the first nuclear submarine. But like his original approach over the Arco project, the 'reluctant dragon' who ran the shipyard was uncooperative, so Rickover again approached Electric Boat.[9] General Manager O. P. (Robbie) Robinson willingly accepted the contract for the building of the USS *Nautilus* in 1951 following completion of design studies. The first atomic submarine was built largely out of public sight in EB's southern harbour. It was Rickover's idea to emphasise the importance of the submarine by asking President Truman to lay the keel of the boat. This the president did on 14 June 1952, with his initials 'HST' being welded into it (strictly speaking, a submarine does not have a keel so one of the lower hull plates was chosen as a substitute). The ceremony reflected an impressive gathering of influential people. In his speech, Truman was generous in his praise of nuclear power and the importance of the naval reactor program, confirming that the *Nautilus* would have an impressive, submerged speed 'of more than 20 knots'. Also present was the chairman of the AEC, Gordon Dean, who in his address paid ample tribute to the distinctive contribution made by Rickover to the overall management of the project. Three weeks later, on 7 July, Rickover was awarded the Gold Star to his Legion of Merit, pinned on him by SecNav Dan A. Kimball—in effect a second bestowal of the award, the first such award made to an engineering officer since the end of the war.

Rickover clearly had friends and admirers in high places but not, it seemed, in the high places of the navy. The following day, a nine-man Naval Selection Committee convened to consider, among other promotions, that of Captain Rickover to rear admiral. This was the second time that Rickover had been considered. His promotion had been turned down the previous year, blamed, it was said, on his single-mindedness and obstructive nature. While this trait was of great benefit to the nuclear project, it had often caused him to overlook the general interests of the navy whereby far the greatest majority of senior officers wanted more surface ships and saw the emergent nuclear submarine as an unwelcome distraction. However, if turned down for a second time, Rickover would have to retire from the navy on 30 June 1953. The committee did not approve his promotion and Rickover was therefore destined to finish his naval career having completed thirty years' active service. The committee kept no records, so no official reason was given for their decision. There was no precedent that would allow him to stay on.[10]

The committee's decision, while surprising some, must be examined in a wider context, for it was not simply the mere turning down of an officer's chance of promotion. Though Rickover had many friends who supported him, his abrasive character had made him enemies who would willingly see his career in the navy brought to a timeous close. However, numbered among his friends were the AEC and the Congressional Joint Committee on Atomic Energy, and he was not without support from elements within the navy, principally via BuShips. These bodies had indeed recommended that his promotion be accepted, but the navy resented its staff infrastructure being determined by outside influence. The most serious aspect of the decision was that it highlighted the existence of a powerful and entrenched anti-nuclear lobby within the navy itself.

Although a decision had been made to proceed with a nuclear submarine and the construction work had started, only limited progress had been made, and without Rickover's driving force, the entire project could, even at that stage, be stillborn and both those for and against the programme knew it. But there was also the question of the likely blow to national technological prestige if the *Nautilus* came to naught. Rickover's carefully cultivated relationship with the media came into play. They found the thought of his retiral unacceptable and once again used their influence by taking a firm stand behind the captain, thus drawing even more public attention to the whole matter of the nuclear submarine and the seeming injustice he had suffered. Adding the power of the press to those who had already declared their support was too much even for the navy, and SecNav Robert B. Anderson ordered that Rickover be retained for a year and that he remain eligible for consideration for promotion. On 1 July 1953, Rickover was promoted to rear admiral. The selection committee had been requested by Anderson to promote to rear admiral an engineering captain with experience in nuclear systems. Even the navy had to accept that there was no better choice than Rickover. The *Nautilus* was secure; as was, at least for the time being, RADM Rickover.

Stemming from the GUPPY studies came some radical ideas about the optimum hull form for maximising submerged efficiency. This showed that a teardrop shaped or 'spindle' hull with blunt bows and a high beam to length ratio would give the highest underwater speed. The conning tower was slimmed down and now enclosed within a streamlined structure called the fin and, together with hydroplanes fore and aft, provided control in three dimensions; more akin to flying than the normal methods of controlling a submerged vessel. The forward hydroplanes were mounted on the fin and this configuration has since been adopted, with only one exception, on all US submarines. The advantage of this design was that it kept the noise of the operating systems for the planes away from the sonar suite in the bow. However, it meant that this operating machinery had to be incorporated in the fin and the planes had to be capable of being moved to the vertical for penetrating the Arctic ice without damage. The Royal Navy, as we shall see, thought differently. There were many who doubted if the theories would prove themselves on an actual vessel, and to examine the practical aspects of the design, the navy ordered submarine hull number 569, still conventionally powered by two diesel motors and one electric motor. She was laid down in March 1952 and was commissioned on 6 December 1963 as the USS *Albacore* (SS-569).

BuShips was responsible for the design of the prototype nuclear submarine and was, of course, well aware of the GUPPY programme's findings and also the plans for the *Albacore*. Tempting though it must have been to consider adopting the spindle hull form on the prototype, it was as yet unproven and there were many other problems that could be anticipated with the new power plant. The *Nautilus* design therefore followed more conventional lines, still inspired by German late-war designs though incorporating certain of the GUPPY modifications that had been proved during the conversion programme.

The design of the reactor and power plant was now agreed. With Rickover firmly in charge, confidence within EB increased and allowed engineers to mock up and check the fit of all internal components, thereby greatly speeding up the work on the *Nautilus* and its STR-2 installation.

Accompanied by the president, Lady Mamie Eisenhower launched the *Nautilus* on a cold and foggy morning, 21 January 1954. Some 30,000 people had arrived to witness the event. 'That many came from great distances is a signal tribute to the scientists, engineers and craftsmen who worked to create this masterpiece of the shipbuilder's art,' commented John J. Hopkins, the chairman and president of the General Dynamics Corporation.[11] This was in fact a very generous description as, perhaps for something heralding new technology, the *Nautilus* could almost be described as being built 'from the spare parts catalogue': 'a diesel submarine already under construction, liquid-holding tanks from a bankrupt New Jersey dairy, emergency diesel engines salvaged from a minesweeper that had spent the last few years sunk at the bottom of a river and a refurbished [destroyer-escort] engine room appropriated from a pre-World War II destroyer'.[12] The design, based as it was on semi-conventional technology, had twin screws but as the engine room had to be squeezed into the submarine hull, the two shafts had to be angled outwards from the centreline, resulting in the width across the screws being slightly greater than the maximum width of the hull. This demanded great skill in coming alongside if damage to the screws was to be avoided—a nicety not always achieved. Total cost of the *Nautilus*: less than $70 million.

Among the official guests were the *Nautilus*'s CO, Commander Eugene P. 'Dennis' Wilkinson, a larger-than-life submarine veteran who had served with distinction in the Pacific theatre in the Second World War and had become something of a naval legend as CO of the USS *Darter* (SS-227). Also present were CDR Beach, later to be appointed CO of the USS *Triton* (SSRN-586)—built to Ship Characteristics Board (SCB) design SCB-132—a unique twin reactor-powered SSN that was to complete a record-breaking circumnavigation of the world (Operation Sandblast) from 24 February to 25 April 1960. He was then the naval aide to the president and had been behind the plans to invite the president's wife to launch the submarine, and, of course, Rickover himself was present, dressed unobtrusively, as was his norm, in civilian clothes.[13] There was now tangible evidence for those involved of all the work they had put into the project, though sadly LT Ray Dick, who had died the previous year, did not live to see it.

At long last, public tributes were paid to Rickover recognising the importance of his part in the whole programme. After the champagne bottle crashed onto the *Nautilus*'s bow, the submarine slid into the Thames River, the fog dispersed, and the sun shone. The sun was always to shine on the *Nautilus*; indeed, this phrase is now enshrined within the US Navy's submarine folklore.

Fitting out took a further year. The *Nautilus*'s sea trials started on 17 January 1955 under Rickover's overall supervision. Successfully completed, USS *Nautilus* was commissioned into the navy on 22 April. Her first fuelling took her a distance of 62,560 miles, including, in August 1958, a transatlantic crossing under the Arctic ice cap to the Royal Navy base at Portland.

On a roughly parallel course, however, the sodium-cooled reactor was running into trouble. Although sodium had certain theoretical advantages, the actual engineering was more challenging. SIR-B went to sea in the submarine USS *Seawolf* (SSN-575), launched at the EB yard on 21 July 1955, but after two years of continual problems, further development was cancelled, and she was retrofitted with a pressurised water reactor—the type of power plant that would become the standard for future US nuclear submarines. Her now redundant reactor vessel and the reactor plant components were dumped into 9,000 feet of water about 120 miles off the Delaware–Maryland coast in the Atlantic Ocean.[14] The navy was now fully committed to the need for nuclear submarines, and although both the *Nautilus* and *Seawolf* were by no means prototypes only (they were fully active elements of the fleet), they remained unique designs, having no sister boats in their class. The first production run of nuclear submarines was the *Skate* class. Four were built: *Skate* (SSN-578), *Sargo* (SSN-583), *Swordfish* (SSN-579) (the first nuclear submarine to be built by the Portsmouth Naval Shipyard, Maine), and *Seadragon* (SSN-574). They still used a GUPPY-type hull, but they were remarkably compact and proved to be highly manoeuvrable. This was a feature that was useful when under the Arctic icecap, which now proved to be an ideal hiding place previously barred to submarines for fear of being unable to reach the surface to recharge their batteries. The designation of the reactors was also changed. The Arco prototype was reclassified as S1W (W for Westinghouse; GE reactors would be suffixed G). The *Nautilus*'s reactor was S2W. The next reactor, S3W, was fitted to the *Skate* class. Perhaps the most spectacular achievement of this class was the double rendezvous at the North Pole on 2 August 1962 between the *Skate* and the *Seadragon*.

By now the experience gained from the *Albacore* could be fully incorporated into the class of submarine designed specifically as high-speed attack boats. These were the submarines of the *Skipjack* class. Powered by a single screw, they displaced 3,500 tons, roughly 1,000 tons more than a Second World War *Gato*-class boat, and this increase in size provided an internal space and comfort on a scale unknown to previous submariners who had endured indifferent food, limited water, and hot, humid environments. Powered by an SW5 reactor, USS *Skipjack* (SSN-585) was launched on 26 May 1958 and on her trials proved to have a record submerged speed of around 30 knots. Before the *Skipjack* had even been launched, however, the keel of submarine number 598 had been laid at Groton on 1 November 1957. The submarine, a sister boat of the *Skipjack*, was to be named USS *Scorpion*. As will be seen later, it was this boat that was redesigned to incorporate a new centre section and was then renamed the USS *George Washington*, the US Navy's first Polaris submarine (SSBN).

2

The V2:
Operation *Prüfstand* XII and
Operation Backfire

Just because something is impossible doesn't mean it doesn't have a solution.

James Albright, USAF

On 15 May 1942, a Spitfire PR IV based at RAF Benson in Oxfordshire, one of two that day tasked with photographing the German naval bases at Kiel and Swinemünde, flew over Peenemünde airfield on the Baltic coast.[1] Attracted by three unusual circular emplacements, the pilot, Flt Lt Donald Steventon, ran the cameras. There had been unconfirmed reports of German rocket developments, but only later could these be reliably linked to the Peenemünde facility. Both the Luftwaffe and the army had a presence at the airfield. The former developing the Fi 103/V1 cruise missile along with various rocket-powered fighters, and the latter, the *Heereswaffenamt* (HWA: Army Weapons Department), engaged in much more ambitious projects. The unit's CO, Maj. Walter R. Dornberger, moved to the secluded location after the rocket testing that had taken place at Kummersdorf on the outskirts of Berlin had reached ranges that were increasingly unsafe for the local population. On 1 December 1932, Dornberger took on a young student engineer called Wernher von Braun. The young man had publicly set his mind on developing a rocket to reach the Moon but willingly saw a military ballistic missile and, later, membership of the SS as possibly opening the way to eventual more peaceful uses of the rocket's potential. Three 'Aggregat' missiles had been developed each showing advances, but it was Aggregat-4 (A-4) that became the focus of attention as a 'wonder weapon' capable of turning the tide of war in favour of the Germans. The A-4, the second of the revenge weapons, was to become better known as the V2.

The photographs of the site alerted the British to investigate further the true nature of the area as a development site for advanced airborne weapons. RAF Bomber Command executed one of its major raids, Operation Hydra, against the area on 17/18 August 1943. The operation was significant as being the first one to use a Master Bomber which reflected the increasing accuracy that bombing was achieving. However, despite a considerable tonnage of bombs being dropped, only limited damage was done. Among the primary targets were the scientists based at the facility, but only two significant members were killed, buried in a slit trench in which they were taking cover, Dr Walter Thiel along with his wife and two children and Chief Engineer Dr Erich Walther.[2] Sadly, there were significant civilian casualties in the nearby Trassenheide labour camp. Little damage was done to the manufacturing or testing facilities and although production of V2s was delayed by some six weeks, the raid did result in the decision to transfer manufacture to a salt mine at Nordhausen in the Harz mountains under the *U-Verlagerungen* programme to house essential industries underground. Here, under the auspices of *Mittelwerk* GmbH, slave labour working in appalling conditions could assemble the missiles completely immune from any further Allied attack. Other research elements, which included personnel, and the supersonic wind tunnel were moved intact by the *Wasserbau Versuchsanstalt* (WVA) to Kochelsee in Bavaria where work continued unhindered until the US Army arrived in 1945.[3]

On 6 June 1944, Operation Overlord saw the Allied landings on the Normandy coast of France. It is said that no plan survives first contact with the enemy and the advance through northern France was in many cases no exception to that rule, but once a foothold had been established the Allies' progress was positive. However, a week later at 3:30 a.m. on 13 June, *Flak-Regiment 155(W)*, under the command of *Oberst* Max Wachtel, began V1 launch operations. The first V1 launched against London landed in Grove Road, Mile End, killing six people, injuring thirty, and making 200 people homeless. The nearby bridge that carried the Great Eastern Railway across Grove Road from Liverpool Street to Essex was badly damaged. The V1, little more than a powered, winged bomb, was in essence an unguided cruise missile. Launched from fixed ramps in northern France which were accurately lined up in the direction of their targets, the V1s fell to earth when a tiny propeller on the nose of the weapon had turned a pre-set number of times calculated by the distance to the target. This caused the auto-pilot to turn down the elevators, sending the V1 into a dive. At a downward pitch of 60 degrees, the fuel supply to its *Argus Motoren Gesellschaft* pulse-jet motor was cut off when the weight of the remaining fuel overcame the pressurisation in the tanks. In its final stage of development, the V1 had a range of around 230 miles and could fly at a speed of 360 mph to deliver its 1,830-lb warhead. Allied progress through France was such that the German garrison in Paris surrendered on 25 August. By the beginning of September, the V1 launch sites in the Pas-de-Calais had all been overrun. A confident Duncan Sandys announced on the 7th that the V1 offensive against London was over. By the time of Sandys's announcement, a total of 8,892 missiles had been launched from ground sites. A further 1,600 V1s were launched from specially converted Heinkel He 111H-22 aircraft operated by III/KG3 and I/KG53 from bases at Venlo and Gilze-Rigen in Holland.[4] Each aircraft carried a single V1 under its inner starboard wing. This proved a dangerous operation as the attrition rate of the carrier aircraft was high. The V1s diminutive size made them more difficult to intercept than conventional aircraft. Flying no higher than 2,500 feet and travelling slower than the latest versions of piston-engined fighters and the first Gloster Meteor jet fighters just entering service, the V1 could be brought down either by anti-aircraft gunfire, snagged by balloons or by wing-to-wing contact. The latter was achieved by a fighter flying with its wingtip just beneath the V1's wing. The V1 could then be brought down by a simple nudge which was sufficient to upset the missile's gyro and send it falling earthwards. Despite this intrinsic vulnerability, one-third of the V1s launched against targets in the south of England evaded interception and inflicted significant death, damage and destruction. Inevitably some V1s had been salvaged and these were sent to America where, as we shall see later, they were reverse engineered and formed the genesis of the first missiles to be launched from submarines and surface ships.

What neither Sandys nor anyone else in the government expected was that as one revenge weapon bowed out, a second deadlier one was to arrive the following day with the operational launches of the first V2s. The V2 campaign lasted until 27 March 1945 when the retreating Germans launched the last of 1,115 V2s fired against London. *Mittelwerk* GmbH had manufactured 5,789 rockets by the time that it was evacuated on 18 March. Aware that a 900,000-square-foot underground production facility existed near to Nordhausen, the Rocket Branch of the US Army Ordnance Corps instructed Col. Holger N. Toftoy to move from his headquarters at the Ordnance Technical Intelligence in Paris to locate and salvage whatever could be found at the site as soon as it was captured. When the US 104th Infantry Division entered Nordhausen on 11 April, they found to their amazement that the plant was still largely intact. To the 329 Medical Battalion fell the harrowing task of liberating the Dora-Mittelbau and Nordhausen *Vernichtungslager* (extermination camps). These housed workers in the underground complex and many years later when their details were fully disclosed were still to haunt the engineers associated with the plant. Toftoy appointed Maj. James P. Hamill of the Ordnance Technical Intelligence department to organise the removal of as much of the rocket materiel as possible. In total this amounted to some 100 rockets in various stages of completion together with a mass of documentation.

Realising that the war was in its final stages and the Soviets were fast approaching, the majority of the senior members of the Peenemünde team, including Dornberger and von Braun, believing that surrender to the US or British forces was preferable to internment by the Soviets, had already left after secretly deciding to move south to be better placed to make contact with the advancing Allied forces. The prevalent chaos within Germany meant that, with care, they could travel with relative ease and avoid the SS roadblocks—only the SS and the *Gestapo* were seemingly able to continue to operate in the confusion. The group made their way to the town of Bleicherode, the headquarters of the *Mittelwerk* production facility. Following Hitler's suicide on 30 April, Dornberger and von Braun agreed that the time had come to make contact with the US forces which were in the area. While the pair enjoyed the hospitality of a local hotel, they sent von Braun's brother, Magnus, who had studied in America and could speak English, to find the advancing US 7th Army. He located the US 44th Infantry Division at the small Austrian town of Reutte which nestled at the foot of the Adolf Hitler Pass and surrendered to them. The other members of the rocket team followed soon afterwards. Supremely confident of their value to the Americans, they demanded to be taken to General Eisenhower, a request that was not, however, fulfilled. The whole group was then taken to Garmisch-Partenkirchen for interrogation. Deprived of their files, many of the statements made appeared to conflict, but gradually a complete picture emerged of the development of the A-4 and also other rockets. Dornberger revealed that he had thoughtfully buried five crates of technical manuals at Bad Sachsa, whence they were salvaged and removed adding to the American's hoard.

* * * * *

Our main objective for a long time was to make it more dangerous to be in the target area than to be with the launch crew.

Wernher von Braun

It was estimated that only some 2,790 V2s were actually fired successfully. Unlike the slow-flying pulsejet powered V1, the V2 was immune to countermeasures, but psychologically it posed less of a threat to the population as, flying faster than the speed of sound, its arrival was signified only by the explosion of the warhead. The V1 announced its imminent arrival by its distinctive sound, causing people to take shelter. There had been much debate around whether to launch the missiles from large, hardened bunkers or from pre-prepared mobile sites that could be hastily commissioned and evacuated after launch. The decision to go for mobile launchers was vindicated: the advancing Allied forces had in any case captured the three fixed launch sites that had been built. Even with Allied air superiority, the mobile launch sites proved difficult to locate. Any firm level area could potentially be used, and the Germans had prepared a number of these, with many more being further disguised by being built into existing country roads. The V2 could be set up, fuelled, and launched in a relatively short space of time. Considering the conditions prevailing in Germany at the time, with a decreasing availability of raw materials and worsening morale as defeat became more and more inevitable, that so many V2s were launched can only be seen as a major technical achievement for such a complex high technology venture. However, the idea of taking such a complex missile to sea to most people would surely be seen as a technological step too far.

As the Third Reich began to crumble under the Allied armies that closed in from east and west, it was surprising that, even with the immense pressures being placed on war production by Armaments Minister Albert Speer, Germany could still field a range of weapons technically far in advance of those of the Allied forces. Jet fighters and bombers, rocket-powered interceptors, cruise missiles, anti-aircraft missiles, ballistic missiles, and advanced closed cycle U-boats were all making their appearance as the Reich's *Götterdämmerung* approached.[5] On 26 April 1945, the advancing Red Army overran the port of Szczecin and found in the shipyard of Vulkan Werft three cigar-shaped concrete containers. One appeared to be complete, with the other two partly completed. These containers, roughly bomb-shaped, were 118 feet long, 18 feet 8 inches in diameter, and had a displacement of around 500 tonnes. They represented the hardware for a highly secret project, set up under the Peenemünde codename *Prüfstand XII*. Georg von Tiesenhausen and Bernhard Tessmann headed up the project (both were later to join von Braun in America). The proposal was to launch V2s from these large submarine containers some distance from the United States' eastern seaboard, thereby bringing the war directly to the American homeland.[6]

A similar American target was being considered by the Luftwaffe through their Messerschmitt Me 264 *Amerika* long-range bomber project. Even to the most optimistic, the U-boat project must have seemed a highly risky venture given the short life expectancy of any U-boat venturing into the Atlantic as a result of Allied anti-submarine capability which had developed rapidly and effectively during the war, helped by the highly secret breaking of the Enigma coded signals and the availability of long-range patrol aircraft. The V2 containers would be towed horizontally by an *Elektroboote* Type XXI U-boat. These were of advanced hull design optimised for submerged speed with a large number of batteries to increase the time they could operate underwater. Some 120 miles off the US coast, the missile container would have been flooded until it was vertical. The launch crew would transfer from the submarine, fuel the missile, return to the submarine, and proceed with the countdown. Some documentation suggests that the later, and still by the end of the war untested, A-8 missile would have been used. This was a stretched V2 with an increased range. Despite the impractical nature of the project, it did prove to be the forerunner of both American and Soviet submarine missile systems.

Peenemünde fell into Soviet hands on 6 May 1944, when the Second Belorussian Front, commanded by General Konstantin Rokossovskii, reached the peninsular.[7] Along with parts of the A-4 were plans and components for other rockets under development including blueprints for the 80-foot-long A-9/A-10 two-stage rocket, the first practical design for an intercontinental missile. Along with the hardware the Soviets captured around 200 rocket scientists including Helmutt Gröttrup, the chief electronics engineer.

* * * * *

Once the rockets go up, who cares where they come down? That's not my department says Wernher von Braun.

Tom Lehrer

During his interrogation, von Braun stated that he considered 'the A-4 rocket developed by us as an intermediate solution conditioned by this war, a solution which still has certain inherent shortcomings and which compares with the future possibilities of the art in about the same way as a bomber plane of the last war compares with a modern bomber.'[8]

The Soviet forces took over Thuringia on 1 June. By this time, the Americans and the British had removed almost all equipment of value from Nordhausen, and of the 1,000 engineers and their families at the site, most had elected to join the Americans. This was part of the USAAF's Operation Lusty (LUfwaffe Secret TechnologY) to garner as much information on German wartime scientific research as possible. When the Soviets—who had a similar objective under Operation Osoaviakim [Осоавиаким]—occupied Nordhausen, they discovered, as Col. Yuri A. Pobedonostsev later admitted, that the Americans had 'cleaned the place out'. Toftoy had, however, not removed the production installations, so that although the Soviets had no actual rockets, they did have the facilities to restart manufacture.

Toftoy had received his orders from Col. Gervais W. Trichel, who had also instructed Maj. Robert Staver to locate the key German rocket engineers and arrange their interrogation. This represented the genesis of what, on 19 July 1945, became Project Overcast, later known as Project Paperclip (often erroneously called Operation Paperclip)—the exploitation of German civilian scientists.[9] It was established under the Chief, Military Intelligence Service on an island in Boston Harbor at a camp formerly known as Fort Standish. A certain degree of discretion had to be exercised as the British—who had directly suffered the effects of the V2 bombardment which had taken over 2,750 lives and seriously injured a further 6,000—were holding Dornberger and von Braun in Maida Vale and were keen to arraign the pair for war crimes.[10] However, rocket development was now a vital area of research, particularly since the Soviets had their own interest in the subject through their quota of captured rockets and engineers. The German scientists were seen as vital to America's interests in this field—and they knew it. Their transfer to work on American projects could not be delayed by the inconvenience of war crimes proceedings. Von Braun and a group of some forty-five colleagues were taken to a new life in America, albeit still under military jurisdiction. The number of Germans was later to increase to 118, including Dornberger who was to join them later after a two-year detention in Bridgend in Wales. It had been agreed that Britain would be allocated a proportion of the captured missiles, but this agreement was conveniently overlooked as the partnerships of the war quickly unravelled. The missiles were loaded onto Liberty ships bound for America before the British could protest.

But it was a British-led project that saw the launch of the first captured V2s by any of the Allies. Operation Backfire took place at the Krupp artillery range at Cuxhaven, on the coast north of Bremerhaven. German security over the deployment of the V2 meant that there were no manuals that covered the full operation of the missiles. Each person in the launch team knew his part and no more, so that, if captured, they could only divulge a small part of the launch procedure. Operation Backfire took place in October 1945 and sought to produce a complete breakdown of the handling and launch procedures of the V2. Using captured V2 personnel to assist, a five-volume report was duly compiled. Although American and Russians observers had been invited to watch the launches, it appeared that these two nations were more prepared to pursue their own paths with the captured missiles than benefit from the British efforts.

Nonetheless, two significant individuals observed the tests. Sergei P. Korolev, dressed as a Soviet Army colonel, was to become the shadowy chief rocket engineer who was later to mastermind the Soviet-manned space programme. A US observer, also masquerading unconvincingly as an (somewhat shambolic) army colonel was Dr Theodor von Kármán from the California Institute of Technology who, foreseeing the future, said to another American observer, CDR Grayson Merrill (the technical director of the Naval Air Missile Test Center): '[N]ow young man, you go home and tell them to get these rockets on ships, including submarines'.[11]

Merrill later commented: 'I believe von Kármán was the only person who was aware of the post-war prospect for nuclear warheads in ballistic missiles'.[12] Merrill did act on the suggestion and wrote a report to the CNO, Fleet Admiral Chester W. Nimitz, recommending that the navy issue an operational requirement to develop ballistic missiles for firing from ships, including submarines, against strategic targets. Although favourably endorsed by the chief of BuAer, Rear Admiral Harold B. Sallada, nothing came of it. In hindsight, it is perhaps odd that the BuAer displayed such enthusiasm for a project that would almost certainly compete for budget with aircraft carriers, which many of the more traditional naval officers saw as the way to restore some of the navy's lost prestige. Conversely, BuOrd under which the project would rest more comfortably were, from the start, pessimistic about the ability to produce such a missile. It may well have been a calculated support by BuAer to at least keep a counter proposal to any air force monopoly in IRBMs. Perversely perhaps, then-Under Secretary of the Navy Thomas S. Gates was later to suggest that the Douglas Skybolt air-launched ballistic missile (ALBM) destined, until cancelled, for SAC and the RAF's V-bombers was an air force reaction to a naval missile.[13] Such was the level of interservice rivalry and suspicion.

The Germans had operationally seen the V2 as a weapon capable of increasing the reach of its artillery battalions, and the US Army viewed it in much the same way. The prize capture of von Braun and his team gave the US Army a potentially commanding lead in the post-war development of missiles. From late 1945, the first of the Germans selected under Project Paperclip were taken under military jurisdiction to El Paso in Texas to start work on the army's rocket programme. Initially, their main purpose was to advise the army and GE who had been appointed supporting contractor for the program, about the launch procedures for the rockets. The program was controlled by Maj. Hamill, now appointed chief of the office of the chief of Ordnance Corps, Research and Development Service (Rocket). Inevitably, the start-up procedures were somewhat haphazard. The Germans, accustomed to all the paraphernalia necessary for rocket development, found little of any use and many were quickly disillusioned. Salvaged components for about 100 V2s had been stored at Las Cruces, New Mexico, while the White Sands Proving Ground had been chosen as the main test area with the overall headquarters for the programme at Fort Bliss. The Germans, however, lacked knowledge of the assembly and operations of the V2s, being mainly part of the design team—Project Paperclip had not covered the technicians involved in the launch procedures. No complete rockets had been salvaged and many of the components had rusted badly during their transatlantic crossing. Requests for help and components left over from Operation Backfire received a frosty response from the British, still irked by the lack of American interest in the British-led project.

But Operation Backfire had employed personnel who had been directly involved with V2 procedures, and von Braun now awaited the arrival of these people once they had been demobbed on completion of Backfire. Thereby possessing the required technical knowledge, the Americans undertook their own series of V2 test launches which started on 16 April 1946 after a static test firing on 14 March, initially merely duplicating what Backfire had already achieved; the Americans still claimed that they had learnt little from the earlier project. The major purpose to which the rockets were put was high-altitude research. The lack of components, however, proved to be a limiting factor as the rockets, not designed for a long shelf life, required a significant amount of maintenance. The Germans were soon to discover that the US Army appeared to have only limited funds available and even the most basic equipment seemed to be lacking. They passed the time with further theoretical studies of the rocket's potential or, by way of interviews, confirmed what they had already achieved. Notwithstanding this, by the end of 1946, the army was content to reveal that the 'willing cooperation of these German scientists and technicians [had] put the United States 10 years ahead of schedule in its research in these fields where before it was lagging behind other countries.'

The US Navy Experiments with Missiles

Navy submarines made a transition from torpedo shooters to missile shooters as well. That's an important milestone.

Captain Grayson Merrill, US Navy

America had already experimented with solid-fuelled rockets pioneered from 1942 by the Naval Powder Factory at Indian Head, Maryland. Though the war had seen advances in solid propellant formulations, these were only useable in short-range rockets.

Notwithstanding the reservations about combining naval vessels and liquid-fuelled missiles, the navy also turned its attention to the other German revenge weapon: the V1. Von Braun had been firmly cemented into the army team, so the navy persuaded Dr Herbert A. Wagner and fifteen of his fellow scientists to join the navy's missile programme. Wagner's involvement during the war was primarily with the Luftwaffe, for whom he had developed the Henschel Hs 293 anti-shipping radio-controlled glide bomb. Although in many ways wartime competitors, there existed mutual respect between the two. Although the Germans had investigated marrying the submarine and the V2, it is perhaps a little surprising that they did not appear to consider adapting the V1 for submarine use; perhaps only because it was a Luftwaffe weapon. The Luftwaffe's He 111-launched missiles were somewhat inaccurate as the aircraft's position and heading at the time of launch could never be determined with sufficient accuracy. A similar problem would affect the directional accuracy of missiles launched from ships or submarines and this therefore contributed an inherent shortcoming of the weapon in a seaborne role and was possibly the reason that the *Kriegsmarine* shied away from considering the idea, although in May 1942, an experiment had been undertaken with *Wurfkörper 42*—the so-called 'Do' 30-cm solid-fuelled rockets used in multiples of six on the army's *Nebelwerfer* rocket launcher. The rockets were mounted externally on a Type IXc U-boat

(*U-511*), which had produced useful and somewhat unexpected results about the positive stability of the rockets when launched underwater, but the rockets were not particularly accurate, and the launch structure adversely affected the U-boats handling.

The biggest US naval late-war missile project was the CTV-N-8 Bumblebee supersonic missile, which eventually took to the air in 1948. Although designed as an anti-aircraft defensive missile, it gives some idea of the direction of naval thinking at the time, and it is therefore not surprising that great interest was shown in captured V1 weapons Some of the resulting experience with the Bumblebee missile was used in the later SSM-N-8 Regulus cruise missile.

But the captured V2s also attracted naval attention. An interview took place at Fort Bliss in mid-1946 when an unidentified naval officer who was visiting the establishment asked to meet von Braun. The German's command of English was still limited and so an interpreter had to be found.[1] Sgt Erich Wormer who had accompanied the first group of Germans agreed to help. The naval officer seemed interested only in knowing of German plans to launch rockets from submarines. It remains unclear as to what had aroused the navy's interest in the possibility of underwater launchings or indeed if it was merely individual curiosity on the part of the officer concerned. However, von Braun gave a full description of the background to *Prüfstand XII* and the work that had taken place by the end of hostilities. Where this interview led to is uncertain, but the navy did express an interest in the V2 as a possible adjunct to naval operations. The NRL undertook a further interview with Germans from Peenemünde when, on 30 August 1946, the laboratory's Milton Rosen arranged a meeting at the Naval Ordnance Laboratory in Maryland at which representatives from the Glenn L. Martin Company were also in attendance. Five Germans were interviewed and demonstrated their willingness to discuss their various areas of research.[2] There was, therefore, some degree of naval interest and this was about to be put to a practical test.

Rear Admiral Daniel V. Gallery was assistant CNO (Guided Missiles).[3] He was somewhat maverick by nature, a characteristic which was not popular among the traditionally minded naval hierarchy, and one that eventually led to his retirement without being given the traditional 'third star'. Gallery was the originator of Operation Sandy, which was to see a V2 launched from the deck of an aircraft carrier. Three missiles, two live and one inert round that would be used for handling trials, were taken from the stock reassembled at the White Sands Missile Range (WSMR) and were transported to the Norfolk Naval Yard, Virginia, where the 45,000-ton USS *Midway* (CVB-41) was berthed.[4, 5] The *Midway* was not only the largest carrier in the US Navy but also the largest ship in the world at that time and was equipped with an armoured flight deck. After taking the missiles on board, the carrier put to sea on 2 September 1947 as part of Task Force 41.16, under the overall command of Gallery. Accompanying the *Midway* were four destroyers from Destroyer Division (DesDiv) 142, which were to be used for tracking, six PB-1W aircraft from VX-4 Squadron, and the SOFAR sound laboratory vessel EPCE(R)-852. The latter's task was to monitor the explosion of a SOFAR bomb placed in the missile. The media were told that the whole project was confidential, and no details could be released, but it was reported that a number of high-ranking army and naval officers were on board to observe the test.[6]

The actual launch structure used original German equipment modified for use on deck. Launch operations were under the overall command of CDR Pliny G. Holt from BuAer where he was a pioneer of aviation navigation systems. The launch crew were navy personnel who had received specialised training at White Sands. Ignition of the missile took place at 3:53 p.m. (X Hour) on 6 September and, watched by some 100 VIP observers headed by Admiral William H. P. Blandy, C-in-C, US Atlantic Fleet (CINCLANTFLT), the rocket rose somewhat erratically—it was believed because of a faulty guidance vane—passing quite close to the ship's superstructure, before heading upwards. This emphasised the danger to a ship's superstructure inherent in the initial slow launch speed characteristic of liquid-fuelled missiles. The missile exploded when it reached 15,000 feet. The erratic trajectory and the unexpected explosion reinforced in the minds of many of the observers the very real dangers that rockets still presented. Nonetheless, one hour and thirteen minutes after the launch, all equipment had been removed from the deck, and twelve minutes later the carrier was ready to accept aircraft again.[7] To prove the point, six F4U Corsair aircraft were launched in rapid succession some eighty-eight minutes after the launch took place.

In the opening paragraph of his report on the launch, Gallery said: 'A large bombardment type rocket was successfully launched for the first time from a ship underway at sea. It was the opening phase of an extensive program leading to the adaptation of naval vessels and the logistics of naval operations to the use of this new weapon—the large vertically launched guided missile'. He envisaged that CVB (*Midway* class) carriers would be able to carry eighty missiles, while the smaller CV (*Essex* class) would manage to deploy fifty. He recommended that an 'aircraft carrier or a seaplane tender be assigned to the Naval Guided Missile Program for the experimental development of ship-borne launching techniques'. However, before further launchings were undertaken, he suggested that more reliable gyros, servos, and computers be used, replacing the German equipment with US-built items where possible. He also indicated that experimental firings should take place on land to investigate the problems of a rolling and pitching ship at sea. 'Operation Sandy,' the report concluded, 'ushers in a new era of naval aviation.' The official statement covering the launch declared: '[The] data and experience ... will bear fruit in the future design of large bombardment type missiles and eventually in the design of guided missile ships. This first launching of a large rocket from a ship at sea is a preview of what will eventually become a routine naval operation'.[8]

The navy was institutionally wary of handling volatile fuels on board ship and the V2 veering off course did little to assuage these fears. If any further proof was needed, then Operation Pushover aptly demonstrated this. Under the direction of LCDR Walter P. 'Pat' Murphy, two tests took place in late 1949 at Launch Complex 35 (LC35) at White Sands.[9] LC35 had been built in 1946, and although no specific requirement had been identified, it was realised that the navy would require an instrumented range facility for its missile experiments. Pushover was literally named as two fully fuelled white-painted V2s were deliberately pushed over on a rig constructed to replicate a ship's deck—one on flat ground and the second test on a replica raised deck. The resulting damage to the thick steel plates, though considered repairable, was far worse than had been predicted and proved beyond any reasonable doubt the extreme dangers of launching liquid-fuelled missiles from ships. The consequences of an explosion taking place inside the confines of a submarine hull were best not considered. There was little, therefore, in the navy's experience of taking a ballistic missile to sea to give them much comfort about the practicality of the idea. For a time, this was to stall any further research on naval ballistic missiles.

The Soviets, rather less concerned perhaps about the nuances of health and safety, had also been keen to exploit German advanced technology and used copies of the A-4 called R-1 (NATO recording name 'SS-1 Scunner') in a variety of adapted programmes. Perhaps the most ambitious was a design based on the Type XXI U-boat, which incorporated vertical launch tubes for a battery of R-1 missiles. Called 'Project P-2', the submarine, not unsurprisingly, never made it beyond the drawing board, but the seeds of the idea of marrying submarine and missile were sown.

In parallel to their interest in the V2, the US had acquired salvaged operational V1 components resulting from the overrunning of the launch sites in northern France and had shipped these to America via London. By September 1944, they had reverse engineered an American version under the Jet Bomb program—the Republic-Ford JB-2 (Jet Bomb-2) Loon—which differed in only minor details from the German missile. The intention was to use it in considerable numbers for the expected invasion of Japan (Operation Downfall).[10] But with the war now over, the production contract for the Loons earmarked for the invasion was terminated on 15 September 1945 after some 1,391 had been delivered to the USAAF. The navy, however, proceeded with a proposal to acquire and deploy the missile aboard submarines. Redesignated LTV-N-2, the missile was deployed in two converted submarines, firstly the USS *Cusk* (SSG-348) later joined by the USS *Carbonero* (SSG-337) (the 'G' suffix was added to the submarines' designation after their conversion to indicate their guided missile role). The Loon's Ford-Schmidt pulse-duct engine was, however, not as powerful as the German engine, resulting in a poorer performance. The modifications to the submarines consisted of a hangar for storage of the Loon and launching rails, both mounted on the after-hull casings. All launch activity had to take place on the surface, and this made the submarine potentially vulnerable during the pre-launch phase, but the relative simplicity of the weapon compared with the V2 in many ways offered a more practical solution than that offered by *Prüfstand XII,* but still one that exposed the submarine's vulnerability.

The first seaborne launch of a Loon took place on 12 February 1947 from the *Cusk* when she was off Point Mugu, California, and marked the first launch of a missile from a US submarine. The first augmented-power launch took place six days later. The Loon was fitted with four RATO (rocket-assisted take-off) rockets to improve its initial performance. In an attempt to overcome some of the guidance problems, the Loons were fitted with a radio-controlled guidance system that allowed them to be guided from the parent submarine. This solution had already been considered by the Germans but had been rejected as being too vulnerable to jamming. A further weakness of the US system was the increase in the submarine's own vulnerability as it needed to remain surfaced to guide the Loon to its target. During the test programme, which continued during February and March, a number of Loons exploded on take-off or soon thereafter, representing as much of a threat to the submarine and its crew as it did to any potential target. Nevertheless, a number were successfully launched, although no single missile covered a distance exceeding 100 miles. In late 1949, a Loon was also successfully launched from the USS *Norton Sound* (AVM-1), a former seaplane tender of the *Currituck* class converted to handle missile test launches which had included the subsonic SAM-N-2 Lark missile developed by Raytheon to counter the wartime threat from Japanese kamikaze aircraft (the Lark was the first ship-to-air missile to destroy a target drone). Although an aircraft carrier and an *Alaska*-class large cruiser had also been considered for conversion, the *Norton Sound* was the cheapest option, and the ship's broad fantail and 30-ton crane made her an ideal subject to have a new life in testing guided missiles. Safety was a major consideration bearing in mind the hazardous materials being handled and because many of the crew were highly specialised in their field, more than a few were later to find their way into the Polaris programme.

The *Cusk* was not to fire any more missiles after the completion of the Loon programme, but she remained involved with missile development, largely because of the specialised on-board guidance equipment. In 1954, after further modification, she reverted to her original, SS-348, designation and was subsequently based at Pearl Harbor.

Although the Loon was not to reach operational status, its concept was proven, and alongside the Loon programme, BuAer was concurrently pursuing the Rigel programme in conjunction with the Grumman Aircraft and Engineering Corporation. The SSM-N-6 Rigel was powered initially by a Marquardt integral ramjet and was designed with a range of some 500 miles at a speed of Mach 2 and could carry a 3,000-lb warhead. The production version would have had two wing-mounted ramjets and would have carried a W-5 nuclear warhead. In a similar manner to the Loon, it could be launched from the casing of a surfaced submarine. Though both programmes contributed to an overall appreciation of the problems surrounding submarine launched missiles, neither proved in real terms to be particularly successful.

The immediate post-war years saw a number of missile projects by each of the three services. The Loon and Rigel programmes can be considered first-generation weapons, so in 1947, not wanting to be caught out by the newly formed USAF who were flexing their newly independent wings by proceeding with the development of a cruise missile called Matador, the navy had initiated development of a turbojet powered cruise missile, called Regulus, named (like Rigel and subsequently Polaris) after a star. In reality, a less challenging design than Rigel, the development of Regulus was given to Chance-Vought Aircraft Inc. at their factory in Dallas, Texas, a company with a long-standing tradition of producing naval aircraft. Regulus I was a cruise missile powered by a small Allison J33 turbo-jet engine for its normal flight envelope and with twin 1,000-lb-thrust RATO packs for the launch phase. The missile had a speed of Mach 1 and a range, like Rigel, of around 400 miles. Initial overland testing took place at Edwards Air Force Base in California before moving to the Navy Air Missile Test Center at Point Mugu with its 11,000-square-mile oversea range. It had been selected over a number of other possible locations as it, 'offered everything the Navy desired—off-shore islands where the Navy could mount instruments to track the flight of missiles; the proximity of the center to aircraft industries in California; its nearness to a seaport and a populated area; and the availability of land affording a large safety area'.[11] This allowed over-water flight testing to take place.

Regulus was, from the start, seen as a strategic weapon and was therefore designed to carry a nuclear warhead. To this end, in January 1950, SecNav Francis P. Matthews approved the development of the 120-kT W-5 warhead for the missile: a warhead that had already been considered for Rigel as well as the USAF's Matador and Rascal missiles. Meanwhile, two Second World War *Gato*-class submarines, the USS *Tunny* (SSG-282) and USS *Barbero* (SSG-317), were being converted to take the missiles. The *Tunny* was recommissioned on 6 March 1953 with the *Barbero* following somewhat later on 28 October 1955. The 33-foot-long Regulus was fitted with folding wings and vertical tail to enable it to be accommodated within the watertight hangars which were installed on the submarines. Two aircraft carriers, USS *Randolph* (CV-15) and USS *Hancock* (CV-19), and four cruisers, USS *Helena* (CA-75), USS *Macon* (CA-132), USS *Toledo* (CA-133), and USS *Los Angeles* (CA-134), were later converted to launch Regulus I. Further proposals were promulgated for the missile to be launched from shore-based batteries and also that the nuclear submarine USS *Nautilus* (SSN-571) be converted to carry it, although neither idea was taken to conclusion.[12]

Regulus incorporated a two-dimensional fairly basic inertial platform. One element kept it in level flight and the other was a vertical gyro to give direction. Guidance was by electronic signal, either from the launch vessel or for longer-range targets, a secondary submarine or alternative vessel giving terminal guidance. The missile was first deployed in 1955 in the Pacific on board the USS *Los Angeles* and a total of five submarines, four heavy cruisers, and ten aircraft carriers were adapted to carry the missiles. There was a clear need, however, for an improved, faster missile with an increased range. The Regulus II programme was therefore instituted to supersede Regulus I. Although bearing the same name, it was essentially a completely new design embodying a much higher performance, although in certain respects, it borrowed from the experience with the earlier missile. Designated SSM-N-9, the 57-foot-long, 12-ton Regulus II was designed with a range of 1,000 miles at a speed of Mach 2 which, it was judged, would considerably improve its chances against counterattack. The prototype was powered by a 7,700-lb-thrust Wright J65 engine. This was replaced with a J79 engine in the production models. This engine was capable of producing, with afterburner, some 15,000 lb thrust.

Two *Darter*-class submarines were completed to carry Regulus II. Improved *Tang*-class boats, these were 'state of the art' conventional submarines, the USS *Grayback* (SSG-574) and USS *Growler* (SSG-577). Although designed principally for Regulus II, Regulus I could also be accommodated. The two submarines had 50-foot bow extensions to allow the incorporation of two large hangars, each of which could hold two Regulus I missiles or one Regulus II (the missiles were colloquially known by their crews as 'birds'). These hangars, like those of the earlier SSGs, presented an element of risk to the submarines in that, if they flooded, the submarine would rapidly capsize. Each submarine was 322 feet long and displaced 2,287 tons. Although limited servicing of the missiles could be undertaken within the hangars when the submarine was submerged, the main parts of the launch operations were yet again conducted on the surface. It was estimated that a well-trained crew should be able to despatch a missile in a maximum of ten minutes. Also taken on as a test ship was the USS *King County*. Originally an LST-542 tank landing ship, the vessel was converted in 1957–8 and reclassified as AG-157 to take part in the Regulus II programme.

The first Regulus II was launched, on land, from Edwards Air Force Base on 13 November 1957 and completed a near perfect flight. This was a version of the missile equipped with a tricycle undercarriage and could be flown to a landing by an accompanying chase plane using radio control thus allowing it to be reused. Chance-Vought was duly authorised to start production. The *Skate*'s innovative teardrop hull had by now found its way into the design of the future submarines. The nuclear-powered USS *Halibut* (SSGN-587) was the first submarine in the US Navy to be designed from the start to launch missiles. Built by the Mare Island Naval Shipyard and launched on 9 January 1959, she could carry either two Regulus II or five Regulus I missiles. Commissioned on 4 January 1960, the *Halibut* was a large submarine (350 feet long) and displaced 5,000 tons submerged. Her bows contained the massive missile hangar that was of much more streamlined shape than those on the *Grayback* and *Growler*. This hangar was nearly 90 feet long and 24 feet high, encompassing a space of some 30,000 cubic feet. Between the hangar and the fin was the retractable launch ramp for the missiles. She was powered by a new design of reactor, the Submarine Fleet Reactor (SFR), powering two shafts. Always wary of the air force's intentions, the navy even considered developing a submarine of similar size to carry eight jet fighters that would be launched vertically.

It was, however, the *Grayback* that had launched the first and, as it turned out, the only operational Regulus II on 16 September 1958 while off the coast of California. As a precursor to the later deterrent patrols of the Polaris fleet, the five submarines equipped to carry Regulus carried out forty-one patrols in the North Pacific between October 1959 and July 1964; by this time, the Polaris programme was well established, and with it, the realisation that Regulus represented a technological path which, at that time, was perceived as holding little further capacity for development. It was not until some years later that the cruise missile concept returned once again to prominence as a weapon complementary to the ballistic missile.

The early termination of Regulus production was announced by SecNav Gates on 12 December 1958. The official statement claimed: 'It is apparent that the ballistic missile has greater growth potential in overall military effectiveness than have air-breathing missiles'. Gates was, however, at pains to point out that Regulus II was 'one of the most successful air-breathing missiles developed'. It still had a powerful following within the navy, which sought to place blame for the cancellation on the US government's economic constraints rather than the developmental limitations of the weapon itself. 'There is always regret at giving up something that really works well.'[13] Gates's response appears, in some way, to accept this for he claimed that the programme had been terminated so as to allow the development of 'the best balance in overall Navy weapon systems within the resources available'. CNO Admiral Elmo R. 'Bud' Zumwalt commented that it was the 'single worst decision about weapons [the Navy] made during my years of service.'[14]

(Incidentally, the USAF suffered a similar termination with its Navaho long-range cruise missile project. Although, in February 1956, SecAF Donald A. Quarles had given the missile national priority second only to the ICBMs and IRBMs, it was soon overtaken by the promising progress of the Atlas ICBM programme.) The *Halibut* completed the final Regulus patrol in July 1964. Although its operational role was finished, the missiles continued to play a valuable training role either as target vehicles, designated KD2U (MQM-15A) or used for other training purposes, designated RGM-15A. Along with Regulus, a subsequent design of submarine, the *Permit* class with four separate hangar tubes to ameliorate the effects of flooding, was also terminated.

It is worthy of note that the Soviets too were moving in a similar direction. Their P-5 'Pyatyorka' (NATO reporting name SS-N-3C 'Shaddock') was a turbojet-powered cruise missile that entered service in 1959 and was designed principally as a bombardment weapon against the US coast. It saw service on Whiskey Single Bin, Twin Bin, and Long Bin submarines as well as Juliet and Echo submarines. Folding wings allowed it to be carried in storage tubes on the submarine casing. It could carry both conventional warheads or nuclear warheads in the 200–350-kt range and like Regulus, the submarine had to surface to launch the missiles.

4

The Germans at White Sands

Back at White Sands, the Germans gradually found their V2 project developing, although eventually only sufficient components could be assembled to allow the launch of sixty-four rockets, the last of which was launched on 19 September 1952. On 24 February 1949, the first of the 'BUMPER WAC' launches took place. This was a two-stage development of the V2 where a WAC Corporal rocket was mounted on what had been the warhead compartment in the nose of the V2. Considerably smaller in size than the A-4, the WAC Corporal had been developed at the California Institute of Technology (Caltech) during the final stages of the war and used a hypergolic (self-igniting) fuel combination of nitric acid and aniline. This two-stage rocket reached record altitudes of around 244 miles and reached a velocity of some 5,150 mph. This achievement represented the technical climax of the White Sands programme.

By early 1950, von Braun's contribution to the White Sands launches was largely complete. The A-4 design had been taken to the limits of its capability and the army was keen to use the Germans' talents on its next generation of rockets. Beginning on 15 April 1950, von Braun and around 130 other German scientists were therefore transferred to the Ordnance Guided Missile Center, which had been set up at the Redstone Arsenal in Huntsville, Alabama, now under the command of Maj. Hamill (promoted to lieutenant colonel on 7 July 1951); Hamill had organised the removal of the V2s from Nordhausen and was involved with the Germans at Fort Bliss. It was a location with which von Braun, now with the position of project director of the center, was to remain closely linked for the rest of his life. The center had already received an instruction in July 1950 from the office of the chief of ordnance to develop a surface-to-surface missile (SSM) with a range capability of 500 miles. The post-war realignment of the wartime Allies and the descent of Churchill's 'Iron Curtain', dividing East and West Germany had called for a full appraisal of the West's political and military aims. The speed with which the Soviet Union had developed its own nuclear capability had also caused widespread alarm and it was clear that the North

German Plain was the likely future battleground. An intermediate range missile was therefore an attractive option as such a weapon could reach a number of Soviet targets. The scientists at the Los Alamos Scientific Laboratory (LASL) who were developing the next generation of nuclear weapons were also promising a reduction in the weight of the weapons such that it was now realistic to design a missile with a nuclear capability. The Mk 1 atom bomb, nicknamed 'Little Boy', which had been dropped on Hiroshima had weighed 8,890 lb, while the Mk III 'Fat Man' allocated to Nagasaki had weighed 10,000 lb. By comparison, the V2 had been limited to a warhead of only 2,200 lb.

In September 1950, GE transferred to Redstone a missile project known as Hercules C1 on which the company had been working since 1946. In overall terms, it was very similar to what the army was seeking. The project was known for the next two years under different code names (Ursa Major, XSSM-G-14, and XSSM-A14) before the missile was officially named 'Redstone' in April 1952. In March 1951, the specification of the missile had been changed to accommodate a heavier payload. Payload weight tended to be inversely proportionate to range so the only way of achieving this was to reduce the range and Redstone therefore ended up with a range of around 250 miles. This was hardly better than the A-4 and in many ways the Redstone could only be considered as a 'glorified V2' incorporating, as it did, so many of the features of the German missile.[1] However, the question of range was later to take on an unexpected significance for army ambitions.

In one respect, however, Redstone was significantly different from the A-4 employing, as it did, an idea which had already been thought out at Peenemünde. In the German rocket's design, the entire missile returned to earth as one unit. This had necessitated a robust enough construction to ensure that the body of the rocket did not break up in flight. But it was, of course, only the warhead that needed to complete the whole path of the trajectory. In the Redstone, therefore, a re-entry section, comprising the warhead and an associated inertial guidance unit, separated from the main body, or thrust unit, which would thereafter burn up in the heat of re-entry caused by the friction of the atmosphere. Steel fabrication was kept to a minimum in the re-entry section with only the thrust unit made from aluminium. Furthermore, whereas the fuel and oxidant tanks in the A-4 design had been separate containers within the outer aerodynamic shell of the rocket, the Redstone design merely used the outer shell of the rocket for the tanks separated by an internal bulkhead. This monocoque construction led to a considerable saving in overall weight, a greater percentage of this overall weight was represented by fuel and therefore a greater payload capacity resulted.

The 69-foot-long missile weighed 62,000 lb, had a range of some 250 miles, and, like the V2, could be launched from mobile sites. It was powered by a version of the rocket motor developed by North American Aviation to power the USAF's Navaho cruise missile and used ethyl alcohol and liquid oxygen.

The inertial guidance unit which controlled the path of the re-entry section as it headed towards its target was the product of Peenemünde research, although only preliminary testing had been achieved during the war. The re-entry section, over 26 feet long and, like the thrust unit, 70 inches in diameter had an all-up weight of 7,900 lb including the nuclear warhead. The nuclear capability of the missile had been determined by the Joint Committee of the US Army-AEC when, on 1 August 1956 they instructed that the Mk 39 RV be modified to carry the warhead for Redstone.

The first, inert, Redstone was fired on 20 August 1953. Thirty-six further test firings followed culminating in two high-altitude nuclear test explosions to prove the W-39 warhead. These two explosions, code-named 'Teak' and 'Orange', were part of the 1958 Hardtack series of nuclear tests. Demonstrating how nuclear science had advanced, these explosions were more than 170 times the power of the Hiroshima and Nagasaki bombs. The tests had originally been planned for Bikini but were moved over concerns about retinal damage among South Pacific islanders. Both launches took place from Johnston Island in the Pacific, some 750 NM south-west of Hawaii and produced airbursts in the 2–2.5-Mt range. Soldiers from the 40th Field Artillery Missile Group fired the army's first Redstone on 16 May 1958 and the missile entered service in Germany the following month. The W-39-YMod1 warhead was released for army use on 8 July 1959. Overall, some sixty W39-YMod1 and -YMod2 warheads, each with a yield of 2–2.5 Mt, were manufactured.

The Redstone project team had been joined in July 1955 by Hermann Oberth.[2] He had joined the Peenemünde group in 1941. He had chosen to stay in Germany after the war but had found little productive use for his noteworthy talents. He therefore willingly accepted an invitation from von Braun, his one-time pupil, to leave Germany and join the Redstone project. The same month as he arrived, proposals were put forward for a follow-on missile to succeed Redstone. Redstone itself, however, was significant in a number of ways. It launched the first American satellite; it carried the first two American astronauts into space; and as the M-8 Field Artillery System and armed with a 3.75-Mt warhead was based in West Germany with the US Army for six years from 1958 and in this form was the most powerful field artillery weapon ever deployed.

* * * * *

Efforts to make economies in national defence budgets have repeatedly attracted politicians to pursue the development of weapons which could be used by more than one service, or which could perform widely differing mission profiles. Such an economy was but one factor in the thinking behind the contents of a report prepared by a secret committee chaired by President Eisenhower's special adviser on science and technology, James R. Killian Jr from MIT. Perhaps not surprisingly for a military man, Eisenhower was deeply interested in how technology was developing and the uses to which it could be put. On 26 July 1954, Killian received a letter from the president:

> I understand that you have been asked by the Science Advisory Committee of the Office of Defense Mobilisation to direct a study of the country's technological capabilities to meet some of its current problems. The project grew out of suggestions which I made to the Science Advisory Committee, and I am keenly interested in it. The results will be of great value to the government.[3]

Eisenhower, prompted by memories of the attack on Pearl Harbor which had brought America into the Second World War, was deeply concerned about the danger of another such surprise attack and the committee's brief was to consider all aspects of strategic defence. The committee, convened under the title of the Technological Capabilities Panel (TCP), considered technological advances, particularly thermonuclear warhead developments and practical inertial guidance systems which led to the conclusion that the development of an IRBM was both feasible and economically practicable. Their report recommended: 'There be developed a ballistic missile (with about 1500 nautical mile range and megaton warhead) for strategic bombardment; both land-basing and ship-basing should be considered'.[4] The report, 'Meeting the Threat of Surprise Attack', was dated 14 February 1955, and was duly considered by the president and the National Security Council (NSC).[5] Killian referred to the dominance that SAC then enjoyed but without a reliable US early warning system SAC was vulnerable and the US open to surprise attack, a scenario which further reminded defence chiefs of the disaster at Pearl Harbor. Robert Cutler, the president's national security advisor, wrote: 'The report's presentation was a high point in the [National Security] Council's record, for it influenced the accelerated development by the U.S. of nuclear capable ICBMs (including later the long-range Polaris missile fired from a submerged submarine)'.[6] IRBMs were also considered, albeit as stopgaps until the more complex ICBMs were available, and this was to lead to the competing, but later largely complementary, ventures by the air force and the army. The NSC accepted the committee's report and, in order to strengthen the breadth of offensive capability, SecDef Charles E. Wilson on 9 September 1955 sanctioned the formation of the Joint Army Navy Ballistic Missile Committee (JANBMC) to develop a missile to be used by both the army and the navy. On 8 November, Wilson issued a directive for the JANBMC to proceed jointly with the development of IRBM #2 'with the dual objective of achieving an early shipboard capability and also providing a land-based alternate to the Air Force program IRBM #1 (THOR)'. The two services thereafter set up their own internal organisations to direct the progress of their respective sides of the development. From the navy's perspective, both BuAer and BuOrd wanted the contract to build the missiles, but CNO Admiral Arleigh A. Burke assisted by ACNO

(Guided Missiles) Rear Admiral John H. Sides, spent a considerable time deciding the correct route and the correct appointment to the position and came down on the side of BuOrd with the instruction to use expertise from BuAer as required. Burke had also assessed the navy's current missile program which concentrated on Regulus I, Regulus II, and Triton. The SSN-M-2 Triton was a ramjet-powered, nuclear land-attack cruise missile project, but the success and rapid development of Regulus II and problems with the ramjet power plant led to its cancellation in 1957 with the funds being transferred to the embryonic fleet ballistic missile (FBM) programme. Burke was meanwhile happy to maintain progress on these providing that enough funds were available. Burke saw his opportunity when SecNav Charles S. Thomas presciently authorised the creation of what was to become the keystone in America's naval missile programme—the Special Projects Office (SP) of the Bureau of Ordnance formed on 17 November 1955 under the command of Rear Admiral William F. 'Red' Raborn Jr who took up his post as Director, Special Projects (SP00) on 5 December. (The designation had been chosen to obscure the true purpose of the organisation, but unlike the Manhattan Project which had proved very successful in masking its real purpose, a second attempt at such a ruse, particularly in peacetime, was unlikely to be as successful, but the name was maintained for many years.) Raborn's appointment also satisfied BuAer. His brief was to determine the problems that might be associated with a naval IRBM. He was an officer with considerable gunnery experience as well as having served on carriers in the Pacific and had been appointed by Burke on the recommendation of Admiral James S. Russell, chief of the BuAer and a keen supporter of a naval IRBM and further endorsed by Sides for whom he had worked as his deputy. It was to prove an inspired choice. SP's *modus operandi* was a departure from the traditional navy set up for such projects and was modelled on US industry methods. Raborn's position was conferred with considerable and wide-ranging authority, reporting directly to Burke and the secretary of the navy. Significant too for the naval missile lobby was that Burke, unlike his predecessor Admiral Robert B. Carney, strongly supported the broad concept of incorporating missiles into the navy's arsenal. Carney had forbidden naval officers from promoting any sea-based ballistic missile project, not wanting a toxic repeat of the icy and destructive relationship between the navy and the air force over the 'bomber or carrier' argument of the late 1940s which led to the 'Revolt of the Admirals'. In this acrimonious debate, the navy's five proposed post-war super carriers lost out to SAC's behemoth Convair B-36 bomber.

This huge 'legacy' aircraft had been developed as a back-up for the B-29 and was in many ways on the road to obsolescence from the start, but it provided a stopgap until the new generation Boeing B-47 and B-52 jet bombers entered service. It had six engines mounted behind the wing with, later, the addition of four turbojets to increase its performance. Beset with maintenance problems which led to a shortage of spares, it was often necessary to cannibalise other B-36s to keep an operational quota. After it was revealed that flying above 40,000 feet was unwise when one of the aircraft lost ten propellor blades, it became the subject of competition between the air force and the navy. This was a time when there was much talk of unifying the services. The US Marines had already felt the chill wind when Air Force General Frank Anderson had warned a group of naval officers in 1947 that, 'as for the Marines, you know what they are. They are a small fouled up army talking Navy lingo. We're going to put those Marines in the Regular Army and make efficient soldiers out of them.' Interservice rivalry reached new heights of bitterness. Both Burke and Sides had been middle-ranked officers in the Revolt of the Admirals when the navy conducted a vicious campaign against the B-36. It was to cost the CNO Admiral Louis E Denfeld his position when the SecNav Francis P. Matthews 'detached him from his job' and replaced him with the more amenable Vice Admiral Forrest P. Sherman. Burke's involvement very nearly brought his naval career to an end. In a further act of retribution, Matthews had personally removed Burke's name from the promotion list to admiral, but when the list was sent to Truman for his approval, the president's naval aide informed the president that Matthews did not have the legal authority to edit the list and Burke was duly reinstated—his career fortuitously saved, although for a time he served at duty stations out of the public eye.

The navy did theoretically have nuclear capability with its North American AJ Savage. A post-war development, the aircraft had two piston engines and a turbojet in the rear fuselage. Its weight determined that it could only be deployed on the larger carriers and in concept it would carry the 'Little Boy' bomb, no longer in production. However, the flagship flush-deck 80,000-ton supercarrier, the USS *United States* (CVA-58), had been summarily cancelled along with the other four similar carriers a few days after its keel had been laid by the unashamedly pro-air force and aggressively ambitious, but widely disliked, SecDef Louis A. Johnson, a staunch supporter of President Truman. This was without any prior consultation with SecNav Sullivan. Although a meeting was promised to discuss the matter, it never took place. This resulted in considerable loss of prestige for the navy. It had nearly cost Burke's subsequent promotion to admiral, but his creation of SP resulted from his concern that the existing naval bureaucracy, still smarting from the loss of the carriers, would stifle the project. SP provided a 'vertical' responsibility which would separate it from BuShips.

Burke was not without considerable opposition from some quarters to his plans for a naval IRBM. Missiles were expensive. Even his appointment to CNO had not been trouble free as a number of more senior admirals had been passed over, and he himself was initially uncertain about whether he possessed the necessary qualifications for the job, even Carney thought that he was getting the top job two years prematurely. However, now in the job and undeterred, he created alongside SP the Navy Ballistic Missile Committee. This committee comprised the secretary of the navy, the assistant secretary of the navy for air, the deputy chief of naval operations for readiness, the director of guided missiles, and the assistant secretary of the navy for financial management. It was tasked with dictating the navy's policy towards the missile as a seaborne IRBM. The inclusion of the assistant secretary of the navy for air was an interesting and significant appointment if taken alongside Raborn's own appointment, for Raborn had spent much of war with the Pacific Fleet's carrier forces. The knowledge of a naval aviator was deemed to be important to provide a liaison facility with the air force, although the icy relationship between the seaborne and the airborne forces had thawed little since the events of recent years. In fact, in July 1952, USAF Deputy Chief of Staff for Operations Lt-Gen. Thomas D. White had gone as far as saying, 'eventually that battle [between the navy and the air force] is going to have to be fought to a finish'.[7] The navy was wary of SAC under LeMay's dynamic and at times maverick leadership, and rightly so. He was determined to ensure that SAC's strategic bombers remained dominant in their ability to deliver the ever-increasing stockpile of nuclear weapons right to the heart of the Soviet Union. His plans, effectively encompassing the United States' nuclear war capability were drawn up with little or no reference either to the joint chiefs of staff (JCS) or indeed to the president himself. His air-atomic plan was to unleash 80 per cent of the US's nuclear arsenal in one massive opening round of the war. Co-operation with the USAF and an understanding of its needs was therefore considered to be important. Fortunately, no such jealousy existed in the navy's relationship with the army, who saw a naval IRBM as no competitor to its own aspirations and, arguably, believed that the involvement of the navy produced a more formidable team even if it added complication to the army programme.

The two services argued their case to the JCS that all three services should be equipped with IRBMs in light of the primary functions allocated to them by the DoD. The air force, however, still claimed the primary role of the IRBM but conceded that the navy could provide a supporting role through a sea-based version in accomplishing the air force's primary mission. The army accepted that its missiles would be used tactically within its areas of operations. SAC's determination to achieve a strategic stranglehold was to be amply demonstrated when, in the early hours of 20 May 1956, after several delays caused by the weather, an RB-52B-1-BO (52-013) named 'Barbara Grace' of the 4925th Test Group (Atomic) from the Air Force Special Weapons Center at Kirkland AFB conducted the first American airborne thermonuclear test when a device was dropped from 40,000 feet. Piloted by Maj. David M. Critchlow, the test article was a TX-15-XI two-stage radiation implosion bomb weighing 6,867 lb. The target was Namu Island, part of Bikini Atoll, but navigational errors caused the target to be missed by 3.6 miles when the bomb-aimer Maj. Dwight E. Durner mistook a nearby lighted island for the target and released the device twenty-one seconds too early. Much of the data on the test, code-named Redwing Cherokee, was therefore lost, but the estimate was an explosion of 3.75 Mt. The test had been witnessed by invited media who were aboard the USS *Mount McKinley* (AGC-7) and the error was initially not disclosed to them, however, regardless of this, it had been a warning to the Soviets of US capability.[8] The test proved that the B-52 was cleared to drop Class 'C' warheads and had also confirmed the optimum parameters, speed, altitude etc., for operational use.[9] At that time, only SAC could field warheads of this weight, but the promised new generation of lighter warheads would change this dimension.

Raborn set up his office in early December, by coincidence in the same building in which Rickover worked. On 2 December 1955, Burke had given him what became known as 'Red Raborn's Hunting License'. This effectively allowed him to co-opt up to forty people he wanted for the project, regardless of where their current posting or position may have been. Such was their influence that, in the fullness of time, many within the navy were to brand Raborn and Rickover as being heads of their own 'private navies'. Raborn would be totally responsible for the management of the project. There was to be no upward responsibility: success or failure of the project would be his and his alone.

> If Rear Admiral Raborn runs into any difficulty with which I can help, I will want to know about it at once along with his recommended course of action for me to take. If more money is needed, we will get it. If he needs more people, those people will be ordered in. If there is anything that slows this project up beyond the capacity of the Navy Department we will immediately take it to the highest level and not work our way up through several days. In taking this type of action we must be reasonably sure we are right and at least know the possible consequences of being wrong because we will be disrupting many other programs in order to make achievement in this one if we are not careful. That is all right if we really make an achievement.[10]

Sensing the urgency of the project in light of the 'tremendous amount of enthusiasm' the Air Force was applying to its IRBM, Burke further commented:

> We must have even more [enthusiasm].... It is quite evident that we must move fast on this fleet ballistic missile and our present schedule for shipborne launches are [*sic*] not good enough. I think that the first service that demonstrates a capability for this is very likely to continue the project and the others may well drop out. This missile must be fired from a ship just as early as possible even though the equipment in the ship is not as desirable as may be conceived.[11]

Raborn had the quality to spot both officers and civilians who possessed the skills he required, and he had soon identified the initial intake of people he needed. Although there were regular meetings to review progress, Burke, by his own admission a somewhat reluctant CNO, had to balance a large number of competing naval projects and largely contented himself in identifying the various areas of naval expenditure that would have to be cut to fund the IRBM programme, and this was to include personnel.[12] One casualty, as we have seen, was the Regulus missile. The navy could not afford to develop both missiles, but the cancellation was made against some stiff opposition from within its own ranks. Regulus II was a successful and proven missile which gave the navy a strategic role, while many saw the FBM as a risky step into the unknown with no proof of success. Burke was to comment, 'Everybody now thinks that there was a lot of push behind these missiles, and there wasn't. People in the Navy pushing, but nobody outside of the Navy gave a damn or a thought or anything at all about a ballistic missile at sea that I ever heard of.'[13]

The army was already planning its own IRBM as, in November 1955, the planning of a missile of, initially, 1,000-NM range to succeed the Redstone had been given to a newly to be created organisation, the Army Ballistic Missile Agency (ABMA) with Maj.-Gen. John B. Medaris as commander designate. This brought von Braun's Redstone team with about 1,700 personnel into a unified army structure. Medaris was a man of not dissimilar characteristics to Rickover. Similarly disliked by many, he had thrice been rejected for promotion to general before this new posting sealed his ascent to that rank. Dignified in appearance and impeccable in dress and behaviour, he had the skill to get the best out of those working under him—even von Braun, his charismatic chief technical officer. The two were to become firm friends.

Medaris disliked the air force, which he believed was far too preoccupied with SAC to the detriment of a battlefield logistic support role, a relationship that had served the marines well in Korea with their allied marine aviation wing. In planning the new missile, he had been conscious that the army and the air force were considering a missile that broadly matched the aspirations of both services, but with the navy now coming on board, the parameters were going to have to change quite drastically. By 28 November, Medaris was able to present an initial proposal to the Office of the Secretary of Defense Ballistic Missile Committee (OSD-BMC), an organisation combining the missile interests of all the services. The DoD had indicated that one missile design was to suit both services and that the operational needs of both were to proceed in parallel, and they were not to favour an earlier deployment of a land-based solution even if that would be easier to achieve. On 20 December, OSD-BMC authorised JANBMC to proceed with the development of the missile. This also released much-needed funding for the project. With this confirmation, Raborn began to form a team under his command. As his deputy (SP01), he appointed CAPT. John B. Colwell, an authority on naval ordnance. Colwell had only recently reported to the office of the CNO and this sudden further move caused some expressions of displeasure from his commander, although Colwell admitted that on reporting to Raborn, he had little idea of what his new role entailed, nor was he aware why he had been chosen as the two officers' paths had not previously crossed.[14] CDR William A. Hasler was soon after appointed to take charge of the naval team that would be working alongside the army. From the start, the army with its team of Germans had very much led the way in terms of ballistic missile development. On 20 August 1953, von Braun had been at Cape Canaveral for the first Redstone I launch. This was, in effect, the first launch of a truly ballistic American missile and indicated the army's lead in this field. For its part, the army had delegated control of its interest to the Redstone Arsenal where the internal reorganisation of the arsenal's missile division saw the full activation, on 1 February 1956, of the ABMA.

The prospect of one weapon system that would answer the needs of more than one service, although attractive to cost-saving politicians, has an uneven history of many such attempts ending in spectacular failures. Was the joint army–navy missile likely to be any different? The proposed missile was given the name Jupiter in April 1956. Echoing the initial proposals that von Braun had already drawn up for a successor to Redstone, and with its existing experience, the army was perhaps unsurprisingly appointed project manager. The desired range of the missile, now determined as 1,500 NM, dictated a length of around 60 feet to accommodate the required fuel load. It was decided that the design would incorporate a new type of nose cone that would be covered in an ablative material to absorb the frictional heat of re-entry. By then, the USAF, intent on dominating what was to become known as strategic warfare—the delivery of nuclear weapons on enemy territory—was developing its own IRBM, the Douglas SM-75 Thor, as well as an ICBM with a 5,000-mile range called Atlas. The latter was viewed by the Redstone Group as potentially a technological step too far and one which might eventually prove too challenging, but like the navy, the army was concerned that the air force might still achieve missile dominance to the detriment of the other two services. ABMA therefore received increasing pressure from within the army's ranks to proceed with the development of Jupiter with utmost speed with the aim of having it operational by 1958 somewhat before the anticipated in-service date of Atlas. This, it was hoped, might secure further funding for a development programme to increase Jupiter's range. As speed was of the essence, with substantial funding already confirmed and progress with the missile well advanced, von Braun and his army team can perhaps be forgiven for being less than enthusiastic about some of the changes dictated by its naval role, which Hasler's team, newly arrived at Huntsville, sought. Nonetheless, the relationship between the two services remained cordial. Von Braun was willing to be pragmatic and saw that the naval presence potentially strengthened the whole project for both services: 'He knew the political value of having Jupiter used by both the Navy and the Army and he did not give up, even as he better understood the submarine environment'.[15] On 28 November 1955, the navy outlined its thoughts on the development of a naval Jupiter but also added a cautionary advice that the navy's cherished aim was the development of a solid-fuelled missile to be operational on surface ships but with the eventual plan to deploy the weapon in submarines. But, '[t]he Jupiter missile was the furthest thing from something anybody would choose for use aboard ship.... Its size was tremendous'. They requested that the OSD allow immediate initiation of a project to produce a solid-fuelled missile so that the serious hazards of handling volatile fuels at sea could be minimised. Nonetheless, when the OSD-BMC authorised the army and the navy to proceed, von Braun added his contribution to the debate by resurrecting the idea of launching missiles from towed barges.[16] It would appear that the navy was unaware of the German origins of this idea, which really seemed as impractical in the mid-1950s as it had been a decade earlier. On 10 January 1956, both the ICBM and the IRBM programmes were accorded the highest national priority.

Operation Sandy had indeed shown that handling a liquid-fuelled missile on board a ship presented complex problems, and thus the navy hoped to limit the overall length of the missile to 55 feet. The eventual agreed length of 58 feet was therefore a compromise that required the diameter be increased to give the required range. The eventual diameter was 8.7 feet, and the overall weight was some 110,000 lb. In view of the navy's wish to launch the Jupiter from tubes, there could be no external fins. Without these, however, the missile would be unstable, and this problem could only be overcome by fitting gimballing exhaust nozzles to the rocket motors, adding further delay and complexity to the project. The navy did in fact correctly point out that fins were only effective during the limited time when the missile was still in the Earth's atmosphere.[17] Guidance would be by an inertial guidance system developed from that used in Redstone. Two uprated versions of Redstone called Jupiter-A and Jupiter-C were used to test various components of the projected missile. Jupiter-C, whose official designation was the Jupiter Composite Re-entry Test Vehicle, first flew on 20 September 1956 and reached a record altitude of 682 miles. Subsequent flights tested the ablative materials, layers of fibreglass, plastic, and asbestos, which were to be used on the nose cone of the IRBM to protect the warhead against the fiery heat of re-entry into the Earth's atmosphere. Raborn's problem was taking someone else's missile that had been specifically designed to be launched from land against land targets, subject it to salt water, and take it to sea. Any modifications thus needed inevitably required elements of redesign, which slowed down the army's progress in its own race with the air force. Still remaining was the concern about the multitude of problems that faced a liquid-fuelled missile, namely the storage of cryogenic fuels on board and the fuelling process which was lengthy and complicated. The relatively slow initial acceleration of the missile after launch was also an unknown area when it came to the various sea-states that would be encountered and the potential problems with this had already been experienced in Operation Sandy.

While it was undoubtedly true that, pound for pound, the technology of solid-fuelled rockets at that time fell far behind their liquid-fuelled equivalents, the initial group of technical staff in SP harboured very grave doubts about the safety of Jupiter if taken to sea on ships let alone in submarines. They likewise remained concerned about the multitude of problems that would have to be overcome before the missiles could be deployed with the minimum of danger to their operators. The missiles could only be loaded with fuel in the vertical position as a fully fuelled missile was not structurally capable of being raised from the horizontal. During fuelling operations on land-based missiles, everyone but the fuelling technicians could retreat to the safety of a concrete blockhouse some distance from the launch pad. On board a ship there was no safe distance, and a fuelling mishap would lead to the almost inevitable serious damage to the ship and danger to the launch crew. Adding further hazard, the super-cooled oxygen would have to be stored onboard. Raborn commented: 'the thought of putting these missiles in the confined spaces of a submarine under the water, would make an internal combustion engine of the whole submarine'.[18] He had every reason to be very wary of fire of any sort aboard a submarine. He was in command of the aircraft carrier USS *Bennington* (CVS-20), 'Big Benn', on 26 May 1954 when the port catapult accumulator burst, killing 103, including a civilian contractor, and injuring a further 118.[19] At that stage, the size and weight of the missile was determined by the weight of the warhead, and this latter determinant produced a missile too big to be accommodated in even the largest submarine. The projected missile was really too fragile to withstand the various stresses that would be imposed on it in heavy seas. Operation Pushover had also shown the dangers from leaking oxidant. Raborn was later to comment, 'conceivably, you'd be in more danger from that than you would [be] if you were under enemy fire.'[20] These ships would also have to address another problem that worried the navy. To have any hope of reaching the target, the accuracy with which the launch ship's exact position had to be established. The missile required two reference points, the location of its target and its own launch position. For land-based missiles, even if mobile, the latter could be accurately identified. For a constantly moving vessel, the same accuracy could not necessarily be provided. Any error in the launch co-ordinates would magnify the dispersion over the target.

By March 1956, it was becoming obvious that a practical naval liquid-fuelled IRBM was never going to be a realistic solution, so consideration was given to a solid-fuelled version of Jupiter, which was to be given the designation Jupiter-S. The design relied on components from Sperry Utah's MGM-29 Sergeant solid-fuelled missile, the US Army's successor to the MGM-5 Corporal. The first stage used six enlarged 40-inch-diameter Sergeant airframes mounted in a cluster around a single Sergeant second stage. Raborn had appointed CAPT. Levering Smith to head up the technical department, and he was asked to manage the development of the missile and the solid-fuelled boost propulsion system. Levering Smith was considered to be the navy's leading exponent on solid-fuelled rockets and was therefore an obvious choice to be seconded to SP. Lockheed was contracted to build the airframe with the rocket motors being manufactured by Aerojet-General, a company that had presciently been set up by von Kármán in 1942. Solid fuels at that time were still inefficient when compared with liquid fuels, and although the Jupiter-S was shorter, it was heavier and wider in diameter than the land-based equivalent—in short, a large, heavy missile well exceeding the liquid-fuelled Jupiter in both size and weight. But if progress could be made with developing more efficient solid fuels, they represented a significant advance on using liquids. No longer would there be the complexity of handling volatile liquids and the time taken in preparing the missile for launch. Solid fuels promised almost instantaneous reaction. Jupiter-S development allowed the army to revert to the original Jupiter design thus speeding its development, and it also took pressure off the supply of the Rocketdyne's S-3D engines which were under contract for supply of sufficient engines for both the Jupiter and the Thor programmes as well as the air force's Atlas.

The path to air force weapons procurement was traditionally undertaken by the Air Research and Development Command (ARDC). Gen. Thomas S. Power had been appointed commander of the ARDC in 1954. He had served as LeMay's deputy during the war and with LeMay had planned the firebombing of Tokyo on 9 March 1945.[21] But it was clear that the processes of the past were no longer adequate for a programme such as Atlas, which introduced new levels of complexity requiring innovative management procedures. The air force therefore set up its Western Development Division (WDD) under the command of Col. Bernard 'Bennie' Schriever, and they were actively pushing ahead with both their

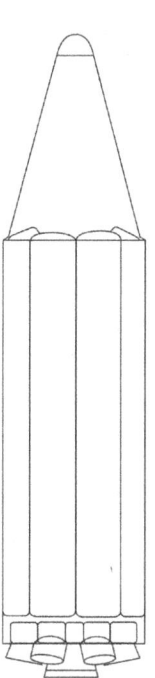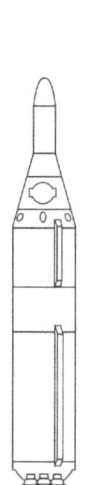

Evolution of Jupiter, Jupiter-S, Polaris A-1. From left to right: Jupiter IRBM, liquid fuel, height 50 feet, diameter 105 inches; Jupiter-S, solid fuel, height 41.3 feet, diameter 120 inches; Polaris A1, height 28.5 feet, diameter 54 inches.

IRBM and ICBM programmes; it was feared by the army that they would lose out in the supply of engines. In the end, a meeting between Schriever and Medaris gave some assurance that Jupiter would not be penalised. There was, however, a caveat added by Schriever that the supply should not ultimately prejudice the WDD's two missile programmes.

Comparison of Specifications			
	Jupiter IRBM	Jupiter-S	Polaris A-1
Length	60 feet	41.3 feet	28.5 feet
Diameter	105 inches	120 inches	54 inches
Gross Weight	110,000 lb	160,000 lb	28,000 lb

Consideration had then to be given to how this missile could be incorporated into a submarine where both size and weight were major considerations, along with safety implications more stringent than on surface ships. This led to a tentative design in which four Jupiter-S would be mounted in an enlarged fin—the maximum number the missile's weight would permit. Launch would take place on the surface. In concept, this was a design not far removed from the Soviet's Project 611, a large ocean-going submarine (NATO reporting name 'Zulu'). The design had been heavily influenced by the German Type XXI, a number of which had been recovered by the advancing Soviet forces. Possessors of the world's largest submarine fleet before the Second World War, the Soviet Navy was now intent on maintaining an even more formidable submarine force. Six of these submarines were converted to carry three liquid-fuelled R-11FM missiles (NATO reporting name SS-N-1 Scud A). On 16 September 1955, one of these missiles was successfully launched from a Zulu V submarine in the White Sea—the first launch of a ballistic missile from a submarine. This prototype Zulu V was fitted with two launch tubes in an extended fin, but the remaining five submarines were fitted with three tubes.

The navy's wish for an advanced solid-fuelled missile had not gone unnoticed. The first report of the Office of the Secretary of Defense Scientific Advisory Committee (OSDSAC) to SecDef Wilson noted: 'the Navy's development of an operating solid fuel IRBM is sufficiently short that this program is a good back-up to the two liquid-fuelled IRBMs even for land-based use.'[22] But on 26 November 1956, the army lost out on any aspirations it may have had to share in a strategic missile programme. Wilson issued a 'Roles and Missions Directive' memorandum for the members of the Armed Forces Policy Council which, among other things, limited the army to the development of SSMs of ranges not exceeding 200 miles, although the Jupiter programme would still go ahead in parallel with the air force's Thor.[23, 24] The 200 miles was based on an army tactical fighting depth of 100 miles, with the launching points 100 miles behind the forward edge of the battle area. This, perhaps inevitably, met some resistance within the services as the navy and the air force would now hold joint responsibility for missiles of greater range—ship-based and land-based respectively. However, the navy meanwhile had been giving very full and serious consideration to the wisdom of its continuing involvement in the Jupiter programme. In March 1956, the JANBMC had been authorised to consider the development of both naval surface and undersea launching platforms, and Raborn's SP was responsible for proposals for these. On 20 March, the OSD-BMC had given approval for a programme to investigate the practicality of solid fuel as an alternative missile propellant for a new missile design.

By now, however, the navy knew the type of missile it needed and how it would be deployed. It had already stated at the start of the Jupiter programme that, 'On a long term basis, the Navy proposes a solid-propellant development program pointed towards surface ships and eventual submarine use.... Development of a solid-propellant missile and submarine system appears feasible, but not on the time scale of the original approach. The solid-propellant is an integral part of the submarine program.'[25] The navy was therefore delighted when, in mid-July 1956, OSDSAC recommended that the navy concentrate on a solid-propellant missile as being within the scope of IRBM #2, in preference to the joint army–navy option, while still retaining the latter as a fall-back option. Burke had previously approached the air force offering to participate in the Thor program if that missile was changed from liquid to solid fuel. The air force rejected this proposal, arguably because a delay in the Thor programme, started a year ahead of the army, could result in Jupiter achieving precedence in the IRBM field. Britain's Lord Louis Mountbatten recalled that after an official visit to the US, Burke drove him to the airport expressing great indignation:

> [Burke] said he wanted to be friends with the USAF and had offered to go shares in their new [IRBM] Thor if they would change the fuel from liquid to solid, to enable it to be fired from submerged submarines. They had categorically refused. He had then and there given the order to start work at once on a solid fuel IRBM to be mounted in a new class of large nuclear submarine[s].

Mountbatten, the arch-intriguer, suggested:

> Since the USAF does not support you would you accept support from the RN? I then offered to send a hand-picked RN officer, with missile experience, to join his team. He accepted, and ever after the First Sea Lord had his own representative in the Polaris project.

The Royal Navy was therefore in from the very start of the nascent FBM programme. This would yield much benefit later on, although at the initial stage, it should be said that there was no intention that the seconded officer would be anything other than an observer, a position which, nonetheless, did not prevent 'prudent staff work' from being undertaken.

Raborn's Special Projects Office

One of Raborn's significant contributions to the Polaris programme was his success in selling the initially unknown project to other departments of the navy, many of which were culturally averse to such a project which in certain cases had been the cause of an unwelcome reduction in their own funding. With the assistance of Thomas J. Watson, president of IBM and known as 'the world's greatest salesman', Raborn and Colwell developed a carefully prepared slideshow and accompanying script which was used to educate people in what the project was about and what it meant to US security.[1] Once it was firmly underway, Colwell commented, 'success brings success, as the project went on and was successful.' Success was essential as more people understood the 'enormous disadvantage with the Russians if we did not have this kind of long-range nuclear capability'.[2] Raborn also sold the project to Congress:

> He did that by himself, and he did a beautiful job. No one should ever take away from Raborn credit for—you can call it a sales job, if you will, but that's not a very good term—the educational job that he did.... I don't know that we ever had any difficulties with Congress at all.[3]

Captain Norvell G. Ward, who had commanded the submarine squadron that had tested Regulus, remembers: 'Raborn was a great salesman; he could go in and talk the pants off of SecNav [Gates and William B. Franke]. He did frequently. I sat in at times and watched him get SecNav to approve funds after Chief Masterton said, "You can't do it."[4] Pressure on Raborn to succeed was very great. Burke had warned him that there was a cut-off if the project was seen to be failing. After receiving some sharp criticism from Raborn at a Saturday meeting, Shugg was invited to have lunch at Raborn's home. As Mrs Raborn prepared the meal, Raborn 'sat down at the organ and just struck thunder and lightning out of that instrument. And when he got up, he said: "Now you see how I feel and there's no need to talk about it any more."'[5] (Raborn was featured on the cover of the *Hammond Times*, the magazine of the organ manufacturer, and featured in an article headed 'Missile-Age Admiral Relaxes at His Hammond.'[6])

Concurrently with these developments was a report from Project Nobska. This was a study forum commissioned by Burke and initiated by the National Academy of Science's Committee on Undersea Warfare. It was named after its location at Nobska Point, Woods Hole, Massachusetts. Chaired by Pennsylvania State University President Eric A. Walker and Columbus O'Donnell Iselin, director of the Woods Hole Oceanographic Institution, the project involved a theoretical assessment of the threat posed by the emerging fleet of Soviet nuclear-powered submarines and the possibility that some of them would be missile armed. To counter this threat, the Nobska report projected that the navy should plan for a state-of-the-art, solid-propellant fleet ballistic missile capability by 1965 and that this should be submarine based, a proposal that impressed Captain Ignatius J. 'Pete' Galantin, head of the Submarine Warfare Branch, Undersea Warfare Division, who commented that the report 'made a very good case that submarines could provide the cheapest, most effective means of naval strategic nuclear weapons delivery.'

It was, however, ultimately the AEC that sealed the fate of the naval Jupiter. In September 1956, it announced that a radical reduction in the size and weight of the next generation of nuclear weapons could realistically be anticipated, indicating that a 600-lb warhead of high yield could be achieved by 1965 or possibly even by 1963. Edmund Teller had already foreseen this when he addressed the Nobska group. He had left LASL in 1952 but had remained a staunch supporter of the project to build a thermonuclear weapon and had moved to the Livermore division of the University of California Radiation Laboratory (UCRL), which had been set up, against considerable opposition from some areas, to provide an alternative centre of research to LASL, and his team at UCRL were confident that the new warhead designs would weigh around 30 per cent of the W-49 warhead then being developed for Jupiter. Yield would be only slightly below one megaton, and this therefore still represented a weapon of significant destructive, and therefore deterrent, power. 'Why', Teller asked, 'are you designing a 1965 weapon system with 1958 warhead technology?'[7] The mid-'60s was a significant date as it was increasingly evident that, by then, there were emerging doubts about the ability of conventional bombers to penetrate the Soviet counter-aircraft missile defences. The inferior performance of solid-propellants, which up until then had been a deciding factor in favour of liquid-fuelled designs, could now be effectively overcome if the payload weight was reduced. Confident that it now had a solution to satisfy its needs, the navy requested permission to withdraw from further involvement in Jupiter. On 8 December 1956, SecDef Wilson granted the appropriate authority. The decision had the full support of Burke and SecNav Thomas. Ten days later, the JANBMC was dissolved and SP was directed to take over the solid-fuelled FBM project. Although grateful to be relieved of its obligations to Jupiter, the navy was not without a degree of disappointment at the severing of the relationship. The navy's project officer, Captain Robert Freitag, wrote to von Braun:

> I sincerely regret that events took the turn they did and that the Army and Navy requirements digressed to the point that our arrangement was forced to end. I sincerely believe that you and your team are the most outstanding group of missile people in this country, or in the world, and regret that the powers-that-be have decided that you will not be working on the Fleet Ballistic Missile.[8]

Medaris even admitted that he 'considered the Polaris system the best bet for the retaliatory striking power for the near future.... Its range, coupled with its underwater capability, provides a flexibility that will meet most requirements.'[9] History tends to understate how the army team's morale was badly affected firstly by the departure of the navy and then the restriction on range. Later von Braun was to leave to head up the US Manned Space program. This left the army able to continue development of Jupiter for its own needs, leading to a $51.8 million contract placed with the Chrysler Corporation on 4 January 1958 to build the missile. But although the 'Roles and Missions Directive' had allowed the army to make 'limited feasibility studies' of missiles with ranges greater than 200 miles, it hardly justified the continued full-scale development of Jupiter. Initially it seemed that this all meant that the only customer for the missile was the air force—and an unlikely one at that. However, it was considered that since work was so far advanced, the missile could be added to the air force inventory, and so ABMA was instructed to continue with the development. Funding was transferred from the army to the USAF via the DoD. The decision was in many ways surprising because Jupiter was undoubtedly complementary to the air force's Thor. Both missiles weighed the same, used the same fuels, had the same range, and used the same W-49 warhead, but work on the latter missile was behind Jupiter, even though the programme, along with the Atlas programme, had been given the highest priority classification.[10] On 27 November 1957, SecDef Neil H. McElroy, who had succeeded Wilson in October, decided to place both Thor and Jupiter into production for operational deployment by December 1958. In due course, sixty Thors operated by RAF crews were to be stationed in eastern England, while the Jupiters were placed in Italy (thirty) and Turkey (fifteen). In all cases, although the missiles were operated by the host countries' air forces, USAF officers controlled the arming of the warheads—the dual key system. It was to be the Jupiters that became the focus of attention during the Cuban Missile Crisis of October 1962. World recognition of the Germans' expertise was, however, eventually accorded when, riding on top of a 363-foot-high NASA Saturn V rocket developed by von Braun and his team, the Apollo 11 astronauts lifted off from Cape Kennedy to achieve the first manned lunar landing on 20 July 1969.

Although cancellation of Regulus committed the navy to a new missile without conclusive evidence that the weapon system would meet its design requirements, initial progress was nonetheless encouraging. The decision to develop what was to become Polaris was in many ways the easiest aspect of the whole programme. Raborn was well aware that the commitment to develop an FBM was also a commitment to new technology, but then it could be argued that that was the very nature of missile development. During the Jupiter programme, consideration had been given to designing a purpose-built submarine, powered by two *Nautilus*-type reactors and with a battery of four Jupiters mounted in vertical tubes in an extended fin. The concept of mounting the missiles in tubes was, in essence, a refinement of the individual hangars of the Regulus boats. However, the hangars together with all the associated launch apparatus had all been external fitments to the pressure hull. The length of the Jupiter dictated that the tubes would reach from the fin down to the bottom of the submarine's hull and would require four large breaches in the pressure hull. Submarine design had always sought to minimise the number of openings in the pressure hull. Some, such as entry and exit hatches and periscope tubes were, of course, inevitable, but large openings of the type needed to accommodate the missile tubes were much more significant than anything previously experienced. Onboard equipment was also required to produce and handle the liquid oxygen. These engineering problems though typical, were, of course, not insurmountable, but showed that a much more stringent approach to production standards would be required.

Mindful of the Nobska Report, thoughts had to be directed towards the specification for the new missile. Some preliminary work had been undertaken by Lockheed Missile Systems Division (LMSD) staffed by a team of young and enthusiastic engineers who had put forward a draft proposal as early as February 1956. In April, Lockheed was asked to take the matter a stage further and consider the configuration of an actual submarine-launched ballistic missile (SLBM). Lockheed had undertaken some preliminary tests using their X-17 three-stage solid-fuelled research rocket and revised their initial thoughts to propose a two-stage solid-fuelled missile with an advanced inertial guidance system. The X-17 had in fact been the result of an air force contract to investigate the problems of re-entry at high velocities. A series of launches of the rocket took place from Launch Complex 3 (LC-3) at Cape Canaveral and were designed to explore aspects of flight dynamics, guidance, nose-cone technology, and thrust reversal at high altitude. Using these 40-foot-long research rockets saved considerable time and cost as problems that arose could be sorted out before commitment was made to the actual naval missile design. Once this missile had received its official name, these X-17 launches were renamed Polaris flight test vehicles (FTV). After April 1958, further tests using a Sergeant rocket were conducted from LC-25A. Although not directly part of the Polaris test series, three modified X-17a test vehicles were launched at sea near to the Falkland Islands from the

USS *Norton Sound* as part of the undisclosed Operation Argus under the auspices of the Defense Nuclear Agency. Taking place in August and September 1958, the launches were designed to explore the effects of high-altitude nuclear detonations on communications equipment, missile performance, and the possibility of blinding future Soviet anti-ballistic missile systems.[11]

The Air Force Missile Test Center at Patrick AFB operated the Eastern Test Range at Cape Canaveral. It was commanded by Maj.-Gen. Donald N. Yates, a meteorologist who, in June 1944, along with the RAF's Grp Capt. James Stagg had correctly predicted the one-day window of calm weather to launch the D-Day landings. Medaris described him as 'one of the most reasonable, co-operative and objective officers I have ever met, and I have nothing but praise for his handling of our problems at the Cape throughout this difficult period.'[12] One of his main problems was handling the press who could see much of what was happening on the flat wide-open spaces of the launch areas. He was later to receive the US Navy's Legion of Merit award for the support given to the ill-fated Vanguard launcher and also the Polaris test launches.

Lockheed's proposal was given to Burke on 4 September 1956, being delivered to the CNO by Raborn who had proposed the name 'Polaris' for the missile, named after the North Star. The name was, in fact, not new, having been favoured by the navy for the Jupiter proposal, but one that the army had demurred as being 'too naval'. The proposal further recommended that the ship-launched option be deleted and that the missiles be designed from the outset only for submarine use. Deleting the shipborne options was calculated to make a saving in the programme of some $50 million. But many of the senior ranks within the navy resisted the proposal. No extra funds would be initially available to get the project off the ground so that money would have to be found from within the existing budget, thereby reducing spending on surface ships and some senior officers disapproved diverting the funds to 'something they were not convinced would be successful'.[13] However, on 1 January 1957, the SLBM programme was officially approved and the name Polaris confirmed. In support of the development programme, the navy was able to capitalise on existing experience with solid propellants which had featured in various missile systems that it had developed since the war. Experience was one thing, but this elevated solid fuel technology to a new dimension. The problem with solid fuel was still the low specific impulse that in no way matched the significant advantages of liquid fuels.

At the conclusion of the meeting with Wilson that had effectively set the course for a naval ballistic missile, Burke had asked Raborn what he thought, to which the enthusiastic Raborn replied: 'If the Navy didn't go ahead with it, it would be the biggest mistake it had ever made.'[14] His views had clearly been vindicated. A programme originally estimated to have taken nine years of development was, with single minded dedication, to be completed in four years. Raborn later reflected:

No one had ever built a stable guidance table for a missile that could be fired from under water, the motors igniting after coming through water, and the missile then on its way to hit a target. No one had done that. No one knew about the launchers. The launch equipment was secret. The missile itself was secret. The formulation of propellants, how do you bind it.

How do you put it in the motors, how do you keep it from cracking, and all that was quite secret. These were military assets of the first order.[15]

As has been previously noted, the decision to proceed with the SLBM was essentially the easiest part of the project. Within the anticipated development span, Polaris represented a project of extraordinary complexity. No precedent existed for the management of such a large and diverse undertaking. Raborn was to comment: 'Our first job was to create a wholly new kind of Team that could develop and build a revolutionary Weapon Concept ... in record time.'[16] He had seen how the USAF had set up its Western Development Division where Schriever had selected a high-calibre team known in the air force as 'Bennie's Colonels' to undertake the development of the air force's IRBM and ICBM missiles: 'They were bold and clever men of initiative, who believed fervently in what "the Boss" was seeking to achieve, and were entrusted with tasks Schriever would not have delegated to anyone else.'[17] Raborn therefore sought to mirror this approach. He commented: 'It's a test of leadership to imbue your people with a sense of urgency. The situation now is urgent now—later it will be frantic.'[18]

Like Schriever, Raborn had *carte blanche* to select whomsoever he wanted to join him: His 'Hunting Licence' allowed him up to forty officers. Burke had told him: 'You have the choice of any forty officers that you want in the Navy. You can pick forty officers and they're yours, but you can't have forty-one.'[19] Raborn had already selected Colwell as his deputy, much to the displeasure of the admiral for whom he was already working. But such niceties could not stand in the way of a major national defence project. Another key appointment was Captain Levering Smith to head up the technical division (SP20), a position which would earn him the temporary rank of rear admiral until it was made substantive in January 1963.[20] He had replaced the first appointee, naval aviator Captain Grayson Merrill, veteran of Operation Backfire and the navy's Loon detachment at the Special Weapons Tactical Test and Evaluation Unit (SWTTEU) at Port Mugu, who, though talented, had limited knowledge of solid fuel technology and had decided to retire from the navy, although later admitting to the difficulties he experienced working with Raborn.[21, 22] Smith had turned down command of a destroyer in order to study ordnance engineering and had served at the Naval Ordnance Test Station, Inyokern in California, where he was in charge of solid rocket research and where he became acquainted with Raborn.[23] Later he had been the naval deputy at the White Sands Missile Range where he had witnessed the army's missile development. By the time he joined Raborn, he was the navy's most experienced officer in rocket development, whom Raborn described as 'a very dedicated and intelligent [man] and I think the best scientist in uniform today.'[24] The appointment of chief engineer went to John B. 'Dick' Buescher, a naval civil servant. He was vested with overall responsibility for the integration of all weapon subsystems into one viable unit. To manage the administration and finance aspects of the project, Raborn selected Gordon Pehrson who was working in the army chief of staff's office where he had proved to be a very astute planner. As a civilian in a military organisation and a non-technical administrator in a technical agency, he could well have faced problems in being accepted, but SP was dedicated to exploring new methodologies. An initial problem resulting from the civil service bureaucracy was his existing management grade in the army. SP had no vacancies for an employee of that grade. Such problems had to be overcome and with the help of Ed Mernone of the BuOrd, they were. Another key appointment was Dr John P. Craven. An enlisted sailor in the Second World War, he had served on board the battleship USS *New Mexico* (BB-40), and on leaving the navy, participated on early work on nuclear submarines at the David Taylor Model Basin at the Naval Surface Warfare Center. In 1958, he was appointed chief scientist at SP, a post he would hold for the next ten years. He was to lead the team that launched the first missile from a submerged submarine. So crucial was his role seen by the Soviets that a full-time KGB agent was detailed to keep a watch on his every move.

An operational solid-fuelled missile had still, of course, to be proved and production and manufacturing criteria established. Suitable submarines had to be designed and built and married to the missile. In addition, a safe method of launching the missiles from the submarines had to be found. Raborn therefore determined that since no significant technology existed from which to derive the missile, it would be designed on the basis of assumed advances in missile technology during the coming five to six years—as indeed Teller had earlier suggested. This embodied with it the risk that problems would of course arise if these advances failed to materialise.

However, at this time, technology was advancing apace, and traditional methods of handling large-scale projects whether by industry or government were fast becoming outdated and unable to cope with this rapid change. It was equally clear that this was going to affect the Polaris project and clear to Raborn that one overall organisation was required to co-ordinate all aspects of the concept, design, testing, and production of the missile, its associated systems, and the submarines and also the training of the crews who would man the boats. Consequently, in early 1956 Raborn had asked the SP's Plans and Programs Division to identify and arrange visits to those businesses known for their managerial effectiveness. Their visits included Chrysler, Dupont, and General Motors but little of value was achieved as it appeared on closer examination that their reputation for management efficiency was largely a self-created myth. It was perhaps somewhat ironic that some years later these companies would be on reciprocal fact-finding visits to SP to learn about the management of the Polaris programme. It was therefore clear that managing Polaris was going to be a problem of considerable magnitude which was going to involve a diverse number of scientific and organisational interests. New management techniques would also be required to ensure that development took place with minimum delays. The line of balance (LOB) was initially used as a management tool. This was a relatively simple graphic process to allow progress as to 'who has to do what' to keep the required progress on schedule. It was soon evident that this was not sophisticated enough. New computerised techniques had to be developed for such requirements and the concepts of critical path analysis (CPA) and program evaluation and review technique (PERT) were born. The navy had traditionally used GANNT charts as a project management tool. But the need to 'sell' the Polaris programme required something more dynamic in concept and of a complexity that it needed to be run on a computer. Washington-based management consultants Booz Allen Hamilton Inc. are usually credited with inventing PERT. This looked at the time each individual process or 'event' would take in its relationship to the whole project. Although these novel management processes did make a contribution, there were those within the program who found the need for information to update the PERT chart was a burdensome diversion of the limited 'thinking' hours that the technical people had available to them. Contractors in particular disliked PERT preferring to use their own experience to determine progress to completion. Merrill commented:

> Simple GANNT charts would have been better. Indirectly PERT also led to regular Saturday morning management review meetings which should have been held on work days. The war was over, and my people felt their family and recreation time was being diverted to support chart making. I championed a change away from Saturday, but Raborn allowed this for only a few weeks.[25]

The Saturday meetings were undoubtedly a contributory factor to Merrill's retirement from the navy. He believed that little value came from these meetings but did concede that it was often when, with its VIP attendance, major 'political' decisions were made. Initially Raborn expressed disappointment at Merrill's decision but recognised that Merrill had helped to 'free him from the Jupiter yoke, organized and jump-started the technical division and helped select the contractors'.[26] In recognition of this, Raborn awarded Merrill the Legion of Merit. Booz Allen Hamilton's involvement was later recognised when, on behalf of ADM Galantin, CAPT. John A. Dudley, head of communications in SP's Technical Division, presented a heavily embroidered blue and gold Polaris program flag to John W. Pocock, the company's president at the Chicago headquarters.

Motivation in wartime is not difficult to achieve, but motivation in peacetime is more difficult to instil. Pehrson, who by then had acquired the nickname of 'Omar the chartmaker', commented that 'the motivation was given to us in part and we built on it. All the presentations on the subject were motivational in purpose, whether they were in a parking lot at Lockheed or Aerojet ... or whether with wives sitting down on a Saturday afternoon listening to why their husbands never showed up for dinner.'[27] Shugg remembered that some of the larger groups were addressed by Raborn over a microphone: 'He was a master at it, but where he was absolutely unique was person-to-person contact with a smaller group, where his dedication came across.'[28] People became convinced this was for the protection of the nation. It had to be done, be done expeditiously, and it had to work. Raborn made regular visits to industry partners in the project. Typical of the team spirit that he engendered was a visit to Hughes Aircraft where components for the inertial table in the guidance units were made. On crossing the factory floor where some 300 girls were busily employed, he noticed that all the girls were dressed in red, white, and blue middy blouses and skirts. The supervisor remarked: 'We're so proud to be part of the Polaris family that we decided on our own that we'd go buy these and we wear them every Wednesday.' Raborn replied that this was Thursday to which he received the response: 'We heard you were coming so we wore them to show you how proud we are to be part of the Polaris program.'[29]

This enthusiasm and impact from people for the task in hand has sometimes over the years been overshadowed by the credit given to PERT which has tended to have become enhanced in the memory. This is often overlooked or misunderstood. Some of the brightest scientists, both civilian and uniformed, sharing a common dedication to making both the ICBM and Polaris work produced two of the finest projects in post-war American history. Burke had bestowed significant authority and responsibility to Raborn who used this to bypass many of the bureaucratic processes that might otherwise have slowed the project. Working with the army team had provided valuable insight into how they controlled their programme and how they had worked the interface with their industry contractors, and this was to prove a vital contribution to the success of the missile project. Harvey Sapolsky is somewhat less complimentary about the attribution of PERT.[30] The myth, as he saw it, of PERT as an effective integrated management system was assiduously reinforced by SP as a sort of 'dark art' and certainly added a protective shield around the organisation which allowed it to get on with the project without undue scrutiny from outside. Raborn, however, strongly objected to Sapolsky's assignment of motives and believed that his book *The Polaris System Development* could be 'quite harmful to the Navy.'[31] In the final analysis, PERT was indeed a 'dark art'. Although much lauded at the time, and examined critically, it was little more than a covert tool to gain political support for the Polaris project: 'PERT did not build Polaris, but it was extremely helpful for those who did build the weapon system to have many people believe that it did.'[32] Raborn's success lay in keeping Polaris separated from the involvement of other departments, or civilian services. This involved the contractors as well who were told, 'You will have a Polaris division and it will be separate from the rest so that it doesn't get contaminated, doesn't get involved, and the people that work on Polaris are going to work on Polaris. I don't want to find any of them any place else in the plant.'[33]

Confirmation of the Polaris programme took place on 8 February when Burke issued the formal requirement for the Polaris system—Operational Requirement SC-16702—for a fleet ballistic missile with a solid propellant motor capable of launch from a submerged submarine and with a 1,500-mile range. The required operational date was confirmed as not later than 1965. The following month saw the formation, on the suggestion of Dr L. T. E. Thompson (known as Dr Tommy) who was serving as Raborn's assistant for engineering services, of the Polaris/Submarine Special Steering Group, later more manageably renamed the Polaris Steering Task Group (PSTG). Chaired by RADM Smith with other senior members from the various contractors, their initial job was to determine the dimensions of the missile and then to translate these into a definition of the dimensions of the submarines.[34] Early confirmation of these parameters was essential to allow concurrent development of missiles and submarines towards a tentative, if ambitious, operational date of the early 1960s.

But there were, almost inevitably, many detractors among those who had lost budget to fund the FBM project, so care had to be taken not to promote the missile as a strategic asset. With such uncertainties within navy circles, the air force had to be watched closely as well, as they considered themselves the sole custodian of the deterrent and indeed enjoyed about half of the defence budget and, given half a chance, sought to lay claim also to the FBM programme:

When [the Navy] said, yes, that's what it is, give us part of your strategic warfare money, they said no. So [the Navy] lost both ways ... for a period of time. The Navy was parading this weapon system as something they were going to use to knock out the submarine pens, even though we knew right from the start that it was a strategic weapon. But there was a roles and missions argument taking place in the Pentagon at that time and [the air force] wanted to get hold of this program ... and the Navy wasn't about to let the Air Force start running the fleet.[35]

The proposal for a surface FBM ship had been deferred and was later to be cancelled. With the powers given to Raborn and his team, the conventional approach of receiving tenders and proposals could be radically revised. SP essentially took the lead in proactively approaching potential contractors, thereby cutting out many months of negotiations. On New Year's Eve, Gates sent a telegram to about forty leading aerospace companies inviting them to an urgent meeting in Washington. All responded, despite an awareness that the Lockheed Aircraft Corporation was likely to be given the main contract and were duly given a two-hour briefing on the project. It proved to be a most productive exchange of views on the overall practicality of what lay ahead. Lockheed were, as expected, duly appointed prime contractor to develop the missile. A new company, Lockheed Missiles and Space Corporation (LMSC) was formed to take on development of both Polaris and all future Lockheed missile work. They were based in Sunnyvale, California, on a 430-acre former greenfield site. Along with Lockheed, a warhead contractor, a guidance contractor, and a missile-launching contractor were also required:

> The selection of various contractors for this widely diversified program involving a missile that had never been built, a navigational system which would precisely locate the position of the submarine, a fire control system to resolve the information to inform the missile what it should do to land on the target, and a missile guidance system which would take this information and steer the missile until it told the solid propellant motors to cut themselves off with precise timing in order that the warhead would follow a ballistic course to the target— all involved pushing back the frontiers of science to a degree and scope which had never before been done.[36]

Without time for the traditional tendering process, an alternative approach was used which examined the identified companies' abilities to fulfil the contracts taking into account their existing capabilities and other factors such as the workload imposed by existing defence work. Here Raborn's direct control of the project paid dividends. Careful to avoid companies whose order books were already well provided for, potential contractors were carefully scrutinised and contracts subsequently placed directly with Lockheed for the missiles and Westinghouse for the submerged launcher. Dr Charles Stark 'Doc' Draper of the MIT Instrumentation Laboratory (IL) agreed to take on the development of the guidance unit with manufacturing and backup support from General Electric and Hughes.[37] Two eminent mathematicians, J. Halcombe 'Hal' Laning Jr. (who was deputy assistant director of the IL) and Assistant Director Richard H. 'Dick' Battin, took on the task. Laning developed Q-guidance which gave an improved line-of-sight targeting and optimised the time for hitting the target. It was critical that the missile was controlled during the thrust stage as under the subsequent coast phase the trajectory was determined by the position at thrust termination. Although this principal applied equally to the Thor IRBM, the navy considered it such an outstanding development that it was treated as highly secret by SP. The main advantage was that critical targeting information could be processed by a large computer in the laboratory and could then be loaded into the missiles which therefore did not need an onboard computer. The problem may not have been quite so complex as the similar problem which faced the air force's troubled Skybolt which had a much more three-dimensional problem, but it was essential for the success of the FBM Program. Remaining submerged so as not to compromise its location, the crew would be unable to rely on conventional ways of determining their position which required at least breaking the surface.

Known by many as 'The Father of Inertial Navigation', Draper had originally aspired to be a pilot, but a tendency to air sickness ruled him out of the air corps, although he later qualified as a civilian pilot. However, his skills led him to explore the use of gyroscopes in what was to become his first significant invention during the war period. In the 1930s, the US Navy had prided itself in its naval gunnery expertise, but the shock sinking on 10 December 1941 of the Royal Navy's battleship HMS *Prince of Wales* and the battlecruiser HMS *Repulse* by Japanese aircraft had caused a rapid reassessment within naval ranks of this new threat to naval authority. This led Draper to develop the Mk 14 gyroscopic lead-computing gunsight, which predicted a target aircraft's future position and was to see widespread deployment in both the US and Royal Navies, dramatically improving the effectiveness of their anti-aircraft weapons.

After the end of the war, and seeing the potential for using gyros in the field of navigation—initially to tell a pilot where he was in cloudy conditions—Draper, by then the chairman of MIT's Aeronautical Engineering Department and head of the IL, sought to develop self-contained inertial guidance units for navigation. The navy indicated its need under a contract issued on 3 September 1948 which became known as Project MAST (Marine Stable System) calling for 'a system capable of establishing the horizontal plane to within half a minute of arc and the geographic meridian to within five minutes of arc under shipboard conditions in north and south latitudes of up to eighty degrees.'[38] Germany had a basic form of gyroscopic navigation in the V2, and Soviet scientists were known to have been working on the problem but 'had most of the idea but not the technology'.[39] On 8 February 1953, a B-29 bomber equipped with a SPIRE (Space Inertial Reference Equipment) unit developed at the IL by Roger Woodbury and Don Attwood took off from Hanscom Field, Massachusetts. Piloted by the lab's flight test unit's chief test pilot 'Chip' Collins, the flight was a coast-to-coast route to be flown using the SPIRE for navigation. All went well until the aircraft encountered turbulence over the Rocky Mountains. Despite fears that SPIRE was taking a wrong course to the right, Draper advised the crew to leave it alone, and when navigation was checked, the plane was still on course. When the target, Los Angeles International Airport, was reached, the error over the 2,600-mile flight was computed as a mere 9 miles. SPIRE had proved what could be done. Function had, however, taken precedence over weight, and SPIRE weighed around 3,000 lb—too heavy at that stage for many applications, but it had been a proof of concept that was to be developed over the next three years into the guidance unit for the Thor IRBM.

The subsequent development of the ships inertial navigation system (SINS) came directly from the Thor unit.

The first prototype for the naval INS was tested on land when it was mounted on board a truck, and in January 1954, it was driven from Boston to Newbury with a number of subsequent runs along roads in the Eastern US. Next, seagoing trials were conducted using the oil tanker USS *Canisteo* (AO-99) and, in February 1955, the cargo vessel USS *Alcor* (AK-259). The success of these trials was such that the navy became involved directly when the USS *Compass Island*, commissioned in 1956, was used for full-scale trials of the prototype SINS. This unit, the N6A-1 Autonavigator, had been developed by North American Aviation's (NAA) Autonetics Division from the N6A used as the guidance package for the NAA's Navaho missile that was the first such active unit to be deployed operationally. Although the much-underrated Navaho programme was cancelled on 11 July 1957, it incorporated much technology that was to find its way into other projects. The N6A-1 was then used in the SSNs *Nautilus*, *Skate*, and *Sargo* and allowed them to navigate under the Arctic icecap to the North Pole.[40]

Raborn added Draper to his Steering Task Group. Range and accuracy were both important challenges for the group. Levering Smith contracted the IL to develop the SINS for the Polaris submarines. Evidencing the Q-guidance science for the air force, Smith believed that this was ideally suited to the FBM project. Although originally planned for the Atlas ICBM, Q-guidance was not used for that missile but was used for Thor. The advantage Smith saw was that much of the computational work was done on land and this placed minimum workload on the submarine's fire control system. Draper was initially sceptical about taking on the contract as his previous experience with military interference had made him wary of their contracts. Raborn, however, assured him that he would be given total authority over the contract, and on that basis, the terms with the IL were duly agreed. However, the laboratory did not have manufacturing capability, and Smith contracted this to GE along with all service and maintenance requirements. This established a pattern that would exist thereafter for all the SSBNs.[41]

With this new approach to contracting, Raborn went to see SecNav Charles Thomas to report the decisions:

> 'Show Admiral Raborn in. He has top priority.' It was a little embarrassing at times to have senior admirals shooed out of his office and walk in.... I went in and told the SecNav that we'd made the selections for the team and that we had put them under contract.[42]

Thomas was somewhat surprised and commented that he thought he had some responsibility for the decisions that had been made, to which Raborn replied that he had been delegated the secretary of the navy's complete authority in the matter and had duly exercised it. Thomas commented, 'They're all good people.'

Vital months had been saved by this direct approach in a way that would be unimaginable in the bureaucracy of today's government procurement processes.

The next major task was to establish the dimensions of the missile. Without confirmation of these, progress on designing the submarine and the launching system could not proceed. The relatively long lead times on these major components would very much determine when operational capability could be achieved. The anticipated date for this was now January 1963. Another regulating aspect (if not a determining one) of the programme was the warhead, but the AEC was becoming confident in its ability to deliver the warhead by 1960. The navy's missile was duly confirmed. Polaris would be a two-stage missile, 28.5 feet long and 54 inches in diameter (small in comparison with other ballistic missiles) and would weigh around 28,000 lb fully fuelled. Range was confirmed at the CNO's required minimum 1,200 nautical miles with the capability to increase this in stages.

The main pressure on the achievement of the target date, however, was the ability to complete the submarines in time. The design of the submarine presented completely new problems in almost every aspect of submarine design and construction. A novel problem was that, on launching the missile, some 16 tons of weight would be lost and then replaced by an inrush off seawater. On a complete salvo this would be repeated over and over again in rapid succession. The resulting effect to the delicate trim of the submarine had no precedent in submarine design. The hatches opening the launch tubes had to overcome pressure of over 2,000 lb per square inch and then shut again. Across the top of each hatch was a seal consisting of Mylar—a product of the DuPont Corporation—and a Styrofoam closure. The tubes themselves needed to have inspection hatches to service the missiles, but these too had to be strong enough to withstand the pressure of launching. As had previously been identified in the embryonic Jupiter-S designs, every breach of the pressure hull represented an inherent weakness in the hull's integrity.

Having confirmed the size of the missile, the dimensions of the submarines to carry them could also be worked out. On this subject, the committee was initially far from unanimous. Some argued that the larger the submarine, the more cost effective would be the fleet. However, a large submarine with so many breaches in its pressure hull represented new technology and, furthermore, there was at that stage no separate budget for the development of Polaris, the funding had to come from within the existing naval budget and so as not to upset the interests of the blue water surface fleet which championed air power and destroyers, the programme would have to demonstrate that it was being run within very strict financial controls: not an easy task when the way ahead was far from defined. Many felt that these submarines would in any case be much larger than anything built to date and that there was therefore a size beyond which it was prudent not to go. Lockheed had by then confirmed that the launch tubes would be in integrated modules of four, so BuShips had produced initial designs showing from four to thirty-two missile configurations as the number of missiles to be carried had yet to be determined. Those seeking a cost-effective decision on the matter strongly argued the case for thirty-two tubes, but this would require a submarine of unprecedented size and existing experience with large submarines had shown that they were difficult to handle when submerged and particularly so near to the surface and it was at this depth that the missile launches would take place. As there was no common consensus as to how many missiles would be carried, to resolve the impasse, each member of the committee was invited to write on a piece of paper the number of missile tubes which he thought the submarine should have. Taking the average of these produced the figure of '16'. The Polaris submarines would therefore go to sea carrying sixteen missiles and the subsequent SSBN designs of the UK, France, and, initially, the Soviet Union all adopted this number (America only moved to twenty-four launch tubes with the advent of the *Ohio*-class Trident SSBNs).

The committee had also determined the method of launching the missile. Theoretically simple though the idea of igniting the missile within its launch tube might be, the danger involved to the submarine was considered to be too great. An alternative had to be found. Torpedoes were already ejected from submarines by compressed gas. It was decided that the missile could be ejected in a similar manner. Sufficient pressure would be generated to eject the missile and force it above sea level from where its first-stage rocket motor could be fired. One idea, not eventually adopted as it was considered unnecessary, even envisaged the missiles being launched through columns of soap bubbles to ease the friction of their passage through the water. Preliminary underwater tests took place in Lockheed's Underwater Missile Facility (LUMF) using sub-scale models, and a series of full-scale tests at a special facility built at San Clemente. The latter was a purpose-built underwater launch facility that was built in the sea at Wilson Cove close to San Clemente Island, 55 miles off the Californian coast. Tests at both these facilities confounded the views of the hydrodynamicists who had insisted that the missile would tumble on its way to the surface, and this would require the incorporation of fins or rudders. In practice, the laws of aerodynamics applied equally to good hydrodynamic design and there was no need for appendages. That covered the missile's underwater performance, but three young Lockheed engineers, Ron Bowlby, Muri Culp, and Harry Bowers believed that more data was required about the missile's subsonic performance once it left the water. They came up with a novel solution. Using a wooden scale model of the A-1 they attached it to a rig mounted on the offside B-pillar of Bowlby's 1956 Ford Victoria car creating a bespoke Rolling Wind Tunnel Facility which must have caused much local interest as they sped down the Bayshore Freeway near Lockheed's Sunnyvale plant![43] (Not entirely new, a similar device had been used in the development of the wing for the B-24 Liberator bomber.)

Ideally the new class of submarine would have been designed from scratch, but speed was of the essence. In its simplest analysis, the SSBN was superficially merely an existing SSN with an added missile compartment and the first SSBNs were indeed based on this premise. Initial studies of the proposed design were completed on 27 May 1957. Made at the request of the assistant secretary of defense, these confirmed that, with the anticipated developments of small high yield warheads, the requirements for Polaris could be met by the anticipated in-service date which at that time was considered to be 1963. Once again, the Soviet Union upstaged America when, on 27 August, it launched the first R-7 ICBM (NATO reporting name SS-6, Sapwood). Although this missile was never used operationally (a derivative, the R-7A, was later deployed with the Soviet Rocket Troops), the USAF's SAC bases were now within range of Soviet ICBMs. With the acceleration of the whole program, the need for earlier delivery of warheads led to the implementation of an emergency capability program to deliver an interim warhead, designated EC-47, by early 1960 with a fully configured W-47 warhead available by October 1960. The Albuquerque Operations Office of the AEC co-ordinated the development of the warhead and, by March 1958, had received from Sandia a full project definition for the prototype XW-47 warhead. The same month, the secretary of defense approved a list of high priority items which would be submitted to the president to request Congress to approve augmentation to the existing 1959 budget. The naval request recommended further accelerating the Polaris programme to include funding for six submarines in addition to the three already approved. In summary, the naval request would provide nine SSBNs by the end of 1961 together with the missiles for these boats, an operating base at Charleston, an FBM tender, facilities for missile testing, personnel training, system development, test, and evaluation, along with communication and associated facilities. However, one-time partner the army, now fighting its corner for its own funding, led the questioning based on the fact that Polaris was unproven and was inaccurate to the extent that it would only be used against area targets rather than specific ones and this opened up the whole debate on the overall operational requirement for ICBMs, IRBMs and atomic capable aircraft. A more belligerent air force, saw this request as an attempt to usurp its primary role and put up a fight, questioning the SSBN's ability to maintain an alert status and thus its ability to respond to its primary role and guarantee its ability to transmit and receive communications from central command. They also cited a submarine's possible inability to establish with sufficient accuracy its position in the ocean, something required to target the missiles accurately, although the forthcoming Skybolt was to be subject to similar doubts. (On 26 May 1959, Douglas had received a contract from the air force for advanced design studies of this missile.) The air force had to admit that deployment of the Atlas ICBM and its successor, the Titan, was a few years off and the solid-fuelled Minuteman even more distant, although they had requested a sizeable $259 million for development of the latter missile. 'It appears that by means of the MINUTEMAN project, the Air Force hopes to kill off our Polaris program.'[44] Despite the argued cases, Polaris survived with the approval of an initial fleet of nine submarines with a 34 per cent allocation of the defence budget, just under two-thirds of which would go to Polaris. This would provide funds for the fourth and fifth submarines along with one FBM tender as well as ancillary equipment, training, missile production, and testing. The navy was by now demonstrably well ahead with the development of solid fuel and their research was to prove invaluable to the development of the Minuteman. Rather than killing off Polaris, the air force's missile was to some considerable degree grateful to the navy for its research.

Adding further impetus to the whole program was the forthcoming nuclear test moratorium, which was due to come into effect on 31 October 1958. The suspension of nuclear testing had first been suggested by Eisenhower in August 1957 and agreement was reached between the US, the USSR, and the UK for a twelve-month hold starting at the end of October. This did, however, place pressure on all three nations to complete necessary testing before the start date. Thus, the first American components to be proved were prototype designs for the primary trigger. These were tested at the Nevada Test Site (NTS) as part of Operation Plumbbob during the late summer of 1957. Testing of the various XW-47 components, however, was included in a series of nuclear tests held under the code name of Operation Hardtack Phase II, also held at the NTS. The first test, taking place on 14 October code-named Neptune, sought to prove the 'one-point safe' design of the warhead. A 'one-point safe' warhead is one that will produce only a negligible nuclear yield if only one of its primaries detonates. This test failed by producing a yield of just over 100 tons. Within two weeks, the UCRL scientists had produced a redesigned primary one-point safe system, which relied on a motor drive and was designated W-47-Y-1. Despite every effort being made to complete the test cycle of the revised warhead, the moratorium came into effect before the full schedule of tests could be conducted to establish if the new warhead was indeed one-point safe. However, two other tests conducted prior to the deadline had proved to be successful and there was therefore relative confidence that the weapon would perform in the way in which it was expected.

With the anticipation that this series of tests would be successful and with the basic parameters now agreed, progress with the complete missile system was given a full appraisal and SP's conclusions allowed Gates to announce on 22 October 1957 that an earlier in-service date for the missile could indeed be achieved. This, however, could only be done by the initial adoption of an emergency capability 1,000–1,200-NM-range A-1 missile which should be operational by the end of 1960. To strike Moscow as a prime target, this first-generation Polaris was limited to a fairly restricted sea area covering the Barents Sea and the western seaboard of Norway. Both the Baltic and the Black Sea, although within range, were considered no-go areas as vulnerable to Soviet anti-submarine forces.

6

The US Submarines

... how vast this ocean ... how formidable a hiding place.

Nicholas Monsarrat, *The Cruel Sea*

Portentous weapons. I really wonder the human mind can bear such a responsibility.

British Prime Minister William Gladstone on being shown the 80-ton main armament on HMS *Inflexible* in 1881

With significant progress being made with the missile, the SSBN programme too could be speeded up with the first deployment of the A-2 1,500-NM-range missile now anticipated to take place sometime in 1962. The full 1,500-mile-range missile should be operational by mid-1963, still two years ahead of the original target date. But confidence within the NAVBMC allowed them to report that the submarine programme would be further accelerated to allow a certain first deployment by October 1960 using the A-1 missile. On 9 December, SecDef McElroy formally approved the acceleration of the programme to achieve this target date. This schedule was obviously extremely tight and allowed for essentially no slippage. SP together with BuShips advised the CNO on 20 December that the schedule would require the most optimistic circumstances assuming that the programme was run under 'national emergency' conditions. Contracts had to be put in place for a submarine to operate an as-yet unproven launching system.

As the navy's pre-eminent submarine constructor, Electric Boat was an obvious choice to be awarded the contract for the lead design of the first SSBN. William Atkinson had been the project engineer for both the *Seawolf* and the *Skate*, which had just been delivered ahead of contract date. At the age of thirty-two, he was one of the country's leading experts on nuclear submarine design and was immediately put in charge of the project. Ahead of him was a task of awesome complexity. To achieve the required in-service date, the SSBN would have to be built in around twenty-four months, but at this time there was not even a completed design. Atkinson pointed out to the navy that the *Skate* had taken twenty-nine months to build. To bring a new design SSBN to completion in less time than this was not possible, even under national emergency conditions. But Atkinson looked again at what the navy wanted. Apart from the missile installation, the rest of the submarine was essentially little different from the attack submarines then entering service. Such an attack submarine, hull number 589, was already under construction at Groton. Laid down on 1 November 1957, she was a *Skipjack*-class boat to be called USS *Scorpion*.

Atkinson and his design team determined that it should be feasible to cut the SSN hull and add a cylindrical section between the rear of the fin and the reactor compartment. This section would contain the sixteen missile tubes in two parallel rows of eight along with the additional subsystems required by the missiles. The missile section would add just under 130 feet to the original length of 252 feet (75 feet for the missile tubes, 45 feet for navigation and missile control, and the remaining 10 feet for extra machinery) and, although cylindrical, would not materially compromise the spindle shaped hull of the original design in streamlining terms. (Cutting a submarine in half was not in fact something new. In 1928 the submarine USS *S-48* had undergone just such surgery to increase her length. By good fortune, on her recommissioning, Rickover had served in her and her 'faulty, sooty, dangerous and repellent engineering' formed the basis of his clinical approach to the high engineering standards he was to require of defence contractors.) This course of action would deprive the navy of an expected SSN, however, the FBM programme took precedence and the *Scorpion* was duly 'reordered' on 31 December 1957 as the USS *George Washington* (SSGN-598)— the first Polaris submarine. The designation was to be changed in June 1958 to SSBN-598—Ship, Submersible, Ballistic, Nuclear. The submarine was built to the BuShips' design number SCB-180A. Rickover wanted as few details of the submarine's configuration to become known so that when the American Revell and Renwal model construction kit companies issued plastic kits of the submarines with a full interior, it was rumoured that Rickover wanted to sue them for breaching US secrecy, claiming to a Joint Atomic Energy Sub-committee that the model had given the Soviets millions of dollars' worth of information about US nuclear submarines. Nonetheless, on the instruction leaflet, the latter manufacturer boasted that, 'We wish to take this opportunity to express our sincere gratitude to the Electric Boat Division of General Dynamics Corporation for generously furnishing complete and accurate data. Without this cooperation ... a completely authentic model would not have been possible.' No doubt this boosted sales accordingly.

Convention would have seen the SSBN fleet named, like the rest of the navy's submarines, after marine life. It was considered, however, that the SSBNs were to be submarines apart from the rest of the submarine fleet and that this fact should be reflected in their names. It was initially proposed that as the SSBNs had in many ways taken on the role of the navy's capital ships, that they should adopt the names of the states of the USA, names previously allocated to the battleships.[1] However, this idea was dropped as there were, at that time, only forty-nine states and the clear belief that this would not provide sufficient names for the SSBN fleet gives some idea of the anticipated size of the eventual fleet. It was originally estimated that to maintain a fleet of thirty submarines operationally at sea at any one time, forty-five would be needed after taking into account deployment, refitting cycles, and the number of identified industrial targets in the Soviet Union. (The Polaris fleet was eventually to number forty-one—the '41 for Freedom'. This may still seem a formidable number, but bearing in mind that there would be an increasing number of submarines in the process of refitting, the number is not excessive in terms of the operational requirement. In a similar vein it is worth remembering that to guarantee the availability of only one boat on patrol, the Royal Navy had to order four.) In the end it was decided, allegedly on Eisenhower's instruction, to name the SSBNs after prominent people who were 'known for their devotion to freedom'. Later on, as the construction of the forty-one submarines was nearing completion, there was a suggestion mooted by the *New York Times* that the final submarine be named the 'Winston Churchill': 'today's generations and those yet to come owe far more to Winston Churchill, honorary citizen of the United States, who presided at Britain's finest hour and whose memory will long be warm in American hearts. His name would be eminently fitting for this mighty submarine, a keeper of the peace.'[2] However, this idea had already been taken up when President Kennedy wrote to the elder statesman in March 1962: 'The people of the United Sates of America would be highly honored if you would allow my country to name a Polaris submarine USS WINSTON CHURCHILL.'[3] This was a departure from US Navy protocol which had never seen a vessel named after a living person. The matter was thereafter handled by David Burke, the US ambassador to London, and Harold Macmillan. However, Clementine Churchill, having seen the letter and while recognising the compliment, nonetheless was somewhat less enthusiastic, telling Macmillan that, 'I fervently hope that you will advise Winston against agreeing [the suggestion]. I should hate to feel that his name should be so closely associated with a weapon whose purpose is mass destruction.'[4] Sir Winston's principal private secretary, Sir Antony Montague Brown, confirmed receipt of the letter, but advised Bruce and onwards to Captain Tazewell T. Shepard, Kennedy's naval aide, that Sir Winston deeply appreciated the proposal but wished time to reflect on the matter.[5] In the end, Lady Churchill's view prevailed. Fortunately, the White House had given no publicity to the proposal, and it was mutually agreed that by giving no reply, the matter could quietly be put to rest with the understanding that no discourtesy was implied.[6] (Appendix I gives a list of other suggested prominent names that were not in the end adopted.)

On the same day that the first SSBN was confirmed, the next hull number, 599, also already assigned to EB, was likewise reordered as the second boat, later named the USS *Patrick Henry*. The 'Scorpion' name was also reinstated in the SSN construction programme retaining its original 589 hull number. Those wary of the superstitions of the sea had subsequent cause to question the wisdom of this decision. The *Scorpion* had a life accentuated by problems which caused her to be called the USS *Scrapiron* by her crew. Returning from a deployment near to the Azores to monitor Soviet naval activity, she was lost in May 1968 with all hands.[7]

After completing his earlier assignments, Shugg would ordinarily have moved on, but aware that Polaris was on the way and that it was 'too hot and too fascinating to miss', he stayed on.[8] Possessed of a restless energy, he was to drive forward the building of the first two SSBNs assigned to EB. The schedule was challenging with the requirement to get the first submarine to sea in twenty-four months. But Shugg later commented that 'the higher the pressure, the better the job will be', citing the very few mistakes and mishaps that happened during the build.

Although significant advances had been made during the war for high notch-toughness steels, (an indication of the capacity of a steel to absorb energy when a stress concentrator or notch is present), the advent of nuclear submarines meant that they now had a wider hull diameter, required to encase the reactor and the associated equipment. This necessitated the use of HY-80 (high yield, 80,000 lb per square inch) low alloy steel for the pressure hull on the recommendation of Ivo Fioriti at BuShips who had implemented a research programme into the use of this steel by the US Navy. It exhibited an extremely good strength to weight ratio, notch-toughness at low temperatures, and anti-ballistic properties when compared with other available steels and theoretically had a collapse depth of 1,000 metres. One major hurdle that had to be understood was welding HY-80 steel in sub-zero temperatures which led to problems that required some rewelding to be done. Laboratory tests showed that the steel could be welded effectively as long as special procedures were carefully followed. However, poor quality control in the shipyards revealed a catalogue of problems with some welds having to be repaired up to six times. The subsequent loss of the USS *Thresher* (SSN-593), however, cast a shadow over the safety of the new steel. EB had already proved its skill and experience in delivering the *Skate* ahead of schedule and did have valuable experience in building a nuclear submarine: a skill that no other yard possessed. Shugg therefore became an additional attendee at Raborn's Saturday conferences. He commented:

> They were the masterpieces of a master leader. Raborn's whole philosophy of dealing with the conglomerate bunch of principal contractors was to get the top men and to have them thoroughly understand their job, and then to give them

some scope, some rope, in executing it.... These meetings were one of his ways to pick the highlights, to search for problems if they weren't self-evident, put on some more pressure, and give each of the contractors a chance to see the other fellow's difficulties, because, particularly at Electric Boat where all things came together, each one had to give a little to accommodate the other. You couldn't do an isolated job. It all had to fit together.[9]

With a definitive plan for submarine construction, the navy now felt confident in committing itself to an in-service date of April 1960 for the *George Washington*. The whole nuclear submarine program was soon to be accorded 'Brick-bat' status—a classification started in the early 1950s to allow the program to have first choice in acquiring that which it needed. Despite this remarkable success, Congress stopped to take breath and appraise progress to date. Five SSBNs, the initial number envisaged by Congress, had been approved without proof that the concept would work. When Eisenhower signed the 1959 Department of Defense Appropriation Act on 22 August 1958 no funds were included for SSBNs 6 to 9. Nonetheless, recognising that certain long-lead items, mainly for the reactors, had to be ordered considerably in advance, authority was given three days later to provide funds in the 1960 Appropriation for advance funding for SSBNs 10 to 14. It was not until 23 December that the president confirmed the order for SSBN 6 to be built by EB. This was to be the first of a class of purpose-designed SSBNs, essentially an improved *George Washington* design. It is not surprising, given the circumstances, that the initial class of SSBNs was to experience some operational problems, in part resulting from the underlying design which was, of course, that of an SSN with a rather different set of requirements. Keeping the submarine level at the very low speeds that were required in the hover mode during launch operations was to prove difficult. A further problem, born of the speed with which the programme was escalated, was that at the time that the *George Washington* design was finalised, it was not even known with any certainty if the missiles could be launched successfully from underwater. Therefore, incorporated in the design, on the presumption that the submarine would possibly need to surface to launch the missiles, was a capability to lean sideways on the surface such that if a round failed on launch it would drop into the ocean rather than back onto the submarine. This had in turn required a large gyroscope which in practice was hardly needed. It was also noisy in operation and was later removed from the early SSBNs. The new class of submarine was slightly larger in size: the hull was based on the *Thresher*-class design still using HY-80 steel to allow an increased diving depth. The BuShips design number was SCB-180. Being purpose designed as SSBNs, the number of torpedo tubes incorporated was reduced to four as the torpedoes would be used only for defensive purposes.

Construction of the *George Washington* proceeded without any serious delays, and, resplendent in orange anti-fouling paint, her launch took place on 9 June

1959. She was launched by her sponsor, Mrs Robert B. Anderson, wife of the former SecNav who had by then been promoted to secretary of the Treasury. Dressed overall, she slipped into the Thames River to the accompaniment of cheering crowds. Also present at the ceremony was Assistant Secretary of Defense Wilfred J. McNeil who gave the official address. The construction of the *George Washington* represented 'an achievement of the highest order', he commented. He went on to say that the submarine incorporated 'into a single weapon system most of the great scientific developments which have so far revolutionised warfare; the nuclear warhead, the ballistic missile, nuclear propulsion, inertial guidance for navigation as well as radical developments in hull design.' Of the Polaris missile itself, he concluded, 'knowing the tremendous destructive potential of the lethal cargoes that will be carried by the submarines, no attacker could hope to escape retribution, even given the advantage of striking the first blow.' This placed Polaris as essentially a retaliatory weapon system. The Soviet Union was, after all, seen as the aggressor likely to strike first and without warning. The anticipated accuracy of Polaris in terms of its CEP was, in any case, still insufficient to guarantee success as a first strike weapon capable of taking out substantial numbers of the Soviet ICBMs still in their silos. Just under three weeks later, on 27 June, Eisenhower gave the authorisation for construction of SSBNs 7, 8, and 9.

EB laid the keel of the *Patrick Henry* on 26 May 1958. Authority to start the construction of the third submarine, subsequently named the USS *Theodore Roosevelt* (SSBN-600), had been given to the Mare Island Division of the San Francisco Bay Naval Shipyard at Vallejo, California. So rapidly had the programme been initiated that funding for the initial costs of construction still had to be found from other navy budgets. To the relief of many in the navy, the need for proper funding had now been recognised and was regularised on 12 February 1958 when the president signed the Supplemental Appropriation Act which included provision for these first three submarines. Nothing was spared in the rush to finish them. Three shifts were worked, twenty-four-hours a day, seven days a week. It had by then been determined that the 598 class would be five in number. This would allow the establishment of an initial Polaris capability and provide time for the follow-on class, purpose-designed from the start. On 29 July, the final two 598-class SSBNs were authorised from the Newport News Shipbuilding and Dry Dock Company in Virginia and the Portsmouth Naval Shipyard in New Hampshire respectively. Funding for these two boats was contained in the 1959 Appropriation Act, signed by the president on 23 August 1958. These two SSBNs were named the USS *Robert E Lee* (SSBN-601) and the USS *Abraham Lincoln* (SSBN-602). These first SSBNs were designed to carry the Polaris A-1 missiles with provision to update to the upgraded A-2 at a later date.

On 22 September 1959, the *Patrick Henry* was launched at Groton. Soon afterwards, the *Theodore Roosevelt* was launched at Mare Island on 3 October, and the fourth SSBN to be launched that year, the *Robert E. Lee*, took to the water on 18 December. This was the first nuclear submarine to be built in the south of the US and the first submarine to be constructed at the Newport News yard in modern times. Meanwhile the complex fitting out of the *George Washington* was being completed and as the USS *George Washington* she was commissioned at Groton on 30 December 1959. She was now ready to take on her complement of sixteen Polaris A-1 missiles when their development was complete. The A-1 (initially known as the Polaris A) was the interim missile designed to prove the concept and allow the seaborne deterrent to become operational at the earliest opportunity.

The five 598-class SSBNs naturally shared many similarities with the *Skipjack*. In the bow section there remained six 21-inch torpedo tubes fitted with Mark 16 MOD 6 or Mark 37 torpedoes. These would allow the SSBNs to protect themselves and would also mean that they could theoretically operate as attack submarines in war after their missiles had been launched. Aft of the torpedo space, three deck levels contained the main control room and attack centre of the submarine together with accommodation and messing facilities for twelve officers and 100 enlisted men. Surfaced displacement of the submarine was 6,019 tons with a submerged displacement of 6,888 tons. Even with this substantially increased displacement over the *Skipjacks* (3,513 tons submerged), the same power plant was used—an S5W PWR reactor supplying steam to a pair of GE geared turbines which delivered 15,000 shp to one propeller. This would give a surfaced speed of 20 knots with an estimated 30 knots submerged. Three Mk 2 Mod 4 SINS comprised the primary navigation system. Bearing in mind the length of time the SSBNs would remain submerged, limited provision was incorporated in the 598 design to allow the crew to maintain their level of fitness. A special inflatable gymnasium was provided, so designed to give protection against protruding parts of the submarine's internal systems. A health physics laboratory monitored levels of radiation within the crew who each carried a personal dosimeter. The recording of the radiation levels was one of the duties of the onboard doctor. Although limited surgical capability existed, any illness would, wherever possible, be suppressed by medication until the end of the patrol. To ensure a comfortable environment, a 300-ton capacity air-conditioning system was incorporated in the design. The life of a Polaris submariner was very different from that usually associated with submarine operations. There was concern that the long patrol periods with very little taking place would lead to boredom and a gradual reduction in operational efficiency. Gates was to admit that 'it was a tough duty on a Polaris submarine'.[10] Shifts were the basis of life on board. Time would also be used for study towards promotion qualifications and attending classes or simply occupying themselves in reading for pleasure. There was a cinema rigged up for the daily film and sing-a-longs could be heard from time to time in the missile compartment. During night hours, the submarine would be 'rigged for red' so as not to compromise night vision should it be necessary to use the periscope. To allow off-duty crew to play poker or bridge, special playing cards were provided as the traditional red hearts and diamonds became invisible under red light.[11] It was after all only the human element that determined how long the SSBNs would be deployed. The next stage was to define the operational parameters.

On 1 July 1958, Submarine Squadron Fourteen (SUBRON 14) was established under the command of CAPT. Norvell G. Ward, with its HQ within the CNO's office. Ward reported to COMSUBLANT as one of the latter's squadron commanders. He had a secondary role in the Pentagon reporting to Rear Admiral Lawrence R. Daspit, director of the navy's Undersea Warfare Branch. Ward had previously been in command of SUBRON 5 tasked with testing Regulus. The initial undertaking was to develop the operational procedures for the submarines, to select crews and organise their training. 'Bub' Ward was an experienced submariner who had won the Navy Cross in World War II for his actions as captain of the USS *Guardfish* (SS-217) in sinking Japanese shipping in the summer of 1943. In 1946 and 1947, he had commanded the submarine USS *Irex* (SS-482), which, in July 1947, became the first operational US submarine to be fitted with a snorkel. He had been aboard the *Nautilus* during a fleet exercise and fully realised the capabilities of nuclear submarines when the SSN tailed the aircraft carrier *Valley Forge* (CV-45) for two days, demonstrating a previously unheard-of capability. Ward had to select staff for his department and selected CDR Harry E. Rice as his missile officer with CDR Roy G. Anderson as his chief staff officer. Despite Anderson failing the Rickover test for submarine duty he was to prove a valuable asset to Ward's staff.

Ward's experience with Rickover was typical of the quirkiness of the admiral. After much persistence in requesting an interview, he was ushered into Rickover's presence whereupon the admiral asked what Ward wanted to see him about. The short conversation went thus:

> 'Admiral I'm Squadron 14 Commander.'
> '*I know that. Now what do you want to see me about?*'
> 'I want to learn a little bit about your nuclear power plants.'
> '*Why?*'
> 'So that at least I'll be able to talk to someone who's running them.'
> '*Fine. Here's a book. Take it and study it.*'

In October 1961, Ward became fully part of the Polaris programme when he was appointed as the head of Navy Plans Branch, Strategic Plans Division, in the office of the DCNO. Here he was tasked with formulating the operating procedures for the increasing numbers of SSBNs being commissioned into the navy. When it came to crewing the submarines, a novel solution had already been proposed and adopted. To maximise the amount of time that the submarines would be on patrol, Vice Admiral Harold P. Smith, chief of the Bureau of Naval Personnel, revealed that each would have two crews. While one crew was at sea on patrol, the other one would be taking leave, training and preparing for the next patrol. In all respects, each crew would mirror the other one. They were to be called 'Blue' and 'Gold' Crews—after the official navy colours—and would each have their own commanding officer. The idea originated from similar manning arrangements adopted by the Royal Navy for their Far East stations. The effect of this was that only a minimum of time would be spent alongside between successive patrols to restore, revictual, and undertake minor repairs to the submarine before its alternate crew took it back to sea. Such was the speed at which the project was progressing that for the first crews, navigation, communications, and supply staff positions were generally filled by non-nuclear qualified personnel. It was inevitable that with strong-willed captains there would some competition between the Blue and Gold crews, but like many intra-service rivalries at first, as the patrol cycle settled into an established pattern, this problem receded. The two-crews system was an idea which was later adopted by the Royal Navy for the British SSBNs, but it was never to be adopted by the Soviet SSBN Fleet. It was also necessary to identify how many people would be needed in each department—communications, navigation, power plant, missiles, catering, etc.—and then double this for each submarine. Smith admitted that this manpower requirement would place considerable pressure on his department and, initially at least, personnel would have to be 'borrowed' from other areas. The influx of personnel led to other problems: 'With the two crews, we had to decide, for instance, how we were going to provide housing for the Polaris crews in the New London, [Connecticut] area.'[12] This problem needed the assistance of the Bureau of Yards and Docks. A further decision had to be made about the duration of the patrols. This tried to minimise any downtime but also recognised the human factor in operating effectively in a broadly alien environment. The decision on both this and on the operating areas fell to Ward. These would be signed off by the CNO, but individual responsibility fell to CINCLANTFLT, taking into account the nature of targeting requirements using information from the Joint Strategic Target Planning Staff (JSTPS) in Omaha. Initially the Polaris submarines would have to use patrol areas in the Norwegian Sea, determined by the range of the A-1. Fortunately, no other US submarines operated in this area. Ward commented:

The plans for employment of nuclear submarines in wartime or times of tension, or even on exercises, were melded into coordination with the Polaris submarine employment. That [was] very necessary at all times to make sure there [was] no mutual interference between submarines.[13]

When the Royal Navy's SSBNs became operational, these plans had to be coordinated with the UK patrol areas as well.

On 1 March 1959, construction of the Team Training Facility began within the naval base at New London. Initial training of crews would later be transferred to the Naval Guided Missile School at Dam Neck, Virginia Beach. The New London base on the Thames River had one strategic disadvantage. It was upstream of the Gold Star Memorial Bridge which carried Interstate 95, the main arterial road on the east coast of America and there was an adjacent railway bridge. A direct hit on these crossings would isolate anything further upriver. The navy therefore made sure that it always had vessels south of the bridge with direct access to the sea.

Appointments of the first four SSBN commanding officers were made shortly afterwards: all being personally selected by Rickover, as were all senior nuclear appointments. The admiral's interview procedure was unusual; at times even bizarre and unforgiving, but it was an essential part of the appointments process. Designed to make interviewees uncomfortable, they were seated on a chair with one leg shorter than the other three. Very often the interview finished with Rickover announcing abruptly, 'You bore me. Get out.' This would be followed a few days later by a letter of appointment to a nuclear role. Others trying to outwit the admiral, suffered accordingly. LT Tombs arrived for interview. Rickover called him Toombs (as in cemetery) whereupon the young officer corrected him, 'Toms, sir.' 'Rubbish', replied the admiral, 'your name is Toombs.' In the interviews, Rickover would usually ask the interviewee if he had any questions, whereupon the lieutenant asked the admiral for his views on 'atomic boombs'. Unsurprisingly, he did not pursue his career in the nuclear division. Even seemingly excellent credentials were not enough. To another aspiring young midshipman who had scored highly at US Naval College, he enquired, 'You are the son of [he named an admiral]?' to which the young man replied 'Yes, sir.' 'Interview over', Rickover replied. Such a rebuff could have a permanent effect on a youngster's career, but there was no appeal. As Rickover became older and more cantankerous, however, it was almost a 'badge of honour' in one's naval career to be rejected.

Like Ward, the first four commanding officers had all seen service in submarines during the Second World War. CDR James B. Osborn (Blue) and CDR John L. From Jr (Gold) were to command the *George Washington*. Osborn already had practical experience of seaborne missile systems for he had previously commanded the *Tunny* before taking command of Guided Missile Unit 50 (Regulus). He therefore already knew well a number of officers and enlisted men who would form the nucleus of the SSBN crews. CAPT. Harold E. Shear (Blue) and CDR Robert L. J. Long (Gold) were to command the USS *Patrick Henry*. Shear was at that time instructing in nuclear power, ballistic missiles, fire control and navigation in connection with the Polaris programme at the Naval Reactors Branch, Division of Reactor Development at the AEC in Washington. In a further appointment, CDR William E. Simms (Blue) and CDR Oliver H. Perry, Jr, (Gold) were to take the USS *Theodore Roosevelt* to sea.

A purpose-built base facility had to be constructed for the submarines. Charleston, South Carolina, an isolated location 16 miles up the Cooper River, was chosen and approval for the Polaris Missile Facility, Atlantic (POMFLANT) was given on 30 September 1958. The $27 million facility was commissioned on 29 March 1960 in a ceremony attended by a large delegation headed by Raborn and Assistant Secretary of the Navy (Materiel) Cecil P. Milne. It would serve as the start point for all the Atlantic-based Polaris submarines before they deployed on their first operational patrol. The navy weapons annex built on an 880-acre site within the Charleston base was to be the link between the manufacture of the missiles, their acceptance by the navy, and loading into the submarines. Most components would be flown to the base with the warheads and motors kept in purpose-built secure underground magazines. The largest building within the complex was the 24,300-square-foot inert processing building where guidance, hydraulics, and electronic systems would be checked and also repaired. Other buildings included the motor inspection building where the motors would be checked for any damage in transit, the re-entry body assembly building where in hospital-like surroundings the warheads would be readied for attaching to the missiles, and finally the 1,500-square-foot missile assembly building where the various different components would be put together before the completed missiles were put into steel 'liners' to protect them against shocks and adverse temperatures. Member of the South Carolina House of Representatives from Charleston County, L. Mendel Rivers, commented:

> Today Charleston becomes the potent thorn in the side of the Soviet Union ... Charleston becomes the deterrent capital of the world. We will also make an indelible mark on the planning maps of the Soviet Union. This is the penalty we must pay for this great honor.[14]

First Lady 'Lady Bird' Johnson later visited Charleston on behalf of the president in October 1964 and commented:

> Just as Charleston has been 'watchdog of the Atlantic,' my husband, with Mendel Rivers, served as watchdog of our defenses. The partnership ... works both ways. It means economic viability for this area and it means strength to the Nation. The new support facility for Polaris missiles puts you on the front line of our defenses and our effort to maintain a stable peace.[15]

Basing the submarines in an American port, however, presented problems in itself. The range of the initial Polaris would be, at best, 1,200 nautical miles: it was essentially an IRBM. This meant that to reach many of the missiles' potential targets within the Soviet Union, including Moscow itself, the submarines would have to deploy to patrol areas within the Norwegian Sea, or the Barents Sea, relatively close, perhaps at times even dangerously close to the Soviet northern coastline. Inevitably, from US bases, a considerable amount of time—up to two weeks on each patrol—would be used up in transiting to and from the patrol area, thereby significantly shortening the sixty-day patrol cycle. To reach these areas, the SSBNs would also have to pass through the Greenland–Iceland–UK Gap (GIUK Gap). As this was the Soviet Northern Fleet's only access to the North Atlantic, it was a relatively active area of shipping, both above and below the surface. It was clearly essential that the boats were not intercepted on their transit routes by Soviet submarines, as the locations of the patrol areas had to be kept a closely guarded secret. Allowance had therefore to be made for this factor in planning the patrol cycle. SSBNs would be accompanied by protective SSNs on departing Charleston. Sonar technology at that time could not detect the difference between the two types of submarine, and in any case, it had been proved difficult, if not impossible, for one submarine to track another for an extended length of time. Nonetheless, every precaution had to be taken to avoid any contact, either deliberate or by chance. Meanwhile, in an impressively short time, the Polaris fleet and its attendant facilities were taking shape.

The Missile

I am here to state what I believe to be right and what I believe to be wrong, and to propose action for correcting what I think wrong.

President Eisenhower
State of the Union Message to Congress
9 January 1958

While the development of the SSBN was to prove remarkable in terms of the speed with which the project was to be accomplished, the development of the Polaris missile represented, if anything, an even greater triumph of technology. The science of solid fuel had to be rapidly brought from prototype to production status and to be married to one of the new generations of small nuclear warheads. Reliability had to be assured, both in terms of the missiles' storage within the SSBNs and, to be a credible deterrent, reliability of the guidance system and the resulting accuracy of the weapon was equally important. While the parameters of the missile had been confirmed in March 1957, the decision seven months later to accelerate the programme to provide a 1,200-NM-range missile to be operational by December 1959 gave only two years to achieve the goal. A target unimaginable in today's defence procurement process.

Before even a prototype of the full-scale Polaris could be considered, a number of test vehicles had to be developed and proved to verify the design of the various sub-systems. Testing the concept of underwater launch entered new and unexplored territory. Land-based and air-launched missiles had been required to operate in two environments—air and space—but a SLBM had to add a third environment, sea, which in many ways was the most challenging of the three. Even if the missile was launched from a surfaced submarine—increasing its vulnerability—there could be the inevitable problems of the sea state, or could the missile be launched from a submerged vessel? Underwater, the missile had to be hydrodynamically stable as it left the submarine and headed for the surface. During this phase, it would be subject to the pressure of the surrounding water and the possibility of cavitation causing it to deviate from its path. Once the missile had broken the surface of the sea, it was still under the influence of compressed gas from the launch tube until it was some 100 feet above the surface. At this stage, the rocket motor would ignite and the guidance unit would set the missile on its planned course. It would then have to breach the sea-surface interface, and after breaking the surface—still under the influence of the compressed gas in the launch tube until some 100 feet or so above the surface—its rocket motor would take over at which stage the missile had to be steerable and aerodynamically stable without the addition of tail fins. The two stages had to separate and shut down as required—a capability yet to be proved—and then warhead separation must take place correctly to ensure that the warhead followed its correct ballistic path to the target.

To explore the initial stages of the flight, a variety of test structures were used to examine the particular characteristics of launching underwater. Operation Peashooter took place at Hunter's Point in San Francisco Bay with the first test launch on 27 September 1957. The facility consisted of an above-the-surface launch tube to test the launching process. Initially using redwood slugs and later dummy missiles filled with concrete to duplicate the mass and the centre of gravity of the real missile, the programme proved the efficacy of compressed gas as a launching system. A concrete pad had been placed on the seabed and above this on a buoyant structure was a launch tube similar to those that would be installed in the submarines. Into the tube were placed the test articles and the loaded tube was then lowered onto the pad and secured. Code-named Operation Pop-Up, the initial test articles were caught in harbour defence nets, but the dummy missiles were expensive and to allow then to be reused, a 186-foot-high crane mounted on the YC-1384 barge, named 'Fishhook', was anchored next to the launch facility and by means of a cable attached to the nose of the missile hydraulically braking the missile until its upward velocity was zero, allowed it to be reeled in and gently lowered.[1] The first test launch using the crane was on 24 April 1959. In later tests to simulate heavy sea conditions, navy cruisers the USS *Los Angeles* (CA-135) and the USS *Helena* (CA-75) would pass by at full speed to generate 8-foot waves. The crane had its detractors who did not believe it would work, but after the successful April demonstration, Rear Admiral Paul D. Stroop, chief of BuOrd, commented: 'This floating monument of the impossible will expedite and assist the Polaris development with resultant savings of many millions of dollars.'

Cameras, both still and television, were mounted under and above the water to record all aspects of the launch and a YFN barge was converted to act as an instrumentation facility. The net-laying ship the USS *Butternut* (AN-9) was allocated to the programme and was used to handle the nets during the early part of the tests and to tow the launch tube and crane into position.

Under Project Hydra, 70-inch wooden dummy missiles filled with lead were launched at the Pacific Missile Range at Point Mugu to further test underwater launching procedures.

By the late summer, sufficient progress had been made to allow construction to start on the series of prototype missiles that would be used for flight-testing. These were designated the Polaris AX series. To undertake these launches, a 36-acre site at Port Canaveral had been identified in the autumn of 1956 and was jointly developed by Lockheed and the Naval Ordnance Test Unit as Launch Complex 25 (LC-25). Two launch pads—Pads 25A and 25B—were constructed. The former was a raised pad so that engine performance could be seen and checked during the launch. To duplicate the various motions to be experienced at sea, a ship motion simulator (SMS) was constructed and designated Pad 25B. The SMS was constructed around a duplicate of one of the launch tubes from the *George Washington* and could move in three planes. Constructed by the Loewy Hydropress division of Baldwin Lima Hamilton, formed from a merger of locomotive manufacturers, this pad consisted of a launch tube supported by vertical hydraulic rams which could be moved to simulate the effects of sea swell. Static firing tests had not gone well as they were plagued by sticking jetevators on the first-stage motors resulting from a build-up of aluminium oxide on the jetevators seals.

[Jetevators control] the thrust vector of solid propellant rocket engines. The device is a semi-spherical shell hinged to the rocket nozzle and rotated, at the command of a sensing unit, into the exhaust flow to produce a control force. Optimum design of the system requires maximum effectiveness with a minimum reduction in thrust.[2]

This delayed the programme by some two months. However, the first hot launch took place on 24 September 1958 from Pad 25A. Designated AX-1, the missile closely resembled the production missile and was identical in size. This initial launch phase was totally successful. The missile lifted off the pad and rose skywards. Shortly after reaching 38,000 feet, the team monitoring the missile's progress via telemetry detected a fault in an electronic circuit. The missile started to veer from its designated course. Twenty-five seconds into the flight and clearly out of control, the range safety officer (RSO) had no choice but to activate the on-board explosive charge to destroy the missile. Although only partially successful, it would have been unrealistic to expect that the programme would have advanced without some setbacks, often referred to in the aerospace industry as 'rapid unscheduled disassembly'. Certainly, in terms of the initial failures of other contemporary missile programmes, it was a not unpromising start.

However, a fortnight later, AX-2 was less successful. After ignition, a systems fault ignited the second stage of the missile. Leaving the first stage to collapse on the launch pad, the second stage set off on an erratic path. Again, the missile had to be destroyed. AX-3 was launched on 30 December. Just over one minute into its flight, it too had to be destroyed when the second stage failed. The reasons for these problems were analysed and modifications made, but as soon as some systems were corrected, other problems arose. The early problems of Polaris were remembered four years later by the pro-Skybolt lobby when one of the reasons for termination of the air force programme was cited as the problems experienced in the early flight trials of the prototypes. Such was the pressure now exerted on the flight test programme that the time between successive launches was not long. AX-4 followed on 19 January 1959. Its flight lasted just over thirty seconds before it turned over on itself and plunged into the Atlantic. This was a clear demonstration of the advantage of siting the Cape Canaveral range so that missiles were launched heading out to sea. On 27 February, AX-5 was launched. It proved to be no more successful than its predecessors when its first stage failed. President John F. Kennedy was later to admit that the technological challenge initially presented by the operational requirement for the missile and its accuracy was beyond current US capability, a charge that he would also levy against Skybolt when it was cancelled.

But despite public euphoria, all was not well. Lockheed, its reputation at stake, was increasingly anxious for some sign of positive progress. Over five months had passed in the flight test programme, and little success had been achieved. All of a sudden, the doubts expressed by Congress during the previous year seemed to have been the product of justified caution. The breakthrough came with AX-6. Launched on 20 April, the flight was fully successful with the missile plunging into the Atlantic after a 300-mile trajectory. Special Project's faith in the FBM concept appeared to have been vindicated. Successful though AX-6 had been there were still many aspects of the missile design to be verified and flight tested. A major sub-system that was crucial to the missile's success was the inertial guidance system which would take Polaris to its target. The guidance system had to be absolutely precise when it came to establishing the launch point. Even the air force had run into problems with its land-based fixed-site missiles in 'matching the plumbing with the missile'.[3] Between 8 May and 29 June, four more missiles were launched—two successes and two failures. Next in line was AX-11, the first missile to be fitted with an integral guidance system. All previous missiles had been guided by an automatic system which had been pre-set before launch with the parameters of the flight. On-board systems would provide a telemetry data downlink so that the operation of the system could be monitored in flight. AX-11 was launched on 15 July. On reaching an altitude of around 40,000 feet, the missile suddenly turned around on itself and the first and second stages separated. The inertial guidance system, mounted in the second stage, automatically took over the guidance of the errant second stage and corrected its trajectory. Although the RSO took the decision to destroy the missile at this stage, the guidance system had demonstrated that it would work.

Despite the various setbacks, it was now considered that the prototype missiles were showing a degree of reliability such that the next stage of the flight development programme could be started. All missiles to date had been launched from stable, fixed launch pads, conditions which obviously would not apply when the missiles went to sea. AX-12 was not a live missile, being used as a facility test vehicle. AX-13 was therefore the first missile to be launched from the SMS on Pad 25B, although it was considered prudent to have the SMS stationary for this, the first test. The launch which took place on 14 August was in all respects a fully successful test. Raborn commented that 'the components which caused the failures are relatively minor ones [which] can be corrected by reengineering certain features. Many of the firing tests have been most successful and have proved beyond any doubt that the solid-propellant fuel is a practical reality.'[4]

A major problem from the navy's point of view continued to be the very real difficulties anticipated because of the effects of a ship's rolling and pitching. The SMS could assist, but only to a degree. To assist with this aspect of the research, two surface support vessels then joined the test programme. In March 1956, the navy had authorised conversion of two C-4 *Mariner*-class merchant ships, USS *Compass Island* (AG-153) and USS *Observation Island* (T-AGM-23), with the idea of the two vessels providing support for the prototype Jupiter-S missiles in investigating the very real technical problems which could arise. The *Observation Island* had been launched in 1952 and had sailed for a short time under charter to US lines as the *Empire State Mariner* before being taken into reserve in 1954. Two years later, the conversion process began, and she entered her new role as the weapons system test ship for Polaris on 5 December 1958 under the command of CAPT. Leslie M. Slack being based at Port Canaveral. Organisationally, the ship belonged to the Eastern Sea Frontier being normally tasked by Commander Operational Development Force, but command was transferred to SUBRON 14 during specific Polaris operations. Original blueprints show provision for the storage of LOX, a throwback to her role in launching the originally conceived liquid fuelled naval Jupiters, a role now superseded. The *Observation Island* was capable of testing at sea all aspects of the launch procedure except, of course, the underwater launching which was to be conducted at another facility. The second C-4 conversion was the *Compass Island* which was converted to the role of FBM navigation development and test ship. Both ships were subsequently to play a major part in the development programme. The two ships along with related land-based facilities were under the command of the Naval Ordnance Test Unit (NOTU) based at Patrick Air Force Station with the ships themselves at Port Canaveral, a man-made harbour at the southern end of Cape Canaveral adjacent to the Atlantic Missile Range. The crews' quarters were within the air force complex and enjoyed the same facilities as the resident air force personnel.

The *Observation Island*'s onboard equipment included two launch tubes on the afterdeck, a complete navigation and fire-control suite, and a missile instrumentation and checkout facility.[5] The twin duplicate missile launch tubes on the afterdeck had a compressed air-launching system together and with the associated navigation and fire-control systems represented in all respects an exact replica of the planned operational submarine configuration. As a safety feature, ballast tanks could be flooded to enable the vessel to list to starboard such that the missile would not fall back onto the deck should the rocket motor fail to ignite. The first seaborne launch of missile AX-22 took place from the *Observation Island* on 27 August 1959 and successfully completed a trajectory of 700 miles. Two further land-based launches from Pad 25A thereafter concluded the initial phase of the test programme. From now on, tactical prototypes of Polaris would be used and were designated A1X. The production missiles would carry the designation Polaris A-1. Reverting back to the launch facility at Cape Canaveral, the first A1X-1 was launched on 21 September from Pad 29A. This was the first launch from the new Launch Complex 29 which had been constructed next to LC-25. Originally designed like LC-25 to have two launch pads, in the event only one was actually built. The missile travelled 900 miles downrange. The test was deemed to be completely successful and verified the overall configuration of the production weapon. This missile was still guided by a pre-programmed guidance system. One week into 1960, the year in which the FBM deterrent was to be deployed, on 7 January, a fully configured A1X-7 complete with an inertial guidance unit was launched from the Cape Canaveral complex and completed a fully successful flight. With these successes under its belt, Lockheed undertook an intensive weight reduction programme to increase the range of the missile. This was engineered as the missiles moved from the test process to operational configuration and was achieved by reducing the weight of the heatshield and the deletion of certain subsystems that were incorporated for the test phase. Meanwhile the flight test programme concentrated on accuracy and reliability rather than range.

Although test flights would continue to be made from Cape Canaveral throughout the programme, late March was set as the date to undertake what was, in effect, the first complete test of the integrated Polaris system with a launch from the *Observation Island*. The systems aboard the support ship had been upgraded to faithfully duplicate the operational systems aboard the *George Washington*. Navigation systems similar to the SSBNs' were used to determine the location of the vessel and this was in turn input to the missile's inertial guidance system. The flight took place on 29 March and was once again declared a success. On the same day, the naval weapons annex was commissioned at the Polaris Missile Facility, the home base of the Polaris fleet.

As yet, no fully configured missile had been launched from the Pop-Up underwater facility. The predominant factor in this test programme was to check the actual performance of the missile once it had left the launch tube, travelled through the water, surfaced, and the characteristics of the subsequent ignition phase. First launch of an A1X from this test facility was accomplished on 14 April 1960. Only sufficient propellant was loaded to allow a six-second firing of the motor before the missile was 'captured' for later reuse. The test was fully successful. On 25 April, A1X-22 was fired from Cape Canaveral and achieved a range of 1,180 miles. The time was fast approaching when the missile could be safely integrated with the parent submarine. The following month, on 14 May, the final 598-class SSBN, the *Abraham Lincoln*, was launched at Portsmouth Naval Shipyard.

Meanwhile, after the commissioning of the *George Washington* on 30 December 1959, a full series of tests had verified the integrity of the missile launch system. Both Blue and Gold crews, under Osborn and From respectively, were fully involved in these tests. The first phase was to prove the compressed air launch system. Instead of missiles, 2,500-lb sabots were used. These were then replaced by 'Dolphins', the same size and weight as Polaris but inert with water being used as ballast. The Dolphins, which according to *Flight* were less attractive in appearance, had been fired 'somewhere in the Atlantic'. The first such launch was witnessed from a navy ZSG-2W airship by photographer Basil Clarke:

At Zero minus 120 seconds we gained our first indication of the exact position of the submarine when a patch of green marker dye spread across the surface. The count went on and at Zero minus 30 a canister surfaced and belched forth green smoke. Zero came. The water boiled. And the 28 foot long Dolphin, test vehicle for Polaris, rose rapidly, in the midst of a gigantic plume of spray, tinged a pale green by the marker dye.[6]

The Dolphin reached a height of 250 feet, somewhat more than the crew of the airship had been advised, which caused a few moments consternation. When a second Dolphin was launched some fifteen minutes later, the airship had prudently moved a little further away. A secondary role for the airship was to detect any evidence that the Russians were monitoring the launch, but it seemed that security provisions had worked and there were no foreign observers. Curiously the navy's official release on the test suggested that it had been unsuccessful, however, Clarke's view was that it had been an 'unqualified success'.[7]

Confidence in Polaris was increasing. The launch of AX1-14 on 9 March 1960 was a successful test of the first prototype 1,200-NM-range missile, and it prompted Congressman Gerald Ford, the future president, to comment:

The successful firing over a 900-mile range of a Polaris test vehicle last week emphasized anew the highly significant Polaris submarine and the diversity of our national weapon system. Out of the last eight attempted firings of the Polaris, seven have been completely successful and one partially successful. One Polaris submarine with its 16 missiles packs more destructive power than all the allied and enemy planes put into the air during the total period of World War II. Because it can operate entirely under the surface of the sea and can direct its destructive power at any spot in enemy territory it has been called a 'truly indestructible retaliatory force.' It combines two revolutionary developments—solid propellant missiles and nuclear-powered submarines. By the end of this year we will have operational at sea two Polaris submarines with 32 ballistic missiles ready for any emergency. It is presently planned to have at least 128 Polaris missiles ready by 1963.[8]

On 28 June 1960, the *George Washington* left Groton for the Eastern Test Range at Cape Canaveral where the actual live test firings would take place at sea at the Atlantic Missile Test Range. This would allow the use of range and tracking instrumentation at the Cape which was already configured for the land-based test flights.

Meanwhile, on 15 July 1960, construction of a further five SSBNs (10–14) was approved by Eisenhower. Three days later the *George Washington*, with two A1E missiles onboard, put to sea from Port Canaveral with her Blue Crew under the command of Osborn with 'Red' Raborn as an observer. She was accompanied by the *Observation Island*, which also fulfilled a secondary role as host to a group of media representatives, and the destroyer the USS *Gearing* (DD-710). The latter vessel was employed to ensure that no Soviet submarines entered the test area and also to ward off any of the Soviet AGI espionage ships, operating under the disguise of fishing trawlers, which might attempt to watch the launch.

The *George Washington* had been fitted with a telemetry mast which was attached to the side of the fin. and it was only the upper extremity of this that was visible above the water when she submerged. It had the added advantage that the attendant vessels knew her exact location. The countdown began but was stopped four minutes ('T minus four') before the scheduled launch. There was a tense fifteen-minute hold before the countdown was resumed. Then, just seven seconds before 'zero', Robert E. Kemelhor of the Johns Hopkins University Applied Physics Laboratory, who was acting as technical adviser to the launch officer, noticed something wrong with a set of warning lights. He urgently told Osborn to cancel the launch. Frustrating though this was, it was the almost inevitable result of taking technology ahead at the rate represented by Polaris. This was not a mere launch pad test shot; this time human lives were potentially at risk as analysis of the problem identified a fault that could have caused the missile to explode in the launch tube with potentially very serious results. Kemelhor later wrote: 'Since we were underwater, this would not have been a very joyful experience.'[9] Osborn recycled the count down, selecting the second missile. This time it was downrange communication problems which stopped the countdown a mere five seconds before launch. Twice more range communication problems stopped the countdown. At 7:45 p.m., batteries in the tracking equipment were running flat and, with darkness fast approaching, the decision was taken to terminate the test for that day. The intercom announced that 'the *George Washington* will not launch.'

The press teams aboard the *Observation Island* were prevailed upon not to report the failure to launch as the group of ships accompanied the SSBN back to Port Canaveral. A further attempt was scheduled for 20 July. On the day in between, a fully configured missile, A1X-41, was launched from the Polaris

Launch Facility at Cape Canaveral and, after a successful flight, landed 1,188 miles downrange in the Atlantic. The missile was now demonstrating both capability and a promising degree of reliability. On the following day, the *George Washington* again put to sea. Her already confined space was now crammed with some 300 personnel, all with their own part to play in the launch process, if only as observers. After a minor technical delay and a further hold when a merchant ship sailed into the area, at 12:39 p.m. the first Polaris missile to be launched from an SSBN broke the surface close to the telemetry mast: it seemed to pause for a moment before its rocket motor ignited sending it soaring skywards. A minute later with the missile already some 15 miles downrange, the first-stage motor was cut and, as this stage fell away into the Atlantic, the second stage ignited. Burning for sixty-five seconds, this stage accelerated the missile a further 55 miles. The dummy warhead which had been fitted to the missile then separated from the second-stage bus and continued the trajectory, eventually landing some 1,100 miles downrange. A flash message was sent to Eisenhower: 'Polaris, from out of the deep to target. Perfect'. The euphoria created both on board the *George Washington* and the accompanying vessels was added to when, two hours and fifty-three minutes later, a second missile was also successfully launched. 'I see a very courageous man [Raborn],' commented Pehrson, 'who set fire two [missiles] when the first one fired ... from the *George Washington*. It would have been so easy just to fire one and go back to port, but he took the chance the second one would work. That takes guts.'[10]

At the ensuing press conference Raborn was asked about the accuracy of the missiles. Clearly they had the range, but had they landed in the correct place? Raborn replied that they had 'adequate accuracy to have done the job if they had been fired on the enemy.' Asked to clarify his meaning of 'accuracy', he added with a wry smile 'you are not much interested in which side of the squirrel's eye you hit.' There was elation in naval circles that after all the planning and hard work, the system in broad terms could perform as required. There was every reason to believe that Polaris could be fully operational and deployed by the end of the year.

RADM Ward commented: '[The launch was] a cause for exultation, feeling that here we had finally accomplished something, got a crew that could do it, got a submarine that could do it and we were almost ready to become fully operational.'[11]

Perhaps spurred on by this success, even the orders for the SSBNs seemed to gather momentum. By 23 July 1960, orders for all of the SSBNs which had so far been authorised had been placed. The first fourteen submarines consisted of three distinct classes. The first five of the 598 class were of the original SCB-180A design. These were followed by 608 class (SCB-180), designed from the start as SSBNs, which consisted of USS *Ethan Allen* (SSBN-608), USS *Sam Houston* (SSBN-609), USS *Thomas A. Edison* (SSBN-610), USS *John Marshall* (SSBN-611), and USS *Thomas Jefferson* (SSBN-618).[12] These boats too were powered by the same Westinghouse S5W PWR reactors used in the 598 class giving around 15,000 shp. The Westinghouse Electric Corporation provided the turbines for the first three submarines with General Electric equivalents being used in the final two boats of the class. Although the diameter of the hull remained the same at 33 feet, this class had an increased length of 410 feet and a submerged displacement of 7,880 tons. The crew was slightly enlarged to fifteen officers and 127 enlisted men. The increased reliability of the SINS allowed the deletion of one of the three units fitted on the 598 class.

The balance of the SSBNs on order were of the 616 class. They were to be named USS *Lafayette* (SSBN-616), USS *Alexander Hamilton* (SSBN-617), USS *Andrew Jackson* (SSBN-619), and USS *John Adams* (SSBN-620). This class would eventually number nine submarines built to BuShips design number SCB-216. Once again, the standard beam measurement of 33 feet was adopted but the total length was further increased to 425 feet. Submerged displacement increased accordingly to 8,250 tons. Much of the extra length was used to make the accommodation more habitable for the crew which consisted of fourteen officers and 126 enlisted men. Bigger bunks were a feature of the design—3.5 inches longer than the standard submarine bunk—and there was increased headroom between the bunks. This latter feature was thanks mainly to Raborn who had found the bunks on the *George Washington* to be too close together and ordered 'more space' in subsequent designs. In many ways, the accommodation on the 616 class was the envy of many surface sailors. Engineering advances resulted in an overall quieter boat and the extra size allowed for a dedicated 'activities room' complete with a variety of fitness equipment. One boat could even boast a slot machine. More space was given over to leisure and study activities with provision being made for lectures and the showing of films.

EB was again responsible for the lead submarine, the *Lafayette*, at that time the largest submarine ever built by the US, whose keel laying ceremony took place six years to the day after the *Nautilus* set sail under nuclear power. John F. Kennedy had been elected president, taking over from Eisenhower, and the submarine, sponsored by First Lady Jacqueline Kennedy, was launched on 8 May 1962. From an engineering point of view, the same Westinghouse S5W reactor was once again used. The initial four submarines on order were all fitted with GE geared turbines. DeLaval was subsequently added to the list of suppliers of these turbines along with Westinghouse. Four torpedo tubes were again incorporated in the design, and these were controlled via a Mark 113 fire-control system. With the constant improvement in sonar capability, increasing attention was paid to sound insulation of the engineering systems and the associated sub-systems. The 616 class was fitted with the BQS-4 Active/Passive sonar array. Navigation was by two Mk 2 Mod6 SINS and a satellite receiver. While on patrol it was necessary to check the positional accuracy of the SINS. This would be done at night after making sure that there were no nearby contacts. An aerial would be extended at periscope depth to enable a satellite fix to be taken. In addition, surveys had been made of the seabed in the patrol areas and these could be verified via discrete echo soundings.

Crucial to the successful targeting of the missile was its inertial guidance system. The inertial guidance developed for Polaris consisted of an inertial platform linked to a digital computer. Once launched the missile had to be completely autonomous of external commands. This was required so that the enemy could not take over control in any way. The SINS used extremely accurate gyroscopes which constantly measured any deviations from the course set by the submarine's fire control system fed in prior to launch and returned the missile to the correct course. Polaris A-1 had a CEP accuracy of 2–4 miles, but this was to improve with later models. This meant, however, that early missiles could not be used on precise targets and like Thor and Jupiter would be targeted at city and larger area targets:

> Draper's miniaturization of the earlier systems was vital to the FBM systems success. Even more importantly, his adamant insistence of maintaining an overall authority from design through prototyping and transition to production and operational usage played a major role in the successful Navy missile program.

The Mk 1 naval guidance system was developed in record time, spurred on by the shock effect of the launch on 4 October 1957 by the Soviet Union of the world's first artificial satellite, Sputnik 1. Weight was still an important issue, so beryllium (Be) was used for its strength and thermal stability although it was not an easy material to handle, and its dust was toxic. The Mk 1 made its first flight on 7 January 1960 on A1X -7: the first fully guided ballistic missile flight using a digital computer for inertial guidance. Pressure to produce the Mk 1 was intense and required the use of existing components which in turn led to manufacturing difficulties. The Mk 1 was used for both the A-1 and A-2 Polaris. The first ten SSBNs allied this to the Mk 80 fire-control system being replaced by the Mk 84 FCS on the remaining thirty-one boats.

Just prior to the successful first sea-launch of Polaris, a further element of the system was put in place when the USS *Proteus* was commissioned as the first of five FBM Tenders.

*****

Polaris A-1 weighed 28,800 lb and had a length of 28 feet 6 inches. It was a two-stage missile. The first stage weighed 18,400 lb and utilised an Aerojet steel motor case with a polyurethane propellant and ammonium perchlorate oxidiser. The second stage weighing 9,400 lb, and likewise used a steel motor case and the same propellant and oxidiser. The remainder of the weight was taken up by the warhead. Each missile was armed with one Mk 47 Mod 0 nuclear warhead. To save vital weight, the warhead was integrated within the re-entry vehicle (RV).

Designated W-47, the RV was given a target weight of 900 lb. Warhead design had been entrusted to Sandia and the University of California Radiation Laboratory (UCRL)—later to be renamed the Lawrence Livermore National Laboratory. The arming and fusing systems came from the Naval Ordnance Laboratory at White Oak. The warhead was 4 feet in length with a rounded nose cone fairing. At its after end the 20-inch-diameter RV was mated to the 54-inch-diameter missile via a truncated conical section which contained the arming and fusing systems and pressurised gas spin rockets design to stabilise the RV after separation from the missile body. Despite the diminutive size of the warhead in comparison with other contemporary designs, it was nonetheless considered essential that UCRL produce, at the very least, a yield of one megaton. Not only would anything less lack sufficient punch to make Polaris credible it was also likely to invoke ridicule from an arrogant LeMay, who, although now VCS of the air force still championed SAC's cause. For him a weapon of one megaton was merely a starting point. In fact, a high-yield version of the warhead design for the BOMARC air defence missile, designated W-40 and also under development by Sandia, was considered as a possible warhead for Polaris but was discounted in favour of a purpose-built design.

The *George Washington* and her Gold Crew under the command of CDR From fired her third and fourth missiles on 31 July and 1 August 1960 with mixed success. The first shot was completely successful with the missile landing on target 1,147 nautical miles from the launch location. The launch on the following day saw first-stage ignition and the missile start on its trajectory correctly, but after forty-five seconds a directional fault caused it to veer off-course and the missile was destroyed on command of range control. No such facility would of course exist with the production missile. Once launched there was no ability to retarget or destroy the missile. Even mature weapon systems could never presume 100 per cent reliability so the failure, though frustrating, was not wholly unexpected.

The *Patrick Henry*, commissioned into the navy on 9 April, was by then ready to join the test programme, being tasked with launching Polaris under operational, rather than test, conditions. Prior to this, however, she was to complete a similar series of test firings off Cape Canaveral to that undertaken by the *George Washington*. Of four missiles fired during September, there were three failures, although two of these were as a result of failures in safety devices and associated circuitry rather than faults within the actual missiles. SP never used the word 'failure' when all did not go to plan. These were deemed a 'non-success from which valuable lessons were learned'.[13] A second series of tests took place between 15 and 18 October with the submarine located some 500 miles into the Atlantic, east of the Florida coast. The test required the launch of four upgraded A1FP missiles but of reduced range capability. Range as such was not a primary consideration as these launches sought to duplicate as far as possible the actual operational launch procedures that would be followed by the submarine's crew. Although these were nominally A-1 test vehicles, with the exception of ballast in place of actual nuclear warheads and certain test circuitry, the missiles were effectively production specification missiles. Lockheed was meanwhile delivering true production A-1 missiles to the Polaris Missile Assembly Facility at Charleston under conditions of the tightest security. Sixteen Mk 47 Mod-0 warheads were delivered during July. These were mated to the missile bodies at the assembly facility.

On 30 August 1960, her test programme completed, the *George Washington* arrived back at Groton for routine servicing, then on 28 October, she proceeded to Charleston arriving shortly after 1 November. Here she was loaded with a full complement of Polaris A-1 missiles, an operation that was completed in about half the expected time, and stored and victualled for her first deterrent patrol. The missiles, each encased in a protective tube, were gently lowered into the waiting submarine and the hatches sealed above them. On 15 November, a few minutes after noon, the USS *George Washington* with her Blue Crew cast off from Charleston and sailed down the Cooper River towards the open sea. Just before departure, VADM Elton W. Grenfell, Commander Submarine Force, U.S. Atlantic Fleet, had awarded the crew the Navy Unit Commendation Ribbon while her captain had received the Legion of Merit. ADM Burke, on board the *Robert E. Lee* in the Atlantic, radioed a message, 'I wish you the best of luck in the most significant journey that any man-of-war has ever taken'.[14] Her departure was by no means as secretive as her subsequent patrols. The full pomp and ceremony of a navy band playing 'Anchors Away' ensured that the SSBN's departure was made fully aware to those against whom the warheads were targeted. With her A-1 missiles capable of a 1,200-NM range, and assuming that Moscow was one of the selected targets, it was possible to interpolate that the submarine could be heading for somewhere in the Norwegian or the Barents Sea which she was expected to reach some ten days later. More than that, only a very few people, including only a very few on board the submarine, would ever know. Sixty miles off the eastern coast of North America, the submarine closed her hatches and would stay submerged and undetected for the next two months. Burke had promised Congress that the first patrol would take place in November 1960: 'We had to scratch and really claw to get the *George Washington* out on the fifteenth, but she made it.'[15]

The development of the definitive version development of the missile, which was to become the Polaris A-3 (UGM-27C) and fulfil the design range aspiration, was approved by SecDef William B. Franke in September 1960 with funding approved the following month. In the interim period, however, Lockheed had developed the Polaris A-2 (UGM-27B). Better performance could be achieved by reducing the weight and improving the specific thrust of the second stage. This missile (initially known as Polaris B) was essentially a stretched A-1, 30 inches longer, with a more powerful second stage which would give the missile a range of 1,500 NM, 300 NM more than the A-1 version initially deployed. The second stage was now made of wound fibreglass and replaced the jetevators with rotating nozzles. Responsible for the improved propellant was the Alleghany Ballistics Laboratory (ABL), West

Virginia, which developed an improved compound using a nitrocellulose/nitro-glycerine mix with the addition of aluminium fuel and ammonium perchlorate oxidiser. This propellant produced higher temperatures and bearing in mind the problems with the jetevators in the hot exhaust, a new system of thrust vector control (TVC) using four rotating nozzles was installed. The warhead remained the same as the A-1. Although perhaps a somewhat modest increase in range, it would nonetheless allow the SSBNs to use much greater areas of ocean, correspondingly reducing their chances of detection. The missile was 31 feet in length with the same 54-inch diameter of the A-1 version and it weighed 30,000 lb fully fuelled. With much of the missile the same as the A-1, the development of the A-2 was considerably easier as was demonstrated by the launch of the first test A-2, A2X-1, on 10 November 1960 which saw the missile achieving a range of 1,628 NM. The first A-2 launch from the *Observation Island* took place on 2 March 1961 when A2X-7 successfully completed a 1,600-NM trajectory.

Two launches from the *Observation Island* were made in March 1961. The test program continued from both LC-25 and 29 as well as a further five launches from the *Observation Island* although not all were deemed successful as problems with the second stage and the guidance system were still being experienced. After a total of seventeen trial launches, the first submarine launch of Polaris A2E-X1 was from the *Ethan Allen* on 23 October 1961 resulting in a perfect downrange flight of 1,500 miles. This SSBN was scheduled to be the first to be operationally

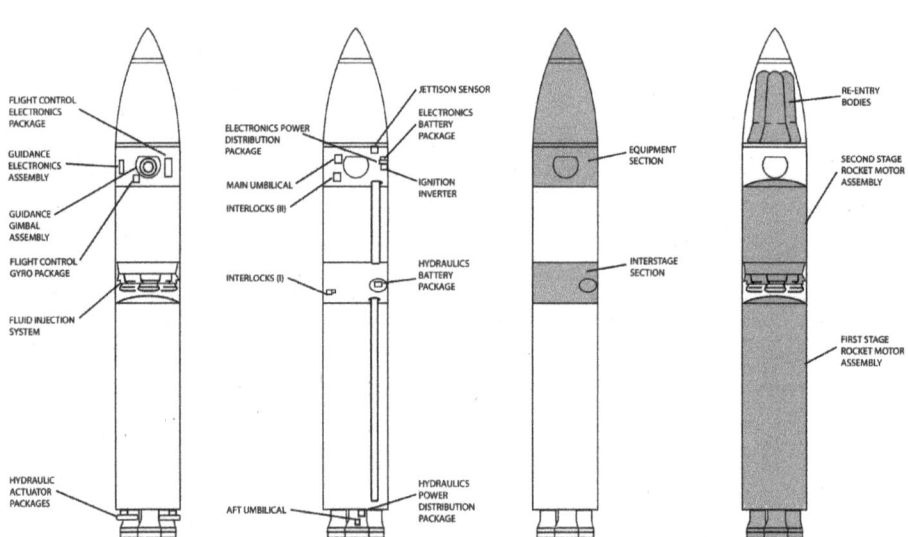

Left and centre left: Guidance, flight controls and electrical sub systems.

Right and centre right: Ballistic shell, re-entry and propulsion sub systems.

equipped with the A-2 missile during 1962 but she was destined to undertake a significant duty as part of Joint Task Force 8.8 operating in support of the largest US Nuclear Test programme, Operation Dominic I, comprising thirty-six atmospheric nuclear tests. On 6 May 1962 under the code name Frigate Bird, the *Ethan Allen,* commanded by CAPT. Paul L. Lacy with VADM Smith on board, launched an A-2 armed with a W47-Y1 thermonuclear warhead. The original plan had been to conduct the test in the Atlantic, but this was superseded by a decision to undertake the operation in the Pacific as part of Dominic. This meant a rapid change of plan for the *Ethan Allen* which left Charleston on 19 April with four of her missiles changed for specially instrumented missiles including a tracking beacon and a command destruct system in case of problems after launch. Extra batteries were added to power these systems. Transiting via the Panama Canal she made good speed to rendezvous with the task force on 2 May. Rehearsals took place on 3 and 4 May with the intention of the live launch taking place on the 5th, however, long-range communication problems which were considered essential for the safety of the launch postponed the actual launch until the following day.[16] Previous target areas at Eniwetok and Bikini atolls were no longer available and with time pressing, the original launch point close to Johnston Island, also a logistic hub for the programme, had to be changed to a point east of the target area about 1,724 miles east–north-east of Christmas Island. Britain had given permission for the use of the island as the logistic hub and use of the Christmas Island Danger Area some 480 miles ENE of the island as a target area for twenty-five of the tests with a reciprocal arrangement to let the UK use the Nevada Test Site and make diagnostic measurements of the explosions. With a range of 1,500 miles care had to be taken in selecting the aiming point far from inhabited Pacific islands. On 6 May, the SSBN submerged to firing depth in preparation for the launch. Poor weather conditions in the target area caused a two-hour delay in initiating the countdown but eventually it was started and proceeded until thirty seconds before launch when the launch control system identified a 'muzzle hatch limit' switch failure and automatically bypassed the primary missile to transfer operations to the second missile. This too failed due to a false 'safe/ready' switch reading. Task Force Commander RADM Lloyd M. Mustin called for a hold to allow monitoring aircraft to reposition themselves. By then the weather at the launch site had deteriorated, further delaying the start of the countdown. Also by this time, the batteries in the first and second missile had run down and required to be replaced, but then the clouds cleared and the decision was quickly taken to launch the third missile which took place successfully just after 1:18 p.m. (local time). The subsequent trajectory reached a height of around 400 miles and a downrange distance of some 1,173 miles. Twelve and a half minutes later, the warhead in a Mk 1 RV detonated successfully at an altitude of around 11,000 feet. Yield was calculated at about 600 kt and was around 1.25 miles from the target zero point. The test was principally designed to launch a nuclear armed missile by a navy crew under simulated wartime conditions, but a number of 'firsts' were also achieved:[17]

The first launch of an armed Polaris.
The first test of the W-47 packaged as a warhead.
The first detonation of a nuclear warhead after ballistic re-entry.
The first operational test of an American nuclear ballistic missile system.

Two submarines, the USS *Carbonero* (SS-337) and the USS *Medregal* (SS-480), submerged 30 miles from the target, took periscope photos of the resultant mushroom cloud as it rose to a height of 60,000 feet.

Following the 1963 Partial Nuclear Test Ban Treaty signed between the US, the Soviet Union, and the UK, this was to be the only atmospheric test of an American nuclear deterrent system. Returning to her operational duties, on 26 June 1962, the *Ethan Allen* left the Charleston base to go on the first patrol carrying sixteen A-2 missiles.

By now, fostered mainly by the embryonic manned Mercury program, US public interest in missiles in general and, in particular, events at 'The Cape' made it a centre of attention. It was considered time to further capitalise on this if only to reassure the nation that the embarrassment of seeing the further Soviet success in launching Yuri Gagarin into space was going to be superseded by

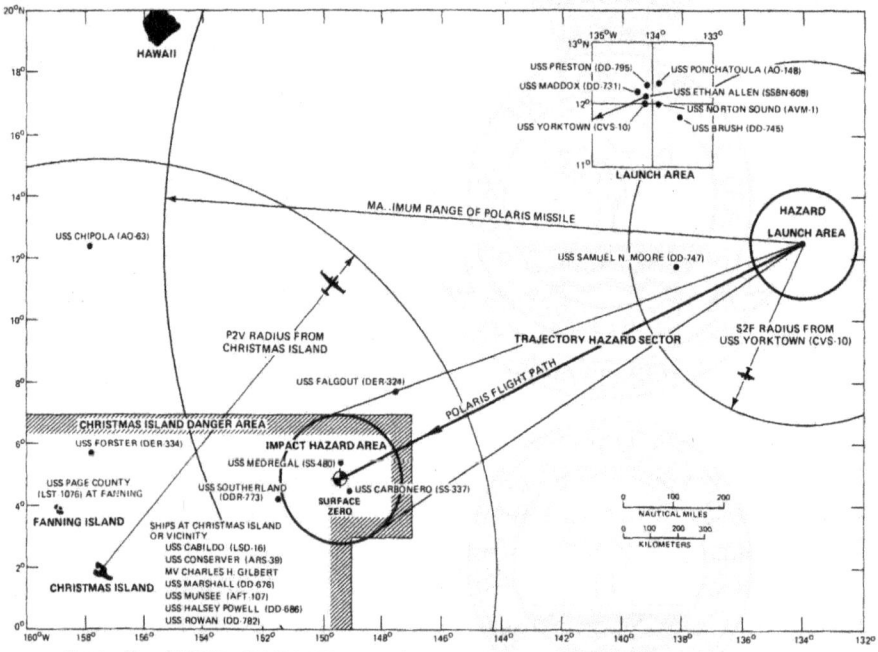

Figure 73. DOMINIC, FRIGATE BIRD operational area showing launch and impact hazard areas, trajectory hazard sector, and ship locations.

forthcoming American successes. In May 1961, therefore, only a few days after Alan Shepard's sub-orbital Mercury launch, the gates were opened to the public for the first time to coincide with Armed Forces Day. According to the *Orlando Sentinel*, people from as far away as California camped outside the entrance to be assured of getting an access ticket when the gates opened at 5:30 a.m. 'Six air-evacuation type helicopters will hover over the thousands of cars to report any difficulties and white-cross trucks will be available for medical care if needed.'[18] A carefully planned itinerary allowed reasonably close access to most of the launch complexes and the guided missile cruiser the USS *Galveston* (CL-93) was tied up at Port Canaveral. Visitors were advised to take plenty of food and iced water on the tour. Public 'space fever' was further fuelled less than a week later when

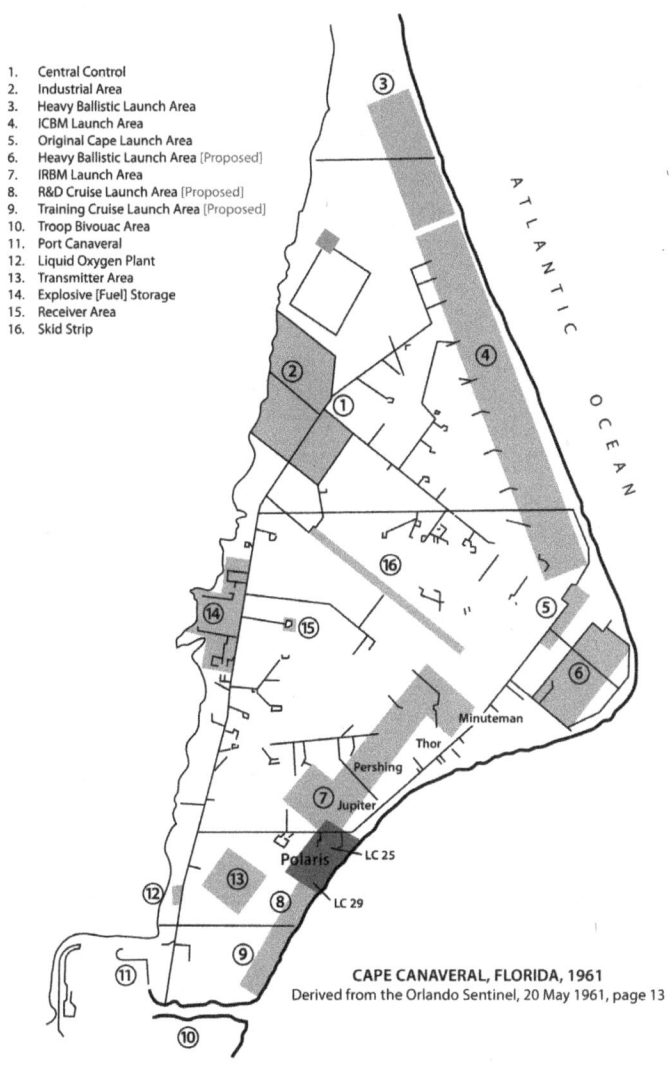

1. Central Control
2. Industrial Area
3. Heavy Ballistic Launch Area
4. ICBM Launch Area
5. Original Cape Launch Area
6. Heavy Ballistic Launch Area [Proposed]
7. IRBM Launch Area
8. R&D Cruise Launch Area [Proposed]
9. Training Cruise Launch Area [Proposed]
10. Troop Bivouac Area
11. Port Canaveral
12. Liquid Oxygen Plant
13. Transmitter Area
14. Explosive [Fuel] Storage
15. Receiver Area
16. Skid Strip

ATLANTIC OCEAN

Minuteman
Thor
Pershing
Jupiter
Polaris
LC 25
LC 29

CAPE CANAVERAL, FLORIDA, 1961
Derived from the Orlando Sentinel, 20 May 1961, page 13

Kennedy announced the intention to go to the Moon. America was catching up on the early Soviet successes, and fast recovering its loss of prestige.

On 16 November 1963, Kennedy arrived at Cape Canaveral for a two-hour visit, receiving first a briefing on the current state of the Apollo program, meeting Gemini astronauts Gus Grissom and Gordon Cooper. He then was driven to LC-37 where he met von Braun and NASA Administrator James Webb. Boarding his Marine Corps VH-3A helicopter along with another Paperclip specialist, Dr Kurt Debus, director of the Launch Operations Center, he overflew the Titan III Launch complex and other launch pads on the 88,000-acre Merritt Island Launch Area including the Polaris pads. It was a rapid tour as the president's helicopter is never allowed to hover. Heading out to sea, the helicopter landed on the *Observation Island* where the president was briefed by RADM Galantin on the forthcoming Polaris launch which the president was to see next. Kennedy watched the successful launch of an A-2 from the *Andrew Jackson* at 11:45 a.m.[19] He later wrote to Galantin: 'It is still incredible to me that a missile can be successfully and accurately fired from beneath the sea. Once you have seen a Polaris firing the efficacy of this weapons system as a deterrent is not debatable.'[20] Six days later, he was assassinated in Dallas, Texas. Vice President Lyndon B. Johnson assumed the presidency and by the time that he was re-elected in the November 1964 presidential election, thirteen SSBNs were fully operational with A-2 missiles when the *John Adams* set sail from Charleston on 3 November—the last of the SSBNs to deploy with that version. Of the eventual fleet of forty-one SSBNs, thirteen would carry A-2 missiles. The remainder were designed from the outset to carry the A-3 version.

Before the *George Washington* had departed on its first patrol, another significant milestone had been achieved in the Polaris programme with approval being given by SecDef Gates for the development of the full range A-3 version of the weapon (initially known as Polaris C). This was to be the definitive version of Polaris fulfilling the range originally envisaged.

On 26 February 1962, Galantin had replaced Raborn as director of SP. Frigate Bird had taken place on his watch and he was now to cover the period of development of the third version of Polaris and would also be destined to conduct the later negotiations with the United Kingdom for the Royal Navy to acquire Polaris.

The ultimate fulfilment of the Polaris project was the A-3 version—the definitive version of the missile with a range of 2,500 miles. Both the A-1 and the A-2 had been the product of urgent need using much existing technology. The Mk 1 guidance system had not been trouble-free in operation. Time taken in developing the A-3 missile insured that in many ways it was an entirely new missile, indeed Lockheed claimed it was 80 per cent new. The shape too was different—the bottle shape of the earlier variants had been changed to a more streamlined bullet shape conforming to the von Kármán minimum drag shape.

The overall size, however, was still constrained by the size of the launch tube. Furthermore, a new nosecone was made from Sitka spruce which protected the three RVs now arming the missile from aerodynamic loads and heating on its re-entering the lower atmosphere. It was fitted to the forward section of the equipment section by an interrupted thread connection. It was strong enough that the whole missile could be raised by a lifting eye in the tip of the nosecone which was covered by a removable fairing. This was required when loading the missiles into the submarine. Inside the top of the nosecone was a small rocket which was fired after a fixed time of around forty seconds during second-stage burn thus separating the nosecone and exposing the RVs. The flight had by then burnt off the outer finish and charred the surface of the wood. Separation of the stages was achieved by line-cutting charges as Lockheed was wary about using separation rockets. Taking advantage of the rapid changes in technology, the updated guidance unit was only one third the size of the unit used in the A-2. In that missile only the second-stage casing was filament-wound fibreglass. In the A-3 the first-stage casing was also fibreglass replacing the steel structure of the earlier missile but still manufactured by Aerojet General. Also derived from the A-2, the first-stage control system saw the jetevators, which had proved troublesome on the A-1, replaced by asymmetric rotating nozzles similar in concept to the directional control system used on the A-2's second stage. Range was almost always a critical factor, and the second stage of the A-3 used a more energetic propellant to achieve improved maximum range. This, however, presented problems which threatened to restrict the A-3's target range. Using this new propellant resulted in higher temperatures and higher chamber pressures which resulted in a destructive effect on the nozzle materials which had to burn for up to sixty-five seconds. The internal cavity in the propellant was star-shaped to give near constant acceleration during the flight phase. This varied from the earlier shapes which provided exponentially increased thrust as the mass of the stage fell. Although Aerojet was the prime contractor, the navy gave Hercules-Allegany Ballistic Laboratory (ABL) a $6 million contract to fund first-stage research and development and to produce ten first-stage motors of Aerojet configuration thus potentially jeopardising Aerojet's contract. Both companies, however, had received research and development contracts for the second stage and these were progressing well.[21] The second stage control had been changed to a system whereby Freon 114 gas, stored in a toroidal tank around the aft end of the stage, was injected into the throats of four buried motor nozzles to alter course. A navy spokesman had confirmed this development but had declined to confirm the type of liquid being used or whether it was combustible, although it was known that during earlier tests, freon, nitrogen tetroxide and bleed-off from the combustion chamber gases had all been tried.[22] This development was in itself not without its problems. Management of the front end's centre of gravity was a critical aspect of the flight path for accurate targeting and the consumption of freon could vary considerably depending on the trajectory. Provision was therefore made for surplus freon to be dumped. Above the second stage was the equipment section, which carried the guidance and control units that controlled the motors along with various batteries and high-voltage firing units for the line-cutting charges. It was made from magnesium alloy—a material subject to corrosion in contact with seawater. An inverter in this section was removed when the submarine was alongside to act as a safety cut-out. Manufactured and initially assembled by LMSC, the A-3's solid propellant motors were manufactured by the Aerojet General Corporation and Hercules Power Company. Even as the Mk 1 guidance unit was being tested, however, chief designer Eldon C. Hall was working on what was to become the much-improved Mk 2. RADM Smith determined that, as the projected A-3 was still a retaliatory weapon, the need for terminal accuracy was not absolute provided the 2,500-NM range could be achieved. In practice, this meant a lighter unit than the Mk 1. The Mk 2 was manufactured by the Pittsfield branch of the General Electric Corporation. This was a unit half the size and one-third the weight of its predecessor. It gave a projected CEP of half a mile.

Despite the considerable advantages now offered by the A-3, the advent of the missile had not stopped inventive proposals being put forward as to how to best deploy it. Aerojet General had, for instance, produced a study on 'Augmenting the Polaris System'. This envisaged two pods attached to each of the flanks of the SSBNs each containing eight A-3s, thereby doubling the submarine's payload. This was presented as an option to cut the SSBN fleet by 50 per cent or alternatively doubling the throw weight of the submarines.[23] The idea was not taken up.

EXTERNAL MISSILE AUGUMENTATION

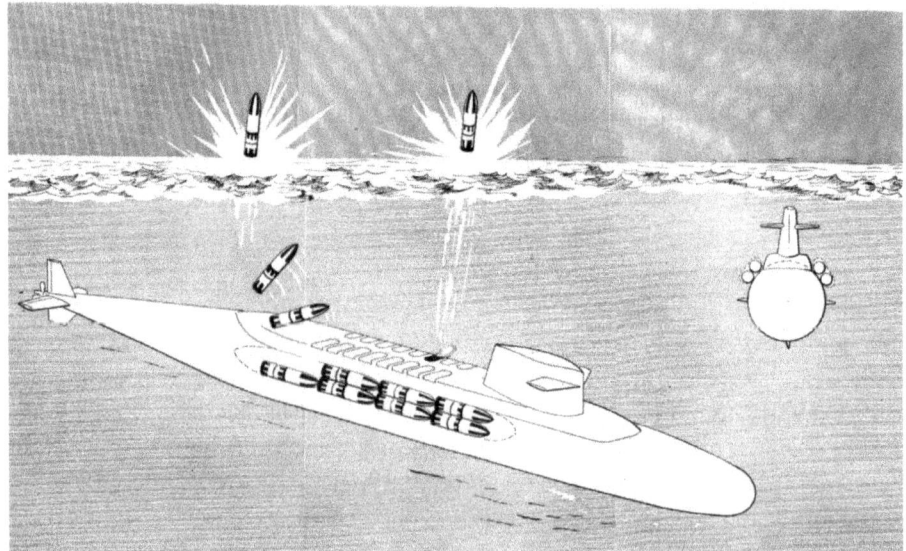

In charge of Polaris development was Lockheed's general manager of the Space and Missile's Division, Stanley W. Burriss. He had joined Lockheed in 1954 and was to become one of the key executives in the Polaris programme contributing a number of significant technical ideas in the development of the missile. His dynamic leadership was one of the main factors that allowed the FBM program to be delivered five years ahead of the original estimates. Rear Admiral Robert H. Wertheim, who was to become technical director of SP, was later to record that 'none of our industrial teammates contributed more to the success of the Polaris program than Stan Burriss'.[24] For the A-3, Burriss advised that leeway and tolerances that had been acceptable for the A-1 and A-2 would not apply to A-3 production—things were much tighter. Although it was planned that all the forty-one SSBNs would be equipped with A-3, the initial operational plan was for the first submarines to carry A-1, the sixth to seventeenth to carry A-2 by which time the A-3 would be ready for the remaining twenty-four. After two unsuccessful attempts at a launch on 31 July (stopped at T-75 minutes) and 2 August (stopped at T-8 minutes), the first launch of an A3 (A3X-1) took place on 7 August 1962 from LC 29A. Range for these first test shots was expected to fall some 200 NM below the 2,500-NM target as a result of a reduction in the flame temperature to 6,000°F to mitigate against the destructive effect on the motors. By this time, over 100 launches had taken place at both LCs and for those who had participated in that number of launches a special '100 Bird Club' was instituted with appropriate membership card.

100 Bird Club membership card.

For the A-3, a new warhead was introduced: the W-58. In March 1960, CNO Burke had approved a triple warhead cluster for the missile to be available by 1965. The AEC had tested a small 200-lb warhead of about 200 kt with the view of scaling this design up to a megaton. Unlike the single warhead of the earlier versions, the A-3 now carried three Mk 2 RVs each with a W-58 warhead with an estimated yield of 200 kt. As part of the Operation Dominic I series of nuclear tests, Device 'White' which took place on 25 May 1962 was probably the test of the W-58 Primary. Device 'Truckee' on 9 June was thought to be a development test of the XW-58 prototype warhead. On 6 October, an airdrop test from a B-52 at Johnston Island was Device 'Bumping', probably a detonation of a W-58 to test the yield-to-weight ratio.[25] Production was sanctioned on 6 November 1962 with manufacture of the warhead and the Mk 2 RV starting in March 1964. Between then and June 1967 when production finished, a total of around 1,400 warheads were manufactured.

Rather than scaling up the warhead, Wertheim preferred to use a device that had been fully tested to its full yield and it was realised that three of these warheads properly spaced in a triangular pattern would have much the same effect on the target as a single warhead of 1 Mt. Thus, multiple re-entry vehicles (MRV) were born—but not yet independently targeted. That was to come later. This was a somewhat unconventional approach, but with warheads properly spaced on re-entry, there was a reduced vulnerability to anti-ballistic missile (ABM) systems multiplying by three the difficulties posed for a defensive system despite there being little substantive information on Soviet ABM intentions or capabilities in this field at the time.[26] That too was to come later. Aware of the potential for an ABM threat, albeit that specific intelligence was limited, James Killian was a non-governmental witness along with George Kistiakowsky, formerly Eisenhower's scientific adviser and director of Defense Research and Engineering, and nuclear physicist Dr Herbert F. York, to a subcommittee of the Senate Foreign Affairs Committee. (York's job as deputy director for research and engineering carried no authority over military operational resources. It had proved a difficult post to fill. Secretary of Defense Special Assistant for Guided Missiles William M. Holladay had described it as a job that 'anyone smart enough to do it was much too smart to accept it'.) Asked if he had been approached by the White House, Killian replied that he had not, nor was he a qualified witness on technology but he had some useful ideas on appraising such large research and development projects and he referred to the earlier study undertaken by the Technological Capabilities Panel and the resulting guidance it had given Eisenhower in his support of the missile programme:

> The committee was interested and asked if we would be willing to present our ideas to the president…. Several hours later we were told that we had a date, not with [P]resident [Nixon] but with Dr. Kissinger, and so we repaired to his office

instead. He commented on our testimony and explained his own views, but was firm in saying that he saw no need for us to see the president. In fact Kissinger, feeling that he was endowed with all the answers, did not want us to see the president, and we never did, to Nixon's disadvantage, I believe.[27]

Wertheim was a little more apprehensive when it came to presenting this solution to the SP: 'The conventional thing would have been to agree with the [AEC] that they would scale up the size of a single warhead, we would have a conventional front end and away we'd go.'[28] He even admitted to certain doubts regarding the three-warhead layout:

> There were technical concerns about whether or not there would be mutual interference among the warheads, if one would detonate and somehow or other sanitize or defeat succeeding warheads, whether they would be far enough apart to avoid mutual interference.[29]

Nonetheless, he put the idea to Smith, who, somewhat it seems to his surprise, was receptive to the idea. Smith saw this as a way of simplifying the design of the A-3 second stage which required considerably more propulsive energy to reach the target range of 2,500 NM. To achieve this was going to require, firstly, a more energetic propellant and, secondly, a reduction in the weight of the motor cases to be achieved by lightening the non-propulsive elements of the missile. In both the A-1 and the A-2, thrust termination ports had to be incorporated in the second stage to slow it down to permit separation of the warhead. With the proposed three-warhead design the Mk 2 RVs could be ejected sideways thus eliminating the need to slow the second stage which could continue through the gap in the centre of the dispersed RVs. This would reduce the complexity and valuable weight would be saved. Wertheim's approach while being unconventional was also in its own way conservative. The warhead was known to work and any departure from this known tested design was treated with caution. 'It permitted the design to be made as a single structure without so-called thrust termination ports being built in. [The warheads could be separated from the second stage] instead of having to terminate the thrust of the second-stage motor when it reached the appropriate velocity.'[30] Wertheim was concerned that the possibilities of forthcoming restrictions on testing could prevent proper opportunities to prove new designs and openly admitted to Smith that his preference for a tested design may have been influenced in part by his Second World War experience of Mk 14 torpedo warheads, not properly tested, and failing in operational use. Spacing would have to be enough that it required three ABMs to destroy the three warheads but not enough to affect the targeting. Political issues were also involved, principally the cost of replacing one warhead with three. The ongoing and intense inter-service rivalry also came into play. The army wanted to develop its Nike-Zeus ABM missile, but the navy was unsupportive of the project whilst also being aware that further development of Polaris would need to take into account advances in Soviet ABM capability. Wertheim commented: '[The air force said] that is inconsistent, you are talking out of both sides of your mouth at once, concerned about the Soviet's anti-ballistic system but unwilling to support the production of a US anti-ballistic system.'[31]

*****

Meanwhile, the DoD budget for the 1963 fiscal year confirmed the provision of funds to construct SSBN numbers thirty to thirty-five with long lead items funded for a remaining six giving a total SSBN fleet of forty-one—the so called '41-For Freedom'. In a letter to Edward J. Bloch, Deputy General Manager of the AEC, Rickover later wrote:

> In addition to the 31 attack type nuclear submarines, we also have 41 Polaris submarines making a total of 72 nuclear submarines in operation. When all nuclear submarines presently authorized by Congress are completed, the United States will have a nuclear submarine fleet of 41 Polaris submarines and 65 attack submarines, and a small submarine [the NR-1] capable of exploring the ocean bottom.[32]

The first test firing of the new missile, A3X-1, took place on 7 August 1962 from Pad 29A. This launch and the two subsequent ones all registered failures of the second stage. Not until 7 February 1963 when A3X-8 was launched was a successful flight achieved, although this was only over a range of 1,600 miles—progress, nonetheless.

A further ten pad launches took place with mixed results, although A3X-7 on 11 February 1963 achieved a range of 2,000 NM, closely followed by A3X-18 on 8 April. Two days later, missile A3X-14 was being readied for launch from the *Observation Island*. After a successful launch, the guidance system failed and the RSO gave the destruct order eighty-five seconds into the flight. A further test flight on 26 April was also unsuccessful when the second stage failed. Three further pad launches took place before AX3-24 launched from the *Observation Island* on 17 June completed a flight of 1,500 NM. By now, many of the technical problems had been identified and rectified so that it was time to undertake a test firing from a submarine. On 26 October, A3X-43 launched from the *Andrew Jackson* completed a flight with a range of 2,288 NM. A range of 2,000 NM was achieved by A3X-42 on 11 November, fired from the same submarine. Confidence was now such that the first underwater launch of a production A-3 took place on 25 May 1964 when the USS *Daniel Webster* (SSBN-626) launched two A3P missiles down the Atlantic Test Range. The same submarine later carried out the first A-3 operational patrol departing Charleston on 28 September 1964. The increased range of the missile meant that any target on the Earth's surface was accessible and also considerably increased the size of the available patrol areas.

With the A-3, Polaris shifted the balance in America's strategic triad of ICBMs, SAC's airborne deterrent and the navy's Polaris. Along with this was the realisation that the nature and doctrine of warfare was changing. But this increasingly required targeting coordination and how would this be done? Anticipating this, on 3 April 1958, Eisenhower had already addressed Congress on the need to reorganise the defence establishment:

[S]eparate ground, sea and air warfare is gone forever. If ever again we should be involved in war, we will fight it in all elements, with all services, as one single concentrated effort. Peacetime preparatory and organizational activity must conform to this fact. Strategic and tactical planning must be completely unified, combat forces organized into unified commands, each equipped with the most efficient weapons systems that science can develop, singly led and prepared to fight as one, regardless of service. The accomplishment of this result is the basic function of the Secretary of Defense, advised and assisted by the Joint Chiefs of Staff and operating under the supervision of the Commander-in-Chief. Additionally, Secretary of Defense authority, especially in respect to the development of new weapons, must be clear and direct, and flexible in the management of funds. Prompt decisions and elimination of wasteful activity must be primary goals. These principles I commend to the Congress. In conformity to them I have formulated and urgently recommend certain changes in our defense establishment. Clearly we should preserve the traditional form and pattern of the services but should regroup and redefine certain service responsibilities. From this will flow the following significant results: Strategic planning will be unified.[33]

This was not SAC's view. It had always considered itself to be the American deterrent force. In the early days SAC alone could carry the bombs to their targets, but as the design of nuclear warheads improved and saw them becoming smaller and lighter, SAC saw itself threatened by both the army and the navy. Their dominant position was, however, not one they intended to relinquish. In July 1957, LeMay had handed over command of SAC to his wartime protégé General Thomas S. Power. Like his predecessor, Power advocated one massive onslaught using most of SAC's resources to eliminate a significant percentage of Sino-Soviet targets in the opening round of a war. But, with Polaris now added to the nation's nuclear capability, the navy also had a strategic weapon, although in the early stages it had lacked the accuracy to be used against pinpoint targets. With no formal coordination of targets and with the SSBNs mobility there was the inevitable risk of wasteful target duplication. Power saw that proper coordination of targets through a centralised targeting policy was the only sensible way of managing the strategic weapon stockpile and he intended that SAC would control this, albeit that this was not a policy to which the navy was likely to accede. This led to the formation of the JSTPS tasked with forming a plan which would be the basis for identifying targets and assigning weapons to them.

On 11 August 1960, SecDef Gates met Eisenhower and his senior defence chiefs to present his plan for a massive coordinated strategic strike against the Sino-Soviet bloc that would take place during the first twenty-four hours of a war. The proposal identified CINCSAC as the prime coordinator for developing the plan, thus taking authority away from the JCS. A National Strategic Target List (NSTL) would be drawn up and incorporated into a Single Integrated Operational Plan (SIOP). It was clearly optimistic to hope that the navy would agree to a single command having control over all nuclear forces which was implicit in the plan. Burke retaliated, objecting strongly to a scenario that would take control of military operations away from the JCS and place it in the hands of one commander and would thereby restrict the authority of individual subordinate theatre commanders. SAC would also be able to exert undue influence on nuclear weapon stockpiles and their allocation. Burke sought a delay on any decision until the JCS had been given time fully to evaluate the plan. His view:

> With their capability to destroy key Soviet targets, the virtually undetectable Polaris submarines could 'inflict terrible punishment' and deter Moscow from launching a surprise attack on the United States or its allies. By contrast Burke saw land-based missiles and bombers as vulnerable to attack, which made the U.S.-Soviet nuclear relationship dangerously unstable.[34]

The JCS chairman, US Air Force Gen. Nathan F. Twining, replied with equal force.[35] He had commanded the Twentieth Air Force, responsible for dropping the two atomic bombs on Japan and was the first airman to be appointed chief of the JCS. In part, the air force argument was that the JCS had failed conspicuously since the advent of atomic weapons to come up with a convincing plan for their co-ordinated use, whereas SAC with LeMay at the helm had become the primary advocate of their use and the primary carrier. SAC had, at least in their view, a clear idea of how they should be used to inflict maximum damage in an attack on the Soviet Union. Both SAC and the US Navy had allies across the Atlantic whose role needed to be taken into account as well, together with target allocation to SACEUR.

The Holy Loch Agreement

Our two governments must understand each other's points of view and do all we can to work together for the common cause, trusting we will be able to build up that common understanding and intimacy which enabled us to go through safely in the past and without which no full settlement of new problems can be reached.

Winston Churchill

We can only see a short distance ahead, but we can see plenty there that needs to be done.

Alan Turing

Considerable impetus had been given to the US missile program by the CIA's assessment of the so called 'missile gap' between the missile forces of the western allies *versus* the Soviet bloc. Early forecasts announced by Director of the CIA Allen Dulles gave a significant balance in favour of the Soviets, fuelled in addition, and as if by confirmation, by the launch in March 1957 of a Soviet R-7 rocket the characteristics of which suggested a capability to deliver a large nuclear warhead to mainland United States, further endorsed in October by the Sputnik launch. Intelligence on Soviet military installations was necessarily incomplete. Much of it at this stage centred on intelligence gathered from Operation Wringer. This was a post-war USAF project which interviewed German and Japanese prisoners that had been captured by the Russians, incarcerated in forced labour camps, and made to help in the rebuilding of the Soviet Union. On their gradual repatriation they were extensively interrogated by air force officers, and this helped to build up some information about Soviet industrial and military facilities and thereby a process of identifying potential targets. But, as reconnaissance overflights by Lockheed's high-flying U-2 spy planes were later to show, the assessment of

Soviet capability was largely illusionary. Eisenhower was unable to reveal that the situation was in fact in favour of the US for fear of revealing this high-flying, highly secret source of the intelligence:

> So, if there was a missile gap, it was created by Mr. [Allen] Dulles in the Eisenhower Administration; and if there was an elimination of the missile gap, it was eliminated by Mr. Dulles, still the head of the CIA agency, in the Kennedy Administration. Let me emphasize, however, that the result of Mr. Dulles' original figures created a tremendous impetus to our own defense programs. We certainly wouldn't have the number of Polaris submarines roaming the seas of the world, which we do have today. Nor would we have the number of Minutemen we now have over this country.... Impetus for the rapid development and production of these weapons came from the so-called missile gap. So there's the silver lining.[1]

US missile programs were the immediate beneficiary of the tiny Soviet spacecraft. The provisional plans to deploy Thor IRBMs to RAF stations in Britain were consolidated and Jupiter IRBMs were to be sent to Italy and Turkey. Plans to mount Polaris missiles in surface ships were cancelled and highest priority given to the SSBN programme. Fortunately, by mid-1957, the outline features of the submarine were already complete, some three months ahead of schedule. It was time also to give consideration to the operational needs of the SSBN fleet.

In April 1955, the socially adventurous British naval war hero Lord Louis Mountbatten became first sea lord, the position which, he believed, was his destiny in life to vindicate the slur placed on his father Prince Louis of Battenberg. The prince had been forced to resign from the post in October 1914 as a result of anti-German feelings within the British population nurtured by the press. After the Second World War, Mountbatten had taken a reduction in rank, becoming junior to many senior officers who had served under him in the war when he was supreme commander of South East Asia Command (SEAC). But this allowed him to continue his naval career in order to further his cherished ambition which he achieved on 18 April 1955. Six months later, on 27 October, accompanied by his notoriously left-wing wife Lady Edwina Mountbatten, the couple arrived in Washington on Mountbatten's first official visit representing the Royal Navy. ADM Burke then presciently took the opportunity to give an update to the Englishman on the current state of missile development in the US.

By 1956, the RAF's new Medium Bomber Force V-bombers were just reaching squadron service. Following the Valiant build-up, the first Vulcan and Victor deliveries to operational conversion units (OCU) were on 20 July 1956 and 28 November 1957 respectively and/or first deliveries to operational units, Nos 83 and 10 Sqns, on 11 July 1957 and 9 April 1958. By then orders were being placed for the B2 uprated versions of the Vulcan and Victor and it was clear to the public at least that Britain's nuclear deterrent was firmly in the hands of this elite force. (By 1962, Bomber Command had more aircraft than Britain's two flag carrying airlines, BOAC and BEA, put together.) But what was not so clear to the public was that a disproportionate amount of the RAF's budget was being spent on the bombers to the significant detriment of other parts of the air force. Mountbatten was concerned that a similar situation could apply if the RN took on the deterrent unless specific separate extra funding was provided to cover the costs. In this respect he, like Chief of the Imperial General Staff (CIGS) Field Marshal Sir Gerald Templer, differed from the Chief of the Air Staff (CAS) Sir Dermot Boyle who believed that an independent British deterrent was of paramount significance even to the detriment of other branches of the RAF.[2] Mountbatten at this stage therefore saw no great need to pursue a naval deterrent, but he was certainly in favour of the Royal Navy commissioning nuclear fleet submarines. SSNs were not cheap and in this respect, he had conjured up support for such a programme from a perhaps unlikely ally in the form of Chancellor of the Exchequer Derick Heathcoat-Amory who came from an old naval family.

In May 1958, Mountbatten was offered the appointment of chief of the defence staff (CDS) with the rank of admiral of the fleet. He formally took over from MRAF Sir William Dickson on 13 July 1959. For him this was a mixed blessing. Although now the head of Britain's armed forces, it meant giving up his naval position to represent the needs of all three services. It also required him to exercise impartiality towards balancing the service budgets. Culturally, of course, he found it difficult to forsake his instinctive loyalty to the Royal Navy, commenting during the press conference held on his appointment, 'It's a very sad day when you leave your own particular profession.' Once more he was back to a tri-service job. Britain, with close ties to the US, inevitably became part of this process of protecting the west against Soviet attack. In March 1959, Prime Minister Harold Macmillan, who had successfully rescued Britain from the shambles of Suez, a campaign that had caused a serious rift in Anglo-American relations, had met Eisenhower for talks on the possible acquisition of Skybolt. Air Vice-Marshal Stewart Menaul, who had been in charge of planning the UK's nuclear tests in Australia and the Pacific, wrote:

> To air strategists [Skybolt] was something long dreamed of and to economists it was the cheapest and most logical course for Britain to adopt. The country could not afford ground-based missiles in hardened silos, [Blue Streak] or a large enough force of expensive and inflexible Polaris submarines with their costly bases and support facilities, which from a cost effectiveness point of view was the least desirable system. So Skybolt emerged as probably the best solution for maintaining an efficient deterrent at a cost within Britain's capacity to meet.[3]

In an unrecorded conversation between the two leaders while *en route* to Eisenhower's son's farm, discussions had taken place about Britain providing a location for a US Navy forward submarine base from which to operate their Polaris boats. Without any European bases closer to the patrol areas, unnecessary time would be wasted on each patrol while the submarine travelled to and from American bases, during which time they would be out of range of their targets. The two elder statesmen were former close wartime colleagues in the North African campaign and enjoyed a cordial friendship. However, without the collaborative support of any witnesses or a record of their discussions it was perhaps inevitable that each man would put a different interpretation on what had, or had not, been agreed. The US memorandum of the agreement stated: 'we welcome the assurance that, in the same spirit of cooperation, the U.K. would be agreeable in principle to making the necessary arrangements for U.S. Polaris tenders in Scottish ports.'[4] Eisenhower believed that their oldest and closest national ally would provide what had been requested and the Americans had even identified their chosen site on the lower reaches of the River Clyde in the sheltered waters of the Gare Loch. Indeed, a possible Clyde base had been mentioned to Macmillan, who, possibly sensing the potential for resistance to such a proposal, noted in his diary his concerns if there was 'some frightful accident which might devastate the whole of Scotland'. To the Americans, one significant advantage of the Clyde area was its relative accessibility from Prestwick Airport where the US Military Air Transport Service (MATS) and from 1966 Military Airlift Command (MAC) had a significant presence, for it was a major staging point for US NATO personnel routing to West German bases.[5] Prestwick was also the only international airport in Scotland and enjoyed a largely fog-free reputation. This location was reinforced in November 1959 when Burke wrote to the British Naval Representative in Washington at which point the Gare Loch was specifically identified. The base would be largely self-sufficient being operated from an FBM tender and a floating dock with a minimum of dependence on shore-based facilities other than appropriate accommodation.

Macmillan was conscious that support for anti-nuclear groups was growing and initially strongly denied that any firm offer had been concluded. Such a base would inevitably be a prime target and Britain could be drawn, by default, into an American war. 'I did not, repeat not agree to this at Camp David', he commented in a note to Foreign Secretary Selwyn Lloyd.[6] But the Americans, sensing British reluctance to commit until Skybolt was a reality, were not wanting to wait. Admiral of the Fleet Sir Charles Lambe, who had succeeded Mountbatten and was a close friend, was keen to promote the 'special relationship' between the US and the UK and also knew that failure to reach agreement on the base would jeopardise the Royal Navy's discrete work 'behind the scenes' to acquire Polaris for the Royal Navy as a replacement for the V-bombers. Lambe, however, was not as enthusiastic as had been his predecessor about pressing too actively for Polaris, preferring to let things take a natural course. Macmillan adamantly ruled out any base adjacent to the Clyde as it was simply too close to Glasgow and privately, he feared the influence of the growing strength of the Campaign for Nuclear Disarmament (CND) which had been formally established on 17 February 1958 at a meeting in Central Hall, Westminster, and the potential of the organisation to disrupt operations. The prime minister had, in the following month, sent a memo to Dr Charles Hill, chancellor of the duchy of Lancaster. It read:

> It is most important that we should find some way of organising and directing an effective campaign to counter the current agitation against this country's possession of nuclear weapons. This is a question on which the natural emotions of ordinary people would lead them to be critical of the Government's policy, and to accept without question or reason the arguments which our opponents use.

He wondered if some influential people such as church leaders or leading scientists could be persuaded to write articles in support of the UK's possession of nuclear weapons.[7]

The Labour opposition leader Hugh Gaitskell had declared that he was not 'in principle' against Polaris, calling it less dangerous to the population than any other nuclear weapon, but the Labour party was culturally against the American base, particularly so close to Glasgow and the ever present, if genuinely remote, chance of a nuclear mishap.[8] Perhaps also reflecting this concern, Macmillan indicated his preferred choice was Loch Linnhe. It was much more remote and therefore less likely to be a target for demonstrators, but Eisenhower advised him that the loch was not acceptable from a technical point of view: the clear preference being for the Gare Loch. The matter also raised the issue of control over the weapons. There was already an agreement over the use of RAF bases by SAC nuclear bombers, but clarity was needed over the SSBNs' presence. The president confirmed that the missiles would not be launched in UK territorial waters without UK consent but extending dual control beyond territorial waters could present problems for both nations. A 100-mile proposal had been discussed, but this could be problematic if applied to the Mediterranean or Caribbean.[9] Some clarification was added later in the year to the effect that 'in the event of an emergency, such as increased tension or the threat of war, the U.S. will take every possible step to consult with Britain and the allies'.[10]

In May 1960, Lambe retired. He had returned home exhausted after a gruelling visit to Australia and suffered a severe heart attack. He was replaced by Admiral of the Fleet Sir Caspar John, a distinguished and talented naval aviator who had worked with Mountbatten in the past, although the relationship now between the CDS and the first sea lord was not always harmonious. In a letter to Sir Edward Playfair, permanent secretary, Ministry of Defence, Adm. John said:

> My own view is that if we deny the United States the use of the Holy Loch there will be an almighty row, not only between the two navies but also, I should have

thought, between the two governments. Personally I think it most probable that the Americans would decide not to base their submarines in this country at all, since the alternatives to the Holy Loch fall so far short of their requirements. This would wreck any prospect we may have of a joint POLARIS venture.[11]

However, he had reservations about the choice of the Gare Loch:

It is far less suitable from the atomic safety point of view. In any case I think the U.S.N. is under a misapprehension about the accommodation advantages of Gareloch [sic]. The major part of their housing and schooling must be met from the South Bank of the Clyde and the difference in boat trips ... from the two places is insignificant. As regards North Bank[,] Holy Loch is nearer Dunoon which is nicer and larger than Helensburgh.[12]

When it came to submarines, John had a staunch supporter in Flag Officer Submarines (FOSM) Rear-Admiral Sir Arthur 'Baldy' Hezlet who like his post-war predecessors had maintained a close relationship with their USN opposite numbers.

Macmillan knew he had to give way, as by giving the Americans the base of operations there was reciprocity in the agreement that America would, by implication, help with the UK deterrent. Moreover, oblique suggestions had been made by the Americans that Bremerhaven could have also been in the running which opened up the complexities of nuclear weapons in West Germany. Although other more remote venues were offered, agreement was eventually reached under the code name Project Lamachus (an Athenian general) to offer facilities in the Holy Loch opposite the town of Dunoon, a favourite holiday spot for Glasgow citizens who went 'doon the watter'.[13] Nearer the open waters of the Clyde estuary this seemed to fulfil the necessary American requirements. On 15 September 1960, Macmillan wrote to Eisenhower:

My Dear Friend ... I am glad to say that although [the Cabinet] were conscious of the considerable difficulties in public presentation they are prepared to accept this project on the general lines which have recently been discussed by our experts. ... it is desirable that the announcement should be made on October the 25th or 26th. ... I should be glad to know as soon as possible whether the Holy Loch is satisfactory in order that unobtrusive preparations can go ahead.[14]

Eisenhower replied:

I am delighted that agreement has been reached on the proposed berthing facilities for our Polaris tender in the Clyde area. I deeply appreciate your splendid cooperation in making a tender site available in [the] Holy Loch which our Navy considers most satisfactory for the purpose.... Your efforts on this regard reflect the understanding and close working relationships between our two countries which we both consider so essential to perpetuate.[15]

The political committee of the Communist Party of Great Britain issued a statement deprecating the decision:

A United States base for submarines equipped with Polaris nuclear missiles on the Clyde would make all Britain a priority target in nuclear war.... Macmillan's shameful attempt at deceit on the control question has been exposed. The U.S. military command alone can decide to launch world war.... All Scotland is joining together in rising angry protest. Extend the movement to every part of Britain! We dare not delay!... Fight now for peace and for Britain's future! No Polaris base in the Clyde or anywhere in Britain! KEEP THEM OUT![16]

Gaitskell found himself under considerable pressure from the unions. Jarrow Trades Council described the establishment of the base as 'a provocative action and a further threat to world peace'. Communist party meetings echoed these sentiments and there were calls for him to resign and make way for someone behind whom the Labour Party could unite.

In response, the US Navy commented that the Holy Loch was not really a 'base' in the usual sense of the word as it would be mobile. Technically, it was not considered part of British territory and was thus subject to border enforcement by HM Customs and Excise—an irritating regulation often a source of much frustration by US Navy crews coming and going from the adjacent mainland! The loch was also tidal and the rise and fall of the water required long jetties to be constructed. The waters were 'sheltered except from occasional north-west gales once or twice per year, and offers no navigational difficulties [and is] fairly open to the south but the steep hills rise up directly from the north shore.'[17] The loch supposedly derived its name from a legend which tells of a ship which foundered there whilst returning from the Holy Land with a casket containing soil on which Christ had walked. It was also a more challenging location for access by potential demonstrators than other suggested sites within the general area of the Clyde estuary. The tender and the drydock could theoretically have been located anywhere, however the loch gave them the protection of calm waters, although there were times when the crew must have thought that the Scottish definition of 'calm' differed from the more universally used description. Winter sun was measured monthly in hours, not days and the vicious wind, known by the sailors as 'The Hawk', in the storm of 1968 dragged the depot ship and its anchors 100 feet towards the shore. At a luncheon before the *George Washington* sailed from Charleston on her first patrol, Rear Admiral Kenmore M. McManes, commandant of the 6th Naval Division and Charleston Naval Base, commented:

We are not—repeat not—establishing a base in Scotland. What we are doing is sending over a tender. When you think of a base the public generally thinks of something like New London or Charleston.

The agreement was formally announced to the House by Macmillan on 1 November 1960 and was the subject of forceful questioning by the Ayrshire MPs Emrys Hughes and Archibald Manuel.[18] Anti-nuclear protests around the world were at a height during the early '60s but particularly strong in Britain through activities of CND, its more militant Direct Action Committee (DAC) offshoot and the Committee of 100. There was much political sensitivity to the likelihood of anti-American protests on the arrival of the American contingent. However, it was not until 24 January 1964 that a meaningful agreement was reached and approved by the Cabinet over the contentious matter of liability in the event of a nuclear accident.

But by then the youthful Kennedy had replaced Eisenhower as president. Morning dress and formality had given way to the lounge suit and a more relaxed approach. The 'special relationship' that had united Macmillan and Eisenhower had died with the latter's retirement from power. A new type of relationship had to be forged with a US administration which no longer benefitted from the wartime camaraderie of its predecessors. Principal among these was reaffirmation of the use of UK bases including the Holy Loch. The then-Senator Kennedy responded that he 'consider[ed] that the understandings in question would continue pending a prompt exchange on the matter immediately after inauguration.'[19] Elected on the back of anti-Communist ideologies, Kennedy needed to form a strong new team of advisers and initially wanted to appoint Robert A. Lovett as secretary of defense. Lovett had served as President Truman's secretary of defense and was highly regarded as one of the 'Wise Men' who crafted American foreign policy and an architect of the Cold War; however, he declined to accept the position on health grounds and suggested instead Ford Motor Company 'whiz kid' executive, forty-four-year-old Robert S. McNamara, who had only recently been appointed president of the company. A businessman who had helped to transform the ailing motor manufacturer, McNamara saw things very differently from his predecessor. He was ruled by logic and rationale, had little experience of national security matters other than serving as a lieutenant colonel in the Army Air Force's Office of Statistical Control, but consciously eschewed military experience and history. President Johnson was later to say of him: 'He's like a jackhammer. No human being can take what he takes. He drives too hard. He is too perfect.'[20] McNamara's view of the air force's ICBMs and the navy's Polaris was that these were strategic assets and effectively a separate subset of the services' offensive capability and would be treated as such.

At a dinner in Admiralty House on 27 February, Macmillan sought to assure the new president's ambassador at large, Averell Harriman, that any negative feelings towards the impending arrival of the American servicemen were only felt by a small, albeit vociferous, minority. It has to be remembered that to most people at the time, America was a remote place and knowledge of the country was generally limited to what was seen at the local cinema. But suddenly, Dunoon was in the international spotlight and the knowledge that it would be 'sitting on a bomb, [and] a nuclear one at that' did not sit comfortably with many of the population.[21] The unexpected arrival of an American ship some months before was now seen cynically as a reconnaissance trip to test local reaction to an American presence. The Argyll County councillor for the Kilmun Ward, Alexander Robertson, had even gone as far as resigning from the local hospital board in protest that the moorings would be within 500 yards of the Dunoon Cottage Hospital. He was angered that no instructions on dealing with a radiation emergency had been given to the hospital or its staff. Local people were also concerned about who would provide compensation in the event of a radiation leak. The advice that the American Government would be responsible under the 1960 Licensing and Insurance Act gave little reassurance.

At the end of the Pacific War, the USS *Proteus* (AS-19) had been one of the US Navy's newest tenders and was selected to enter Japanese waters to support US submarine operations. She was later transferred to the reserve fleet but when the urgent need for a tender to support forward operations of the planned SSBNs was identified and the timeline of the programme would not allow for the construction of new ships, she was withdrawn from reserve and in 1959 was towed to the Charleston Naval Yard for a year-long conversion. Cut in half, a 44-foot section was added amidships for magazines in which the missiles would be stored. The crew comprised 980 officers and men. Comprehensive workshop facilities were added to service all aspects of the submarines' missiles and navigational systems along with the nuclear reactors making the operations of the forward bases fully self-sufficient. A crane with port and starboard outriggers was added for handling the missiles and loading them into the submarines. Some 80,000 line items would be carried in stock against the 25,000 needed for conventional submarine support. Live proving of the *Proteus*'s capability was to come when the *George Washington* returned to the US from her first patrol and tied up beside the tender arriving at New London, Connecticut, on 21 January 1961. On this first deterrent patrol, the *George Washington* established a record for submerged operations—sixty-six days and ten hours without coming up for air—when she berthed alongside the *Proteus,* not yet departed for Scotland. The support ship was due to sail exactly one month later to take up her duties in the Holy Loch, so the arrival of the *George Washington* provided her with the opportunity for a dress rehearsal of her support functions including missile servicing, resupplying the submarine, and rectifying the various faults which had been reported.

The *Proteus* set sail for the Holy Loch arriving on 3 March 1961 blown in by a westerly gale. She was towed stern first into position by tugs. Her arrival was accompanied by ten naval launches to protect the ship, while the protesters fielded four canoes and a dinghy along with other small craft determined to disrupt the event. One by one the canoes, perhaps inevitably, capsized when they were hit by the wash of the naval launches with the occupants requiring rescue by the naval patrols, no doubt much to the amusement of schoolchildren who had been given the day off school to watch her arrival. Six protesters were arrested and charged with breach of the peace. As the ship approached its mooring two kayaks joined the affray and managed to elude capture for a while before boathooks succeeded in catching them. Two naval frogmen had to come to their assistance. Also watching at a safe distance was a not-so-innocent Russian trawler sporting a number of fittings not usually associated with the fishing industry. Differences had arisen in how the *Proteus*'s arrival should be announced. Wanting to minimise any possible protest, the Scottish Office wanted a low-key announcement, but the Admiralty saw the event as a positive public relations opportunity. Flag Officer Scotland and Northern Ireland (FOSNI) Vice-Admiral Sir Royston Wright wrote: 'we badly need some good counter-blast to the Unilateralists and Anti-Polaris elements, whose publicity at present is virtually unchallenged'.[22] The navy view prevailed.

Despite these local exhortations for protest, it did not take long for fleet ballistic missile Refit Site 1 to become operational. The *Proteus*'s motto was 'Prepared, Productive, Precise' and her role was to support SUBRON 14, US Atlantic Fleet—unofficially now known as the 'Highland Squadron'.

The *Proteus*'s captain, Captain Richard B. Laning, had commented, perhaps a little unhelpfully before leaving Charleston bound for Scotland:

> We're not vital. We would like to think we are *absolutely* [author's italics] vital to the Polaris system, but we're not. They don't need us. They could come home. We don't have an umbilical cord at all. We have a few piers that we can use if we want. A number of our men will live ashore with their families. But we can go anywhere. It's a matter of convenience, not necessity. We're not a fixed base.[23]

Laning was a veteran submariner who reputedly always carried a .45-calibre pistol. He had served with distinction in the war and had attended the 1946 US Operation Crossroads Bikini Atoll atomic tests. Impressed by what he saw, he had discussed the possible development of a nuclear submarine with naval consultant and nuclear physicist Dr George Gamow—unaware that the idea was already being considered. Despite volunteering through the chain of command to be involved in the nuclear programme, he did not receive a reply.

Initially the *Proteus* was to service the *George Washington* and the *Patrick Henry*. This would rise to a full squadron of ten SSBNs with no more than three alongside at any one time. There is in fact evidence that the original concept of resupplying the submarines was for the tenders to indeed be 'not a fixed base', but they would secretly rendezvous with the submarines somewhere in the Atlantic.[24]

(This basic idea had been the practice of the Germans in the Second World War when '*Milchkuh*' [Milk-Cow] submarines had resupplied the U-boat fleets to enable them to stay at sea for as long as possible.) However, the prospect of offloading and replacing faulty missiles in anything other than a calm sea would seem to have been fundamentally impracticable.

The *Proteus*'s arrival was just in time to accept her first customer, the *Patrick Henry*, the submarine arriving five days later after a record sixty-six-day, twenty-two-hour underwater patrol. SUBRON 14 CO CAPT. Ward joined the SSBN off Campbeltown for the final leg of her journey. Careful arrangements had been made to protect against protesters, even as far as greasing the submarine's rudders to stop efforts to climb onto them. The arrival itself was coordinated with the Royal Navy's captain-in-charge Clyde, Captain Robert Mayo, and was treated as a low-key event but, inevitably, some protesters were in evidence. Recognising that Ward, although in overall command, had a wide range of duties which would require regular commuting back and forth to New London the *Patrick Henry*'s captain, Hal Shear, and Laning from the *Proteus* gave a press conference on board the tender. Once the patrol cycle had settled into a routine, by July Ward would spend most of his time at the Holy Loch.

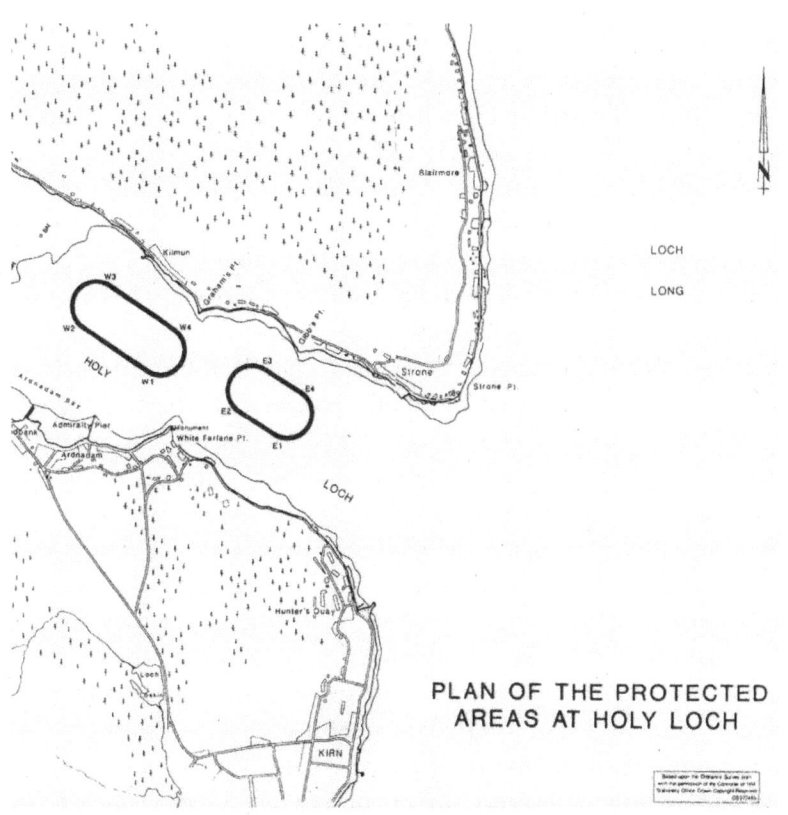

**PLAN OF THE PROTECTED
AREAS AT HOLY LOCH**

Full facilities were available from November 1961 when the drydock *Los Alamos* (AFDB-7) was commissioned. The dock had originally been designed and constructed during the Second Word War by the Bureau of Yards and Docks as an advanced base sectional dock (ABSD) but only served in the latter months of the conflict. Reclassified as an auxiliary floating dock big (AFDB), she was disassembled and placed on the Atlantic Reserve Fleet in 1947. With the need for drydocking facilities in the Holy Loch, four of her seven sections were towed across the Atlantic and then assembled in situ by Seabees from Naval Mobile Construction Battalion 4 (NMCB-4), a process that took five and a half months. This piece of equipment was the only major component to be present throughout the thirty-one years that Site I operated. It was in its own right an impressive structure. Each one of its four sections measured 110 feet long by 101 feet wide with four ballast tanks and the whole assembled dock could theoretically support a 32,000-ton vessel. Collapsible wingwalls each weighing 450-tons were folded during the trans-Atlantic journey. The completed dock was anchored with 15-ton anchors designed to withstand 100-mph winds. A separate section provided domestic facilities and work areas for the enlisted men operating the dock. From time to time, sections were replaced with other upgraded sections—eventually all four original sections were changed—and throughout its years of operations, the diesel engines which provided power also required to be upgraded as the power requirement constantly increased. Eventually locally sourced Greco generators were rented to provide electrical power to submarines berthed alongside. The dock was built with wartime knowledge and some aspects of its equipment struggled to keep up with advances in technology. Necessary upgrades included the replacement of the two original gantry cranes in 1988 with state-of-the-art electronically controlled portal cranes. A giant 310-ton SMIT International floating crane was used to hoist the new cranes into position. The *Los Alamos* crew had a reputation for being rowdy and liked partying, but this did not prevent a number of female crew members being added during the later years of operation. The dock was able to accommodate up to five submarines, one in the dock and four moored alongside. Inevitably, however, the working environment was a dangerous one and regrettably Site I did not escape without some fatalities.

On return from patrol, each submarine submitted a complete report on the patrol, based very much on that used during the Second World War. These were then distributed amongst the technical offices and SP to evaluate the performance of the various departments. In addition, each captain was debriefed by Ward so that in total a complete picture of the patrol was obtained and any problems could be identified and responded to. In addition, the tender would provide its own report for any items identified during the submarine's time alongside. Change of crews took place over a four-day period and relevant factors would be discussed over this period and any factors bearing on the next patrol would be fully understood by the other crew. In this way a process of constant improvement fine-tuned the deployments and led to an established routine.

The *Proteus*'s presence and the comings and goings of the early deployments inevitably attracted attention during the first months. 'Peaceniks', as they were called, would row around the submarines and the tender, trying to climb on board and photographing their efforts. Others would simply sit down on the pier shoulder to shoulder and attempt to block access. Such an event took place one afternoon while Ward was visiting the lady provost of Dunoon, Miss Catherine McPhail—the first lady to hold the post. Some 500 demonstrators had blocked the pier ready for some form of confrontation, with photographers on hand to witness the event. Undeterred, the local police who adopted a suitably robust approach to protest told Ward not to worry, adding that they would get him back to the boat and no photos would be taken and indeed, by the time Ward reached the pier, the police had removed all the photographers. The sergeant in charge told Ward to follow him and they walked over the backs of the protesters to get to the barge. Ward was supported by two policemen and remembered, 'The bobbies have heavy boots.' After the initial novelty of protesting had worn off, the majority of 'Sussexniks' as the Scots called them had returned home to England, a move welcomed by most of the Scots who, unsurprisingly, had little time for the sassenach English contingent.[25]

Most of the anti-nuclear protests passed off peacefully. On 14 May 1961, some 2,000 protesters left Kirn to march to Dunoon, led by the mildly eccentric, and later Labour Party Leader Michael Foot MP and William Scholes, Scottish secretary of the Transport and General Workers Union. Before leaving Kirn, the marchers scuffled with a group of counter-protesters but generally the protest was peaceful, although there were differences even within the ranks of the protesters. The *Glasgow Herald* reported:

> There were cries of protest from some of the marchers when Mr Scholes gave some 'advice' to Miss Pat Arrowsmith and members of the Direct Action Group who [were] marching from London to Holy Loch to protest against the base. 'The best help she can give us in Scotland is by going back to London,' he said. 'We will achieve our objective through the democratic machinery of this country and we will not be influenced by cranks or anyone of that nature.'[26]

There were to be many such marches over the coming years. Typical of these was one over the Whitsun weekend in 1962. Organised this time by the Scottish Committee of 100, An appeal went out for 2,000 supporters to close the Ardnadam Pier for twenty-four hours. Special trains were put on along with a ferry to take the protesters from Gourock to Dunoon. A helicopter had even been chartered apparently to try and disrupt the activities of an oiler moored alongside the tender. In May 1963, the British Peace Committee and the Scottish Peace

Council chartered a steamer from British Rail to take some 1,200 protesters to Ardnadam Pier. On the day the steamer was bulging with around 2,000 protesters accompanied by railway police. A further 300 had made their way by other means. The MoD tug *Empire Ace* was put on standby in the event of any threatening action against the US facility. 'The fine weather and the bargain fare for the voyage down the Clyde probably contributed to the attendance.'[27] The day went off peacefully, many apparently seeing it merely as a day out. But gradually the novelty of these events receded and left the Holy Loch in relative peace. Fine weather was not always typical of the loch. Many remember seeing the entrance to the loch wreathed in mist as they either approached or left. Such was the damp atmosphere that special black paint had to be developed to coat the submarines as the normal oil-based formula would struggle to dry properly.

On 3 April 1961, Labour Deputy Leader George Brown accompanied by local MP Dr Dickson Mabon had paid a four-and-a-half-hour visit to the *Proteus*. Still believing that Loch Ewe would have been a better location, Brown was nonetheless satisfied by what the two had seen:

> When I report to the Shadow Cabinet I shall be able to say that I was completely reassured by the protective measures adopted. Though a good deal has been said about risks to the neighbourhood, in the light of what we have seen and the procedures to be adopted the chances of an accident happening are a good deal less than is normally believed.

Brown also commented on rumours about Russian spy-ships operating off the west of Scotland providing reassurance that 'everyone in the ship knows the Russians are there and that they will be watching these ships coming in and out. The Proteus has picked up signals, but the Americans are not perturbed.'[28] A regular observer was the 700-ton *Okean*-class AGI trawler *Krenometr*. With a crew of thirty-two, the vessel, part of the Soviet Northern Fleet based at Murmansk, was a complicated electronic intelligence gathering vessel which lurked off Malin Head, the northern-most tip of Ireland, seeking to acquire and track the SSBNs leaving the Clyde and relay the information to Soviet *Victor*-class SSNs that were known to operate in the Clyde Approaches attempting to track the emerging submarines. No pretence as to its purpose was made, such as the occasional appearance of a fishing net. As an added precaution, on a regular basis and certainly before they left on patrol, divers checked the hulls of the SSBNs in case tracking devices had been secretly attached. In November 1981, the Royal Navy took a group of journalists on a Sea King helicopter from Prestwick based 819 Naval Air Squadron to search for the *Krenometr* reported to have been sighted between Northern Ireland and the Inner Hebrides. Sadly, the vessel was not found. It was known that it monitored telephone calls routed via the post office microwave system and had possibly picked up the calls making arrangements for the journalists. In the early days, the Soviet ship had on occasion got too close to their prey although collisions had fortunately been avoided. This practice was 'dropped when the Royal Navy deployed escort vessels to see the[m] off. Polaris submarines [made] a point of sailing out of sight of the trawler before diving, and a number of diversionary tactics [were] employed, including the escort vessel making a lot of noise to stop any Russian submarines locking on to British vessels with their sonar.'[29] From 1976, an ocean-going tug, HMS *Wakeful*, was assigned to Faslane after a £1.6 million refit. The tug covered a variety of duties which included deterring the Soviet spy-ships.

Getting the SSBNs out of the Firth of Clyde and into the open sea with the minimum of fuss required careful planning and coordination. The complex pattern of islands off Scotland's western coast allowed four exit routes. Making sure that the exit routes were free of any sensors, or in wartime any sea mines, mine countermeasures vessels (MCMs) would regularly sweep the seabed initially to identify any objects already there and thereafter to search for any new or previously unknown objects. Minimum indication of departure times would be given and slow speed would minimise sonar contact with any opposing SSNs trying to track the departing submarine. The bomber could be accompanied by an SSN or possibly a noisy merchant vessel to mask its sonar profile. As soon as possible the SSBN would want to go deep to check the integrity of the hull for any leaks. Thereafter, it would make its way undetected by any opposing SSNs and it has always been the boast of the British government that no SSBN has ever been detected or followed.

The agreement over the Scottish base had given the Americans a very significant military advantage in operating their 'boomers' by maximising the time the submarines could be on active patrol and reducing the wear and tear on the propulsion systems, but inevitably this was a time of learning from experience and during the coming two years there was 'refit after refit, problem after problem and hours of back-breaking work'.[30] Some of the onboard procedures were not without a certain risk, albeit controlled. Deep inside the tenders were special room to handle 'hot' i.e., radioactive, repair work. Wearing special protective suits and badges to monitor their exposure to radioactivity, their working time in the compartments was closely regulated. Security was tight. The armed deck guards were under orders to shout 'Halt!' once and then were permitted to fire if necessary. In March 1963, with forty-two SSBN visits under her belt, the *Proteus* returned to Charleston for a much-needed overhaul which included a number of modifications based on the initial experience of operations at the Scottish base. Additional crew accommodation was added as the initial berthing provision was found to be inadequate for a full wartime complement of 1,130 officers and enlisted men needed for forward based operations. So much had the *Proteus*'s crew become embedded in Scottish culture that the commanding officer, Captain Walter F. Schlech, authorised the introduction of a 'Polaris Military' tartan.

Designed by Alexander MacIntyre of Strone, such tartans had to be approved by Scotland's heraldic expert Lord Lyon King of Arms who is quoted as saying, 'We don't record tartans for submarines. It is nonsense. I have never heard of a ship's tartan in the whole history of Scotland!' Nonetheless it was approved.[31] But by the time the *Proteus* had finished its first duty cycle, the *New York Times* reported that some 100 members of the crew had married Scottish girls.[32]

The advent of the Americans had indeed brought together two very dissimilar cultures. Dunoon was 'twenty to thirty years' behind America. Suddenly there was an influx of hundreds of sailors and when accommodation was sorted out, their families too. Many saw this as a commercial opportunity. Houses traditionally let out for summer rent could now be occupied all the year round at a higher price. Taxi companies thrived as did local hostelries. American generosity introduced Dunoon's youngsters to the delights of free cola, hamburgers, and hot dogs. Local girls were charmed by the Americans' polite manners, sparking resentment and rivalry amongst the local youth. Americans' more liberal attitude to sex attracted prostitutes from Glasgow which was obviously seen as the less appealing side of the new arrivals. Some local businesses were less optimistic claiming little benefit from 'the "invading forces", who do their food shopping in the Commissary, a non-profit making supermarket run by the US government, where prime beef cuts cost about half the going rate'.[33] What was not yet realised, however, was that Spain was becoming an increasingly popular holiday destination for Glaswegians who began to forsake their traditional holidays 'doon the watter'. To the more commercially minded, the arrival of the Americans was a godsend. Inevitably, of course, many still resented and would continue to resent the 'invasion'. As a way of fostering local integration, the first Polaris Regatta was held in the autumn of 1961. It was jointly sponsored by SUBRON 14, the *Proteus*, and the Holy Loch Sailing Club. The regatta's modest beginnings when only about twenty dinghies took part attracted much attention, and the event which continued to be sponsored by the resident depot ship had grown by 1969 to four classes of racing with some 100 entrants. On its tenth anniversary, the sponsoring ship, the *Canopus*, invited all competitors, their crew members and their families to a tour of the tender before the event concluded with the Holy Loch Sailing Club dance at the nearby Glenmorag Hotel where the winners' trophies were presented by SUBRON 14 commander, CAPT. F. D. McMullen and the CDR R. M. Hoover, CO of the *Canopus* both accompanied by their wives.[34]

As the Cuban Missile Crisis developed on October 1962, three of SUBRON 14's SSBNs were already at sea. On 22 October, the two that were in the Holy Loch were rapidly sent to sea when Kennedy raised the alert status to DEFCON 3 (except for the USAREUR). The *Proteus* left her mooring the following day and headed for the north of Scotland, remaining at sea for ten days.[35] This arguably reduced the chance of the Clyde estuary being attacked. A month later Macmillan responded to a question from William Warbey, MP for Ashfield:

Polaris Regatta programme.

British naval authorities are informed whenever it is proposed that *Proteus* should enter or leave Holy Loch. They were also consulted about the area to which *Proteus* should proceed when she left Holy Loch on 23rd October.[36]

Although McNamara perceived that the Cuban Missile Crisis was political rather than strategic, the world had approached the nuclear edge and perhaps by way of reassurance post-crisis, on 28 February 1963, the British media were hosted aboard the *Ethan Allen* and taken on a short journey to sea on the submarine to experience life aboard.[37] Some months earlier, political journalist Martin Agronsky and five other news correspondents from the US National Broadcasting Company had spent sixteen days aboard the *George Washington* to film a documentary *Polaris Submarine: Journal of an Undersea Voyage*. It depicted in detail a realistic training exercise culminating in the launching of Polaris missiles into the Atlantic Missile Range. The documentary received a prize at the Venice Film Festival. The navy was now prepared to show the general public what Polaris meant for the security of the country.

Consideration was also given to deploying Polaris in the Mediterranean to cover targets in the south of the Soviet Union. Initially it was agreed that the existing Jupiter IRBMs stationed in Turkey and Italy could continue to fulfil this function and it was not, therefore, until 1963, by which time the Jupiters had been deactivated following a secret agreement reached during the Cuban Missile Crisis, that Polaris found itself in warmer waters. An arrangement similar in concept to the Holy Loch agreement was concluded with Spain and allowed the Polaris submarines of SUBRON 16 to operate from Rota. Originally the Moroccan naval base at Port Lyautey where the US Navy already had a presence had been the possible choice, but the base was due to be handed over to the Moroccan Air Force which forced an alternative site to be found. The Spanish government had an agreement with the USAF to build Spanish bases and a pipeline to distribute fuel. The pipeline came in through Rota which then became the preferred choice as a base. Gates and John Lodge, the US ambassador to Spain, both inspected the area and in due course 'We spent a lot of money and we built a hell of a fine naval base at Rota', although Gates felt that it was 'very unprotected'.[38] A third advance FBM anchorage site was established at Apra Harbor, Guam, the largest island in the Western Pacific between Hawaii and the Philippines, to support the Pacific Fleet SSBNs of SUBRON 15 operating from Pearl Harbor, Hawaii. The base was established on 1 September 1963 under the command of Captain Charles B. Almy, at which point four of the seven SSBNs that would be assigned to the squadron were being built. The initial months were spent undertaking the groundwork required to make the base operational. On 23 April 1964, the USS *Daniel Boone* (SSBN-629) was commissioned at Mare Island whereupon she became the flagship of the Pacific SSBN fleet. On her arrival at the base on 27 May, she rendered honours to the Arizona Memorial which commemorated military personnel killed in the Pearl Harbor attack. In October, the permanent assignment of commander SUBRON 15 was transferred from Pearl Harbor to Guam in preparation for the arrival of the *Proteus* at Apra Harbor on 29 November. On a visit to Australia in October 1964, commander of US forces in the Pacific (CINCPAC), Admiral US Grant Sharp, Jr, announced that a Polaris submarine would be operating from the base by the end of the year at a time when the US presence in Vietnam was increasing. The first operational Pacific patrol started on Christmas Day 1964 when the *Daniel Boone* left Guam armed with sixteen A-3 missiles.

Each base had its own characteristics: Scottish cold wind and rain; Spanish heavy ocean swell and desert winds; typhoon threats and humidity in the Pacific.

On 6 March, the supply ship USS *Betelgeuse* (AK-260) arrived in the Holy Loch and made her first transfer of stores.[39] Launched in 1944 as the SS *Colombia Victory*, she was used as a cargo ship by the US Merchant Navy until in 1952 when she was purchased by the US Navy, renamed *Betelgeuse* (and nicknamed 'Goose'), and placed under the command of the Atlantic Fleet. Then, in the summer of 1960, she was to undergo a substantial modification program to transport Polaris missiles which were stored vertically in one of her holds. She supplied both the Holy Loch and the Rota sites with missiles and various equipment and victuals required for the operation of the support sites. A further vessel, the USNS *Marshfield* (T-AK-282), was converted to a fleet ballistic missile cargo ship in 1968 and, operated by the Military Sealift Command, was able to resupply Rota and the Holy Lock with Poseidon missiles. The Holy Loch site alone required some 2,300 metric tons of resupply each year. Whereas all ships in the Royal Navy of a certain class were all essentially identical in terms of specified equipment, American tradition was to confirm what was needed but allow the shipbuilders to source their own equipment to satisfy the contract. This meant that even within each class, the American SSBNs were not all identical, a factor which required a far greater breadth of inventory to be kept. A further refit in 1962 allowed the *Betelgeuse* to carry a total of twenty-three missiles—fourteen in number three hold, five in number four hold, and a further four in containers on the deck. The shipping containers had been approved for use following a technical evaluation aboard the ammunition ship the USS *Shasta* (AE-6) in March 1960.[40] A second Victory supply ship, the USS *Alcor* (AK-259)—formerly the SS *Rockland Victory*—was similarly converted and fulfilled a parallel role to the *Betelgeuse*. One crewmember described the Site I complex as 'an industrial Las Vegas open to customers 24-hours a day, 365 days a year'. On 15 February 1963, the 19,000-ton USS *Hunley* (AS-31) arrived in the Holy Loch and took over duties from the *Proteus*. Captain Douglas N. Syverson, another veteran submariner, gave a press conference, but still wary of opposition to the base and American perception of the CND as a subversive organisation, refused entry to a journalist from the communist *Daily Worker*.[41] Assistant Materiel Officer LCDR Bobby Cox aboard the *Hunley* commented:

> … with a submarine leaving every 10 days, weekends and holidays don't mean anything. We don't have weeks to work with, so when we get a tough problem everyone works until it's resolved…. [The] Holy Loch has a long logistic support chain. We don't have all of the assets that you would find in a stateside site, but we get tremendous support from SUBLANT [U.S. Submarine Force, Atlantic]. We have called them in an afternoon and they have had things turned on and people flying out on the next thing moving.

Launched on 28 September 1961, the *Hunley* was the largest tender in the USN and, unlike the *Proteus*, had been designed from the start to service nuclear submarines. It was now commonplace for more than one SSBN to be moored alongside. These were tied-up 'Chinese style', bow to stern, to protect the propellers of adjacent boats. Even *Proteus*'s commanding officer admitted that '*Hunley* will make us look old fashioned'.[42] To keep track of the *c.* 80,000 inventory lines kept on board, a state-of-the-art machine accounting system was tended by the specialised talents of sixteen enlisted men backed up by nine storekeepers. Little had been left to chance, and with fifty-two specialist repair shops, the *Hunley* could match a shipyard in its repair capability including the intricate SINS for which the tender carried two spare units. For any repairs required underwater, a compression chamber was available for two officers and twelve enlisted men who were qualified divers. A 32-ton hammerhead crane was used to load Polaris missiles onto submarines or offload faulty units. Crew comforts were carefully thought out for the full complement of fifty-eight officers, 1,023 enlisted men, and a detachment of thirty Marines: creature comforts included an ice cream manufacturing plant and 'bug juice' (fruit juice). Food became an important item, and the galley was kept busy providing meals to suit the needs of the various watches. Inevitably, most of the crew wanted the standard favourites of burgers or 'fried seagull' (fried chicken) and chips. The frying for the latter was, by its very nature, a potential fire hazard and a CO_2 extinguisher was incorporated into the fryer unit. A fallback was the ubiquitous PB&J (peanut butter and jelly) sandwich. As many chefs within the armed forces were to find out, there was usually little demand for dishes that demonstrated their culinary skills. The crew slept on bunk-over-locker beds with hampers in their quarters for soiled clothes. Everyday working clothes for the crew were dark blue 'poopy suits', which were practical and did not show stains. Officers' staterooms were big, bright, and airy. Extra sleeping quarters were available for the visiting submarines' crews. In the mess, tables folded out of the way when not in use to provide easy access to torpedo storage spaces. No accommodation was to be found in the repair shops as had previously been the case in tenders. This allowed twenty-four-hour operation if required.[43]

After the secret agreement made between Kennedy and Khrushchev to resolve the Cuban Missile Crisis, and therefore unaware of the reasons why, the JCS were instructed to draw up a plan to remove the Jupiter missiles stationed in Italy and Turkey and replace them with Polaris submarines in the Mediterranean on or about 1 April 1963, although in practical terms this was to prove easier for the Italians to achieve than the Turks. It was the latter's Jupiters that had caused a particular problem to the Soviets. Targeting would be undertaken by SACEUR on the same basis as the Jupiters, but it was acknowledged that forty-five targets covered by the Italian and Turkish IRBMs together with the loss of availability of sixteen Polaris missiles while the SSBNs were out of range in transit would have to be taken into account. Acceptance by Italy (see Chapter 21) thus proved easier than by Turkey where there was political unhappiness at the removal of the IRBMs from their territory unless a substitute weapon could be provided. In part, this was achieved by confirming an acceleration in the delivery of Lockheed F-104G Starfighters to the Turkish Air Force, but the question of an IRBM replacement was resolved by the promise that one Polaris submarine should be in the Mediterranean by 28 March 1963 and a second one by 10 April. But it was noted:

> ... the efficiency of use of available POLARIS submarines will be degraded when they are deployed in the Mediterranean before the ROTA POLARIS base is completed [as they would need to travel from the Holy Loch]. Hence it will be to our over-all advantage to keep the number of submarines so employed to a minimum.[44]

It was expected that the Rota Base could be operational by the end of the year once the *Proteus*'s refit was completed.

First Mediterranean Deployment to Replace the Turkish Jupiters

		Depart Holy Loch	Mediterranean	Return Holy Loch
USS *Sam Houston*	SSBN 609	23 March	28 March–13 May	18 May
		16 June	20 June–5 August	10 August
USS *Ethan Allen*	SSBN 603	5 April	10 April–1 June	5 June
		19 August	24 August–9 October	14 October
USS *John Marshall*	SSBN 611	27 May	1 June–17 July	22 July
Note 1		31 July	5 August–20 September	25 September

Note 1: It is planned that the USS *Thomas A. Edison* (SSBN-610) would temporarily replace SSBN-611 which was due to undergo operational readiness and reliability tests (ORRT).

USS *Sam Houston* manned by her blue crew and commanded by CAPT. William P. Willis paid a three-day visit to the Turkish port of Izmir (replacing the original choice of Gölcük) in mid-April 1963. This was the first occasion when a missile submarine had entered the Mediterranean. Attached to SUBRON 16, the Mediterranean Polaris squadron, the submarine was temporarily based at the Holy Loch before moving to Rota on the commissioning of that base on 28 January 1964. The SSBNs came under the command of SACEUR, Gen. Lyman Lemnitzer. A Turkish naval expert reported in the Turkish newspaper *Cumhuriyet* that a submarine in the Sea of Marmara had sixteen major Soviet cities within range of its missiles including Moscow, Leningrad, and Volgograd. The US embassy in Ankara reported to US Secretary of State Dean Rusk:

> Visit of Polaris Submarine Sam Houston to Izmir was success from all points of view. Turkish press gave maximum favorable coverage ... totaled 1600 col[umn]/in[che]s equivalent two complete Turkish newspapers.... Typical headlines 'Most powerful guardian of freedom.... Powerful weapons for preserving peace.[45]

When the two Polaris sites were becoming established in Scotland and Spain, attention turned to speculating when bases in the Pacific would be made available. Presence in the Pacific had been planned from the start, and by early 1963, the press was beginning to seek answers. On 30 January 1963, Admiral Harry D. Felt, CINCPAC, had commented: 'I'm not sure that this is public information yet, so if you don't mind, I would like to answer it in this way: The [Pacific] Fleet does not yet have Polaris submarines, as you know, and is probably not scheduled [to receive them] for another year or two.' (Felt had a reputation as a rather prickly character and was unofficially known within his command as CINCFELT.) As SUBRON 16 was being established at Rota, the *Lafayette* became the first submarine to use the base when she arrived on 25 May 1964. The same day, the USS *Daniel Boone* (SSBN-616) arrived in Hawaii to inaugurate the Pacific contingent. This SSBN was thereafter permanently assigned to the Commander, Submarine Force, US Pacific Fleet (COMSUBPAC). The *Proteus* had now established all three advanced sites and thereafter became the permanent support ship in Apra along with the USS *Hunley*, apart from a period of refit.

The three sites were serviced by five submarine tenders. The *Proteus* had the task of setting up all three sites and was joined by *Hunley*-class tenders: USS *Hunley* and USS *Holland* (AS-32); and *Simon Lake*-class tenders: USS *Simon Lake* (AS-33) and USS *Canopus* (AS-34). On 7–8 August 1963, the *Holland* was completing its official sea trials under the supervision of the Navy Board of Inspection and Survey before heading for Spain to take up station with SUBRON 16 at Rota.

US Navy Polaris Submarine Tenders

Holy Loch Base, Scotland—Site I: Subron 14		
USS *Proteus* (AS-19)	March 1961	March 1963
USS *Hunley* (AS-31)	January 1963	August 1966
USS *Proteus* (AS-19)	December 1963	February 1964
USS *Simon Lake* (AS-33)	July 1966	May 1970
USS *Canopus* (AS-34)	May 1970	November 1975
USS *Holland* (AS-32)	November 1975	February 1982
USS *Hunley* (AS-31)	January 1982	June 1987
USS *Simon Lake* (AS-33)	May 1987	June 1992

Rota Base, Spain—Site II: Subron 16		
USS *Holland* (AS-32)	August 1963	November 1966
USS *Proteus* (AS-19)	March 1964	August 1964
USS *Canopus* (AS-34)	August 1966	April 1969
USS *Holland* (AS-32)	October 1969	December 1972
USS *Simon Lake* (AS-33)	November 1972	December 1976
USS *Canopus* (AS-34)	December 1976	June 1979

Apra Harbour, Guam—Site III: Subron 15		
USS *Proteus* (AS-19)	November 1964	November 1971
USS *Hunley* (AS-31)	January 1968	June 1968
USS *Hunley* (AS-31)	October 1971	January 1973
USS *Proteus* (AS-19)	January 1973	December 1975
USS *Hunley* (AS-31)	November 1978	July 1980
USS *Proteus* (AS-19)	January 1973	September 1981

Security on the Holy Loch was naturally very strict, but with so many servicemen involved, the risk of espionage or illegal access was ever present. In May 1967, a lovesick sixteen-year-old girl disguised herself as a sailor to get on board the *Simon Lake* to see her US sailor fiancé. Sadly for her, she got no further than the landing stage. Something more serious took place at the end of the month when British Special Branch detectives posing as fishermen were involved in the arrest of an American shipfitter, Garry Lee Ledbetter. CAPT. George F. Ellis, commander of the *Simon Lake*, confirmed that an American sailor was being held on board in connection with the incident.[46] A spokesman said that the arrest was connected to the court appearance earlier in the week of an East German, Peter Dorschel, accused under the UK Official Secrets Act. Dorschel was working legally in Britain and had been instructed by two compatriots working for the USSR to acquire a property overlooking the Polaris base. Ledbetter was found guilty of supplying, via a third party, a training booklet and other material to Dorschel, sentenced to six month's hard labour, and discharged from the navy. Dorschel received a prison sentence of seven years but was deported to East Germany three years later. Security around the area was maintained at a very high level, but in April 1988, a lady from Helensburgh was collecting shells from the foreshore near Rhu and came across a bag on the beach at Kidston Park just north of Helensburgh which on examination was seen to contain some 800 pages of confidential documents relating to the expenditure on maintaining the tender and detailed costs of parts supply for the submarines. The documents were handed in to *The Scotsman* offices. United States authorities dismissed the documents as being of no interest.[47] Fodder for the anti-nuclear campaigners, nonetheless.

The Holy Loch site was constantly under observation from CND and related groups, and the protesters were quick to react when a fire broke out on the *Canopus* on 29 November 1970. 'U.S. Prisoners in Holy Loch horror. Polaris Ship Ablaze: 3 Dead', headlined the *Scottish Daily Express*. Two submarines, the *Francis Scott Key* and the *James K. Polk*, were alongside at the time, one on either side of the tender with the former undergoing a change of crew. Records show that the submarine's CO ordered the *Key* to be cast off and moved away to a safe distance. The fire, though severe, was contained and brought under control within four hours. Two teenage sailors, who claimed they were 'cheesed off' with life on board the ship, had been confined for minor misdemeanours during a weekend run ashore and died along with a crew member who was guarding them. He had released the pair as the fire approached, but all three sadly succumbed to smoke inhalation. Ten other sailors received minor injuries. Unsurprisingly, it did not take long for the anti-nuclear brigade to play up their concerns on what might have happened. Local veteran protester Margaret Robertson said she would be writing to her MP to find out when British authorities were alerted to the hazard. Also in print was William Wolfe, chairman of the Scottish National Party (SNP), who criticised BBC Scotland for their report on the fire. Writing to *The Times*, he said:

On whose behalf was the B.B.C. trying to lull fears by referring to the site of this accident as being 'in a remote Scottish loch'? Of all the main sea lochs in the whole of Scotland, the Holy Loch is about the least remote. lying as it does only two miles from the busy sea lanes of the Clyde and only thirty miles from the centre of a conurbation of at least two million people. The dangers of siting the Polaris base so near to the majority of Scotland's population and industry have been recited time and time again. Now we have clear proof that serious accidents can happen there.[48]

Perhaps by the very nature of their operations, the SSBNs were no less prone to accidents. Potentially the most serious occurred on 3 November 1974 when the *James Madison* collided with an unidentified Soviet submarine in the North Sea. In January 1975, investigative journalist Jack Anderson reported in the *Washington Post* that the collision had left a 9-foot scar on the side of the American boat and the collision could well have led to the sinking of both submarines. The damage was sufficient to require the *Madison* to return to the Holy Loch for repairs. The CIA later reported:

> The SSBN *James Madison* was departing Holy Loch to take up station when it collided with a Soviet submarine waiting outside the port to take up trail. Both submarines surfaced and the Soviet boat subsequently submerged again. There is no report yet of the extent of damage. Will keep you posted.[49]

More diplomatically concerning was the incident on 9 April 1981 when the *George Washington* collided with a Japanese freighter, the *Nissho Maru*, in the East China Sea some 110 miles off the southern coast of Japan. On surfacing the submarine scraped the bottom of the freighter's hull, leading to it sinking with the loss of two lives. The US Navy issued a report accepting liability but claiming that the submarine was unaware that the freighter was sinking, however, it was said to be 'unconvincing'. 'There is a vast gap between the testimony of the survivors from the *Nissho Maru* and the Navy's preliminary report', said Shunichi Tagawa, a lawyer for the thirteen surviving crewmen, 'I can hardly believe what the submarine skipper says, according to this report.'[50] Diplomatic relations between the US and Japan were strained for a month and further antagonised when no explanation was given as to why the submarine was operating so close to Japan or whether it was carrying nuclear missiles. It also raised a complex question of maritime law over the obligation to render assistance to the Japanese vessel's crew.[51] Writing to *The Times*, Professor Colonel G. I. A. D. Draper questioned, 'is there any duty laid on the commander of a Polaris submarine on patrol not to disclose the identity or position of his boat such as to raise a qualification in his mind about the common duty to render assistance and pick up survivors?'[52] He concluded, however, that under international law the USA was not required to render assistance to the *Nissho Maru*, a merchant ship of Japanese nationality, while, by US domestic maritime law, the commander of the *George Washington* submarine lay under such a duty.

It was, of course, essential that the location of the patrol areas was not compromised. The only guaranteed chance to intercept an SSBN was to catch it emerging from its home base before it could seek the vastness of the ocean in which to hide. There was, therefore, a chance, albeit a small one, that Soviet submarines could be lurking close in, in wait for the SSBNs' departure—as the *James Madison* had found to its cost. To confuse this potential situation, SSNs would deploy along with the SSBNs to provide a number of conflicting contacts for any opposing submarines. Sonar equipment at the time was unable to distinguish between the two types of submarines, and it would therefore not be able to determine which contact represented their main quarry. Even if it was determined to follow one contact, it was known to have proved impossible for one submarine to follow another for any length of time. The SSBN was therefore effectively guaranteed an undetected passage to the patrol area. Once there, the submarine would reduce speed to only a few knots, thereby emitting very little noise to betray its presence. At this minimal speed, it would spend the majority of its patrol loitering out of sight, undetected.

Although specific dates were not published, it was known that the nominal length of each patrol would be between sixty and seventy days. With the *George Washington* returning in mid-January and to maintain an unbroken, and therefore credible, deterrent, a second SSBN would have to be in position to take over the function. This was achieved when, on 30 December, the *Patrick Henry*, under the command of CDR Shear, left Charleston with a full complement of missiles. For a short time, thirty-two missiles were ranged against targets in the Soviet Union. By August 1961, all five SSBNs of the 598 class had successfully launched A-1 missiles in the Atlantic Test Range. The *Patrick Henry* arrived at the Holy Loch on 8 March 1961.

As the first A-3 flight test took place, three days later on 10 August 1962, Kennedy signed the DoD Appropriations for fiscal year 1963 which authorised funds for SSBNs 30 to 35 with long lead items for the final six, thus completing the forty-one planned fleet. Two months later on 10 October, the *Sam Houston* left Charleston with a full complement of A-2 missiles.

The Poseidon Adventure

Throughout the gestation of Polaris, SAC under the guidance of General Power had sought to confirm its dominance of the American strategic deterrent: having gained autonomy from the army, there was a compulsive wish to dominate the deeply divisive inter-service rivalries which were preoccupied with 'who does what?' Warheads were now much smaller, the Thor and Jupiter IRBMs were nearing operational capability, but the ultimate vulnerability of manned bombers was beginning to show itself. Starting in 1958, SAC tested the airborne alert mission using its squadrons of B-52 bombers to maintain a continuous alert posture. This was consolidated and publicly announced in January 1961 as Operation Chrome Dome. A force of B-52s supported by KC-135 tankers would be constantly airborne, loitering around the Soviet border to give immediate response to a 'bolt from the blue' attack. The programme got off to an inauspicious start when on 24 January a B-52 lost a wing during a refuelling operation and crashed along with two Mk 39 nuclear weapons. Both were eventually recovered but it caused unwelcome publicity. Nonetheless, it was a bold assertion of nuclear capability which even Premier Khrushchev acknowledged during the Cuban Missile Crisis. 'About 20 percent of all Strategic Air Command planes, carrying atomic and hydrogen bombs, were kept aloft around the clock', he later wrote.

Starting in 1959, SAC commenced its build-up of operational ICBM squadrons using the Convair SM-65D Atlas. This was shortly followed by the silo-based Titan 1 (borrowing British silo technology proposed for the cancelled Blue Streak MRBM). Having concentrated its efforts on Atlas, the air force was some way behind the navy's development of solid fuels having to wait until 1963 for the Minuteman 1 to enter service. But, as far as the bombers were concerned, there were increasing doubts about how much longer the B-52s could hope to evade Soviet surface-to-air missiles (SAM) *en route* to their targets. It was not only the aircraft that were becoming vulnerable, as intelligence sources identified the development of Soviet ABMs which would threaten the ICBMs and also Polaris.

Despite the lack of detailed specific intelligence on the subject, concerns were by then developing over progress in Soviet ABM capability. In 1961, consideration had been given to deploying Polaris A-2 with a suit of six PX-1 penetration aids (penaids) in the Mk 1 re-entry vehicle to confuse Soviet ABM radar. This would allow the ejection of decoys and chaff in mid-trajectory and electronic jammers would be activated early in the re-entry phase. The PX-1 test programme took place between July and December 1962 with twelve launches on A-2T and A-1 missiles. Seven of these were deemed successes allowing the overall performance of the PX-1 system to be considered adequate in providing significant improvement in the penetrability of the A-2. The PX-1 mounted six decoys and two chaff packages on a 4.5-inch extension ring. These were ejected after second-stage separation when the RVs were a sufficient distance from the equipment section. Two electronic counter-countermeasure (ECCM) packages were mounted in the flare section of the RV and were released along with a chaff package after the RV separation rocket was expended. A contract for 221 sets was issued and these were manufactured between July 1962 and July 1963. In the event, only one submarine went to sea with a PX-1 fitted warhead. Range was adversely affected by this variant at a time when increasing the range of the missile to enlarge its patrol area was considered a priority and the presumed ABM threat had not, as yet, materialised.

With the advent of the much more capable A-3, however, progress in ABM capability demanded that a more sophisticated solution was found to ensure the effectiveness of the new missile in reaching its targets. In April 1962, development of the PX-2 was initiated. This was designed to improve the penetrability of the Mk 2 RV and consisted of six decoys and six chaff dispensers while deleting the electronic jammers of the PX-1 which had proved an unreliable addition. The adoption of the A-3's three warheads was, in itself, a step in the right direction as these would theoretically have to draw more than three interceptors per missile to fully defeat the attack, although without much data on the known characteristics of an ABM system, certain assumptions would have to be theorised. The resulting concept was relatively simple. Saturate an ABM system with so many indiscriminable targets which were a mixture of penetration aids, decoys, and live warheads that it would be overwhelmed. Incorporation of anti-ABM measures had in fact been specified in the original Polaris specification but only with the advent of the A-3 was the threat becoming a significant consideration. The PX-2 test programme started in July 1963. This too consisted of twelve flights and was assessed as being capable of significantly improving the A-3 penetrability. Production started in May 1965, but a month later, the programme was put on standby in view of the Pen-X committee's reassessment of the Soviet ABM threat. Polaris A-3 with PX-2 would offer little resistance to a VHF area defence. However, DoD recommended that the cluster system of warheads should be adopted for future missile designs. PX-2 was no longer considered suitable and the first alternative step in countering the ABM threat was to harden the missile itself to protect it against the effects of radiation and the electromagnetic pulse (EMP) caused by an explosion from a nuclear armed ABM. This hardening process was undertaken in a project known as Topsy, and missiles thus treated were designated A-3T.

Topsy addressed the safety of the missile in response to a scenario whereby the Soviets might seek to suppress the Polaris SSBNs by nuclear detonations over the patrol areas, thereby rendering the submarines *hors de combat* before the missiles had even been launched. It made no changes to the warhead, so proposals to further counter the threat were urged by the OSD and the navy responded with plans to development a warhead package to include a range of penaids. These were a variety of devices such as metal shards, chaff, or balloons designed to look like warheads to the radar systems controlling the ABMs. This program was started in 1965 and was named Exo-PAC—reflecting the assumed problems of exoatmospheric ABM interceptors. It involved replacing one of the three warheads with a penetration aid carrier (PAC) which was jettisoned from the missile along with the two warheads. The PAC would thereafter eject a number of solid rocket-propelled decoys and chaff. On completion of its task, the PAC would fire a further solid rocket motor to separate it from the cloud of dispersed warheads and decoys. A parallel program called Mark-Up using Mk 2 Mod 2 RVs sought to further harden the two remaining warheads to make them more difficult targets. In July 1965, the Exo-PAC and Mark-Up projects were combined into a further project called Hexo. Later, in October 1965 yet another project called Antelope was introduced. This combined Hexo and Topsy into a unified approach to weapon hardening. Missiles thus equipped would have been designated Polaris A3A and sought to improve the chances of the missile and RV surviving a nuclear environment in the launch area. In the event, Antelope was never operational, although five test flights (three A3TX and two A3TY missiles) took place from Pad 29A between November 1966 and January 1968. A further four large endoatmospheric decoys developed under Project Impala, originally part of the Hexo programme, could have been carried above the thermal barrier on the second stage and were ejected at the same time, following the path of the RVs into the atmosphere by which time the other decoys or balloons would have burnt up. In September 1966, Impala was incorporated into the Antelope system for Mk 2 Mod 3 RVs.

Part of the reason that Antelope-equipped missiles never went to sea was that with Polaris A-3, the original FBM had effectively reached the limit of its development potential. In a meeting on 28 May 1964, SP Chief Scientist Dr John P. Craven had commented:

> With the start of the DASO [Demonstration and Shakedown Operation] program ... I [felt] that the POLARIS program [had] reached a major milestone. If the Russians do not do anything to counter the threat posed by the POLARIS

ANTELOPE/IMPALA THREAT TUBE STRUCTURE

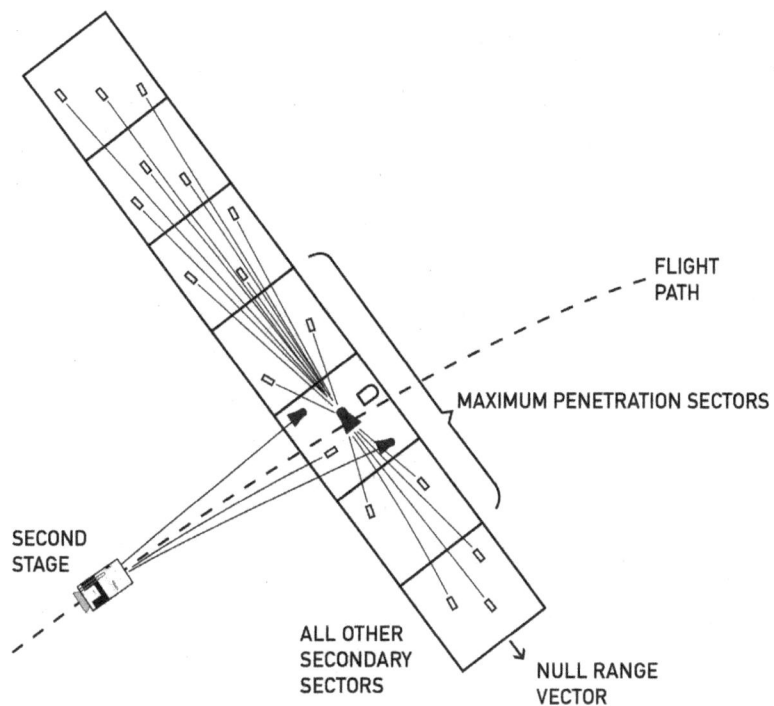

Deployment:
Mk 2 Mod 3 PAC ejected from A-3 missile body
Mk 2 Mod 3 ejects modules into threat tube
- - Cylindrical: 125nm long by 10nm diameter
- - Divided into seven equal sectors with specular reflector and chaff in each one
Ref: LMSC

Impala warhead deployment.

missile, then our responsibility in developing and producing a deterrent weapon system is finished. We will not need the B3 or any other follow-on program. The DASO's [sic] are themselves an indication that we have reached the end of our development program, and this is a major milestone indeed.

But it was, of course, wishful thinking to suppose that the Russians would not make a major effort to counter the threat to Mother Russia. Craven went on to say:

> But the Russians will and are doing things to confront and counter the threat posed by our program. We must accept this fact; we must identify the tasks that face us; we must choose from the alternatives confronting us; we must do this in full cognizance of what the Russians are doing and will have to do.[1]

Dr Harold Brown, director of Defense Research and Engineering (DDR&E), had introduced a formula to assess the effectiveness of the deterrent: Survivability + Reliability + Penetrability = System Dependability. Knowledge of what the Russians might be doing to counter the threat was necessarily limited, but it was known that they would be prepared to devote considerable resource to the problem. What this resource came up with, while out of US control, would affect the ability to ensure that the warheads both survived and achieved a successful penetration.

Lockheed's Space and Missiles Division had undertaken a variety of studies under the codename of Hydra, to extend Polaris's range even further—broadly identified as Polaris A-4. The navy, though aware of these studies, showed little interest as they were satisfied with the 2,500-NM range which gave ample sea area for safe SSBN operations and greater range perversely gave the enemy more time to detect the incoming missiles. The A-4 would still be a two-stage missile but would use only a single nozzle in each stage. Aside from the need for a yet more energetic fuel which had already troubled the A-3 development, the required modifications to the submarines' launch tubes or mount tubes would be prohibitive. Furthermore, as the proposed missile's range would exceed 3,000 NM, it would have moved out of the IRBM classification. Undeterred, Lockheed felt that such a missile could be of interest to the USAF, although this idea was never developed. SAC was by now well advanced in its deployment of Minuteman ICBMs and saw little need for a further missile in its arsenal.

Navy disinterest in the A-4 did not mean as such that they were averse to realising that Polaris would in due course become vulnerable to Soviet ABM systems. As early as April 1962, Assistant Defense Secretary Charles J. Hitch confirmed that studies of a successor to Polaris were already underway, although at that stage it was a relatively small study project and no specific type of weapon system had been identified.[2] Experience had shown that the fibreglass spacers in the launch tubes were not needed, and starting in 1963, this allowed the concept studies to be made around a missile of greater diameter. Twenty inches could be added to the diameter of the new missile giving it a diameter of 74 inches and 3 feet was added to its length resulting in an increase in weight of 30,000 lb. At this early stage, it was envisaged that the warhead would be the Los Alamos-designed W-67 multimegaton which, in a Mk 17 RV produced by the Avco Corporation, would have been common to both the naval application and SAC's Minuteman III. However, this idea never reached more than the design stage when the air force chose instead to use the W-62 warhead in a Mk 12 RV. Considering the way ahead, there were differing views within the navy. Inside the office of the CNO, a strong contingent advocated using the capabilities of the new missile to allow for a few very large warheads. This would allow the navy to compete with SAC—inter-service rivalry being never far below the surface—for the targeting of very hard targets such as missile silos, but Polaris had always been seen primarily as a retaliatory weapon where terminal accuracy was less critical. As such, the submarine launched missile lacked absolute accuracy, but a large warhead could overcome this shortcoming by sheer explosive force. However, this proposal would limit the warheads carried to a maximum of three which in turn brought back the problem of overcoming Soviet ABM systems. While many within the navy hierarchy wanted this large warhead, McNamara was strongly against this option and turned it down, leaving the path clear for Levering Smith to put forward proposals for the next generation of Polaris—the B-3 with multiple warheads.

From the start of the ballistic missile era, it had been understood that a single warhead would, in time, be vulnerable to interception by an ABM system. In tests, America's US Army developed Nike-Zeus ABM system had no difficulty in destroying individual re-entering objects. The world's first known successful interception took place on 19 July 1962 when a Nike-Zeus fired from Kwajalein Island hit an Atlas nosecone above the Pacific. The target Atlas had been launched from Vandenberg AFB by Francis E. Warren AFB's 565 Strategic Missile Squadron (SMS). Various research programmes had explored ways of obscuring the warheads from enemy radar. Once the Soviet deployment of the ABM ring around Moscow was established, the Antelope programme along with its derivatives sought to address the problem of getting the warheads to their targets. These penetration aids would be technically sophisticated, costly, and heavy. They had to be developed using the available intelligence on the Soviet system and there was always the fear that some unknown feature might have been developed by the Soviets to unscramble the radar data on the incoming targets and reveal the actual warheads. But even in the most pessimistic scenario, there was only a finite number of targets that could be followed and multiplicity of targets would overwhelm the ability to track them, and in parallel thinking there was only a finite number of interceptors as a counterforce. However, the addition of decoys necessarily reduced the space and payload available for the actual warheads:

If all available payload on a ballistic missile is utilized for small nuclear warheads, each one capable of producing great damage, then several missiles can be used, each with multiple warheads to exhaust the supply of the opposing ABM interceptors. After that, the remaining warheads get no opposition.... Consequently, the Department of Defense committed itself to the full exploitation of multiple warheads, probably the ultimate in penetration aids.[3]

The original B-3 specification envisaged either one large warhead or three smaller ones following the layout of the A-3. The air force's Skybolt had one large warhead and incorporated a star seeker for navigation and the question was raised as to whether the B-3 should incorporate this feature as a means of achieving greater terminal accuracy. This was a solution developed by the Kearfott Division of Singer Business Corporation. Experiments had taken place under the Stellar Acquisition Flight Feasibility (STAFF) program which used recycled A-2 missiles that had been retired from service. This tested a Kearfott stellar-inertial system with a Northrop star sensor. The first such flight was on 14 April 1965, and although not wholly successful, telemetry indicated that the tracker had locked on to the Pole Star (appropriately enough also called Polaris). However, the flight had taken place at night and therefore failed to prove if the experiment could be repeated in daylight. Opinions were divided, Draper believing that it was not necessary, and the seeker may in fact be blinded by an exoatmospheric nuclear explosion, although his critics would claim this was a 'not invented here' response. Smith's view, supporting Draper, believed that the existing IL systems were proven and accurate enough already. After Skybolt, there was no indication that the air force was going to employ any ICBM system other than from fixed sites and would therefore have no need for star tracking navigation (although the early thoughts on the MX missile which became the 7000-NM-range LGM-118 Peacekeeper envisaged a certain mobility to confuse Soviet targeting). Additionally, unless the SSBN role was changed, there was no absolute need for precise terminal accuracy. Was there too perhaps a cultural reluctance to use a system designed for the air force? Nonetheless, a new guidance unit was needed for the missile. The IL had been developing a new SINS as a follow-on to the A-3's Mk 2 unit. The navy had asked for a 'strapdown' system that would be cheaper and easier to build. Such a system would be attached rigidly to the missile's structure. The computer acted as an analytical gimbal eliminating the need for a stable platform. Although the IL demonstrated the feasibility of this idea, it did not lead to a navy contract, however, that did not rule out their further involvement, for on 1 April 1966, the IL issued a press release:

Contracts totalling more than one million dollars for [the] guidance system for the new [B-3] missile, to be developed by the Instrumentation Laboratory ...

with support from General Electric Co. and Raytheon Co., were awarded today by the Navy's Special Projects Office in Washington.... The guidance system consists of two major subassemblies—the inertial platform and the guidance system with associated electronics.[4]

From the naval point of view on the B-3 proposal, they chose to disregard any increase in range to concentrate of developing the warhead package, so while the missile body was a development of the earlier version, the front end would incorporate radically new technology in the form of multiple independently targetable re-entry vehicles (MIRV). Some would argue that increase in the B-3's range should not be disregarded as some designated targets were still outside the range of the A-3. Developing warhead technology, however, was producing ever smaller warheads, and it would now be possible for the B-3 to carry fourteen Mk 3 RVs, ten mounted in a ring and a further four in a raised central platform. As previously noted, the DoD had argued for the Mk 12 RV being developed under the Pave Pepper programme, but SP preferred to retain the tried-and-trusted RV used on Polaris. The UK's Assistant Under-Secretary of State (Ministry of Defence) Sir Frank Cooper later commented that the 'US was euphoric about the MIRVs which they believed no one else could develop'.[5] But it was complex cutting-edge technology. One of the considerations was how to disperse the warheads on separation from the missile. Three possibilities were considered. 'Mailman' used technology based on the USAF Minuteman and employed a bus on which were both guidance and propulsion systems which would release the RVs individually, but this required a change from the Polaris approach to one where the missile's position was known. 'Blue Angels' retained the Q-guidance used on Polaris, but each RV would need its own guidance and propulsion system. 'Carousel' appropriately envisaged a rotating missile ejecting the RV by centrifugal force. The bus system was considered the most appropriate and was duly approved by the SecNav Paul Nitze. It promised greater accuracy and thereby a move towards the level of accuracy that the air force's land-based missiles could achieve. In November, design settled on a MIRV system with ten to fourteen warhead capability: fewer warheads giving greater range. W-68 warheads with Mk 3 RVs could give ranges of: 1,740 NM (fourteen RVs), 2,200 NM (ten RVs), or even 3,000 NM (one RV). The system used loft to maintain the in-flight separation of the RVs at shorter ranges. The Mk 3 RV was 54.75 inches long, with a 15.25-inch base diameter and 140-lb weight, and it was hardened to about the same level as the A-3A.[6] Yield of the Livermore-designed W-68 warheads was believed to be 40 kt (some sources quote 50 kt) with an accuracy of 2,000 feet, although accuracy deteriorated the further north the launch point was, due to limitations within the navigation system. Pinpoint accuracy was considered less important as it was hoped that it would encourage the Soviets to think that the missile was not seen as a first strike weapon which would ideally need to be sufficiently accurate to take out specific critical targets. Nominal missile performance was usually quoted based on a ten-warhead configuration. If these ten warheads hit a city, it was estimated that there would be one million deaths and a similar number of casualties. In comparison with the hardened Mk 2 RVs of Polaris, and assuming that damage area was proportional to yield to a two-thirds power, then the number of the smaller warheads to achieve the same level of destruction would be approximately as follows:

Warhead Yield/Range Details						
Yield kt		1,000	350	200	100	50
Ratio	1.0	0.35	0.2	0.1	0.05	0.025
Rounded	1	2	3	5	8	12

Thus, it would need three to four times the number of Mk 3 RVs to produce the same result as the Mk 2s. The decision to go for a number of smaller warheads was by no means unanimous. Polaris B-3 had twice the payload capacity of the earlier missiles and by adopting the MIRV warhead package it was both modular and flexible. MIRV technology spaced the RVs in such a way that each would have to be targeted by individual ABM interceptors. It was this flexibility that rendered the Antelope warhead obsolete. Wertheim commented that Antelope 'was never put into production. Not because it failed but simply because it was overtaken by a superior system.'[7]

As regards the motors, Lockheed concluded a three-month project definition phase with Aerojet for both stages: Hercules for the second stage with Hercules and Thiokol jointly studying the first stage. Still at this stage called Polaris B-3, with the navy's intention that it would be called Polaris II, the missile was actually to be given a new name: 'Poseidon C-3'. This was largely for political reasons. The Johnson administration was being heavily criticised for not starting any new defence projects, as indeed had been the previous Kennedy administration, and McNamara refused to accept the navy's choice of designation for the new missile claiming that it was a huge step forward in weaponry—in essence a new weapon. It doubled the accuracy and doubled the payload of Polaris, and it was more versatile. Special Assistant to the Secretary and Deputy Secretary of Defense Joseph A. Califano remembered:

We were so burned by [the LGM-30F] Minute Man [*sic*] II. Goldwater claiming that Minute Man II was not a new weapons system that when the navy was all set to name something Polaris II which *was* a new weapon system for the subs and I remember being called in by McNamara and [being told] 'We're not going to do what we did on Minute Man II again. You go down, change, get a new name for this thing for the President to announce.' And I went down.

I think there was an admiral named [Horacio] Rivero [who was VCNO] and sat with him with a book. We went through a book of naval expressions or nautical things. The navy was really p***ed. They were very p***ed off about the change in the name. And he and I came up with Poseidon right out of the book that day. I came back to McNamara and said, 'How about Poseidon?' I called [White House Press Secretary Bill] Moyers or [White House Special Assistant Jack] Valenti and said, 'Here's a new weapons system for the President to announce, Poseidon.'[8]

After an exchange of views with CNO Admiral David L. McDonald who refused to accept that the defense secretary had the authority to name weapons, the matter was transferred to Rivero who eventually relented after pointing out that the navy, which was fully geared up to announce the Polaris II name, would undoubtedly leak the fact that they had been overruled for political reasons. McNamara forcibly indicated that he could not care, and a new name would have to be found. The president duly announced the new missile programme, now to be called Poseidon, to Congress on 18 January 1965:[9]

President Johnson sent Congress a special message on defense today, disclosing plans to develop a new submarine-carried ballistic missile with twice the destructive power of the Polaris. Called the Poseidon, the new missile was one of a range of strategic weapons outlined by the president as means of keeping American retaliatory power ever ready to deter attack.... The president described 'remarkable' developments for existing strategic missiles—penetration aids to help them reach their targets, guidance and nose cone designs to increase their effectiveness and communications devices enabling missiles to report their arrival on target 'up to and even including the time of explosion.'[10]

Johnson later commented that, 'the Poseidon will be eight times more effective a deterrent than the most advanced Polaris—the A-3.... It will have twice the payload of the Polaris and more than twice the accuracy.'[11]

Wertheim remembered: 'I woke up one morning, I remember very well, reading in the newspaper that the president had just announced his approval for a new project called POSEIDON.'[12] Recalling the time when he was at China Lake Naval Air Station, he further commented 'whether you call it CHAPARRAL [a self-propelled surface-to-air missile system based on the AIM-9 Sidewinder air-to-air missile system] or POSEIDON there is some value in taking an old idea and giving it a new name.'[13] McNamara approved production of Poseidon on 17 December 1966.

First launch of a Poseidon test vehicle, STV-4K, took place on 7 April 1967 from the Peashooter facility. By 5 July, the first-stage motor was successfully fired at the Magna, Utah, facility of Hercules Inc. with the initial second-stage firing taking place there on 3 February 1968. Thus encouraged, the navy awarded Lockheed a $456.1 million contract for the development and production of Poseidon. On 16 August 1968, the first test flight aimed at basic missile development took place from LC-25C and was deemed a success even though a malfunction delayed the launch by twenty-four hours. The day's postponement meant that the navy's new weapon was tested the same day as the first test of the air force's Titan III ICBM.[14] (This was one of the iconic US launch vehicles which also found a role in the Gemini manned spacecraft programme.) This demonstration of capability was calculated to show that the US had a commanding lead over Soviet missile technology. But there was internal protest by some who believed that the tests might delay discussions on a bilateral missile freeze. Along with certain voices within the Johnson administration, Dr Jerome B. Wiesner of MIT, a former White House science adviser, had unsuccessfully petitioned the Pentagon to delay the tests.[15]

However, by this time, the final Polaris A-3 had left the Lockheed production line and was handed over to the navy on 1 July. In anticipation of the changeover to Poseidon, the SSBNs had to be duly upgraded. The *James Madison* was the first to enter Groton on 2 February 1969. The modifications were quite significant. As well as alterations to the mount tubes—or launchers—the Mk-84 fire control system on the thirty-one *Lafayette*-class SSBNs had to be replaced by the later Mk 88 Mod 1. Consideration also had to be given to what updates were required to allow Poseidon-armed submarines to operate from the Holy Loch. Prime Minister Edward Heath gave UK authorisation in a letter of 7 April 1971 which confirmed that 'US Fleet Ballistic Missile submarines (Poseidon-equipped)' could use the Holy Loch 'in the same way as their sisters Polaris and under the same arrangements as are set out in the memorandum of understanding on Holy Loch.'[16]

Meanwhile, the *Observation Island* too had been converted to support the Poseidon test programme. She completed the refit at the Norfolk Naval Yard on 1 May 1969 and on 3 August 1970 was the headquarters ship for the first submarine launch of the new missile. As well as the press who were accommodated aboard the *Observation Island*, the launch, taking place some 30 miles east of Cape Canaveral, had an unwelcome observer in the form of the Soviet AGI 'trawler' the *Khariton Laptev*, a regular attender of US missile launches, which stood 3 miles from the launch location. As soon as the missile had been successfully launched the Soviet ship headed for the launch position and with a net and grappling hook attempted to recover debris, specifically the ten-piece Styrofoam closure membrane that sealed the launch tube. The American destroyer the USS *Calcaterra* (DE-390) attempted to head off the Soviet vessel coming as close as 100 yards in the process. Nine pieces were recovered by sailors from the *Observation Island*, but it was uncertain if the tenth had indeed been retrieved by the Soviet vessel. 'There was no indication of the material's value, but one official was overheard to say that its manufacturer, Westinghouse Electric Company ... wanted it' to see if it had split into sections as its was designed to do.[17] Further modifications to the *Observation Island* in 1985 saw the installation of the AN/SPQ-11 Cobra Judy phased array radar to detect and monitor Russian SSBN activity in the Pacific.

Poseidon's development was not an easy one and the nascent MIRV technology, perhaps not unsurprisingly, proved challenging. To fit inside the nosecone, the RVs were necessarily small, and this caused dynamic motion problems on entering the atmosphere. By April 1973, there had been a concerning 58 per cent failure in the operational test programme and the cause was proving difficult to isolate. VADM Smith had testified before the Senate and House Armed Services Committee that in the twenty-eight demonstration tests of the production version, five had failed and there had been a further fourteen failures in the twenty-four operational test programme launches. He recommended that 'it would be appropriate for us to essentially recall all of the missiles that are now deployed to disassemble and test the various components, perhaps even to tear down the components and get to the basic bits and pieces.'[18] Smith added that with nineteen SSBNs converted to Poseidon, this represented 3,040 warheads and was still something the 'Russians would be foolish not to pay attention to it'. His recall suggestion was considered too dramatic, and the missiles would be examined over a period of time once a solution to the problem had been identified. DoD officials were not deeply concerned, although they did admit that there was a lesser probability of a Poseidon warhead hitting the target than they would have liked. In a letter to John L. McClennan, chairman of the Senate Appropriations Committee, dated 7 September, Under Secretary of the Navy John W. Warner confirmed that an upgrade programme similar to that applied to the A-3 which had also experienced problems would be spread over a period of time.[19] The operational launching programme had been stopped for the time being, resulting in a reduction in the immediate purchase of some twenty missiles. Further reassurance had been given by Secretary of State James R. Schlesinger during a 'Meet the Press' interview on 26 August when he had said:

> There has been no significant weakening of the US deterrent. It may be desirable, over a period of time, to refit these missiles to ensure they work more satisfactorily, but one should not be deeply concerned about such a development in terms of its reducing America's deterrent.

To support Poseidon operations, a further four VC-2 Victory ships were converted to FBM supply ships, offering a 'one stop shop' capability to the Holy Loch and Rota. They were:

US Navy Fleet Ballistic Missile Supply Ships			
Ship	Formerly	Hull Number	In Service
USNS *Norwalk*	SS *Norwalk Victory*	T-AK-279	December 1963–1970
USNS *Furman*	SS *Furman Victory*	T-AK-280	October 1964–October 1986
USNS *Victoria*	SS *Ethiopia Victory*	T-AK-281	October 1965–August 1984
USNS *Marshfield*	SS *Marshfield Victory*	T-AK-282	May 1970–October 1992

Operated by the Military Sea Transportation Service (MSTS)—renamed the Military Sealift Command in 1970—with civilian crews and a small naval detachment to provide security and technical support, these somewhat elderly ex-Second World War transport ships were converted to carry sixteen Poseidon missiles, stored vertically, in their No. 3 hold and the deckhouse was increased in size to accommodate the enlarged crew. Torpedoes and other associated support equipment were also carried. Making their regular transatlantic crossings, the crews were able to experience what life must have been like on the wartime convoys as the ships reacted badly to heavy swell. The ships operating base was the discreet Charleston Naval Weapons Station pier on the Cooper River.

A more modern ship was also converted as a supply ship for the Holy Loch and Rota. This was the USNS *Vega* (A-TK-286), laid down in April 1981 and launched as the SS *Mormacbay*, she was acquired by the US Navy in March 1983 and, following conversion, was taken on by the Military Sealift Command.

The A-2 had gradually replaced the A-1 which was officially retired on 14 October 1965 when the *Abraham Lincoln* returned to Charleston having completed her final patrol before her overhaul. Likewise, the A-3 superseded the A-2 which was taken out of service in September 1974 when the *John Marshall* returned from patrol. The SSBN fleet then comprised a mixture of A-3 and C-3 equipped boats. The *James Madison* had inaugurated the Poseidon patrols, leaving Charleston on 31 March 1971 with a full complement of sixteen C-3 missiles. Polaris A-3 was to continue in service until February 1982 when the first nine boats were re-designated SSNs under the SALT II agreement to make way for the new twenty-four-missile *Ohio* class. The 1,000th deterrent patrol completed by the *John C Calhoun* (SSBN-630) occurred on 16 May 1972, when she returned to the Holy Loch. Twenty-five of these had been with Poseidon missiles.

The Human Element, Admiral Zumwalt, and Farewell to Foreign Bases

With the commissioning of the USS *Will Rogers* (SSBN-659)—named after an American cowboy entertainer—on 1 April 1967, the US Navy had commissioned its complete complement of forty-one Polaris SSBNs. On 3 October 1967, the submarine left on its first patrol armed with sixteen A-3 missiles marking the moment when the entire fleet had become operational. Manned by eighty-two crews, it had by no means been an easy feat to find the officers for these crews and became more so as the Polaris patrols became increasingly seen as 'routine'. Nonetheless, the navy possessed a core of personnel with better general knowledge of nuclear systems that did the air force. However, rather than the challenging task of the SSNs in seeking out the enemy with the concurrent excitement of the chase, the SSBNs by comparison were actively trying to avoid any possible contact with opposing submarines. The job risked becoming one of boredom and therefore unappealing to the recruitment of younger officers, but it was a job essential for national security and one that required a strong professional ability. But it still had to offer the chance of promotion, and for some, the achievement of command of a submarine. To those with an established family life the regularity and predictability of 'shore time' was undoubtedly attractive, but more likely to appeal to the more senior personnel. The commanding officers had all been chosen with Rickover's direct involvement, and for the early appointees it was a challenging assignment in bringing the boats to operational efficiency. Engineering officers required specific nuclear training—engineering skills becoming second placed—whereas the navigation and weapons officers did not require nuclear expertise and had the advantage of using the very latest of naval technology. However, without such nuclear knowledge, they would not become executive or commanding officers, a position, in fairness, not seen by all as the ultimate career achievement. As the Polaris boats became older and with the upgrading to Poseidon there was little need and in fact little justification in updating the submarines, meaning less and less challenge to the crews operating them. At the start of the Polaris programme, finding crews with some form of submarine experience was not difficult to the extent that for the first decade of operations, there had been no training officers on the strength of the SSBN squadrons. The commanding officers had all had former submarine command. Similarly, all the officers in the 1960s had previous experience on diesel submarines, some even on surface ships. By the 1970s, there was a noticeable decline. Rickover could no longer select from an experienced pool of qualified submarine officers:

> All officers reporting on board, below department head were fresh out of Naval Academy or NROTC [Naval Reserve Officers Training Corps]. Even the submarine school course had been reduced from 6 months to 6 weeks in length. What really triggered the need for a training and readiness officer for each squadron was when SSBNs started failing their operational reactor safeguards examination. Also about one fourth of the crew were transferred off after each patrol and the replacements needed to be trained to become an integral part of the ship's organisation.[1]

In April 1970, CNO ADM Thomas H. Moorer was promoted to be chairman of the joint chiefs of staff and was replaced by Rear Admiral (Admiral from 1 July 1970) Elmo R. Zumwalt. Moorer, an aviator, had been suspicious of Zumwalt, a 'surface sailor', and the latter's close relationship with Secretary of the Navy Paul Nitze. Fearing that this duo might thwart his plans, he had appointed him to Vietnam where he carried out President Johnson's Vietnamization. His successful ACTOV (Accelerated Turnover to Vietnam) programme brought him to the attention of SecDef Melvin Laird, and, against Moorer's advice, he became the youngest CNO at the age of forty-nine. Zumwalt had inherited a poisoned chalice. Morale within the navy was low. Social attitudes, not least the effects of the Vietnam War, were changing and the traditional approach of the navy was affecting recruitment and retention. Insubordination was commonplace and the age of the navy's ships was becoming an increasing factor, whilst the Soviet Navy under Admiral of the Fleet Sergei Gorshkov was an increasing and real threat. Zumwalt was tasked with bringing the navy into the modern age: this was to include the recruitment of blacks, Hispanics, and females: 'Zumwalt was a public charmer and burned with an energy that threatened to outshine the sun.'[2] Much of the fleet was now facing block obsolescence causing significant gaps in its operational capabilities. While new equipment was being ordered—such as the F-14 fighters, *Nimitz*-class aircraft carriers, *Spruance*-class destroyers, and the 688 (*Los Angeles*)-class nuclear attack submarines—these were all extremely capable but also extremely expensive. But nothing had changed the navy's role post-Second World War more than the assumption of the strategic deterrent role. All forty-one SSBNs were now in service, but the navy's interest in insuring a survivable SSBN force resulted in ongoing expenditure as Poseidon missiles took over the role of Polaris. However, this necessary cost continued to come out of the navy's general budget, and this inflicted damage on other naval procurement programmes. Surface ships were a visible means of projecting US naval power in peacetime and would be required in times of war for force protection and keeping the sea-lines of communication (SLOC) open. On acceding to the position of CNO, Zumwalt initiated Project Sixty, a plan of action for the duration of his term of office. The report opened with: 'The initial Navy capability is the contribution it can make to an assured Second Strike potential. Strategic deterrence must come first.'[3]

In March 1971, Zumwalt confirmed this view during testimony before the US Senate Committee on Armed Services, saying, 'Admiral Moorer has cogently pointed out that continuing provisions for an assured second-strike nuclear capability must have our first priority.' He went on to outline the concerning growth in Soviet naval capability, and commenting on the US SSBN fleet, he said:

> The Navy strategic deterrent force of 41 SSBNs and associated support ships is adequate. The rate of POSEIDON conversions is proceeding as programmed. Our most recent assessments have concluded that the U.S. fleet ballistic missile force at sea will be virtually invulnerable until at least the mid 1970's and almost certainly the late 70's.[4]

But what did life in the SSBN force offer to its crews. For submarines based at the Holy Loch, duty crews would be flown across the Atlantic on a 180-day cycle for each period of duty at the loch. Rickover had determined that the crews being flown from America for the changeover would be split into two similar groups and bussed and flown across the Atlantic separately in case of any accident. This ensured that a core crew would be ready to take over the next patrol and be relatively easily supplemented by additional personnel in such an emergency. Accommodation would be on board the tender during the Blue–Gold transfer whereafter they would take over the submarine for the next patrol. Leaving most of their kit and uniforms on board the tender, they would wear 'poopy suits', blue Dacron overalls for the duration of the patrol. Dacron, a proprietary polyester material developed by DuPont, has the advantage of being quick and easy to wash and dry and is almost indestructible. It is also hypoallergenic and is waterproof thereby being resistant to mould and mildew. It also sheds very little lint, an important consideration in the confines of the submarine. Oxygen was produced from seawater by electrolysis and carbon dioxide removed by scrubbers within the air conditioning system. Accommodation, thanks to VADM Raborn, was the best in the submarine force equal or better than on many surface ships. There was an open galley policy which allowed the crew to make a sandwich at any time and reflecting the home comforts of their homeland, there were ice cream and popcorn machines. During each 180-day cycle, the crews could expect to be home stateside for up to seventy-five days, again, an arrangement that many of the older personnel found attractive. However, the downside was that there was no communication with families during the patrol which some found this regular absence challenging. Only in the most extreme situation would the submarine leave its designated patrol and to cope with all but the direst emergencies there was a doctor on board who had the additional duty of monitoring radiation levels on the dosimeters worn by everyone.

The Zumwalt Era

Having expressed himself confident about the SSBN fleet, Zumwalt continued by showing concern over weaknesses in the conventionally armed fleet. The Soviets had in effect achieved nuclear parity with the US rendering nuclear conflict 'self-destructively unattractive'. This raised the importance of US conventional forces which would become 'the deciding factor in future conflicts of interest, other than those involving national survival'.[5] With the withdrawal of US forces from Vietnam, it was also essential that the navy maintained an international presence to reinforce confidence within its allies. He no longer believed that for the first time in twenty-five years, the navy could no longer guarantee winning a war at sea.

With a restricting budget and ever-increasing costs, traditional bureaucracy within the navy became a buffer against progress. Functionally, the navy was divided into three 'unions' each with a deputy CNO at its head—aviators, surface sailors, and submariners. Zumwalt noted that 'intense competition for resources and recognition among the three unions—for there is never enough of either to satisfy everybody, or even anybody.'[6] But there was one other power base within the navy that Zumwalt had to contend with: Admiral Rickover. The two admirals met on 2 June 1970 and the new CNO offered to support accelerated procurement of 688-class SSNs in return for Rickover's support for the inexpensive sea control ships, which Zumwalt hoped to start building in 1973/4. Rickover also raised the question of a new class of SSBN to replace Polaris/Poseidon. Zumwalt indicated that if Soviet advances in missile technology and deployment continued at their present pace, then he too would support such a programme. The resulting somewhat tense relationship did not last for long. Personally and professionally, the two leaders were poles apart: a relationship which never thawed. Zumwalt was later to say that he had three enemies: the air force, the Soviet Union, and Hyman Rickover.[7] Nonetheless, the 688 class represented yet more work for EB and yet despite this, union demarcation lines became a serious obstacle to forward progress. Poseidon DASO launches started in August 1970 with the *James Madison*, the lead ship in the Poseidon conversion programme. Both the *James Madison* and *Daniel Boone* had been converted to the new missile with the intention of starting patrol cycles at the start of 1971. But USN sources indicated that the first patrols of submarines carrying Poseidon missiles would not start until middle or late spring. The navy attributed the deployment setback to 'problems frequently associated with the initial production of a new weapons system'. The difficulties—which were not set forth—had delayed assembly of the missiles.[8]

The *James Madison* set off from Charleston on 31 March 1971 to undertake the first operational patrol with the new missile. Further SSBNs completed their conversions followed by DASO launches. It would be unrealistic to expect that no problems would be encountered. On 10 May 1973 with the media and some 200 naval guests on board the USNS *Range Sentinel* 30 miles east of Cape Canaveral, the *Henry L. Stimson* prepared to routinely launch a C-3. As was often the occasion, a Soviet AGI, the *Prymor'ye*-class *Zakarpatye*, had also turned up and placed itself a mile from the submarine to observe proceedings:

> The 34-foot Poseidon, carrying a dummy warhead, popped out of one of the Stimson's 16 submerged launching tubes, ignited normally and roared into the cloudy sky toward an Atlantic target area more than 1,500 miles to the southeast. But after about 15 to 20 seconds of flight, the stubby black and white rocket wheeled off course. It appeared to recover, gained altitude and then began fishtailing wildly, its brilliant exhaust spewing from side to side. Range safety officers at Cape Kennedy allowed the rocket to perform in this fashion for about a half-minute as it gained altitude and distance from the *Range Sentinel* and the Soviet vessel. Then, 57 seconds after launching, a radio signal was sent to the missile, which detonated an emergency explosive charge and severed the rocket.[9]

The Soviet ship then sent out a small boat to collect any floating debris from the launch, while the disappointed onlookers returned to port.

Despite the significant advances offered by MIRV, it was inevitable that a new missile and a new class of submarine would be needed in due course. Curiously, however, it was not the navy that started the ball rolling. In 1966, the DoD had initiated a study under the title Strat-X. Undertaken by the Institute of Defense Analyses (IDA) with support from the office of the secretary of defense, the military, industry, and academia, its brief being to consider the next generation of strategic missiles—either land-based or sea-based. The trigger for Strat-X was a desire by Deputy Director of Defense Research and Engineering Dr Lloyd Wilson to find if there was an alternative to Boeing's proposed WS120A Advanced ICBM (AICBM) intended as a successor to Minuteman. The Boeing missile was a very large solid-fuelled missile carrying between ten and twenty MIRV warheads, but Wilson considered it no more survivable than Minuteman in its fixed silos. The study group was headed by Fred Payne of the IDA and in August 1967 produced a twenty-five-volume report. A total of 125 concepts were studied and narrowed down to nine of varying types. Two naval options were identified: the ballistic missile ship (BMS) and the undersea long-range missile system (ULMS). Conceptually, the ULMS submarine was very different from the Polaris SSBNs, which were in essence converted attack submarines and designed for speeds far higher than was needed for the low speeds typical of the missile boats. The new type of submarine would be large, slow moving (maximum speed 11–13 knots), quiet, and, controversially, would carry the missiles horizontally outside the pressure hull thereby allowing extra space inside the hull for equipment access which promised increased time between overhauls and decreased time in port between patrols.

VADM Smith as head of SP was tasked with evaluating the ULMS. With the acknowledged success of the Polaris/Poseidon projects, SP enjoyed a certain amount of influence and independence within the navy. Smith had represented the navy on the Strat-X board and not surprisingly was given the position of project manager for the new missile. He was also known to be very conscious of costs, an aspect that would appeal to McNamara and his successor from March 1968, Clark Clifford.[10] So he was well aware that he must keep tight control over his staff, believing that 'any good engineer will volunteer his opinion that he sees a way to design and build more capability than in the current equipment. It is then up to others to decide whether or not the design goal should reflect that opinion.'[11] Concentrating on the form the submarine would take soon resulted in a conceptual design of 18,000 tons displacement—over twice that of the later Poseidon boats. Using an existing reactor design would minimise costs but would result in a slower top speed of 20 knots, some 4 knots slower than the Polaris/Poseidon SSBNs. Eschewing the Strat-X idea of horizontal externally mounted missiles, the ULMS missiles would continue to be mounted vertically within the submarine's hull, but these missiles would be considerably larger than Poseidon C-3.

But when it came to the reactor to be used, Rickover's department would hold sway and the extraordinary position held by the admiral with significant political support from Congress still defied naval attempts to force his retirement: even a powerful 1967 triumvirate of Johnson, McNamara, and Nitze had failed to achieve his departure. In many ways, it was not Rickover himself that was the problem, more the inability of those in positions of authority to understand how to cope with Rickover's authority. Thus, Rickover remained in power with supreme jurisdiction over all matters nuclear through the Division of Nuclear Propulsion. Presumed advances in Soviet anti-submarine passive sonar detection techniques determined that the new design should operate as quietly as possible. If the noise generated by the coolant pumps could be reduced, this would be a major step in the right direction. Or, of course, eliminate the pumps completely. Such a design potentially existed in the S5G reactor aboard the experimental USS *Narwhal* (SSN-671) commissioned on 12 July 1969. This reactor design was a natural circulation reactor (NCR), and although coolant pumps were fitted, these were only required for high-speed operations. With the low speeds required for normal operations, the NCR seemed to suggest a solution, but Rickover, who wanted more powerful reactors and higher speeds for all submarines, made the point that even the SSBNs may have to evade a pursuing Soviet SSN and at that stage passive sonar could not function at speeds greater than 24 knots. Compromise became the order of the day, and as will so often happen in such cases, the proposal received little enthusiastic support from any quarter. The ULMS SSBN would be of around 30,000 tons of displacement—Polaris SSBNs were around 8,000 tons. Two reactors of a new NCR design and capable of delivering 30,000 shp would be required to provide a top speed of up to 27 knots. However impracticable this leviathan may have been, the Soviets followed a roughly similar path in their Project 941 *Akula* SSBN (NATO reporting name: Typhoon).

The key contributing determinants in the studies for the ULMS submarine were the size of the missile and the design of the propulsion system which would lead to a conceptual outline of the submarine. Each aspect had an influence on the other factors. In early August 1970, the CNO's office released a document 'Undersea Long Range Missile Concept', which encapsulated the programmes goals:

> High force effectiveness with emphasis on survivability and high utilization of each ULMS submarine for economy.... High survivability is to be achieved through the use of advanced submarine technology and by deployment in large ocean areas.

Later that year, Warner discussed the planned 30,000-ton submarine with Deputy Secretary of Defense David Packard who quickly dismissed the idea of such a large, complex and expensive submarine thus putting a question mark over the whole ULMS programme.[12] Smith maintained that the missile capability had first to be finalised before work could be undertaken on the design of the submarine. However, as with most of the navy's nuclear ships, Rickover's proactive nature had ensured that his reactor design was completed first thereby determining the nature of the vessel. ADM Zumwalt indicated that a study should be made of a submarine design based on using only one of Rickover's proposed large reactors and this idea was developed, becoming known as the 'Super-640 class'—based on the final batch of Polaris/Poseidon SSBNs of the *Benjamin Franklin* class. But it was becoming clear that within the constraints of the budget, the cost of high-speed capability outweighed the operational value. Gradually the proposal was being whittled down in size and complexity. SP's continuing study of the proposed missile showed that with the ever-emerging improvements in missile technology, an Extended Range Poseidon (EXPO) was fast becoming a realistic proposition. This gave the advantages of reduced transit time to and from the patrol areas which could be closer to the US mainland and therefore easier to protect against anti-submarine warfare (ASW) operations. Initially the idea was to retrofit the new missile to make full use of the space available within the Polaris/Poseidon launch tubes. A missile two inches wider in diameter and 3–4 feet longer in length could still fit inside the existing tubes. EXPO could balance payload against range to achieve the range projected for the ULMS although without the potential for improved accuracy and hard target kill capability promised by the ULMS. Using existing SSBNs clearly represented a significant cost saving although some updating, including a new sonar suite, would have to be undertaken to maintain their invulnerability in the face of improved Soviet ASW capability. If, however, the existing Polaris/Poseidon boats needed to be retired, 'the EXPO could be deployed on new, updated Polaris/Poseidon ships [which would] retain most of the design of the old Polaris/Poseidon vessels, but would probably be improved with the latest "quieting" technology to reduce detectability. No new ULMS submarine would be needed.'[13]

SP analysts concluded that an improved Polaris/Poseidon-type submarine utilising one S5G reactor could be operational by late 1978 and a missile substantially more capable than Poseidon could indeed be fitted into existing size tubes. But other ideas were still being considered and a meeting of the Naval Warfare Panel held on 19 November 1970 reviewed the latest configuration studies and agreed to initiate studies on the latest Soviet submarine threat profile and ways that this may be countered.[14] This, of course, was a factor in choosing the next generation of SSBN. There was now increasing pressure to consider Rickover's latest 688-class SSNs as potential carriers and the possibility of equipping them with the ULMS. But the alternative 'Super-640' proposal still remained on the table for consideration and by January 1971 had been defined as a 12,000-ton submarine—roughly half as big again as the *Benjamin Franklin*-class SSBNs. Rickover's response was that such a proposal, powered by a single-shaft 30,000-shp reactor, was acceptable but any non-advanced state-of-the-art submarine would not be. With his typical energy Rickover was keen to stop the discussions and proceed to project definition even casting a side-swipe at SP by claiming their analysis was not objective and was tainted by some (unnamed) vested interest. Zumwalt ordered RADM Stansfield Turner, director, Systems Analysis Division, office of the CNO, to report on this accusation, but Turner could find no supporting evidence. That was not to say that there were political manoeuvrings within the SP. Smith was unconvinced by the need to push ahead with the 'Super-640' believing that there was a possibility of embarking on an expensive programme based on hurried studies and an undefined Soviet ASW capability. He was also aware that although a new SSBN programme had much support from within the navy, Zumwalt was keen to devote a greater proportion of funds to conventional forces, but he was also under pressure to reach a decision.[15] As well as the intra-service rivalry over funds, SecDef Clifford had given a warning that there was to be no interservice squabbles over requirements and that no project was to be started without approved funding to complete it.

Meanwhile, a report ('Detailed Review of the ULMS Decision') prepared by the navy's Systems Analysis and Long-Range Objective Division was discussed by the ULMS Steering Group on 27 January. The report commented:

We conclude from these studies that if an ULMS force is to be significantly threatened, it will probably be as a result of some unpredictable technological breakthrough in the ASW field.

Unfortunately, most of the important choices to be made between competing ULMS designs are strongly influenced by survivability considerations. The choices regarding missile range, submarine speed, acoustic signature, and the number of missiles per submarine are four of the most important. Given that the threat is unpredictable, it is not clear how analysis can play an important role.

However, the review recommended that 'Although there is limited information for a decision, we recognize that circumstances dictate that one is made.'

On 31 March 1971, the ULMS project manager was established under the chief of material. By this time the ever-advancing technology of solid propellants allowed LMSC to design an increased range missile which was identical to the C-3 in dimensions and weight but promised a range of 4,000 NM. This was the C-4 missile which became a new generation of weapons under the name 'Trident'.

With the increased range now promised firstly by Poseidon and later by Trident, the navy no longer needed forward basing. The Rota base closed on 1 July 1979 after the Spanish government insisted on removal of all nuclear weapons from the country. The local community which had enjoyed the employment opportunities afforded by the base were less enthusiastic and the closure provoked angry demonstrations and a two-week sit-in by the newly unemployed in the town council building. Guam closed on 30 September 1981. But it was to be a further decade before Scotland bade farewell to SUBRON 15. Whitham argues that this may well have been because of the more relaxed approach to overall safety.[16]

CND still drew attention to the area and what was really their final sizeable peace cruise (aboard the veteran PS *Waverley*) and march to the Holy Loch had taken place on 10 September 1977, marking the twenty-fifth anniversary of Britain's first nuclear test. The Royal Navy marked the anniversary by launching the first Chevaline test vehicle. CND reported that some 1,200 people had attended, and every sort of person had come to 'protest at the American nuclear base. Christians and anarchists, Communists and Conservatives, Liberals and Socialists, Buddhists and Nationalists.' Headed by the Monktonhall colliery band, the walkers wound around the shoreline and were later addressed by the usual band of left-wing political worthies. A total of £200 was raised to support Scottish CND.[17]

But Site I's end was nigh. On 9 November 1991, on a sunny day, the USS *Will Rogers* left the Holy Loch and sailed to her New London base after first carrying out exercises in the Atlantic. Accompanied by two dinghies full of peace protesters and the media, with more press securely accommodated in a naval tug, she had been based there for some twenty years and was the final US submarine to leave Scottish waters: 'There was a festive air as the sub sailed down a flat-calm Clyde, a small flotilla in her wake [including a rubber inflatable flying the CND banner].... Commander Ronald W. Dennis looked back from the conning tower and waved Scotland a final fond farewell.'[18] CAPT. Ronald D. Gumbert, the nineteenth and last CO of SUBRON 14, commented: 'It us with some sorrow that we have to pack up our things and go home. There have been a number of tearful farewells, but over the years many men have married Scottish girls and gone to live in the United States. I like to think there has been an exchange of American and Scottish culture.' While the peace protesters may have expressed joy at her departure, some 1,500 jobs that had been filled by the local population were lost in an area of high unemployment.[19] In recognition of the time that Eisenhower had spent at Culzean Castle where he was given lifetime tenancy of the top floor, Glasgow and Strathclyde University Officers' Training Corps (GSUOTC) provided a three light-gun salute to the departing Americans, a compliment that was duly recognised and returned.

Decommissioning of Site I was completed the following year almost exactly thirty years since the arrival of its first 'customer'. The *Los Alamos* had undertaken over 2,800 submarine docking operations. It was partially dismantled and taken back to America aboard the 27,000-ton *Mighty Servant 3*, a semi-submersible heavy-lift ship designed to carry oil rigs and operated by the Dutch firm Wijsmuller Transport.

There had been increasing concerns over the previous thirty years about what the Americans had dumped overboard and under pressure, a team of marine investigators conducted an underwater camera survey of the seabed. Apart from the roughly sixty drums containing unknown substances, a further survey showed that levels of zinc, cadmium, and selenium were above national averages. Possible dangers to the local environment delayed further action until 24 February 1989, when a multi-million-pound salvage operation started to remove some 2,700 tonnes of assorted debris from the bed of the loch using the electro-magnetic crane on the barge *Molly McGill*. Although some local opposition wished the debris to remain undisturbed under its covering of silt, the MoD had an obligation to effect the clean-up under the Host Nation Agreement—a common obligation during the Cold War whereby the UK agreed to bear any clean-up costs entailed by guest forces such as the United States Navy.[20] The MoD duly handed over responsibility for the Holy Loch to the Clyde Port Authority in April 2002.

On 6 March 1972, VADM Smith attended a reception on board HMS *Resolution* to celebrate the successful completion of DASO 9.[21] On 30 March, he officially retired from active duty, but he had consented to be recalled so that his unique experience could continue to be of use to the US strategic defense programme. He had received a congratulatory letter from President Richard Nixon, which said:

> First the Polaris Program and now the Poseidon Program have and will provide immeasurably for the protection of the free world. Through your personal contribution, both of these programs have experienced continued success. Such devotion to duty, perseverance, and your exceptional ability will long serve as inspirations to all who share the responsibilities of national and military leadership. On behalf of a grateful Nation, I extend my personal best wishes for your continued success, good health and happiness.[22]

Some three months previously, Smith had been honoured for his part in the British Polaris programme by being made an Honorary Knight Commander of the Most Excellent Order of the British Empire (KBE). Nor was he forgotten by his British friends as during the queen and Prince Philip's official visit to the US Bicentennial Celebrations in July 1976, he and Lady Smith attended a reception held at the British Embassy on 8 July which was attended by their majesties.[23] Some years later, the *Washington Post*'s obituary of Smith commented:

> Navy leaders consider Adm. Smith on a par with the late Adm. Hyman G. Rickover in pushing submarine technology to unprecedented heights. Adm. Smith quietly developed the Polaris, Poseidon and Trident ballistic missiles for submarines, while Rickover flamboyantly championed nuclear propulsion.[24]

The Royal Navy's Path to Polaris

Although Britain was initially in the forefront of atomic research, the needs of war determined that scientific resource had to be channelled towards projects with a quicker return and Britain was therefore quite willing to let the far vaster resources of America develop this emerging technology, albeit with the skilled assistance of a team of British and Canadian scientists. However, the expediency of the wartime alliances quickly fractured after the cessation of hostilities. Particularly marked in this respect was the question of further cooperation on atomic weapons. Maj.-Gen. Groves who headed the Manhattan Project had never been enthusiastic about British involvement and now jealously guarded American atomic knowledge, repeatedly down-playing the part that non-Americans had played. America possessed the atom bomb, and he was not alone in deciding to keep it away from others. The wartime alliance between Britain and the US was governed by the Quebec Agreement between Churchill and Roosevelt, but this ended with the signing of unconditional surrender. The Atomic Energy Act of 1946—commonly referred to as the McMahon Act after the strongly religious Senator Brien McMahon who sponsored the act—brought any hope of further collaboration between America, Britain and Canada to an abrupt end. The British contingent returned from Los Alamos without a full understanding of the complex technology of the atom bomb. Groves had deliberately kept them away from involvement in the production of plutonium which was a key factor in the manufacture of the necessary fissile material. America now held a significant strategic advantage and was determined that the science of the atom should not be subject to proliferation. Churchill, to the surprise of many, had been defeated in the General Election of 1945 and the wartime Deputy Prime Minister Clement Attlee now headed a Labour government. Britain was financially impoverished, but Attlee saw that the country's future influence in world affairs would become linked to possession of atomic weapons and pressed the Americans for a renewed atomic partnership but faced only repeated humiliating rebuttals. The British population had experienced a level of national organisation and provision during

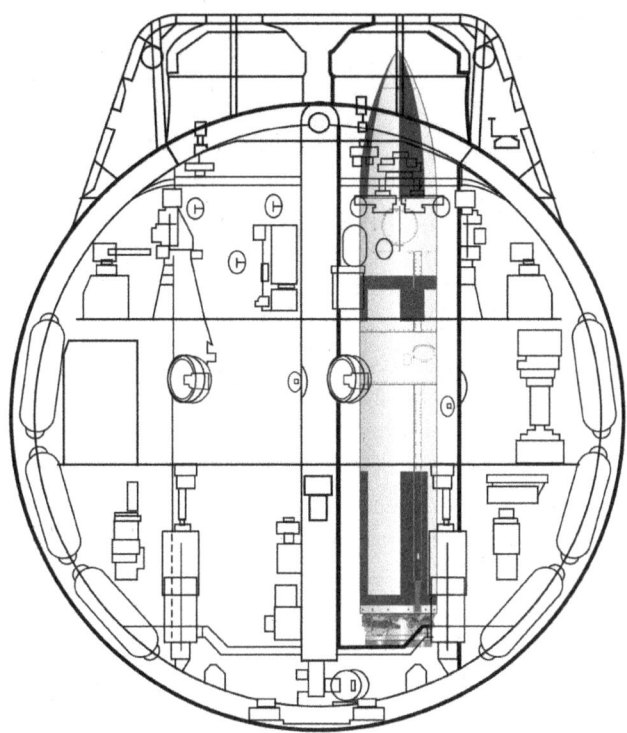

HMS *Resolution*
cross-section of missile
compartment—Frame
86 looking forward.

the war and looked for a similar scenario in the post-war period. Those who had fought through the war and survived now had to rebuild their country. But with a fragmenting empire and an increasing call from many of the colonies for independence, could Britain effectively maintain its position as a world power? Despite clear indications that the future enemy lay to the east, many members of Attlee's socialist Cabinet had pro-communist tendencies, a fact lost neither on Attlee nor the Americans.

In November 1944, the British chiefs of staff, anticipating the victory that was to come had asked the Technical Warfare Committee to anticipate the doctrine of future warfare and advise on how they saw weapons evolving in the face of future changes. An *ad hoc* sub-committee (the Tizard Committee) was set up under the chairmanship of eminent scientist Sir Henry Tizard to report on its recommendations. Although without any official access to Los Alamos, it foresaw the concept of nuclear deterrence such that the threat of the atomic bomb could only be countered by an equal threat by way of possession of such a weapon of proven capability and the willingness, in the eyes of the enemy, to use it.

Taking into account that the war had brought Britain to the brink of bankruptcy, it was a brave but also an almost inevitable decision to pursue the development of a UK nuclear weapons policy. This was undertaken by the highly secret GEN 163 Committee which was itself a sub-committee of the GEN 75 Committee, known by Attlee as 'The Atom Bomb Committee'. To further protect its secrecy, the committee met initially at Shell Mex House on The Strand where the directorate of Tube Alloys—the British atomic research programme—was also based. Under the chairmanship of the prime minister, the committee numbered among its members Foreign Secretary Ernest Bevin, Minister of Defence Albert Alexander, Lord Privy Seal Christopher Addison, Lord President of the Council and Leader of the House of Commons Sir Herbert Morrison, and Minister of Supply and former Minister of Aircraft Production John Wilmot. Also advising the committee was Viscount Portal, the former and longest serving of the chiefs of the air staff (CAS). He was CAS during most of the war and had answered directly to Churchill. He was therefore closely involved with the many implications of the atom bomb and was the obvious choice to be appointed to the new position of controller of production (atomic energy) (CPAE), and although a somewhat reluctant controller, his prestige and knowledge were to inject much needed authority into the programme.[1] Attlee agreed that the confidentiality of the discussions was such that a fifty-year embargo, rather than the usual thirty years, be placed on public access to the minutes of the committee. This was agreed and Secretary to the Committee D. H. F. Rickett, an assistant secretary on the civil staff of the offices of the War Cabinet and the Minister of Defence, endorsed the minutes in such manner when they were archived. Suffice to say that at the meeting of GEN 163 on 8 January 1947 the decision was taken to develop a British nuclear capability without undue delay. Coincidentally on the same day the Ministry of Supply (MoS) issued invitations to selected aircraft manufacturers to submit tenders for Specification B.35/46 which was to become the basis of the RAF's Avro Vulcan and Handley Page Victor medium bombers. Bevin, regarded as one of Britain's best foreign secretaries, in particular was convinced that the United States should not be allowed a monopoly of the power of the atom in the West. Public awareness of the project had to wait until 12 May 1948 when, in reply to a question from Winchester MP George Jeger, an announcement was made in the House of Commons by Alexander:

> As was made clear in the Statement Relating to Defence, 1948 [Command 7327], research and development continue to receive the highest priority in the defence field, and all types of modern weapons, including atomic weapons, are being developed.[2]

Alexander then added it would not be in the public interest to give any more information.

The German-born mathematical physicist Rudolf Peierls who had migrated to Britain in the late 1930s and had worked at Los Alamos since 1943 was arguably the most suitable candidate to head up the British project but he had openly promoted the interests of the supposedly left-leaning Atomic Scientists Association (ASA), an activity which had led to his exclusion from the project and the selection of modestly unassuming William Penney as its head. Penney who had led the British delegation at Los Alamos was put in charge of the British atomic bomb project. He had accompanied Group Captain Leonard Cheshire aboard one of the observation B-29-40-MOs (named *Big Stink*: Serial 44-27354) that witnessed the Nagasaki bomb—Operation Centerboard II—the design on which the British weapon was to be based.[3] As with their Russian opposite numbers, both nations now benefitted from the knowledge that, if they got the physics right, it would work. Initial investigations were carried out at Fort Halstead near Sevenoaks in Kent, an existing Armaments Research Facility, before the team working on the bomb was found a new home at the former RAF Aldermaston in Berkshire where the Atomic Weapon Research Establishment (AWRE) was created.

On 29 August 1949, the Soviets took the West by surprise by conducting a successful nuclear test—RDS-1—at the Semipalatinsk Test Site in Kazakhstan. Known in the West as 'Joe-1', this was some five years ahead of the best estimates by western intelligence of how advanced the Soviet programme was. The air force had predicted 1952 as the earliest date, the army 1960 and the navy 1965. America was quickly alerted to the event, initially when an RB-29A (44-62214) assigned to 375th Reconnaissance Squadron (VLR) Weather on a reconnaissance flight on 3 September 1949, first picked up evidence of the test. Mounted at various points in the plane were photographic plates designed to record and thus measure cosmic ray penetration of the Earth's atmosphere. The returned plates on analysis showed that the aircraft had flown through a radiation hotspot that could not have been explained by extraterrestrial origins. It could only have been a Soviet nuclear test and it showed up how awesome was the gap in US intelligence. Independent British analysis confirmed the findings.

In April 1947, former Wall Street banker Admiral Lewis Strauss (pronounced 'Straws') joined the AEC. Conscious that at some stage the Soviets would surely detonate an atomic bomb, he asked SecDef James V. Forrestal if any provision had been put in place to detect such an explosion. This resulted in the Office of Naval Research implementing the highly secret and unofficially named Operation Rainbarrel. Dr Peter King at the NRL organised the collection of rainwater samples from various locations including the remote areas of the Aleutians. Samples were flown monthly to Seattle, loaded on a navy aircraft and flown to the NRL in Washington, DC. When, shortly after the Soviet detonation, USAF sniffer planes brought back more evidence of a suspected nuclear explosion, King immediately ordered rainwater samples taken between 6 and 16 September. These were urgently flown to the NRL and confirmed that indeed the test had taken place. With negligible intelligence information on the inner workings of the Soviet nuclear programme, it had been assumed that, with agricultural and industrial capacity severely reduced by the war, the Soviets would not have the capacity to instigate a rapid nuclear programme. However, Stalin appointed feared NKVD Chief Lavrentiy Beria to oversee the overall management of the programme. With thousands of gulag labourers available to him and his ever-present threat of the implications of failure, the programme made rapid progress, aided of course by the knowledge that the various technical cul-de-sacs that the MED had explored to find the right answer were unnecessary and that if the physics was right, the bomb would work. In fact, an alternative improvement on the American design was put forward but this was shelved to concentrate on a bomb that needed no experimental stage before a successful first test. There were some improvements, however, as the Soviet bomb was around ten per cent more powerful than the Fat Man dropped on Nagasaki. Despite claims that the bomb was an original Soviet design, it was to all intents, a Fat Man copy, the result of information that had for some time been passed on by the British nuclear physicist Klaus Fuchs who had been a senior member of the British team at the MED.

The following February, he was identified and arrested on espionage charges for giving atomic information to the Soviets. Revealed through the Venona decrypted Soviet diplomatic communications, his reports to Moscow had gone back to his time at Los Alamos and, although by no means the only person to have communicated with the Soviets, (for example, some thirty Canadians working at the Metallurgical Laboratory in Chicago had also been passing information) his information had been a material help in advancing the Soviet bomb programme, hence the similarity between Fat Man and Joe-1. It proved embarrassing that Fuchs was one of the very few people to have been part of the initial British atom bomb project and was accorded the highest security clearance by the MED. Taking what he saw as the moral high ground and motivated by a desire to ensure that no nation had a monopoly of nuclear capability, he had been feeding information to the Soviets since the early days of his secondment to the MED. Not only were his knowledge and exemplary skills now much needed by Britain in its own nuclear developments, but he had returned from Los Alamos with, possibly, more information—including the initial thoughts on a hydrogen bomb—than any of the others in the British team. It was therefore reasonable to suppose that his knowledge of the hydrogen bomb was now known to the Soviets. This was a predicament for the politicians. They needed the power of the atom for both civilian and defence projects, but they did not understand how to handle the scientists to whom they were beholden, many of whom showed left-wing, and therefore potentially communist, tendencies.

Fuchs importance to the British project was of little interest to many Americans who saw this as more than justifying the wisdom of the McMahon Act in proving the laxity of British security arrangements which had further failed to identify the Canadian-based traitor, Alan Nunn May. Distrust of British security was further endorsed with the sudden defection, shortly afterwards, of Bruno Pontecorvo, who was working on reactor design at the Atomic Energy Research Establishment (AERE) based at the former RAF Harwell. In September 1950, he disappeared suddenly to the Soviet Union. But the Americans Julius and Ethel Rosenberg and David Greenglass, Ethel's brother, were also convicted of passing secrets. Both the Rosenbergs were executed by electrocution, while Greenglass served a prison sentence before being released in 1960. All this together with communist sympathiser John Strachey as Attlee's secretary of state for war made any prospect of information exchange even more unlikely as agencies on both sides of the Atlantic sought to shift blame for their shortcomings onto others. But, restricting though the McMahon Act was in appealing to an American wish to ringfence its nuclear lead, discreet contact had been maintained between the two nations and was proving mutually beneficial. Following the unexpected detonation of Joe-1, just over a month later the Chinese Communist Party (CCP) was established as the ruling authority in China under the leadership of Mao Zedong. The, perhaps tenuous, hope for a more peaceful world was quickly receding. The immediate reaction to these events was that the question of the 'Super' (the hydrogen bomb) became a topic of heated debate. There was a marked division between those who thought that morally the production of a weapon that was significantly more powerful that the Hiroshima bomb was unacceptable versus those who believed that the Soviet Union would not be bound my such lofty ideals and having mastered the atom bomb, would almost certainly pursue thermonuclear science thereby giving it a distinct military advantage. More concerning perhaps was the fact that at an *ad hoc* meeting in 1946 to discuss the theory of the Super, Fuchs had been present and had no doubt passed vital information on the subject to the Soviets. Speaking on 9 October 1948 at the Tory party conference held at Llandudno in Wales, Churchill said:

> If it were not for the stocks of atomic bombs now in the trusteeship of the United States, there would be no means of stopping the subjugation of Western Europe by Communist machinations backed by Russian armies and enforced by political police.... If the United States were to consent, in reliance upon any paper agreement, to destroy the stocks of atomic bombs which they have accumulated, they would be guilty of murdering human freedom and committing suicide themselves.[4]

Such thoughts merely confirmed that the risks of not developing the Super were just too great.

Along with the United States, Britain had been keen to acquire uranium for its atomic energy plans and wanted to 'secure all accessible supplies and deny this strategic material to others, particularly the Soviet Union'.[5] The two nations had therefore reached a tripartite agreement in 1944 with Belgium on supply—

the Belgian Congo being the major producer. This allowed the two nations first access to the Congo's uranium. During the war, Britain allowed all the uranium to go to Los Alamos to advance the Manhattan Project, but after the war, this allocation was revised on a roughly equal parts basis. With its developing atomic weapons programme, American supplies were less than was required, so in 1948 a '*modus vivendi*' agreement was reached to allow US access to British stockpiles, which were in excess of its needs, in exchange for limited atomic information. That the two nations were in such contact was of mutual benefit. Perhaps initially Britain had little knowledge it could give to America other than as an independent observer, but in any case, after the Fuchs and Pontecorvo cases, all communications essentially ceased for the next eight years. This was certainly true for military know-how, but the less sensitive civilian dimension was not so rigorously policed. From a military perspective, it can be argued that the embargo acted against American interests, as by 1954 Britain had established considerable expertise in analysing the fallout from nuclear tests: expertise which the US lacked. Security interest in Peierls, as a close friend of Fuchs and with a Russian wife, was to continue although no action was ever taken against him. After his release from a fourteen-year prison sentence for breach of the Official Secrets Acts, Fuchs went to the German Democratic Republic where he lived for the remainder of his life. He never spoke to Peierls again nor did he gain any recognition for his contribution to the Soviet bomb programme, no doubt because his new masters did not want to admit that a foreigner was the chief agent of their nuclear programme's early successes.

Churchill was returned to power in the October 1951 General Election. Writing to his close personal friend, Lord Cherwell, his paymaster general and coordinator for atomic energy, he expressed willingness to accept America as the principal arsenal of democracy, but he also stated that, 'I have never wished, since our decision during the war, that England should start the manufacture of atomic bombs. Research, however must be energetically pursued. We should have the art rather than the article.' Both men were disappointed that the McMahon Act had disallowed the exchange of nuclear information and this no doubt contributed to his decision to appoint a secret 'A Committee' to plan for Britain's first atomic test. Achieving this milestone and demonstrating British intent, Churchill hoped, would make the Americans more flexible. Chancellor of the Exchequer Rab Butler was careful not to take on the defence sector directly but warned that to be a great power needed economic strength as well as armaments and Britain was still far from being free from the edge of bankruptcy. Things came to a head at the North Atlantic Council meeting held in Lisbon in February 1952. Britain was forced to declare that it was unable to contribute its forces to the level demanded, thus placing the government, as one of the architects of the proposed NATO European force, in an awkward position. Churchill now clearly saw that it was not enough to have the art. Britain had to have the article as well. Arguably, while this approach was an easy way to balance the defence budget, it was a brave decision. There was no actual British bomb as yet, nor were the Americans likely to offer assistance. This decision also required a rethink of Britain's defence objectives, and in March, Churchill directed newly appointed Minister of Defence Earl Alexander of Tunis to initiate a study to formulate a defence policy based on nuclear weapons. This task he delegated to the three service chiefs, MRAF Sir John Slessor, Field Marshal Sir William Slim, and Admiral Sir Rhoderick McGrigor, the latter a strong believer in carrier-based offensive air power. Fortunately avoiding any internal conflicts of the type that had riven the US forces and could so easily have arisen over a restricted UK budget, the chiefs came up with a plan that balanced defence needs against harsh economic reality, although they did admit that, 'these risks are only justifiable in the face of the threat of economic disaster'.[6]

Meanwhile, Harwell had not been idle in its research, although Fuchs's position there was not filled until 1952 when the ambitious Brian Flowers was appointed. Plans for a nuclear test were well underway and in a remarkably short space of time, the art became the article and resulted in the first British nuclear test, code-named Operation Hurricane, which took place the same year on 3 October. The explosion which produced a yield of around 20 kt took place off the island of Trimoulle, part of the Monte Bello Islands off Australia's western coast. The prototype bomb was a plutonium implosion bomb of similar but improved design to the Nagasaki Mk III Fat Man device. Viscount Swinton, minister for war materials, advised the House of Lords:

> The object of the test was to investigate the effects of an atomic explosion in a harbour [because there were concerns a bomb might be brought in onboard a ship]. The weapon was accordingly placed in H.M.S. '*Plym*', a frigate of 1,450 tons, which was anchored in the Monte Bello Islands. Conditions were favourable and care was taken to wait for southerly winds, so as to avoid the possibility of any significant concentration of radioactive particles spreading over the Australian mainland. Specimen structures of importance to civil defence and to the Armed Services were erected at various distances. Instruments were set up to record the effect of contamination, blast, heat flash, gamma ray flash and other factors of interest.[7]

With this successful explosion, Britain became the third nuclear power—although without, as yet, a means of delivery. The British public were now also aware that atomic bombs were being manufactured in Britain. The rate of progress in nuclear developments was a constant cause of concern to the British programme, nonetheless, the first British atomic weapon, the 'Bomb, Aircraft, HE, 10,000lb MC', more commonly known as Blue Danube, fulfilling Air Ministry Operational Requirement OR.1001 was delivered to the Bomber Command Armaments

School (BCAS) at RAF Wittering on 7 November 1953. The ongoing irony was that the bomb had preceded its carrier aircraft, the future V-bombers, and was used initially only for training purposes.[8] The bomb had been rushed into service and many felt it was not an intrinsically safe weapon and was certainly one that required regular servicing and one that was to be subject to some 150 in-service modifications. It was very much a stopgap weapon but claiming to be a nuclear power was no good without having both the weapon and the means of delivery. Aylen describes it as 'not one weapon—more a sequence of modifications in response to a succession of problems'.[9] There were delays with the development of the first of the V-bombers, the Vickers Valiant, not helped by the crash of the first prototype on 12 January 1952 and the first one did not enter service until 138 Squadron was reformed at RAF Gaydon on 1 January 1955 with their first Valiant B.1 being flown in from Wisley on 8 February.[10] Understandably proud of their new acquisition, the squadron CO, Wg Cdr Rupert Oakley, a doyen of the handlebar moustache, gave a flying display at the RAF College Cranwell on 18 March. By the end of the year, the squadron was achieving over 200 flying hours per month.

The first live air drop test of a Blue Danube bomb, code-named Kite, was part of the Operation Buffalo series of atomic tests, which took place at the Maralinga range in southern Australia on 11 October 1956 when a Valiant B.1 (WZ366) of 'B' Flight, 49 Squadron, dropped the device from 35,000 feet. The pilot for the test was Sqn Ldr Edwin 'Ted' Flavell.[11] The resulting explosion was measured at 3 kt. This was a deliberate reduction from the planned operational 16-Kt weapon. The bomb weighed *c.* 10,000 lb and was inside an aerodynamic shell some 5 feet in diameter. This was essentially the weapon that was to enter RAF service. The explosion placed Britain in the 'Nuclear Club', but nuclear science had moved on.

On 1 November 1952, America had tested a thermonuclear bomb, code-named Mike, at Eniwetok Atoll in the Pacific as part of the 'Ivy' series of tests. On 12 August 1953, the Soviets detonated their first thermonuclear device, 'Joe-4', much to the consternation of many Americans. Whatever qualitative advantage in weaponry the US possessed had been considerably eroded.

A nuclear bomb was still a weapon of considerable size and could only be delivered by strategic bombers. Strategic Air Command's strength lay in its fleet of jet bombers, built up under the forceful leadership of Gen. LeMay. SAC's backbone in the early '50s was still the B-36, a huge and complex aircraft that had suffered a host of development problems, but it was capable of carrying a heavy bomb load to an altitude of 60,000 feet.[12] Convair had proposed a swept wing version, the YB-60 in competition to Boeing's B-52, but the latter proved faster and handled better. However, even as the formidable Boeing B-52, was still in prototype form, it was realised that the days of the manned bomber seeking to penetrate enemy airspace would eventually be numbered as enemy air defences became ever more capable.[13] Various programmes confirmed the awareness of this threat. Typical of this was the Fairchild XSM-73 Bull Goose, a delta-winged decoy missile designed to simulate a bomber to enemy radar, but in the end the project was not brought to operational status. SAC's capability and its ability to present itself as the prestige element of the American nuclear force, was enhanced when the B-52 Stratofortress first became operational on 29 June 1955 on which date B-52B (52-8711) joined the 93rd Bomb Wing at Castle AFB, California.

* * * * *

The realisation that ballistic missiles represented the future had to some been clear ever since the German V2 campaign of the latter days of the Second World War and both the US Army and the embryonic USAF started, soon after the war finished, to set up missile development programmes, but the air force, commanded by those who had served in the war, was culturally somewhat against any device that did not require a pilot to fly it and its attitude to missiles was initially cautious. Nonetheless, the decision was made to proceed with the ICBM programme that was to become the Convair Atlas. There had been various discussions about an IRBM weapon that would be easier and quicker to develop and provide stop-gap coverage although it would have to be sited in client countries within range of the Soviet targets. So as not to dilute the ICBM programme, it was hoped to persuade Britain to develop a missile of 1,500-mile range and productive meetings were held between Britain's Minister of Supply Duncan Sandys and US SecDef Charles E. Wilson in December 1953. The former, conditioned perhaps by his direct experience of the V2 bombardment on London, was to become a staunch supporter of missiles both for defence and also offence.

There were those in America who were concerned about Britain's ability to take on such a complex project, given the country's economic situation and the budget that had to be committed to its more conventional defence needs in the dying days of empire, but the talks resulted in the Wilson-Sandys agreement whereby there would be a technology transfer covering missile structure and engine technology. The McMahon Act still resolutely precluded any warhead related assistance. However, unconvinced about Britain's ability to develop a medium-range missile and in the face of an aggressive interest by the US Army in its own IRBM, the USAF decided to proceed with an air force IRBM, contracting with Douglas late in 1955 to produce the SM-75 Thor. Nonetheless, in the same year, the British Air Ministry issued a not dissimilar operational requirement, OR.1139, for a medium-range ballistic missile (MRBM) with a range of 1,500 miles extending later to 2,000 miles. This 'home grown' liquid-fuelled missile called Blue Streak would be fitted with a British warhead—still to be developed—and would provide Britain with a fully independent deterrent, something that appealed to those who feared overreliance on American bought-in systems. However, it was a missile that Zuckerman described as 'technically and operationally obsolete almost from the start'.[14] British warhead expertise may have been developing fast, but when it came to the means of delivery, America was the expert. The missile was therefore very much influenced by the transfer of American technology from their missile programmes. The requirement called for the missiles to be based in underground launchers which meant entering new, unknown areas of technology. Sandys, by now appointed minister of defence in Harold Macmillan's government, in his controversial 1957 Defence White Paper set out a future where missiles were dominant—not in fact as new an idea as many have, over the years, sought to suggest. The UK defence policy was 'the power to threaten retaliation with nuclear weapons'.[15] It also chimed with Macmillan who was averse to excessive spending on defence. The task of building the MRBM along with its rocket engine was greatly assisted by the Wilson-Sandys Agreement, but it still presented a major technical challenge.

In October 1956, Britain had been humiliated by its handling of the Suez Campaign and as a way of restoring good relations with America, newly elected Prime Minister Macmillan and President Eisenhower had reached tentative agreement early in 1957 to site US IRBMs in Britain: later identified as the Thor. Then, in October 1957, came the shock of Sputnik 1. Not for the first time, nor the last, the American population witnessed the ignominy of the communist enemy upstaging them. With this launch and its military significance still making headlines, in late October Macmillan visited Washington to discuss with Eisenhower increasing the availability of nuclear technology, materials, and weapons within the NATO arena. It was increasingly recognised that the restrictions on the sharing of nuclear knowledge between the US and the UK was leading to Britain wastefully duplicating US weapons development and testing and was preventing the efficient use of scientists, materials, and industrial resources in fulfilling the two countries' common national security objectives. Such changes would require Congress to agree amendments to the Atomic Energy Act, but in the meantime, the US would explore 'with the U.K. any steps which can be taken to improve existing cooperation (e.g., ... sale of submarine nuclear propulsion reactors if desired.)' Indeed, the US position was that if there was liberalisation of the Atomic Energy Act then 'advantage would be taken ... [by] interested and qualified NATO countries by provision of nuclear materials and technology for nuclear submarines'.[16] At the meeting of the two leaders on 24 October, things moved with much speed. Also in attendance were RADM Strauss and Quarles on the American side and Sir Edwin Plowden, chairman of the Atomic Energy Authority and Sir Richard Powell, permanent secretary at the MoD representing British interests. The latter four were tasked with coming up with a recommendation by the end of the day for future US–UK cooperation. This they did, producing the 'Strauss-Plowden Memorandum', but information on boosting, radiation implosion and fusion would not be included unless it left Britain behind known Soviet current knowledge where their recent tests seemed 'to indicate familiarity with the two-stage thermonuclear weapon and boosting'.[17] On being advised of these restrictions, Macmillan voiced understanding and acceptance.

Along with this, the Thor deployment—code-named Project Emily—was confirmed and launch sites for sixty of the missiles soon started to be built in the eastern counties of England. These missiles were operated by RAF personnel, although it was an American key that armed the warhead under 'dual-key' arrangements thus fulfilling US regulations on warhead security. Although not welcomed by many of the RAF's senior ranks who still struggled to accept anything that did not require a pilot, others saw this as a way of giving experience in handling ballistic missiles which could subsequently be of use when Blue Streak entered service in the mid-1960s. Notwithstanding this and with the passionate support and backing of Sandys and Sir Frederick Brundrett, the chief scientific adviser to the Ministry of Defence, Blue Streak struggled against unequal odds. There was ultimately no one factor that led to the missile's cancellation in April 1960, the victim of politics, an unconvinced RAF and the missile's vulnerability to collateral damage from a determined Soviet attack on the underground launchers, although to balance the argument, this could also be applied to the V-bombers and the Thor sites. Zuckerman, who succeeded Brundrett in 1960 and not unknown for his often-heterodox views on defence issues, believed that Blue Streak 'had ceased to make sense from the moment that the Government had decided that it should be buried in concrete silos'.[18] This was arguably the main reason for its cancellation: its vulnerability in the face of fast developing technology. But the positive legacy of Blue Streak was that much of the work that had been completed led the way to future British nuclear developments including the warheads for Polaris. But with the cancellation of Blue Streak, Britain took itself out of fixed-site nuclear missiles. Blue Streak enjoyed a brief and successful second life as the first stage in a European satellite launcher programme which eventually too was cancelled. The debate surrounding the missile's demise as a weapon resulted in heated exchanges in the Commons with even Black Rod forbidden entry until the speaker's fortitude brought some order back to the proceedings. Viewing the row from the Distinguished Strangers' Gallery in the Commons, Australia's Prime Minister Bob Menzies, whose country's fortunes had been linked to the missile, was somewhat bemused at the exchanges commenting later that this was a minor ripple compared with what could go on in Canberra.[19]

But while work on Blue Streak was still proceeding, and perhaps anticipating uncertainties in its development programme, the RAF had been undertaking 'prudent staff work' on another American missile, the Douglas GAM-87 Skybolt. The relationship between the two air forces had always been cordial after Project Encircle had been instituted in 1946. This was an informal agreement between US General Carl Spaatz and MRAF Lord Tedder and saw the stationing of SAC bombers on RAF bases in the UK. Skybolt was a stand-off air-launched ballistic missile (ALBM) which would offer an element of protection to the SAC bomber force. At this time the Soviet Union's western boundary was protected by the most densely packed air defence cover in the world, predominantly in Eastern Germany. The RAF saw Skybolt as an ideal way of extending the life of its V-bombers, the then bearers of Britain's nuclear deterrent and a force on which a great deal of money had been, and would be, spent. RAF officers had been in close liaison with their American counterparts since the inception of the Skybolt programme and the missile was even being configured with both air forces in mind. But the missile's accuracy depended on the ability of the launch aircraft, travelling at high subsonic speed, to determine its position in three dimensions at the time of launch. Test launches did not go well. This was, even for the Americans, challenging technology that was ultimately to seal the missile's fate. Somewhat presciently, ADM Arleigh Burke had anticipated Skybolt's problems when he wrote to Mountbatten:

> It [took] a great deal of courage for the Prime Minister to announce in Parliament the abandonment of the BLUE STREAK program in view of the amount spent on it. The rationalization is that the V-bomber program will still get a long range air-to-surface missile, but a new one called SKYBOLT. This missile is technically feasible provided enough research and development is done on it, but it is a very expensive and vulnerable system. I believe you will find it advisable to shift to Polaris in the end.[20]

Even the influential *Flight* magazine, which could have been expected to support an air-launched missile, believed:

> ... there is little doubt that, had he more money, [the Minister of Defence] would have given the Royal Navy Polaris; and, in fact, a somewhat indefinite feasibility study for Polaris has now been authorized. There are many who consider the submarine-launched ballistic missile the least vulnerable deterrent in the world.[21]

Nonetheless, Kennedy had given apparent support to the ALBM when, in March 1961, he had asked for Congress's approval to rationalise SAC's fleet by putting 50 per cent of the bombers on ground alert, speed up the phasing out of the B-47s, reducing the B-70 Valkyrie Mach 3 deep penetration nuclear bomber to an R&D effort only, and phase out the Snark and Hound Dog missiles, the latter to be replaced by Skybolt.[22] From an American standpoint, there was little opposition to Britain's involvement with the missile. By the mid-1960s, Soviet air defence capability would render the V-force obsolescent even with Skybolt and would effectively bring Britain's nuclear capability to a natural conclusion by the end of the decade. Polaris was quite a different matter and would extend the capability for some considerable time into the future. But already, by November 1960, Minister of Defence Harold Watkinson who had replaced Sandys, and was initially a staunch supporter of Skybolt, informed the Commons on 22 June 1960 after a visit to America:

Skybolt is a new and very advanced weapon system, but if our forces are to be armed with up-to-date weapons, we must decide in favour of projects that are at a relatively early stage in their development. In the case of Skybolt, my belief in this means of maintaining the deterrent is much reinforced by what I saw during my visit and by the first technical assessment of the project by British experts. Another important consideration is that fact that the techniques necessary to develop Skybolt have already been proven in the course of the development of other missiles such as Snark, Hound Dog and Bold Orion.[23]

Nonetheless, he warned Mountbatten of disquieting rumours beginning to circulate about the weapon's future. Mountbatten's view of Polaris was far from straightforward. He was largely unconvinced by the argument for, or the practicality of, an 'independent' British deterrent but seemed not averse to a British contribution to a Western deterrent force. Watkinson had joined the Royal Navy Volunteer Reserve during the war and had thereafter become a highly successful businessman. His appointment by Macmillan had been with the intention of running defence matters on a more business-like manner as well as implementing a unified system to avoid the interservice rivalry that plagued both British and American defence management. Watkinson saw value in maintaining a British-made deterrent under British control and indicated there were options in both a missile-carrying TSR2 and the Blue Steel stand-off weapon, both of which were capable of future development. While the CAS MRAF Sir Dermot Boyle was understandably in favour of a British deterrent based on the V-force, both Mountbatten, carefully maintaining a pro-naval view, and the then-CIGS Field Marshal Sir Gerald Templer had previously taken an opposing view. Templer's successor, Field Marshal Sir Francis Festing, had taken time to fully acquaint himself with his new duties and, somewhat alone, Mountbatten therefore duly advised Zuckerman, perhaps a little theatrically, that he had 'strongly advised [Watkinson] to use the same money (over £100,000,000) to buy a couple of American built Polaris submarines by 1964 when Blue Steel Mk 1 runs out.'[24] Coincidentally, First Sea Lord Adm. Sir Caspar John was at that time in Washington being updated on Polaris progress by Burke. John's underlying concern was that buying Polaris would decimate the navy estimates and would result in the end of any carrier replacement programme, and thereby, the end of the Royal Navy's capital ships.[25] Mountbatten concluded his note to Zuckerman, who strongly believed that nuclear weapons could only deter, not defend and was also abroad at the time, by adding: 'I have told Harold that he must on no account attempt to take a decision about the future British deterrent until you are back, as your advice is vital.' However, things were ever changing, and Mountbatten added a handwritten PS: 'I now hear that Ike is going ahead with Skybolt, so Harold will not be writing to you, but he said I could send this letter for you to keep in touch with Caspar.' With such rumour and uncertainty, the RAF, almost alone in their confidence in Skybolt, was, nonetheless, preparing a fallback position with the Bristol X-12 'Pandora', a ramjet-powered air-launched missile capable of Mach 3. Cdr James Kennon, Mountbatten's military assistant (MA), warned: 'It would be foolish to cast doubts on PANDORA at this stage as we have no evidence to show it won't be successful.'[26]

Despite his support for Skybolt, Watkinson had not been blind to developments in the US and had more or less accepted that at some time, Polaris was the likely replacement for Skybolt if Britain wanted to remain in the nuclear business when the V-force became obsolete, but he did not expect such events to force themselves quite so quickly on him or his successor. Watkinson's experience with Blue Streak and Skybolt was that the more independent the British deterrent, the more acceptable it would have been to the British public. Still at this stage believing in Skybolt, he saw that it would prolong the life of aircraft and when the TSR2 reached operational service the weapon it carried would be a British nuclear weapon. 'In the case of the Polaris submarine the carrier (unless of course we build it ourselves which would take a very long time,) would also be American.' Thinking at this time was that the submarines would either be purchased or leased from America as part of an all-in-one deal. However, the British Nuclear Deterrent Study Group (BNDSG), known colloquially as 'Benders', had already rejected the idea of TSR2 as a follow-on deterrent system. Mountbatten commented: 'Any weapons can be said to deter but the results of the investigation, I think, show that to consider the TSR2, even with a free falling bomb, as a nuclear deterrent, was merely playing with words.' Mountbatten still favoured Polaris as a weapon that the Royal Navy would in due course get and he prudently requested the controller of the navy, Sir Peter Reid, to produce a report which would detail what would be involved in building a fleet of Polaris submarines in Britain. Reid gave the task to Rear-Admiral Michael Le Fanu, director-general weapons at the Admiralty. Le Fanu therefore produced the blueprint that would later be adopted when Polaris became a reality. However, the report elicited little comment at the time, and as he set off in July 1960 for his next appointment as flag officer, second in command of Far East Fleet, promoted to vice-admiral, he wondered if perhaps he had got it wrong.[27] But at this stage, the Royal Navy was preoccupied with thoughts of a large aircraft carrier—looking with envy at the US Navy's supercarriers—and development of Skybolt seemed to most people, and certainly the Royal Air Force, to be on track.

The Skybolt Crisis

In January 1961, the US presidency had changed from Eisenhower to Kennedy, a generation apart in age. Atlas ICBMs were by then operational, and the next generation of Titan missiles was well advanced.[1] McNamara took an empirical approach to defence spending and Skybolt did not score well in the process—perhaps nice to have but not essential, particularly in a time of fiscal restraint. However, Britain had placed all its eggs in the Skybolt basket, and the RAF had fallen for the siren calls from its SAC colleagues and, without a fall-back option, was mortified when rumours of cancellation began to circulate. Watkinson was equally horrified by this news as the only credible alternative was Polaris which he was at that stage adamantly against.[2] Zuckerman's view on Skybolt was unequivocal:

The events which led up to the Skybolt affair were absolutely straightforward and simple. We had the V bomber force—and V bombers are flown by pilots, and pilots are good things and manned bombers are good things in this country as they are in the United States. And for some years to come people are going to the stake for manned aircraft in this country as they will in the United States.

There were also missiles. The United States had embarked upon a very ambitious missile program which was brought to a real and successful fruition. We in this country had only one big missile called Blue Streak, which was becoming very much more costly than we'd bargained for. At the same time it was perfectly apparent to everybody—well, not to everybody—that strategically it was a nonsense. So then the moment arrives through the collision of the right individuals at the right moment in time, and Blue Streak's cancelled. We don't want Blue Streak. The [RAF] then sees itself stuck. They were going to have Blue Streak as well as their V bombers. Somebody knows about Skybolt, and so Skybolt comes into the picture. And the plan then is that we have got to have Skybolt.

I had a lot to do with this. But almost immediately I started inquiring into Skybolt. I knew that Skybolt was as much a nonsense as the manned bomber in a missile age.... I wasn't getting my information from somebody in Douglas who wanted to sell Skybolt, nor was I getting my information from some Air Force general who wanted Skybolt because he could fly Skybolt off a B-52. I was getting the real information from men whose opinion I trusted and who trusted my view.[3]

The disquieting rumours about Skybolt persisted. Further complicating matters, Watkinson was replaced by Peter Thorneycroft in July 1962 in Macmillan's 'Night of the Long Knives' cabinet reshuffle.[4] Macmillan was increasingly apprehensive about his party's chances in the forthcoming general election, having suffered badly in recent by-elections, and he had decided that the principles of business that Watkinson had attempted to apply to the 'emotional, and often tortuous, handling of political affairs' were not going to work for the political establishment.[5] Watkinson himself had arguably been unwise in earlier confiding in a weary prime minister about his fears of losing his Cabinet position in the event of the Conservatives losing the election. He was to discover that the politics of political appointments was even more aggressive than the politics of the boardroom.

The axe summarily fell on Skybolt in December 1962. America had, understandably, been distracted by the Cuban Missile Crisis and had failed to fully understand or concentrate on the British position of absolute dependence on Skybolt. While en route to a NATO summit meeting in Paris, McNamara stopped off in London to meet with Thorneycroft. Going against instructions, he delivered a press statement on his arrival at Gatwick airport fuelling an already simmering media. Threats of perfidy added to an already charged atmosphere. Was America seeking to emasculate Britain's nuclear deterrent? As McNamara departed for Paris, arrangements were already in hand for a fortuitously already arranged meeting between Kennedy and Macmillan—'Jack and Mac'—later in the month in Nassau. At the presidential press briefing on 12 December, Kennedy had been questioned on Britain's role should Skybolt be cancelled. He was positive in response saying that 'the British have a very important equity in the matter', adding that 'that is why McNamara went to Britain. I am sure it is a matter that will be discussed with the Prime Minister in Nassau.'[6]

The meeting duly took place in the balmy atmosphere of the Bahamas. The original agenda to discuss world affairs in general was scrapped to allow the Skybolt Crisis to take centre stage. Despite the outward show of friendship, the atmosphere between the two nations was, from the start, tense. The two leaders had carefully picked those who were to accompany them. Kennedy had requested that the meeting took place without interference from military representatives. John Rubel, deputy to Harold Brown, US director of Defense Research Engineering in the Department of Defense, advised the president. Rubel was called in at the last minute as someone who knew the historical background to the Skybolt programme as he had been associated with the project from the start and therefore knew what ongoing understanding there had been between the two countries. An indignant RAF had not been invited although naval interests were represented by Adm. Le Fanu, now promoted to controller of the navy. He had been given less than a day's notice to accompany the British delegation.[7] His naval responsibility extended to ships and equipment and was included as an advisor, although he was later to report that there was little discussion on the technicalities of the weapons under review and no equivalent USN representative with whom he could exchange notes.[8] Also present was Zuckerman who commented:

I had a second source of information in Jerry Wiesner, the President's science adviser, and he, like my Pentagon friends was sure that Skybolt would never materialise. The project was not only highly doubtful technologically but strategically redundant in the light of the rest of the US's vast nuclear weapons programme.[9]

Zuckerman was well known to the president and had previously been involved in joint discussions with Wiesner on the nuclear test ban treaty. He described Kennedy as 'one of the friendliest people I've ever met—one of the easiest to meet':

The other characteristic I carried straight away—if one may elaborate what one means by friendly and what one means by welcoming and all that; different people have different words for this—the other thing which was very, very clear about him was his directness. He was very forthright. He was always trying to get straightaway to what to him was the kernel of any problem, the main issue. And he didn't appear to be pulling any punches in the questions he put to you or in the comments he made.[10]

Nonetheless, Zuckerman ensured that the prime minister remained on an even keel in the discussions. The RAF, apparently completely blind to the warning signs about Skybolt coming from Washington, became convinced that Zuckerman had plotted with Mountbatten from the start to enable the Royal Navy to take over the deterrent role. An unimpressed former CAS, MRAF Sir John Slessor, wrote: 'It is a really appalling thought that a couple of Ministers and a zoologist can slip off to the Bahamas and, without a single member of the Chiefs of Staff Committee present, commit us to a military monstrosity [Polaris] on the purely political issue of independence which anyway is a myth.'[11] The RAF, reckoning that they had been side-lined and outmanoeuvred by CDS had to go and lick their wounds.

Macmillan reminded Kennedy that the atomic bomb had been developed almost entirely in the beginning by British scientists and Churchill and Roosevelt had agreed that development should be carried out in the relative security of the US. The prime minister's erudition eloquently explained to Kennedy the tenuous position his government would be placed in as a result of Skybolt's cancellation, a situation which he believed could lead to the government's fall. He was also well aware that many within Kennedy's administration wanted to curtail the possession of nuclear weapons outside the two superpowers. But the wily politician with very many years of experience of diplomatic negotiations—perhaps more so that anyone else there—knew there was a way to resolve the issue: let Britain purchase Polaris, a decision that Harold Brown described being used as a palliative.[12] The ground had already been well prepared by 'building on the goodwill carefully nurtured by Lord Mountbatten among American submariners'.[13]

Of course, Polaris had for some time been in the background and the Royal Navy likewise maintained its representative in the US Navy SP through whom 'prudent staff work' had been undertaken. McNamara was unsupportive of the idea of giving the missile to Britain. George W. Ball, Kennedy's under-secretary of state, in particular wanted to rein in the nuclear aspirations of countries other than the two superpowers, but neither did either side want to unduly antagonise the other European NATO allies. Ball strongly believed in the unity of all European nations and Britain's stance was at odds with this belief and not in America's interest. The president, however, appreciated the parlous situation in which America's friend and ally now found itself. It threatened the special relationship when only a few weeks before, the world had seen how easy it might have been to slip into actual nuclear conflict and Kennedy had sought and received British support throughout. 'Would a switch of horses from Skybolt to Polaris upset the principal allies?' Macmillan thought not. 'If it did, we could make some gesture' the prime minister suggested. 'All these things we were discussing were gestures. in a sense, since the only reality was U.S. power.' Kennedy was sensitive to French reaction to any agreement on Polaris; however, Lord Home did not share this anxiety as France under Charles de Gaulle was going ahead with its deterrent programme regardless. If there were to be a rift, it would be far less damaging to NATO than a rift between the United States and Britain:[14]

> After careful review, the President and the Prime Minister agreed that a decision on POLARIS must be considered in the widest context both of the future defense of the Atlantic Alliance and of the safety of the whole Free world. They reached the decision that this issue created an opportunity for the development of new and closer arrangements for the organization and control of strategic western defense and that such arrangements in turn could make a major contribution to political cohesion among the nations of the Alliance.[15]

Kennedy saw the provision of Polaris as the way to creating a multi-national NATO nuclear force in the closest consultation with the other NATO allies including the French and using their 'best endeavours'—from Macmillan's point of view a usefully vague promise. Indeed, the memorandum of the initial discussion between Eisenhower and Macmillan on the acquisition of Skybolt had noted:

> As the U.K. is aware, the United States is offering at the current NATO Defense Ministers meeting to make mobile Polaris missiles—minus warheads—

Operation Sandy, V2
launch, USS *Midway*,
6 September 1947.

Regulus II aboard the
USS *Grayback*.

Admiral Hyman G. Rickover.

Above left: Polaris FTV-1.

Above right: Polaris A-1 on test stand LC29.

Above left: Polaris A-2 STAFF, 14 April 1965.

Above right: Polaris inside its container being lowered into the launch tube on the USS *Observation Island*.

Left: Polaris launch from the
USS *Observation Island*.

Below left: Project Hydra,
Point Mugu, May 1960.

Below right: Polaris AX-20,
2 October 1959.

Launch of the USS *George Washington*, 9 June 1959.

USS *Robert E. Lee en route* to the fitting out dock.

USS *George Washington* at sea.

FLOTUS Jacqueline Kennedy launches the USS *Lafayette*, 8 May 1962. Looking on are Roger Lewis, chairman and president of General Dynamics, and naval aide to the president, Capt. Tazewell Shepard.

Polaris A-3 on its transport trailer.

USS *Stonewall Jackson* under construction at Mare Island Naval Shipyard.

'The Famous Five': VADM Galantin, ADM Burke, VADM Schade, VADM Raborn, and RADM Smith at the commissioning of the USS *Will Rogers*. (*General Dynamics*)

Tri-Service meeting: Dr Kurt Debus, Maj.-Gen. Samuel Phillips (USAF) seconded to NASA as director of the Apollo Program, Dr Wernher von Braun, and CDR John Wise (port crew), USS *Von Steuben*.

View from the USS *Proteus* as the USS *Patrick Henry* arrives in the Holy Loch, 8 March 1961. At the top right is her escort frigate HMS *Exmouth*.

USS *Proteus* with the USS *Hunley* behind, Holy Loch, January 1964.

USS *Los Alamos* floating drydock next to the USS *Simon Lake*, Holy Loch. (*US Navy Submarine Force Museum*)

CND protest march through Glasgow.

Above: USNS *Marshfield.*
Fleet Ballistic Missile
Cargo Ship.

Right: Missile loading on
the USS *Abraham Lincoln.*

A-3 launch.

President Eisenhower watches a water sabot launch from the USS *George Washington*.

Right: 'Frigate Bird' nuclear mushroom cloud, photographed by the USS *Carbonero*.

Below: USS *Theodore Roosevelt* transits the Panama Canal's Pedro Miguel Locks *en route* to its Pacific base at Guam, 25 October 1962.

Above left: Poseidon C-3,
19 February 1969.

Above right: First Poseidon
launch from the USS *Observation
Island*, 18 December 1969.

Left: Poseidon launch at sea. Note
the telemetry mast on the left.

Above: Viewed from the USS *Observation Island*, the radar picket escort ship USS *Calcaterra* (DER-390) and the Soviet AGI ship *Khariton Laptev* (right) await the launch of a Poseidon C3P-1 missile from the USS *James Madison*. The Russian ship caused the subsequent postponement of the launch.

Right: Returning to the Holy Loch.

Left: Dr Charles Draper dons protective footwear after being 'fired' from the Instrumentation Lab as a result of anti-war protests fuelled by the war in Vietnam.

Below: HMS *Excalibur*.

'You really need Polaris.' Rear Admiral Ignatius J. Galantin, Sir Solly Zuckerman, and Vice Admiral Sir Varyl Begg.

Lord and Lady Mountbatten meeting Admiral Burke, 27 October 1955.

Left: Dr Kirchner (Bureau of Naval Weapons), RADM Smith, and VAdm. Mackenzie in lighter mood.

Below: Herschel J. Brown (Lockheed), Sir Harold Watkinson, Admiral Burke, and Sir Solly Zuckerman.

Keel laying of the *Resolution. From left to right*: RAdm. Sir Horace Law, Sir Alfred Sims, Leonard Redshaw, VAdm. Sir Hugh Mackenzie, and Rowland Baker.

The launch of the *Resolution*, 15 September 1966.

'I name this ship *Resolution*.' HRH The Queen Mother, 15 September 1966.

The launch of the *Repulse* did not all go to plan, 4 November 1967.

Right: HMS *Repulse* leaves Barrow-in-Furness after her commissioning service, 28 September 1968.

Below: HMS *Repulse* at sea.

VAdm. Mackenzie with Defence Secretary Roy Mason. The *Renown* is under construction in the background, January 1967.

Lord Mountbatten retires, handing over to Field Marshal Sir Richard Hull.

All but one of HMS *Renown*'s launch tube hatches are open.

Polaris control panel.

Polaris systems console on a Royal Navy SSBN (note cigarette!).

HMS *Repulse* returns to Faslane flying her decommissioning pennant.

HMS *Repulse* arrives at Rosyth for her refit, 15 September 1984.

HMS *Renown* in Rosyth refitting dock.

HMS *Repulse* recommissioning ceremony, Rosyth.

HMS *Repulse*, DSRV trials.

Right: Polaris A3RTKE Chevaline P-Body eject test, launched from HMS *Revenge*, 1 August 1986. (*US National Archives*)

Below: RFA *Fort Langley* missile supply ship.

Above: AFDO Faslane's 600th docking, HMS *Repulse*. (*Photographic Section HMS Neptune*)

Left: TCPU on the test rig at Westcott 'E' Site. (*E. Andrews*)

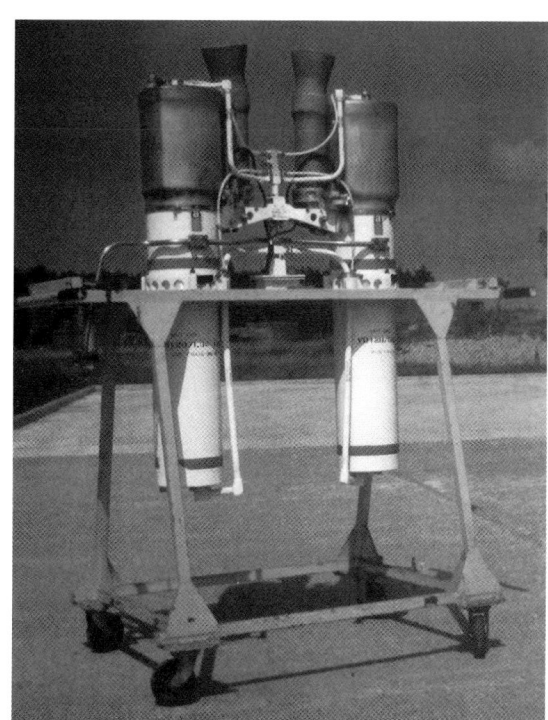

Right: TCPU. (*Via John Harlow*)

Below: Chevaline warhead at JSCSC Shrivenham. (*Sgt P. Marr*)

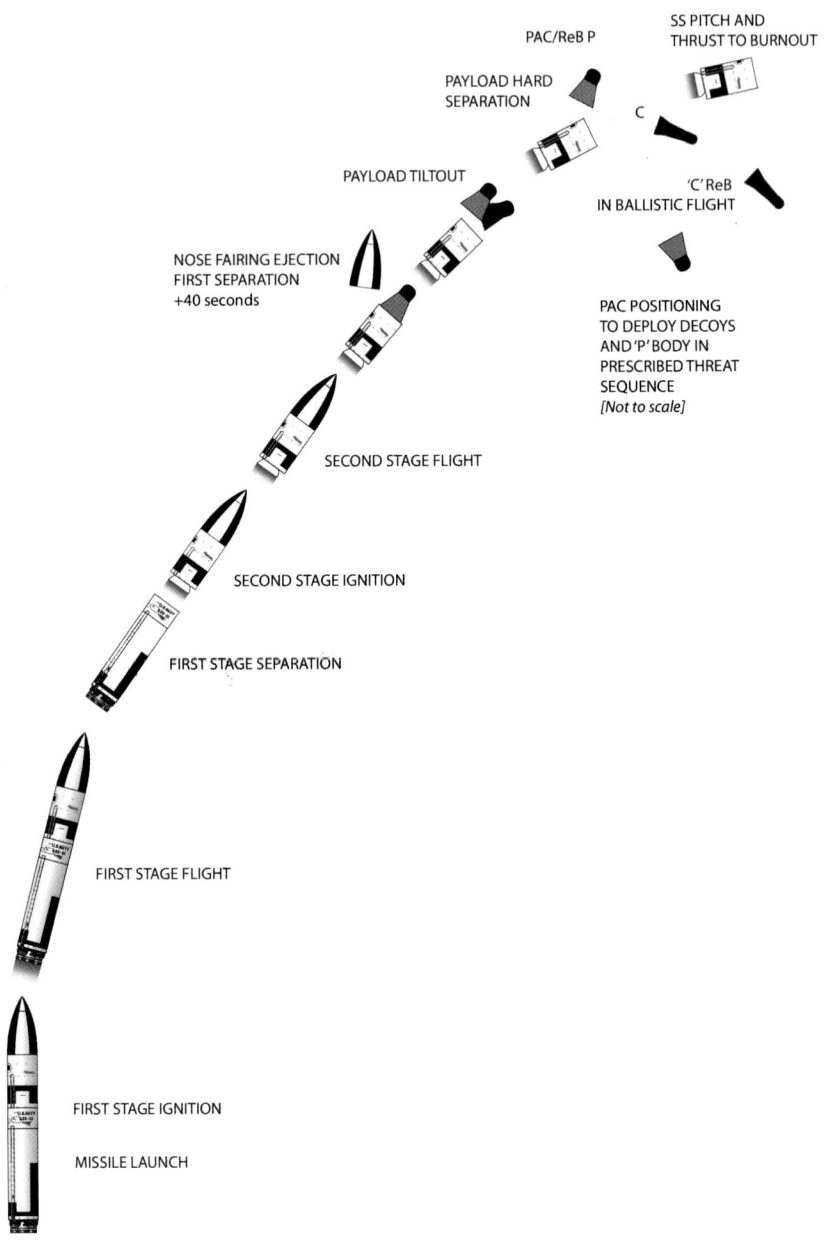

SS PITCH AND
THRUST TO BURNOUT

PAC/ReB P

PAYLOAD HARD
SEPARATION

C

PAYLOAD TILTOUT

'C' ReB
IN BALLISTIC FLIGHT

NOSE FAIRING EJECTION
FIRST SEPARATION
+40 seconds

PAC POSITIONING
TO DEPLOY DECOYS
AND 'P' BODY IN
PRESCRIBED THREAT
SEQUENCE
[Not to scale]

SECOND STAGE FLIGHT

SECOND STAGE IGNITION

FIRST STAGE SEPARATION

FIRST STAGE FLIGHT

FIRST STAGE IGNITION

MISSILE LAUNCH

Polaris A3TK/Chevaline launch to separation sequence.

HMS *Resolution* being nudged into place at Faslane. (*Crown Copyright, 1996*)

Watchful eyes are kept on Prime Minister John Major on the day of HMS *Repulse*'s final decommissioning, 28 August 1996. (*Crown Copyright, 1996*)

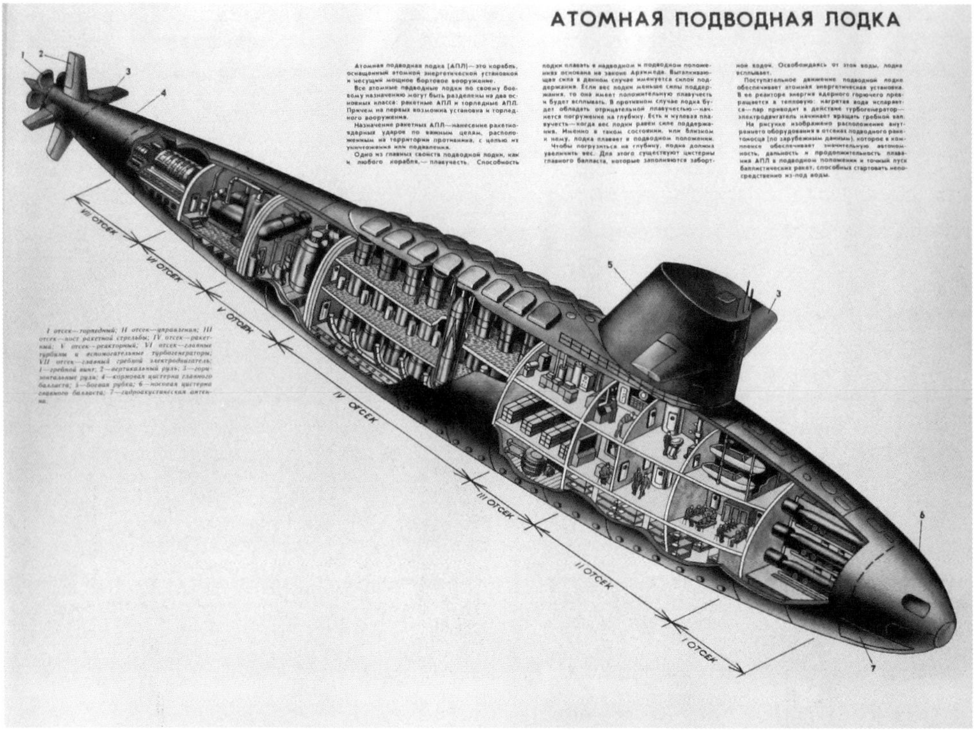

АТОМНАЯ ПОДВОДНАЯ ЛОДКА

How Soviet intelligence interpreted the Polaris SSBN.

HMS *Revenge* in dry dock at Rosyth after her final decommissioning. (*BFBS/Forces News*)

available from U.S. production to NATO countries in order to meet SACEUR's requirement for MRBMs. The U.S. is also offering to assist in joint European production of Polaris if our preference for U.S. production proves unacceptable. It does not appear appropriate to consider a bilateral understanding on Polaris until the problem of SACEUR's MRBM requirements has been satisfactorily disposed of in NATO.[16]

As so often happened in such discussions, each side interpreted what had been understood somewhat differently when it came to enacting the agreement. Thorneycroft, there as adviser to Macmillan, commented on Kennedy's technique:

I think the main thing that struck me about Nassau, leaving aside the Skybolt issue and concentrating in the mass on the President himself, the real thing that struck me was this technique of his, and the relationship between these two men and countries. Whether you could call it a special relationship or not I don't know but what his technique was—which was unique really was to ask the English some damned awful questions and make them answer it in front of the Americans and then turn to the Americans and cross-examine them up hill and down dale and make them answer in front of the English. This was a method which I had never seen adopted between two foreign countries in my life and it was the most refreshing thing I have ever seen.[17]

With no service representatives present in the talks, the agreement has to be seen primarily as a political settlement rather than a military one and the task of drafting the necessary documents was given to Macmillan's private secretary Philip de Zulueta and Kennedy's National Security Advisor McGeorge Bundy, but Zuckerman and Sir Robert Scott, the new permanent secretary at the MoD, explored the various drafts for any ambiguities. The two men composed a memo outlining certain concerns before the final session took place and addressed it to Thorneycroft. On their arrival back in the UK, a small group of MPs including Julian Amery, minister of state (Ministry of Aviation), was on the tarmac to welcome the prime minister's party. Noting Zuckerman's addition of 'on a continuing basis', Amery said to him: 'One day you will be proud of that minute: not that it made any difference.'[18] Zuckerman's prescient and careful wording was in future years to open the door to replacing the UK Polaris with Trident.

Macmillan by semantic sleight of hand and playing on Kennedy's respect for the older man had returned home with a deal second to none. He had obtained his 'great prize' and had sidestepped the potential ignominy of losing both Skybolt and his own premiership which, he believed, would surely have otherwise followed. He had allowed Kennedy's Multilateral Force proposal to be recognised and he had reinforced the special relationship and retained an independent deterrent—depending on how optimistically the degree of 'independence' was interpreted. The airborne missile, like the RAF's sixty Thors, had been a symbol of British influence on the world stage rather than a military necessity.[19] Polaris now took things to the next higher level of such influence. Chapman Pincher commented, 'no sensible punter would have backed the Navy to win the battle against the RAF but it had a powerful ally in the form of the "Zuckbatten axis".'[20] Despite his excellent contacts, Pincher had perhaps failed to see the gentle and discrete pressure that had been applied by the Royal Navy over the preceding years. Some less blinkered senior RAF officers had already seen the inevitability of where the future lay:

> One of the lessons we should have learned from the operations of V1 and V2 in 1943–44 was that the weapon fired from a fixed emplacement—the V1—could in the end be dealt with. The V2, that could be discharged from any hardstanding—a road, from the bottom of a quarry, almost from a concrete carwash—could be neutralised only by the occupation of territory or the destruction of its sources of supply—both long-drawn-out operations. In my view the only effective method of employing missiles is to place them on a mobile base—an aircraft, a war vessel or, perhaps best of all, in a submarine.[21]

In the subsequent Commons debate on defence, 330 members voted in support of the agreement with 236 voting against. It had been a heated debate, but it was confirmed that the UK would pay no development costs for either the A-1 or A-2, but a 5 per cent surcharge should the A-3 be selected, and this would be a contribution towards R&D costs. It was further confirmed that Bomber Command's V-force, on which some £2.8 billion had been spent since 1948, would remain under RAF command but would be integrated into NATO control subject to suitable agreements being reached with the allies, but would revert to UK control under extreme circumstances.[22]

However, as the V-bombers aged, credibility of the V-force was bound to come under increasing scrutiny as the decade progressed. In a pre-emptive attack, the bombers could arguably even be destroyed on their bases or dispersal sites. During the Westminster debate on the fiftieth anniversary of the Continuous At-Sea Deterrent, MP Anne-Marie Trevelyan reprised (and slightly misattributed to Arleigh Burke) a cartoon that had been sent to Mountbatten with the caption 'Move deterrents out to sea where the real estate is free and where they are far away from me.'[23] Therein lay the argument for a strong case to be presented for Polaris. The reality was that the Royal Navy had effectively won their fifty-year battle against the RAF. The cancellation of Skybolt sounded the death knell of the manned bomber as an effective deterrent, both for the RAF and for SAC. America and the Soviet Union now both had an arsenal of ICBMs. SAC was phasing out the B-47 with the B-52 as its primary weapon, but in the event of war, its mission would be preceded by missiles designed to soften up the air defence sites. When Article 360 reconnaissance flight by Gary 'Frank' Power's U-2C (56-6693) was shot down near Sverdlovsk by an SA-2 SAM on 1 May 1960, it was a timely and unexpected warning sign of Soviet air defence capability and a seminal event in Cold War history as well as causing the midnight oil to be burned in the MoD as there was secret RAF involvement in the U-2 surveillance flights. With no equivalent softening-up capability, this was a stark demonstration of the vulnerability of the V-force, but from the mid-1960s when the V-force role became essentially untenable until Polaris became operational, there would be a gap in Britain's defence. In response to this vulnerability, in 1964 the V-force, designed from the start for high-altitude operations, changed to low-level under-the-radar flights. Denis Healey was in combative mood during the Commons debate on that year's defence budget:

> We all know that the V-bombers are unlikely to be able to penetrate Soviet territory even now with free-falling bombs.... The sort of poetry which we got in 'Golden Eagles which can skim the ground' at the Bomber Command briefing is no substitute for power or performance and many people feel rather unhappy about the possible life of the V-bombers if they are going to be used at low-level. [24]

Not being designed for low-level operations, the Valiants were the first to suffer when serious main spar fatigue problems saw them phased out by the end of 1964. Victors too were found to be unsuitable at low-level and were phased out in 1968 but found a new role as aerial tankers and reconnaissance aircraft, a task in which they excelled during the Falklands conflict. The Vulcans maintained the deterrent role armed with the complex liquid-fuelled Blue Steel stand-off bomb, but the missile, designed to be launched from high altitude, found being re-roled for low-level operations severely compromised its range. Even then both SAC and the RAF faced the 'densest and most intricate anti-aircraft defence system in the world'.[25] The management of Soviet air defence had grown in the 1950s under the authority of the Troops for National Defence (PVO). Relying on interceptors and SAMs, they had created a formidable defensive shield covering most of the USSR land mass. By the early 1960s, this proved to be an ever-increasing threat to NATO strategic bombers at a time of increasing tensions between the superpowers. By this time, too, the Soviets were aware that ballistic missiles would also need to be targeted.

The Soviet Air Defence Forces (V-PVO), under the command of Marshal of the Soviet Union Vladimir Sudets, numbered some 250,000 personnel. That was not to say that the bomber was outdated in conventional warfare terms as was later to be evidenced by the Black Buck operations against Port Stanley airfield during the Falklands campaign.

France's General de Gaulle did baulk at the Nassau outcome, which was in part at least to lead to his later veto of Britain's entry into the European Economic Community (EEC). The Conservative government's defence strategy had now been dismantled, first by the cancellation of Blue Streak and then

Skybolt. Macmillan remained convinced that Britain's influence in world affairs could only come with the possession of an independent deterrent. Polaris now gave them that continued assurance as the RAF's V-force, 'for what that was worth', became increasingly vulnerable.[26] With the 1957 Defence White Paper, Duncan Sandys had placed Britain's future in nuclear hands with an independent deterrent as the cornerstone. As was becoming ever more obvious, there was now little 'independence' in Britain's deterrent. The unliked confidant of Harold Wilson, Lord George Wigg, who was the Labour paymaster-general in Wilson's government, later commented that the idea was based on a deterrent 'we did not possess, do not possess now and, I forecast, will not possess in the foreseeable future.'[27] The question of a NATO multinational force was a different matter and one that raised little enthusiasm from Britain, but Kennedy saw it as solving various problems within the NATO allies to such an extent that it was beginning to shape his government's thinking. What the Americans had envisaged was:

A US national component comprising Atlantic-based Polaris submarines.

A UK national component consisting of the RAF's V-force and in due time Royal Navy Polaris submarines.

The NATO Multilateral Force. This was envisaged as a force of around twenty-five warships manned by crews from NATO countries. Kennedy hoped this would encourage the non-nuclear members of NATO to take a greater part in nuclear planning and operations.

Secretary of State Dean Rusk had already confirmed at the North Atlantic Council Meeting in May 1962 that 'We are already deploying POLARIS submarines in European Waters, and are planning to add more to this deployment. We will commit POLARIS to NATO, so that the most modern and invulnerable strategic weapons systems can be formally added to the arsenal of the Alliance.'[28]

Foreign Secretary Lord Home and Lord Privy Seal Edward Heath indicated that the government would attempt to assist the Americans form the force in the manner that was planned, but the sticking point could well be the position that the West Germans were reportedly seeking to take whereby the force would have an independent nuclear capability. This question had already been raised some years previously when the siting of US IRBMs was being considered and it was clear then that the Soviets would have reacted badly, seeing this as destabilising. Home believed that the Germans did not have nuclear aspirations but knowing that if they forced the issue, they could well threaten the break-up of NATO and find their only ally in the French. The stage was now set for the Royal Navy to take on the mantle of Britain's nuclear deterrent.

13

The Polaris Sales Agreement

The U.S. will make available on a continuing basis Polaris missiles (less warheads) for British submarines. The U.S. will also study the feasibility of making available certain support facilities for such submarines. The U.K. Government will construct the submarines in which these weapons will be placed and they will also provide the nuclear warheads for the Polaris missiles.[1]

It was one thing to issue what was in effect a statement of intent. A formal agreement had then to be drawn up followed by the challenging task of building the submarines. With British representation in SP, much intellectual work had been done, but little practical work to prepare for the task now in hand. During the intervening time span, the RAF would continue to provide the strategic deterrent albeit that this was in the form of the complex, unreliable liquid-fuelled Blue Steel stand-off weapon and its ability to reach targets in the Soviet Union would progressively diminish. Britain's now fragmented missile program was to be labelled 'another defence miscalculation' when the new atomic 'wonder bomb' for the RAF's forthcoming TSR2 was publicly denounced by ACM Sir Philip Joubert de la Ferté, a former air officer commanding-in-chief Coastal Command, saying it was 'a complete fraud on the British public'.[2]

The agreement inevitably featured in a lengthy six-hour debate on defence which Macmillan presented to parliament on 30 January 1963 which sought to approve the agreement reached in the Bahamas. He gave some justification for confidence in Skybolt saying that 'the whole American bomber force was looking to the Skybolt missile with considerable impatience to give the United States Air Force a new life and strength, as one of the main props of the American defensive system.' Having accepted the demise of Skybolt and having rejected the American offer of the Hound Dog, 'It was a good weapon but, unfortunately, technical reasons connected with the construction of this cruise-type missile—it was not a ballistic missile—and with the construction of our own bombers made this impracticable.' Macmillan concluded:

The only alternative, therefore, was the Polaris complex—the submarine, of course, to be of British manufacture, the warhead to be British-made, and the rocket and its accompaniments to be sold to us by the Americans, like Skybolt. Under our agreement we shall be able to obtain the latest model of Polaris available at the time. This arrangement is made practicable because any new mark of Polaris will have to be designed to fit into the existing submarines, in which so great an investment has been made by the Americans.[3]

Shadow Home Secretary George Brown was tasked with responding for the opposition—although Sir Arthur Harvey noted '[He] made a very fine speech, [he]did not, however, speak with his usual conviction on this subject. I do not think his heart was in it.' Brown said:

Nothing ever does 'all go well' [quoting an expression Macmillan had used] in this highly complicated era of rocketry, guidance systems, computers and the rest. The A.3—the bird, exists. It is not a question of minor changes. The projected A.3 Polaris is, in the words of its manufacturers—who must be presumed to know—80 per cent, a new bird. Heaven knows what will be involved before it ever arrives, whether it will ever arrive or what it will have cost by the time it does arrive. It is as speculative at this stage and as uncertain as Skybolt ever was, and the Government are repeating exactly the same blindness over this as they did over Skybolt.... I thought that the Prime Minister seemed to accept, by implication, that we shall not have any submarines to put even the existing ones in before they are out of date. I recall that the other day an hon. Member opposite suggested that we could get over the difficulty by renting a submarine. You can rent a telly, you can rent a car; but, good God, you cannot rent a nuclear independent deterrent.[4]

Nonetheless, following Macmillan's return from Nassau, things had gathered pace despite the Christmas and New Year holiday periods, and by the time this debate took place, the project was well under way. The task was daunting. The Royal Navy representative within SP who regularly reported back on US progress had kept the navy well informed, but little specific planning had been put in place in anticipation of any deal actually being struck. Now, without Skybolt, the credibility of Britain's strategic deterrent would increasingly come under pressure as the decade continued. The RAF were left bewildered and angry at what it saw as its summary execution without a fair trial. Considerable funds had been invested in the V-force, which to many people was the RAF, and there were many residual resentments on both sides of the Atlantic about the nature of the deal and the way in which it had been concluded. In addition, AWRE would have to design the warheads for the missile as this was not part of the agreement. There was some concern that Calder Hall nuclear power station would not be able to supply sufficient fissile material until the end of the decade. Despite this doubt, it did not take long for the government to declare that it wanted the Polaris force 'to deploy on station the first RN Ballistic Missile Submarine with its missiles and with full support, in July 1968 and thereafter the remainder at six monthly intervals. These dates cannot be allowed to slip.' Fortunately, there was a good knowledge of how the Americans were managing their Polaris operations and there was of course already a model organisation that Britain could follow, namely the US Navy's SP. However, British and American working methods were different, so it was not simply a matter of creating a carbon copy.

Such was the urgent momentum of the project that, by the close of 1962, the organisation to manage the project, the Polaris Executive (PE), had been promulgated and the position of Chief Polaris Executive (CPE) had been filled by Rear-Admiral Hugh 'Red' Mackenzie—a highly experienced and successful submarine commander.[5] He had been appointed to the post after a somewhat brief tenure as FOSM and was now to benefit from a visit made to Washington the previous year during which he had received a comprehensive briefing from RADM Galantin on the operation of the SP. He appointed Captain Rae McKaig as his deputy, with Captain Charles Shepherd as his weapons director.[6] Office space was allocated in the Old Admiralty Building with little more than a couple of desks and chairs. The Americans meanwhile would set up a Special Projects Liaison Office to work with the Royal Navy, sending their representative, CAPT. Phill Rollings, to London. There was still a degree of suspicion about the project. The RAF were understandably still smarting from the cancellation of Skybolt and the knock-on problems that this created and even within the navy's ranks there were still those preoccupied with thoughts of aircraft carriers and the possible implications on their budget of this new intruder. There was no indication that a separate budget would be created to cover the costs which at that stage were estimated to be around £500 million for the first ten years. Within the British population, CND was attracting much support and many of those who did not actively support the movement were concerned that in contracting for Polaris, Britain had prejudiced the independence of its deterrent, and if it was to purchase a weapon system from abroad, then it should at least be a proven system, a stage which the A-3 had yet to reach: an argument in which the even less proven Skybolt seemed to be conveniently forgotten. Even within America, there was far from universal support for this joint venture—despite the 'special relationship'.

The sudden change in events initially left the Royal Navy a little bewildered as well. Their naval architects had to design a totally new type of submarine and have it operational by 1968. Events were to move rapidly. In December 1962, R. J. 'Jack' Daniel was looking forward to taking up the prestigious position of professor of naval architecture at the Royal Naval College at Greenwich. It was not, however, to be. Instead, he received the Christmas present of a request to form a new group to take on the design of the Royal Navy's Polaris submarine and look after the construction, using the DPT name again but this time standing for Director Polaris Technical.[7] In January 1963, a number of people flew to Washington, DC, forming a delegation headed by VCNS Vice-Admiral Sir Varyl Begg to start the process of integration between the two nations. Daniel led the Deep Technical Mission. The start of the visit was somewhat inauspicious when it was found that the chosen accommodation was also being used by the outgoing Skybolt team. Daniel's team needed definitive information on the systems required for them to start the design process. Much of the initial time was spent at SP where they met Galantin and Smith. Daniel commented: 'it came as a cultural shock to find the submarine was regarded as a sub-system but I soon got used to it'. Of Smith, who was to become a close friend, he said:

> [The] first visit to Levering was, well, unusual. Our staff officer in Washington, had warned me in advance 'Ask your question and wait, don't repeat it, just wait'. But it was still a little unnerving to sit opposite a man and ask a question and wait 30 seconds, 60 seconds and sometimes more with his bright blue eyes fixed on one but doubtless far away, until he spoke and then out would come the complete answer arranged chronologically with all the facts that also answered the three or so follow up questions that one had in mind.[8]

Ward had similar advice:

> Levering would listen. You could see the wheels in his head turning over as he was listening and he would say, 'Well, I don't know. I'm not sure that is correct. I think that …' And then in his very quiet voice he would say, 'I think you should look at it this way or do something this way.' He was the technical brains behind Polaris.[9]

Thereafter, Daniel's team visited EB at Groton and then headed by train to Boston and were then driven further north to the Portsmouth Naval Yard. Here the basin was covered in ice, but a visit was arranged to the USS *John Adams* (SSBN-620).[10] Daniel also met some of the crew of the ill-fated *Thresher* which was in refit. Armed with a wealth of technical detail and much to think about the team returned to the UK:

> We started the design in March and released the structural drawings to Vickers in April–May to enable them to order the steel. Deliveries commenced in September and fabrication began. The Resolution Class design was approved by the Board of the Admiralty in December; a quite remarkable achievement.[11]

Daniel had returned from America convinced that the A-3 version of the missile was the one for Britain. His views were by no means unanimously held as many senior officials wanted the proven A-2 missile. Certainly, the A-1 version was not in contention as the US Navy was in the process of converting their fleet to the upgraded A-2. However, the A-3 which promised much greater operational capability was in the pipeline, but unproven. On 4 March 1964, Lord Carrington was pressing for a decision on the matter which would have a knock-on effect on the design of the warhead and the re-entry body (ReB) as well as the submarine itself on which the Royal Corps of Naval Constructors (RCNC) had already started work. Galantin had also indicated that a decision would be 'helpful' before the forthcoming visit by a joint Admiralty, Ministry of Aviation, and AWRE visit to Washington. Carrington had clearly made up his mind in favour of the A-3. A much wider and consequently safer patrol area would be available. The A-2 necessarily restricted operations to the north-east Atlantic and close to the Soviet submarine bases in areas not covered by naval anti-submarine assets. The Mediterranean was also a consideration as an operational area, but time would be lost in transit to and from the patrol area. The A-3 promised greater accuracy and could carry penetration aids (penaids) which would give some assurance against a Soviet ABM breakthrough. The A-2 production would cease in 1964 and Carrington noted, still no doubt smarting from the Skybolt crisis, that '[previous] experience in using U.S. weapon systems which the U.S. forces have abandoned has been far from happy'. Still, however, remembering Skybolt and the potential problems of choosing a weapon still under development, he fended off possible detractors of the A-3 in his belief that it was not a fair comparison. Unlike Skybolt, many of the A-3 subsystems had already been proved satisfactory using A2X missiles, and although the complete missile was still to be tested, the American incentive to complete the A-3 was considerably greater than it had been for the air-launched missile. In sending a copy of his minute to Minister of Aviation Julian Amery, Carrington concluded: 'I strongly recommend an immediate decision in favour of the A-3.'[12]

In assessing the choice of version for the Royal Navy, it had been noted that 'the major area of difficulty with the A3 is the reliability of its motors'.[13] The empty weight of the missile was very low, and needed to be if the required range was to be achieved. This placed safety restrictions in regards to strength and heat insulation. Unfortunately, this had caused limitations on the flight test programme and it had not been possible to investigate the flight performance of the A-3 on aerodynamic heating on exiting the atmosphere or the performance of the warhead and RV. While the navy had every confidence that the problems could be resolved, the fallback position would be to reopen production of the A-2 or re-motor the first A-3s with 'cooler' A-2 motors accepting that this would reduce the range to around 1,900 NM. Nonetheless, culturally the Royal Navy had tended towards commonality of systems with its allies. By the time that the British SSBNs were ready to put to sea, the US Navy would, short of some major unforeseen problem, be wholly converted to the A-3. This presented a strong case for the later missile and support was also forthcoming from Air Marshal Sir Edouard Grundy, controller of guided weapons and electronics (CGWL), who advised Le Fanu, 'on operational grounds alone, we should go wholeheartedly for A.3. I understand that an admiralty recommendation to this effect is already on its way to the Ministry of Defence, and you may rest assured that, if asked, we in M.O.A. shall give it our full support.'[14]

There was, of course, a financial aspect as well. A-2 production was due to be completed in 1964 at the time when production of the A-3 started. By 1968, as the UK's submarines were nearing completion, all A-2 missiles in the US fleet would have been replaced. Re-establishing A-2 production would have been difficult, and the costs would have to be paid by the UK along with ongoing servicing and replacement costs. Opting for the A-3 would allow production costs to be shared with the US as well as obtaining a much better missile.[15]

The decision on which missile was chosen had a knock-on effect on the design of the warhead which was not part of the sales agreement. The fact-finding mission to Washington had noted that the Americans had two re-entry systems. The Mk 1 used on the A-1 and A-2 carried a large warhead but had no penaids. The Mk 2 proposed for the A-3 carried a different warhead of lower yield and three of these were mounted on the front end of the missile. These warheads carried some degree of penetration capability and further developments in this respect were to be expected. In certain areas, UK manufacturing facilities did not parallel those of the US. This was considered particularly so in the case of the Mk II guidance units and the inertial navigation components. Should problems with these units threaten progress with the demanding schedule in building the submarines, they may have to be sourced from America. It was initially calculated that for the originally planned fleet of seven SSBNs with sixteen missiles, 183 missiles would be needed for deployment, pipeline, System Development Analysis Programme (SDAP), and warhead development. This calculation was reduced to 120 missiles for a seven boat, eight missile fleet and was of course further reduced when only four submarines were ordered.

The Warhead

AWRE had benefitted considerably from a relaxation of the rules on exchange of nuclear data which came about from the 1958 UK–US Mutual Defence Agreement (MDA). America had been shaken by events coming from the Soviet Union which had removed the last vestige of America's isolationism and the protective barriers of the Atlantic and Pacific Oceans. The time was considered right for combining resources. Discussions between representatives of both countries showed that British knowledge was well advanced, but America was able to benefit by being able to undertake many more tests. US Public Law 85-479 allowed the DoD, with the assistance of the AEC, to cooperate with another nation in exchanging nuclear information where 'it would not constitute a risk to the common defense and security of the United States'. In furtherance of this, Quarles had advised Eisenhower that the DoD desired to transmit information to the UK in connection with the development of a delivery system capability in the navy of the UK— although the items in question are redacted in the filed copy of the letter.[16]

British warhead design rested on the 'Granite' series of shots undertaken by Britain in the Pacific, but Dommett notes that this was an ultra-conservative design. Nonetheless, it was in no way 'one-way-traffic' as has often been cited. The following month, Gates advised the president:

> There have now been a number of high altitude, subkiloton, underground and underwater tests conducted by both the United States and the United Kingdom and we have previously exchanged with the United Kingdom some of the data obtained from these tests. The stage has now been reached where a further exchange of information between experts on both sides will be beneficial to both nations.... The [DoD] and [AEC] believe that this information will enhance British development of future defense capability against potential enemies and in return will provide the United States with actual and theoretical data obtained by the United Kingdom.[17]

America could now offer details of its W28 two stage warhead that was used in the US Mk28 weapon. The UK Ordnance Board, however, were concerned about the high energy explosives used in the US design. This would require the reworking of the design but resulted in a bigger warhead which was given the name Red Snow. Notwithstanding its size, it was fitted into the RAF's Yellow Sun Mk 2 free-fall bomb with room to spare. It went on to be used in the Blue Steel stand-off bomb and would have been used in the RAF's Skybolt. By 1962, Aldermaston had the IBM 7030 Stretch computer, at the time the fastest in the world. This greatly assisted its calculations as it approached its new task. The proposed Skybolt warhead was suitable for both A-1 and A-2, which, it was believed, could be fitted into the Mk1 RV without serious modification. However, this combination was unsuitable for the A-3. The Skybolt warhead could still be used but would need major redesign in a number of ways and then flight tested. The USN had estimated a cost of £30–40 million for these modifications which could be undertaken in America, but this assistance was considered politically sensitive. Space within the warhead section of the missile was very limited and would likewise place limitations on the nature of any penaid package that was envisaged. A Joint Re-Entry Systems Working Group (JRSWG) report on the issue advised that '[t]he effectiveness of these systems which we can only deploy in the late 60's or early 70's and thus much later than the equivalent U.S. system, need careful study in the light of likely deployments of U.S.S.R. anti-ballistic missile defence'. Alternatively, the Mk 2 RV, or a later version developed by the time of the UK SSBN deployment, could be used, but this would require a new warhead to be developed by AWRE although the US could test this re-entry system at an estimated cost of £10 million.[18]

The US W-58 warhead used on the A-3 would, on the face of it, be equivalent to the required UK warhead, but UK safety authorities were once again concerned about certain safety aspects and production techniques not used in the UK and this resulted in a different warhead being developed, designated ET.317. In this design, the fission primary, code-named Katie, that would have been used in the Skybolt warhead was substituted for the American design and a fusion secondary, code-named Reggie, completed the reworked warhead. Thus, the triple warhead configuration of the US front end was retained but was adapted to comply with British safety requirements.

The Royal Navy Submarines

The necessity for a dual system lies in the fact that no satisfactory prime mover adaptable to both conditions has yet been devised, although therein lies the obvious course for the future improvement and development of the submarine.

Unattributed comment made in 1918

Despite the significant impact that the German Navy's U-boats had made during the First World War, advances in submarine design had progressed at a relatively moderate pace compared, for instance, with the advances made in the field of aeronautics. By the end of the Second World War, the Royal Navy's A-class submarines were very similar to the *Kriegsmarine*'s long-range Type IXD which had been the backbone of the German *Rudeltaktik* 'wolfpacks', taking over from the Type VIIC which by then was becoming outdated.

Comparison of Representative German, British, and American Second World War Submarines			
	German Type IXD	British A class	US Gato class
Range	23,700 NM	10,500 NM	11,000 NM
Torpedo tubes	6	10	10
Displacement submerged	1,800 tons	1,620 tons	2,460 tons
Speed (submerged)	7 knots	8 knots	9 knots

But the knowledge that Britain could potentially be starved into submission if the Atlantic convoys could be seriously interrupted had encouraged the Germans to take a lead in innovative submarine design. As previously mentioned, conventional diesel-electric designs had been a compromise between surface running and submerged performance. The goal was a design independent of the need to surface. Despite the formidable success of the wolfpacks during the early years of the war, by 1943 the tide was at last turning against them. April of that year saw the climax of the Battle of the Atlantic, with over 600,000 tons of Allied shipping sunk. It was a level of loss which the Allies could not continue to sustain, but it had been achieved at the cost of most of the U-boats on patrol. *Großadmiral* Karl Dönitz, who since the 1930s had single-mindedly pursued the cause of the U-boats against an initially indifferent Adolf Hitler, reluctantly recalled the remaining U-boats on 24 May. The adoption of the snorkel was one solution. It certainly reduced the vulnerability to aircraft but did not eliminate it altogether and restricted the U-boat to a speed of 6 knots when in use. The only proper solution was the development of a closed-cycle system, independent of the need for an external supply of air—in fact, a true submarine. It was, perhaps surprisingly, not an entirely new idea. The Germans had conducted laboratory tests as far back as 1911, but the technology to transfer this to a full-scale prototype simply did not exist. It was therefore not until the mid-1930s that Dr Hellmuth Walter initiated a series of general experiments to investigate the viability of using hydrogen peroxide—or *T-stoff* to use its German name. Although the principal route of his investigations was aimed at producing a rocket engine which was eventually to be used operationally in the Messerschmitt Me 163 single-seat interceptor, he expanded his experiments in 1937 to include the possibility of using *T-stoff* in a closed-cycle submarine power plant. For this purpose, Walter proposed the use of perhydrol, a refined peroxide fuel. The perhydrol would be pumped from fuel tanks into a reaction chamber containing a catalyst which would cause it to decompose into oxygen and steam which could be used to power a turbine to drive the submarine. Walter's experiments showed that a practical and compact power plant could be produced. The major drawback was the substantial quantity of fuel which would be required, and this limitation was clearly only going to allow the design to put to sea in U-boats of a coastal type. By 1940, a prototype, the V80, had been built. In trials it achieved the remarkable speed of 28 knots submerged, but the range was limited to only 58 miles. Nevertheless, a production class, the Type XVII, went ahead. The design employed two pressure hulls in a figure of eight configuration, the lower hull being used as the fuel tank. No longer requiring surface operation, the Type XVII could be designed for optimum underwater performance and so began the evolutionary change towards the shape of today's submarines.

By the end of the war, only four Type XVIIAs (U792-795) and three Type XVIIBs (U1405-1407) had been commissioned, although others were in various stages of completion. The 50 tons of perhydrol stored on board gave these U-boats a range of 114 miles at an average speed of 20 knots. The Germans had, however, really shown the way to the future with the Type XXI *Elektroboote* introduced in 1944. Designed with increased battery capacity to enable it to spend most of the time submerged or relying on its snorkel, its hull shape too was optimised for underwater speed. It could dive deeper, manoeuvre and keep up with its intended prey, and attack while submerged.

However, to the victors went the spoils of war including a large number of U-boats. Most of these had been interned in the Baltic ports when Stettin and Danzig had fallen to the advancing Soviet forces. There they found more than 100 U-boats in various stages of completion. Among them two Type XXIs (U-2513 and U-3008) were extensively tested by the Americans, and these trials resulted in the USS *Tang* (SS-563). Designed from the start under the Greater Underwater Propulsion Power Program (GUPPY), the *Tang* heralded the US Navy's transition to the modern submarine. Still equipped with a snorkel, but not suffering a number of problems previously experienced with the earlier snorkel-equipped boats, the *Tang* could dive to 700 feet. By the mid-1950s, however, nuclear propulsion was to become a reality for the US Navy with the launch of the USS *Nautilus*.

The Royal Navy had also grasped the opportunity to examine the captured U-boats. Their distribution was discussed at the Potsdam Conference in July 1945 when it was agreed to allocate a number of them amongst the Allies under the auspices of Operation Deadlight. The Royal Navy received seventeen, subsequently disposing of eight, but only after they had been subject to a complete design and engineering appraisal. Of the remaining boats, one was given to the Royal Canadian Navy, two to the French Navy, and four to the Royal Norwegian Navy. The remaining two were scuttled. The British tested both the Type XXI and the Type XXIII—both diesel-electric boats but capable of speeds of up to 17 knots submerged. One of the those retained by the Royal Navy was the Type XVIIB U-1407. This coastal research U-boat used the Walter HTP propulsion system. Her salvaged remains were towed to Sheerness by a German tug whereafter she was taken to the Vickers-Armstrongs Ltd's shipyard at Barrow-in-Furness and was rebuilt with the assistance of Professor Walter and a number of his design team who had been brought over from Germany.[1] After completion, she was commissioned into the Royal Navy as HMS *Meteorite*. In her subsequent trials programme, she demonstrated the viability of the closed-cycle system to the Royal Navy which had also reached agreement with the United States to pass on the results of the *Meteorite* trials. However, by the time that the information was available, the US Navy had embarked on their programme to design a nuclear reactor for naval use, and as this represented a far more significant development, they, perhaps understandably, viewed the British information with only limited interest.

	HMS *Meteorite*	HMS *Explorer*	USS *Albacore*
Displacement submerged	415 tons	1,120 tons	1,824 tons
Speed (Submerged)	25 knots (HTP)	25 knots (HTP)	33 knots

The development of submarine warfare during the Second World War had shown the Submarine Service that they had acquired a new primary role as an anti-submarine force and would become increasingly influential as the post-war Soviet submarine fleet rapidly expanded. Thus, despite stringent budget cutbacks, the Admiralty determined to pursue submarine development and initiated a programme to produce its own closed-cycle design. To handle this, a joint enterprise between the Admiralty and Vickers was set up. Named the Admiralty Development Establishment Barrow (ADEB), it was headed up by Dr George H. Forsyth, 'a brilliant engineer who made enemies because he was always right'.[2] He quickly recruited as his deputy an ex-submarine engineering officer, Peter Scott Maxwell, and was further helped by six Germans who had moved to Barrow with their families. Reflecting the secrecy of the department's task, it was located remotely from the shipyard. ADEB's facilities for design, development, and subsequent testing of prototype and production heralded an innovative approach to the complex engineering problems that new technology would present, and was to prove a solid foundation 'on which some years later the nuclear submarine propulsion machinery would be developed'.[3] The task in question was to evaluate Germany's submarine technology in general and in particular their use of hydrogen peroxide. This led to a request to design an HTP power plant which in due course would lead to Admiralty contracts being awarded to Barrow on 26 August 1947 for the design of two experimental high-speed '*Ex*-class' submarines.

HMS *Explorer* (S30) was launched on 5 March 1954 by Lady Reid Young, wife of Vickers-Armstrongs' chairman, Sir James Reid Young. HMS *Excalibur* (S40) followed, launched on 25 February 1955 by Lady Mason, wife of the engineer-in-chief of the fleet, Vice-Admiral Sir Frank Mason. Both were based on the larger German Type XXVI design and in engineering terms were complex. Their hull shapes represented a further evolution in the post-war design of submarines, being much more streamlined for underwater efficiency and based on the post-war Royal Navy diesel-electric *Porpoise*-class hull. They also introduced a new type of carbon manganese molybdenum steel, UXW. They featured a comparatively low fin, somewhat reminiscent of the U-boats from which their design was derived, but this had the downside in that during rough seas, anyone on the bridge was likely to get very wet. Particular attention was paid to reducing their noise signature to a minimum in view of the rapid advances being made in the acoustic detection of submarines. Using high test peroxide (HTP) (perhydrol) which gave rise to them being referred to as the 'blonde' submarines, the pair were among the fastest in the world at that time, but they were troublesome from the start to the extent that the *Explorer*'s first captain never got the chance to take her to sea. The perhydrol resulted in a number of 'incidents', even though in 1945 the Germans had been handling the fuel safely on a routine basis. The feelings of the crews about these recurring problems can be gauged from the nicknames that they gave to the two submarines—Exploder and Excruciator—though it is reasonable to suppose that these problems resulted, at least in part, from inexperience. Perhaps unsurprisingly, the latest in submarine escape gear was incorporated, a one-man escape chamber and state-of-the-art breathing apparatus. The loss of HMS *Sidon* (P259) on 16 June 1955 when a high-test peroxide-powered torpedo ran hot and exploded resulting in thirteen fatalities underscored the dangers of the volatile fuel and gave the Royal Navy an almost pathological fear of liquid fuels aboard a submarine. The subsequent board of inquiry recommended that no liquids be on board submarines and this culture was to remain as part of Royal Navy lore. But, nonetheless, *Explorer* held the record for submarine surface speed of 26.25 knots. The HTP turbine produced considerable heat, not a problem in cold northern waters but there were doubts that this would be suitable for Royal Navy operations in warmer climes where the availability of HTP stocks would also present difficulties.

In view of the known imminence of nuclear power, it may seem strange that the limited funds available should be spent on the project—annual fuel bill alone for the two submarines was estimated to be £1 million, and although nominally attached to the 3rd Submarine Squadron, they required their own depot ship, HMS *Kingfisher* (A291), and a fuel tender, the converted water carrier RFA *Spabeck* (A227) which could carry 111 tons of perhydrol. But nuclear power for Britain was an even more expensive route to follow. In many respects, it could be argued that the two submarines were obsolete by the time that they were commissioned, but they spent much of their time usefully acting as high-speed targets for both surface and airborne ASW training. However, traditional diesel-electric power was by no means obsolete and the Royal Navy maintained a number of 'conventional' submarines until the four boats of the later *Upholder* class were paid off in 1994, all subsequently being sold to the Royal Canadian Navy. Clearly the direction towards nuclear power that the Americans were taking was known in reasonable detail, but the British stopped what little research they had done on nuclear power for naval vessels in 1952, preferring to concentrate with the limited funds available on improving diesel-electric submarines, this leading to the Royal Navy's next submarines of the *Porpoise* and *Oberon* classes, therefore bypassing the possible use of a closed-cycle system.

It was impossible, however, to avoid facing the fact that nuclear power represented the future, and the Royal Navy maintained an interest in British nuclear research with a naval section resident at the AERE site at Harwell under the command of Captain (E) Sydney Harrison-Smith. Initial proposals for a gas-cooled reactor could not be reduced sufficiently in size to fit a submarine, even though the US had achieved a practical design for the *Nautilus*. But the advantages of nuclear power were obvious and, somewhat frustratingly, the Americans were clearly well ahead and access to their technology, should it be made available, would cut out expensive and time-consuming duplicated research. In this respect, First Sea Lord Earl Mountbatten had an ally in his close friend US CNO ADM Arleigh Burke. But Mountbatten also needed support from

RADM Rickover. Such was Rickover's influence that when Mountbatten visited America in October 1955, Burke had intended to take him to sea on the *Nautilus* as the first British officer so to do—an idea firmly supported by RADM Frank T. Watkins, Commander Submarine Forces, US Atlantic Fleet (COMSUBLANT). Preliminary arrangements were made for Mountbatten to meet Rickover, which Captain John Coote, handling the British side, said was like 'briefing a Romanov to meet Rasputin'.[4] The request and the meeting were firmly refused by Rickover who claimed that it was not covered by the US/UK Military Atomic Co-operation Agreement which had been ratified by Congress on 20 June 1955, and even Burke's position and Mountbatten's impeccable provenance as a grandson to Queen Victoria were insufficient to sway Rickover's decision. 'Rickie snubs Dickie.' Mountbatten had to be content with a non-nuclear submarine experience when, on 4 November he flew to Key West to go to sea on the non-nuclear *Albacore*.[5] Commanded by LT CDR Jon L. Boyes (no relation), Mountbatten experienced something of the capabilities of the teardrop shaped submarine, far in excess of any capability of previous submarines and he therefore firmly pressed the cause of this significant advance in hull shape in discussing future British submarine design. Rickover upset many people in his single-minded objective of a nuclear submarine force, but there were ways of softening even the hardest of iconoclasts. In August 1956, he visited London and at last met Mountbatten who had described him as 'the stormy petrel of the American Navy'.[6] Charmed by the Englishman, 'Rickover didn't give a damn whether we as a country got the submarine or not, but he did care whether Lord Mountbatten got one or not.'[7] Equally, Mountbatten knew that Britain had entered the nuclear submarine business late in the day and would find it almost impossible not to fall further behind developments in America and the Soviet Union. Furthermore, Mountbatten was also aware that British SSNs would add quantity and influence to NATO's offensive capability in the face of a rapidly developing Soviet Navy.

Rickover again visited the UK in May 1957 and a limited exchange of information began which opened the door for British representatives to visit the US, but the decisive meeting was on 24 January 1958 when Rickover was due to meet the Special Nuclear Committee whose members consisted of representatives of the firms involved in the British nuclear programme: Vickers, Rolls-Royce, Foster Wheeler, and Vickers Nuclear Engineering, a new company formed by the other three involved. The meeting was discussing the problems being encountered with progress on the propulsion system when Mountbatten and Rickover entered the room to announce that they had just agreed a deal to supply a complete *Skate* power plant for the prototype British nuclear submarine, HMS *Dreadnought*—in many ways a very appropriate name as the former vessel that bore that name heralded the revolutionary age of the dreadnought battleships. Rickover was later to comment that he told Mountbatten '[D]o you want a working reactor plant now, or would you rather preserve British pride?' Mountbatten replied unequivocally that he wanted to get a nuclear submarine as quickly as possible.[7] Thus the deal was apparently done. Attractive though this story is, it could not have been quite so simple. To allow the deal, the Atomic Energy Act would have to be modified which required Congressional agreement. Rickover could not afford to fall out with his many supporters in Congress, so would have had to tread carefully however much he may have been willing to help the Englishman. It was not until 3 July 1958 that the act was modified to enable the sale of a submarine reactor to Britain. In return, Britain gave information on the design of the fuel cans used in the Calder Hall nuclear power station.

Not everyone in Britain was happy with the decision which some saw as undermining the nascent British 'home grown' project and therefore a waste of time and resource. But without this American assistance, it would have been naïve to expect an all-British nuclear submarine going to sea by 1963. Liaison with America was swiftly acted upon. Keith Foulger from the Royal Corps of Naval Constructors (RCNC) was put in charge of a team that went to EB to discuss the implications of marrying the *Dreadnought* fore end with the American-designed aft end. Foulger had already been involved in the design of HMS *Explorer* and had a very wide-ranging knowledge of submarine construction. Inevitably there were many differences in the approach to submarine design by the two nations. *Dreadnought* was designed to dive deeper than its predecessors and this required stronger torpedo tubes. British submarines had hydroplanes on the front hull—a design philosophy that remains to this day—and this placed the fin further back than on the US design. Things got off to an uncomfortable start when Rickover intervened and refused to accept Foulger until an understanding acceptable to the admiral was reached. The new submarines required a reassessment of the steel needed for the hulls as it was already known that America was using HY-80. Fully welded submarine hulls had been introduced with the 'T' class in 1942. The post-war 'O' and 'P' classes used an upgraded QT28 steel, but this caused lamellar tearing during construction, although the significance was not fully understood at the time. For the *Dreadnought*, a further upgrade led to the adoption of a special low-alloy heat-treated QT35 quenched and tempered steel—similar to, and in due course superseded by, the HY-80 used by America. However, this steel required great cleanliness in manufacture, standards which were difficult to achieve, and it therefore suffered cracking. HY-80 had been specified for the US Navy's submarines which were designed for greater depth than was considered necessary by the Royal Navy for their operations. There were only two suppliers, one in County Durham and one in Scotland, and the pressure vessels would be made at Renfrew in Scotland by Babcock and Wilcox. This steel eliminated the lamellar tearing problem.

But the wise decision was made to continue development of the UK reactor design incorporating, where necessary, experience from the American one. The demands made on the programme, however, meant that many of the modifications incorporated as a result of comparing the S5W with the British design were not fully incorporated until the later *Swiftsure* class of SSNs—also the responsibility of Foulger. In August, it was deemed time to have formal RN representation within SP. Cdr Michael Simeon, a gunnery officer, was appointed to the position of SPRN based in Washington. Initially he was a little sceptical about the longevity of the posting, given that this was a time of defence cutbacks. But this was an agreement between two senior naval officers and not subject to budgetary constraints.

In October 1957, the *Nautilus* had visited the Royal Navy base at Portland after taking part in Operation Strikeback which exercised NATO ships in the eastern Atlantic. Macmillan had not been told in advance of the intended visit, originally scheduled for Portsmouth. Concerned at the possibility that the Americans would use this as a platform to showcase their nuclear capability, he agreed to the visit being made to the more remote Dorset base. This did not stop CDR William Anderson giving a news conference saying that during the ten-day exercise he had left behind a trail of theoretically damaged and sinking capital ships. The submarine threat was coming of age and unlike the diesel submarines that spent most of their time on the surface, the *Nautilus* had spent all the duration of the exercise underwater.[9] Mountbatten was present and had invited Sandys who was greatly impressed with this example of the latest technology to the extent that Mountbatten feared that the defence minister might suddenly declare that the present navy had been made obsolete by the advent of the nuclear submarine.[10] The message was further brought home by respected Washington columnist Jack Anderson who revealed that after Strikeback, the Royal Navy had borrowed *Nautilus* for its own exercises:

> The obliging *Nautilus* had simply pulled up under a British aircraft carrier and hung about 20 feet beneath it like a sucker fish. From this hiding place it launched simulated torpedo attacks against the surrounding ships. Official reports show that the *Nautilus* theoretically sank the whole giant task force three times.[11]

It took two days to locate the submarine and to have 'theoretically' destroyed her would have also eliminated her shielding carrier. Such activities were not, however, without a certain danger. On 10 November 1966, the *Nautilus* collided with the USS *Essex* (CV-9). One submariner was injured.

Rickover had offered the Westinghouse S3W *Skate* reactor, which was tried and tested but was a low-power unit more suited to a smaller submarine than *Dreadnought*.[12] It was also designed for two propeller shafts rather than the one planned for the British submarine. At a meeting held on 29 January 1958 and chaired by the controller of the navy, the question of which reactor was most appropriate for *Dreadnought* was put forth, bearing in mind the work that had already been undertaken in assuming a British reactor would be used. Rear-Admiral Guy Wilson, rear-admiral of nuclear propulsion, spoke strongly in favour of the later S5W *Skipjack* plant which, although not fully tested, was a more powerful single shaft unit and was the reactor used in the latest USN SSNs as well as being selected for their proposed Polaris boats.[13] Wilson had been seconded to the *Dreadnought* project after it suffered a series of setbacks so was well informed on the pros and cons of submarine nuclear propulsion. The minutes of the Admiralty Board meeting on 13 February records, 'subject to the concurrence of the Ministry of Defence and the sanction of the Treasury, the *Skipjack* propulsion unit was to be preferred.'[14]

The contract for the *Dreadnought* (Ship No.1062) had already been placed with Vickers-Armstrongs (Shipbuilders) Ltd on 22 February 1957 and the design was, in a number of ways, very similar to the *Skipjack* to the extent that some Americans suspected, but were never able to prove, espionage. Design of the *Dreadnought* was undertaken by the *Dreadnought* project team (DPT) headed by Rowland Baker, under the leadership of Louis Rydill, and despite many challenges, it was, by this time, well advanced but would inevitably have to be reassessed to incorporate the American power plant. The forward end had to incorporate the innovative Type 2001 conformal radar mounted around the upper bow of the submarine and above the torpedo tubes. The aft end, from bulkhead 44, tapered quite sharply to conform to the American design. The original design had anticipated a larger reactor compartment and transition sections had to be added to join the two sections.[15] Furthermore, the British design was 3 inches wider than the American. All this gave the submarine a unique whale-like profile. The reactor compartment had a sign over its access hatch, '*Achtung!* You are now entering the American Sektor' and, for those so entitled, was entered, somewhat appropriately, through 'Check-point Charlie'.

HMS *Dreadnought*'s keel—a prefabricated circular section of plating—had been laid down on 12 June 1959 by HRH the duke of Edinburgh accompanied by Leonard Redshaw, the yard's shipbuilding manager.[16] Redshaw was described by Daniel as 'a remarkably gifted man, a giant in an industry populated by pigmies'. But at times his vision of the wider world beyond the Furness peninsular seemed blinkered. National Service was still in operation as *Dreadnought* was being constructed, and the Barrow workforce had to play its part in this. Having seen what was on offer in the outside world, however, few returned to the shipyard in the one-industry town.

While construction was taking place, the submarine's commander-designate Commander 'Peter' Sambourne had spent some nine months in the *Skipjack* to acquaint himself with the novel experience of operating a nuclear submarine. In mid-May 1960, the *Skipjack* made an eight-day visit to Faslane for what was described as a 'routine visit'. Local authorities' fears and misapprehensions about anything nuclear made visits to UK ports highly controversial but *The Times* noted that the visit 'may well afford an interesting opportunity to see how such an addition can be handled there among the present conventional types'.[17]

Dreadnought's launch took place on a rain-threatened Trafalgar Day, 21 October 1960, when, in the presence, it seemed, of most of the population of Barrow, the queen broke a bottle of Empire wine across the bows of the submarine. It was the 295th launch of a submarine by the company. Also present were Lord Mountbatten and Lord Carrington who, at the post-launch lunch, accurately summed up the significance of the day by saying 'we have seen not just the launch of a new ship but of a new era'. Rickover, a VIP guest to the occasion, was held somewhat in awe by the British working with him and enjoyed immense respect but he was careful not to override this relationship, commenting at the launch, 'we should be careful not to look as if we were trying to grab any glory from them. She's their ship, let them have full credit.' Surrounded at the launch by Royal Navy officers in full dress, he had elected to assume a discreet presence dressed in his customary business suit. Nonetheless in her speech, the queen did recognise the part played by American technology in the project and the Barrow Shipyard Band reflected on this new technology by playing, 'Fings ain't wot they used to be'.[18] By this time Vickers had already received the order for the second British SSN—this time an all-British design—setting the shipyard on the path of being the principal builder of British nuclear submarines.

But not everyone welcomed the royal party. Ever willing to bite the hand that fed them, Barrow Trades Council had invited two Russians to the ceremony, but Vickers refused entry passes to the delegation who had to watch the launch from nearby Walney Island. Protocol required that Barrow's mayor, Alderman John Miller, greeted the queen on her arrival but, somewhat incongruously, he had also been the architect behind the invitation to the Russians who, as a result, saw Britain's first nuclear submarine at close quarters. There were many left-wing activists within both the community and the shipyard, and their enthusiasm was nurtured by the Russians' visit. Unable to officially attend the launch, the Russians nonetheless were entertained to lunch with the mayor the following day and a special meeting of the Trades Council was held at which they both gave short addresses before a resolution was approved 'That we call upon the Trades Union Congress to arrange inter-visits with Trades Unionists from other Countries.'[19] The two visitors were no doubt fully debriefed on what they had seen when they returned home.

The *Dreadnought*'s sea trials took place in mid-December 1962. A model of the submarine had been tested in the tank at the Admiralty Experiment Works as Haslar to ascertain the hydrodynamic effects of this revolutionary hull shape. Her underwater speed had been calculated but her surface speed was less certain. Matching the best of the predicted speeds, she was to achieve 20 knots on the surface riding a huge bow wave which left her forward casing dry. HMS *Dreadnought* was commissioned into the Royal Navy on 17 April 1963. The three years in between had seen the submarine involved in extensive proving tests as the crew came to terms with the new technology. Although her first twelve months were taken up with further testing of the equipment, *Dreadnought* was to become fully integrated with the RN's surface fleet when she took part in September's Exercise Unison. In December 1963, she was joined by conventional submarines from the 1st and 3rd Submarine Squadrons for Exercise Lime Jug. Such exercises were in due course to become routine fare for the fleet submarines (SSNs) but, inevitably, understanding and dealing with such new technology was not without its various problems, but this was valuable experience which could be translated into Vickers' second SSN, HMS *Valiant* (S102). She was launched on 3 December 1963 by Lady Thorneycroft. Power came from a Rolls-Royce PWR1 pressurised water reactor of all British design, although much of the technology used benefitted from technology transfers from America. Along with this were now three sets of nuclear cores. Core A was to power the two *Valiant*-class boats and the four subsequent Polaris boats. Broadly similar to the *Dreadnought*, but more in line with British design practices, *Valiant* was some 20 feet longer and had a submerged displacement of 4,500 tons. The SSN was one of two fleet 'hunter-killer' submarines of her class, the second being HMS *Warspite* (S103) which was launched on 25 September 1965.

Like the Americans, British scientists had reached the conclusion that the most promising reactor design was a light water moderated reactor fuelled by enriched uranium. This would make Britain along with America the only two nations to use weapons-grade uranium for naval propulsion. The British project had been initiated in 1956, by which time the US was already working on its fifth-generation naval reactor—such was progress within the nuclear industry. To test this reactor design, the MoD had built the Naval Reactor Test Establishment (NRTE) at Dounreay on Scotland's remote northern coast about 10 miles west of Thurso. It was next to the UKAEA's civilian fast breeder reactor project which could provide support for its new naval neighbour. Formerly RAF Dounreay, a Coastal Command station, it was handed over to the RN in 1944 and renamed HMS *Tern (II)*. Now renamed yet again as HMS *Vulcan*, Rolls-Royce had built the prototype of the PWR1, the Dounreay Submarine Prototype 1 (DSMP1), with a target date of January 1960 for the prototype reactor to reach criticality. Despite its relative remoteness which some at times began to regret, it became the centre of naval nuclear reactor research for many years to come until the decommissioning process started in 2015.[20] Its location, in logistic terms, was far from ideal. Staff needed to have freedom of travel between Portsmouth, Bath, Barrow, and Dounreay, and the only sensible way to maximise time available was by air. In the early days of the nuclear project, British United Airways offered some flights, if at intermittent intervals. There was an airstrip on Walney Island, formerly RAF Walney Island, which had been sold to Vickers in 1959. Unfortunately, the airstrip was unsuitable for the de Havilland Heron that the company used, so Blackpool became the operating hub. To streamline the service, Vickers later acquired two DH.125 business jets. The nearest airfield to Dounreay was Wick where the Heron had to be taxied straight into a hangar as in strong winds the aircraft could have been blown over. Progress to Dounreay—a distance of some 30 miles—was then by single-track road with passing places. When the new jets arrived, there was a twice daily service between Barrow and Bath with an additional one or two flights per week to Wick. RAF Colerne was conveniently close to Bath, but permission to use it was not granted as the station shut down at 5:30 p.m. and the last Vickers flight would have come in at 6:00. Bristol had to be used instead. When sometime later an offer to use Colerne was received, the naval grapevine discovered that the RAF station was due to be closed. Sadly, the moment had passed.[21]

But progress was not without its problems. The British reactor was quieter than the S5W, an increasingly important factor as ASW capability improved, but was to prove more troublesome in use than the American plant. Zuckerman was soon involved in a request to seek urgent advice from Rickover. When the Dounreay reactor was in the last stages of pre-criticality with the core inserted, some of the Inconel welds in small bore tubing failed. 'The trouble is not calamitous but serious enough to warrant our asking you to contact Rickover.'[22] The American S5W reactor used in *Dreadnought* had used stainless steel in its primary and auxiliary primary systems. Part of the agreement on the supply of the reactor was that America would supply information relating to any problems encountered in operation. In practice, assistance seems to have been somewhat limited, perhaps because part of Rickover's motivation in giving Britain the S5W reactor was along the lines of 'there it is, now get on with it yourselves'. Rolls-Royce had used chrome-molybdenum steel for the primary and Inconel for the auxiliary system. This change in material was justified as it was known that stainless steel was subject to stress corrosion in contact with sea water. Rickover had already advised against the change for the primary circuit for *Valiant*, as a running boat, however, it was unclear what Rickover's view was on using Inconel for the auxiliary system. But such problems were, perhaps, an inevitable side effect of the technology of nuclear reactors which required safety standards in advance of anything that had previously existed. Solutions could be tried at Dounreay, but such an approach would be unacceptable on operational boats, and both *Valiant* and her sister fleet submarine *Warspite* were affected by these problems.[23] The request to Rickover was for two stainless steel auxiliary primary systems from US stocks. Zuckerman, by now the principal and trusted contact with Rickover, duly discussed the problem with the admiral, but the latter, a stickler for detail and process and by now becoming increasingly autocratic, was not prepared to assist until various ongoing safety related issues over the Holy Loch facility were resolved.[24] To address the situation, Zuckerman agreed a one-page safety protocol which would allow US nuclear-powered warships to visit the Holy Loch base, and this formed the basis of a reciprocal arrangement for British vessels visiting US ports. However, neither country had the right of inspection.[25]

Committing to build the Royal Navy's SSBNs presented considerable challenges, but the previous foresight in commissioning Le Fanu's report now came into its own. He described it as 'the toughest job our Navy has ever tackled in peace'. In terms of maintaining a credible UK deterrent, time was short, but Le Fanu had countered any doubts Macmillan may have harboured in Nassau by assuring him, 'It'll be alright—I've got friends.'[26] The admiral was known for injecting humour into long-winded meetings, a trait that his US counterparts never quite came to terms with, and no doubt his confident assurance was all that the prime minister needed. The ability of the V-force to successfully penetrate Soviet airspace would be considerably compromised by the mid-1960s and a credible deterrent depended on the complex Blue Steel Mk 1 stand-off bomb. Liquid fuelled and unreliable, it was of doubtful credibility, so the navy's Polaris force was needed as soon as was realistically possible. This question had been discussed in January 1963 in a meeting between McNamara and Secretary of State for War John Profumo.[27] The American view was that the V-bombers along with their counterparts in SAC would have real difficulty in penetrating Soviet air defences by 1967 and recognising that this would create a gap in the British deterrent McNamara was anxious that the Americans should do all they could to achieve commissioning of the British submarines as near to that date as possible. Profumo had doubts that this date could realistically be achieved, but McNamara had assured him that there were various ways in which practical assistance could be given to minimize the deterrent gap.

A memo from Zuckerman suggests that the original projected British Polaris fleet would number seven SSBNs each carrying eight missiles, although he cautiously noted that '[t]his is not an assumption that I provided, whatever its source the information related to it is highly illustrative.' Even more illustrative were the wildly differing assumptions of the number of boats required provided by Polaris's detractors. Arch-detractor Menaul even suggested a force of twenty would be required to equate with Bomber Command's (theoretical) ability to deliver 230 megatons.[28] Seven boats would allow three to be on patrol simultaneously. The idea for an eight-missile boat had almost certainly originated in the idea of making the navy's planned fleet of SSNs dual role. Inserting an eight-missile section would, it was hoped, not compromise the design too much, resulting in a submarine with a strategic role that would still be sufficiently fast and manoeuvrable to enable it to fulfil a hunter-killer role as well. In fact, Lord Carrington, as first lord of the Admiralty, had conveyed these options to the Cabinet shortly before Christmas 1962 and only days after the cancellation of Skybolt had been announced.[29] The navy had clearly not been letting the grass grow under its feet. Four submarines with sixteen missiles operational from 1969 or seven each with eight missiles and a dual role available from 1971.

Examination of this proposal, however, revealed many shortcomings. To be a credible deterrent required the submarine to be readily available at all times and to be untraceable by the enemy. Should the submarine be required to revert to an ASW role, this would *de facto* compromise its deterrent stance. Although theoretically offering a cost-effective solution, the two requirements were essentially incompatible. Furthermore, from a size point of view, much of the hardware involved in the navigational and fire controls systems of Polaris was the same regardless of the number of missiles. However, any changes required in either of these systems as a result of varying the number of missiles would require a disproportionate amount of effort and was likely to inject significant delays on the programme. Therefore, sixteen missiles in the 'rocket shop' it was to be. There were also purely practical reasons for adopting the American layout. Zuckerman assumed that the British sixteen-missile SSBN would be similar to the *James Madison* class. This was the upgraded *Lafayette* class designed to carry Polaris A-3 missiles. He was enthusiastic about the opportunity for an Anglo-American project commenting that 'the establishment of a British Polaris Submarine Fleet would provide the largest field of technical co-operation between the two countries since the war'. He considered that, in two fields in particular which touched upon the vulnerability of the weapon system—anti-submarine detection and anti-ballistic missile systems—it was necessary for the scientists of both sides to work as closely as possible.[30]

On 30 January 1963, Ian Orr-Ewing, civil lord of the Admiralty, announced in parliament:

> The Polaris programme will call for additional submarine building capacity. Its extent and the need for additional builders has not yet been decided, but firms which have had recent experience of submarine construction will certainly be considered along with others which have the necessary technical resources.[31]

It was estimated that even a straightforward copy of the American system would require many thousands of extra drawings to merge the fore and aft sections of a British design—effectively a derivative of the *Valiant* design—with a Polaris centre section. The 'unexpected' arrival of the need to build the Polaris submarines had not been provided for in the forward planning of the SSN fleet; so how best to incorporate both types with the minimum of compromise? Initially the thought was to copy the Americans. HMS *Valiant* had been laid down on 22 January 1962 in Vickers' Barrow shipyard and, like the *Scorpion*, could arguably be cut in half and the Polaris section inserted. This almost certainly would result in down time at the shipyard while the necessary drawings and background work were completed. On the face of it, this may seem to have had a degree of validity, but there were in practice many problems. The main one was that *Valiant* was 3 inches wider than the *George Washington*, but the hull frames would need to match and furthermore it incorporated the first reactor of UK design. The nature of the Polaris patrols needed expanded crew accommodation. *Valiant*'s external ballast tanks were considered insufficient for the SSBN which needed to incorporate two extra internal tanks. It was therefore decided to continue with the *Valiant* and allow it to be launched and proceed to sea trials which would in any case be useful in assessing the operational effectiveness of the reactor before committing it to the SSBN. Taking a longer, and perhaps more realistic, view, there would even be time to build the *Warspite* on the slipway freed up by the launch of the *Valiant* before the first SSBN was laid down. There was also a strong view within the navy that the SSN programme should not be unduly delayed. By the time that the SSBNs became operational, there would be three SSNs which would assist in the training of the SSBN crews, but more importantly would be available to clear the exit routes from the Clyde of any 'foreign' observers as the Polaris boats set sail for their patrol areas. It was therefore decided to proceed with a new design, albeit that it adopted much of the *Valiant* layout, although the beam was reduced to match the US 33 feet. It could also benefit from knowledge of the later American *Lafayette* design.

In the parliamentary debate on defence on 4 March 1963, Mr Simon Digby MP for Dorset West and a former civil lord of the Admiralty observed:

Are we merely to lengthen the '*Dreadnought*' hull, or are we to go one further? The '*Ethan Allen*', which we visited, is already being followed by two further classes of Polaris submarines in the American Navy. I think that the hull of the '*Dreadnought*' goes back to something earlier. The hull of a submarine is not complicated to design compared with that of a surface ship. I hope that we shall not plunge into something which is already based on an out-of-date American idea, as I understand the hull of the '*Dreadnought*' is based on an earlier American one. I am delighted that we are not to cut down the number of missiles to be carried but are to stick to the number of 16, the same number as are carried on American submarines.

I come to the vexed question of the reactor. The successor to the '*Dreadnought*' is to have a British reactor. I am sure that in submarines we should stick to a form of pressurised water reactor which is most suitable for this purpose. I hope that here again we shall not slavishly follow the American design and have an out-of-date reactor. It must be a totally different kind of reactor from the one we have been talking about for merchant ships. The Americans have had a number of submarines with pressurised reactors. It would be folly if we did not try to learn from that experience in our submarines which will not be commissioned for four years.

I believe that the success of the nuclear-powered submarines in the American Navy has been largely due to one man, Admiral Rickover, who has applied tremendous drive and foresight to this problem. We want someone like him. We must try to find an Admiral Rickover to put pep into this programme and to get the best results.

Next, there will be the manning problem. In manning and training I believe that we have rather a larger task than has been envisaged in some of the newspapers which have written on the subject. I was at first surprised to learn the high average age of both officers and enlisted men in the '*Ethan Allen*', but I understood it when I was told about the amount of technological training and attachment which they had had. I am sure that we must do the same thing here. We cannot afford to waste any time in starting, even though some of these officers and men may have to do attachments to outside industry in order that they thoroughly understand the very complicated apparatus which they must handle. I believe that the men must be of a very high standard. I was most impressed by the high standard of the officers and enlisted men in that submarine—and with a submarine costing such a large amount of money we can afford to have nothing but the best.

It is a challenge to us technologically to make the best of this Polaris submarine but it is also a great opportunity for our shipbuilding industry, which sadly needs the orders. It could not have come at a better time. It is a challenge to our electronic industry, too, and lastly, it is a challenge to our nuclear engineering.[32]

It was important to determine the number of submarines required to guarantee a deterrent force of sufficient capability and to integrate the building programme to minimise disruption to the concurrent construction of the SSNs. A general naval rule-of-thumb was that three vessels were needed to ensure one was always available, leading Adm. Mackenzie to argue that a fleet of five boats would be required to ensure one was on active patrol at all times. He believed that this was essential to allow for unforeseen problems arising such as equipment failures or delays in the refitting cycle or, in the extreme, the loss of one of the submarines. This would allow two boats to be on patrol at the same time—a factor that would prove to be of more significance in a few years' time. Theory was fine in principle, but this theoretical logic would have to convince the chiefs of staff, the shortly to be formed MoD (1 April 1964), and, perhaps most importantly, the Treasury. As the force got older and problems were more likely to arise, even five may not have been enough to guarantee that two would be on patrol. Four submarines were to be initially approved, with a fifth one to be ordered at a later date. On 27 February 1964, George Brown, Labour's deputy leader and at that time a much more forceful individual than the rather avuncular and not always sober figure he was later to become, said in response to the government's Defence White Paper:

When the bombers have gone, what is the size of our force to be? It was to have been four Polaris submarines. It is now to be five Polaris submarines. We do not at the moment know whether we shall have any other aeroplanes with a bonus nuclear carrying capacity.... Why were the four submarines put up to five yesterday? I hazard a guess, I suspect that it was because, with four submarines, we cannot guarantee to have two or more on station at any one time. When refitting is allowed for, when going out and coming in is allowed for, and when accidents are allowed for, it might be that only one would be on station. If only one was on station, vulnerability becomes a possibility, even with a Polaris submarine, because there is the whole question of routes out and home. I suspect that it was, therefore, decided that it would be better to have five.

Whether we have one submarine on station or two submarines on station, how, having been refused the use of the major deterrent, are we then going to bring about a great decision that nobody else is interested in by the threatened use of that force? The Minister is right in saying that it can do substantial damage. Even 16 Polarises fired off could do damage. It is an altogether different matter whether they would do the thing that the deterrent has to be able to do—to inflict such damage that it is unacceptable, because that is what gives it credibility, that is what gives its deterrent effect.[33]

For the time being, the fifth boat was safe and as a result, some long lead items, including the launch tubes, were ordered.

The submarines, considered to be the navy's new capital ships, were to be called after famous predecessor battleships, and it had originally been proposed to call the first boat *Revenge*, but due consideration suggested that this was not perhaps the most apt title in the current deterrent age and the name was duly changed to *Resolution*. *Revenge* was kept for the fourth boat, by which time, it was hoped, the name would have borne lesser significance.

Then a decision needed to be made as to who would build the submarines. Vickers Shipbuilding and Engineering Ltd at Barrow-in-Furness were the most experienced British submarine builder and, almost without saying, would be the lead contractor, although there were some concerns about the depth of the Walney for manoeuvring a submarine of such draught. Early on in the project a replica of the Walney Channel had been set up in the Dumbarton Testing Tank to calculate the degree of necessary dredging needed in the Channel.[34] The tank was a Vickers owned facility situated on the northern bank of the River Clyde estuary. In fact, and perhaps unsurprisingly, deputy managing director Leonard Redshaw had already made approaches to the Admiralty. These contracts would have to factor in the inevitable rescheduling of the building of the next class of fleet submarines. Essentially an improved *Valiant* design, these were to be the three SSNs of the *Churchill* class which were to use Core B.

The placing of these significant Polaris contracts had wider political implications regarding the distribution of sub-contracts within the shipbuilding industry. Lord Carrington advised Quintin Hogg, who was minister with responsibility for unemployment in the north-east, that the prime contractors were all required to place work in development areas wherever possible, but with the specialist nature of the Polaris work, it was recognised that this may well be difficult and some of the support would inevitably have to come from the US. Aware of the risks in putting all the eggs in one defence basket, Vickers was also already committed to building a 100,000-ton tanker for BP at Barrow but had agreed in principle to switch construction of a *Leander*-class frigate to Tyneside to free up space in the former yard for submarine construction.[35] Running a close second to Vickers was Cammell Laird of Birkenhead. This shipbuilder had been a key player in the battle of the Atlantic during the Second World War and was by then a large firm with modern facilities and a dry dock suitable for the deep draught of the submarines. However, they had no nuclear experience and certain works would have to be undertaken with regards to special nuclear facilities that would be needed in the dockyard. The River Mersey was a busy thoroughfare which some considered a limiting factor in the awarding of the contract. It was accepted that the greatest degree of cooperation and pooling of resources would have to exist between these two firms with Vickers providing 'lead services'. Sadly, the Birkenhead shipbuilder was known for the disruptive activities of the trade unions in the shipyard and the often less than honest activities of its workforce; a concern amply demonstrated when the first batch of bronze castings for the submarines was delivered. These items were placed in secure storage on Friday, but by Monday morning, they had disappeared. Nonetheless, these two shipbuilders were to become the only British shipyards capable of building nuclear submarines. Consideration was also given to using an additional third contractor. Belfast's Harland and Wolff, the largest British shipbuilder had many strengths including favourable labour relations and a good safety record but had no experience in building submarines. Swan Hunter on the Tyne had modern warship facilities, but it had not built a submarine since the First World War and had no suitable dry dock for fitting out. Clyde shipyards were also major contenders. These were John Brown and Company and Fairfields, both of whom had warship experience, but it would appear that Scotts of Greenock seemed to be the preferred choice if a third contractor was chosen.[36] In fact, a meeting had taken place on 19 March at Barrow at which Scotts and Cammells were present and both received a briefing on the requirements of the contract.[37] While there was an argument that three yards would be able to complete the project quicker than two, it may well have turned out to be a fallacy as it was unlikely that the three yards would move with the same momentum. Writing to Le Fanu, Sir Alfred Sims, director-general ships, underlined his comment that only two contractors should be employed: 'The key consideration must be the prompt and efficient fulfilment of the severely tight programme, and I must propose, therefore, that two firms only are employed.'[38] There had been thoughts of establishing a purpose-built Admiralty facility at Devonport in which to build the submarines and thereafter use this for the refitting programme thus eliminating the need for Rosyth Dockyard involvement. But there were political advantages in diversifying the work and expanding the capacity for nuclear shipbuilding, and speed of completion remained a major consideration, 'that was the dominant factor in this tremendous programme' and, in the end, the contracts were placed with Vickers and Cammell Laird for two SSBNs each.[39] Sims advised that in the interests of fairness, 'it is considered that firms securing POLARIS submarine contracts should be omitted from future tendering exercises for frigates and they should be so informed at the discussions'.[40]

The contracts for the four submarines were placed on 8 May 1963.[41] HMS *Resolution* (S22) and HMS *Repulse* (S23), the first and third, would be built by Vickers, with HMS *Renown* (S26) and HMS *Revenge* (S27), the second and fourth, by Cammell Laird. Each launch would be six months apart. Unsurprisingly, Vickers were naturally keen to build all four SSBNs, but this would no doubt have had political repercussions as well as putting yet more pressure on the SSN build programme. Furthermore, Mackenzie was of the firm opinion that they had neither the resource nor the capacity to achieve this within the tight timescale.[42] The Admiralty with understandable but perhaps unrealistically aspirational objectives had sought to make the contract with Vickers subject to there being no hold-ups as a result of union demarcation disputes, a problem that beset Barrow, but Redshaw, understandably, was reluctant to give such assurances.[43] It is easy nowadays to overlook the power that the unions held over industrial relations in those days, but 'who does what' regularly brought union against union until the line of demarcation was agreed, often after costly delays. In the case of the submarines, the unions at Barrow far preferred to see their members constructing ocean-going liners which employed a much wider range of skills but were in the fullness of time to agree to embrace the demanding skills required in building nuclear submarines. Cammell Laird was also to receive an Admiralty contract for the SSN HMS *Conqueror* (S48) to increase their knowledge of building nuclear submarines.

For both shipyards, the contracts represented something far in excess of any previous construction experience. Mackenzie commented:

It was something far more complicated than anything they had dealt with before, involving the assembly, installation and rigorous testing of thousands and thousands of items of equipment, many highly technical, to be supplied by several hundred contractors, some in the United Kingdom, some in America, all to be achieved in a strict timescale.[44]

Without a complete change in attitude and operating procedures, Mackenzie realised that there was little or no hope of completing the submarines in time. It was to take much persuasion, no doubt at the sacrifice of much time, by Mackenzie and Baker to convince the two shipbuilders that their traditional approach would no longer apply in the evolving age of modern technology. The *Daily Express*, an influential and well-respected newspaper, reported on the new type of worker that was appearing in the shipyards of the north-west clad no longer in grimy overalls but 'white clad and clinically clean'. Vickers' management was reminded of the effect the unions could have on the project, when, on 23 December 1963, the welders, by now aware of the premium the 'nuclear' tag could invoke, passed a resolution demanding a satisfactory increase in wage or all work in the nuclear welding department would cease. This also resulted in an immediate overtime ban which fortunately was lifted in January.

The whole British Polaris development plan, nonetheless, needed to lean heavily on American support, generously given. Thus it was that the design of the British SSBN was largely based on the USS *Benjamin Franklin*, 640-class missile section. This class was a development of the earlier *Lafayette* design and incorporated revised features as a result of experience in the adverse handling characteristics experienced near to the surface. The SSBN had to operate with one mast exposed above the surface in Sea State 5 (Rough—wave height 2.5 to 4 metres) without the submarine broaching the surface. The top of the fairwater was now lower in the water and the whole submarine was 10 feet deeper in the water which reduced the surface suction effect. As the missile section used HY-80 (British near equivalent was QT35) steel this necessarily had to be now specified for the construction of the whole of the British hull.

Steel Plate Composition: Royal Navy Post-War Submarines										
Submarine Class	Steel Type	C	Mn	Si	S	P	Ni	Cr	Mo	V
O-Class	QT28	0.15	1.15	0.08	0.03	0.02	0.40	0.25	-	-
Dreadnought	QT35	0.15	0.20	0.30	0.04	0.04	1.20	1.00	0.50	0.12
SSBN	HY-80	0.14	0.32	0.25	0.01	0.01	3.20	1.60	0.45	0.01

As if to emphasise the end of the old order, the launch of HMS *Osiris* (S13) on 29 November 1962 was thought by many to have signalled the conclusion of conventional submarine building at Barrow. (This was true, at least for the Royal Navy, but in the early 1970s three improved *Oberon*-class submarines were to be built at Barrow for the Brazilian Navy.) In early 1973, an order was received from the Ecuadorean Navy for two Type 209 submarines. These were to a licensed design by the German *Howaldswerke-Deutsche Werft* company. Concurrent and preferential orders from the MoD unfortunately rendered this contract impossible to honour and unfortunately soured Vickers relationship with potential international customers.

Mackenzie harboured grave concerns about the full understanding of the complexities of the project within Vickers' management. He received some degree of comfort from the announcement by Redshaw on 25 February 1964 of the formation of a Polaris Project Office under the control of Australian Greg Mott who had accepted a move to Barrow from Vickers' High Walker shipyard on the Tyne in 1957 to be part of the team developing the nuclear reactor for submarine use. In certain areas, British and American practices differed, such as the welding of the launch tubes into the hull which Redshaw insisted being done under workshop conditions to ensure a higher quality weld. The decision provoked considerable debate, much of it against the proposal. At one of the quarterly progress meetings, the naval constructor's overseer, Arthur Sharpe, caused himself much embarrassment by leaping to his feet and declaring: 'If Vickers persist in using this building method it will be over my dead body.' There was silence for a moment before Redshaw quietly said, 'Yes, if necessary.'[45] Cammell Laird, however, took a different approach and used the EB method. Cleanliness and checking were the new guidelines for working in the nuclear shipyards although grimy work, traditional within many areas of heavy industry, still took its place on the construction floor.

Nonetheless, the keel laying of the first Polaris submarine, HMS *Resolution*, took place on 26 February 1964. Sims performed the ceremony. Redshaw visited the US late in the summer of 1964 to observe the training that Vickers' employees were receiving. He realised that the success of the British project would very much depend on the relationship with the American sub-contractors and their commitment to the transfer of knowledge and technology. But 'defence of the realm' seemed of little importance to the unions and persistent strike action continued during the autumn of 1964. Further evidence of this vulnerability had been evident in April when work on the production line of the Handley Page Victor, the third of the RAF's V-bombers, was halted by a strike of 100 aircraft inspectors demanding more pay.

Yet more uncertainty was brought about with the general election in October. Maybe as a result of the various fiascos over Blue Streak and Skybolt and the resultant adverse publicity, the unified support for a British deterrent shown by both Conservatives and Labour was beginning to crumble and was to become an election manifesto issue. Labour support for the atomic bomb put in train after the war, and the resulting party policy on nuclear weapons, had, unhindered, paved the way for a Conservative government to proceed to develop the hydrogen bomb. Prime Minister Churchill had reminded the Commons in March 1955:

Owing to the breakdown in the exchange of information between us and the United States since 1946 we have had to start again independently on our own. Fortunately, executive action was taken promptly by the right hon. Gentleman the Leader of the Opposition [Attlee] to reduce as far as possible the delay in our nuclear development and production.[46]

By 1964, however, views on the deterrent had polarised. Labour was now against continuing with the national deterrent as with the demise of Blue Streak, any belief in the cornerstone policy of 'independence' had become wafer thin, while Conservative influence on the world stage was predicated by possession of nuclear power at the expense, if necessary, of conventional forces. Both parties had experienced a change in leadership with Sir Alec Douglas-Home, seen by many as a somewhat surprising choice, taking over from an ailing Macmillan and Harold Wilson becoming Labour leader after the premature death of Gaitskell following complications from a flare up of an auto-immune disease. In his first speech as prime minister, after a twelve-year absence from the House of Commons, Douglas-Home said: 'At the start of this Session I must make the position of the Government crystal clear on this matter. The Government mean to retain our long-range nuclear forces—our V-bombers and our Polaris submarines—under our own control.'[47] This issue became central to the Conservative election campaign, forcing Labour, who had wanted to focus on domestic matters, to declare its opposition and be accused of pandering to its left-wing and its pacifists. World events conspired against the Conservatives as Election Day loomed. What effect would it have had on the outcome if China had tested its first nuclear device before, rather than the day after, the election? Furthermore, the news of Khrushchev's 'retirement' arrived only late on the day of the election which saw a Labour government assume power with a slender majority of four seats. Harold Wilson was now prime minister, and the future of the Polaris Agreement was in new hands. Wilson along with his wife had met Johnson earlier in the year. The president had been briefed by his assistant secretary of state for international organization affairs, Harlan Cleveland, who had recently dined with Wilson in the House of Commons noting that there was a possibility of the Labour leader becoming the next prime minister. Cleveland had been a student under Wilson when the latter was a tutor at Oxford University. He described him as 'Rather shy':

> Ten years later, when he was a very young Minister (as President of the Board of Trade), he seemed rather too pleased with himself, and a little pompous. Now, fifteen years after that, he is still very sure of his own brilliance, but has settled into a mood of relaxed confidence, seemingly in command of himself and of the situation in which he finds himself. He retains that joy of rapid and fancy intellectual footwork which has long been his trademark whether in the House of Commons or in private conversation.[48]

Thus armed, Johnson met Wilson, his wife, and son in Washington on 2 March 1964. Neither man really knew the nuances of the close relationship that existed between the two nations, but Wilson spoke as if a Labour victory at the forthcoming general election was a foregone conclusion. In a *tour d'horizon* meeting, there were differences. Johnson started by wondering why Britain continued to trade with Cuba, but when it came to the question of defence and *inter alia* therefore the question of the deterrent, Wilson used a standard argument he had previously used with Secretary of State Dean Rusk. He said a Labour government 'would want to. get rid of the national deterrent which made no sense at all for England today. This would save 300 million pounds which could be used to put back the British fleet on the high seas, and would permit an increase in conventional forces so that the UK could play an active role in putting out brush fires when necessary.' The president then sought Wilson's views on the MLF which Kennedy had been so keen to promote. Wilson indicated:

> The only circumstances in which a Labour government would support the MLF would be if this were [sic] the only way to prevent Germany from acquiring a national nuclear force. He said that he did not think the German government wanted this, or that there was any support for this in German public opinion. The president asked Mr Wilson whether he really thought that Germans had abandoned their desire to play a dominant role and Mr Wilson said that even if they wanted to do so, the West had the means of preventing this from happening. He felt that the MLF did have the result of putting the German finger on the nuclear trigger. He was apprehensive of a possible development whereby the United States would no longer retain the veto and Germany might.[49]

The MLF had never really gathered momentum in Europe. The German question usually being the stumbling block and it gradually faded into the background.

With the Labour victory, thirteen years of Conservative government was brought to an end. Questions were naturally asked about the future of the British deterrent under a Labour government led by Wilson. The 'intellectual thug' Denis Healey (so called by the Speaker Betty Boothroyd) was appointed defence secretary. In early 1964, the contract had not yet been placed for the fifth boat: provisionally named HMS *Redoubtable* (although many within the Royal Navy believed that HMS *Churchill* was the senior service's preferred name). Was this perhaps a name too close to the French SSBN *Le Redoutable* (S611) as it was changed by the Ships Names Committee in 1964 to *Royal Sovereign*?[50] Or had those concerned forgotten that it was from the French seventy-four-gun ship of that name that the fatal shot had been fired at Admiral Lord Nelson during the Battle of Trafalgar? The Labour Party had campaigned on the basis of cancelling Polaris, thus putting the new prime minister in a potentially awkward position. Wilson, who had wherever possible played down referring to the deterrent in his campaign, had nonetheless given a pre-election pledge, albeit that this was not reflected by the majority of his party, that the submarines would be built 'come what may'. Perhaps he did not trust American integrity in suggesting the opposite to Johnson.

The French, too, were concerned at what might happen if the Wilson government cancelled Britain's deterrent. On 21 October, somewhat auspiciously on the anniversary of the Battle of Trafalgar, the American embassy in London outlined its thoughts on Polaris under a Labour government, copying the report to their embassy in Paris and quoting Healey's comments in parliament the previous February when he said:

> I cannot say yet whether or not we will cancel the Polaris submarine. What I will say is that we will certainly not continue the programme in its capacity as an independent British force and, secondly, if we decided that there was no alliance requirement for a British Polaris component we would not have the slightest difficulty in converting these submarines into hunter-killer submarines, a programme of certain and immediate value to the British Navy and to national defence which has been set back five years by the Polaris programme.[51]

Perhaps an easy statement to make in political opposition, but it would take a brave or perhaps foolhardy defence secretary to remove Britain from the nuclear club. The American report noted that Labour had never 'flatly stated that it would abandon the Polaris program, but has adopted a wait and see attitude':

> ... We believe that Labor has not yet taken a firm decision on the future of the UK Polaris program, nor is the Government likely to make up its mind until after the defense talks Prime Minister is planning to have with President Johnson. From a purely technical standpoint ... Labor has about until midsummer of 1965 to decide, without major program delays, whether to continue with Polaris ... submarines or to convert them to hunter-killer types ... (t)hrough its determination of cancellation costs.

In summary, the report concluded that cancellation costs if Labour terminated Polaris might outweigh the costs of converting the submarines. Conversely, if the US minimised these costs, it could encourage Labour to abandon the Polaris programme. In this respect, the Americans potentially held all the cards. 'If we wish to effect the elimination of the British nuclear deterrent, as a part of a general policy to bring about the demise of national nuclear deterrents, low cancellation costs would help the Labor Government to convert its Polaris program to a hunter-killer submarine program.'

Despite persistently circulating rumours that Wilson was an agent of the Soviets, he was patriotic and clearly saw that from the standpoint of national prestige he had to support the deterrent. He therefore sought the advice of CDS Lord Mountbatten who presented a strong case not only for keeping Polaris, but also for the fifth boat.

Douglas-Home had also stressed in parliament that 'no force less than five is viable'.[52] Furthermore, it was estimated that cancellation of the programme would cost some £200 million in charges and other losses, not to say the jobs that would also be forfeit. Indeed, the Conservatives had been active in the Barrow constituency in the run up to the election, warning people in the area of the dire consequences of cancelling the submarines. Nevertheless, cancellation was taken seriously enough that plans were put in place to consider the complexities of converting the SSBN orders to fleet submarines—cynically referred to as the 'Wilson' class.

Notwithstanding this, Healey had determined that apart from some long lead items, little had been ordered for the fifth boat—the launch tubes were later purchased back by the US for use in their own programme. But making manifesto declarations and being confronted by these from the government's front bench was a somewhat different matter. The political repercussions of relinquishing the deterrent were manifest and complex. When put to cabinet, Wilson discovered that even dyed-in-the-wool anti-nuclear colleagues could fall for the argument, albeit based on some economy of facts, that cancelling the deterrent was too politically risky, both on the domestic and international stages. As a degree of compromise, it was further agreed that a four-boat fleet would suffice, with some even arguing for a three-boat fleet. However, three submarines would barely guarantee a submarine on station at all times and could be severely compromised by any accident or mechanical problems. Writing to Wilson on 6 January 1965, Healey said: 'I propose that we should take, and announce, a decision to complete the four submarines already building but to cancel the proposal for the fifth boat.'[53]

The Royal Navy seemed to have put up little resistance—manning the SSBNs alone was likely to be a problem and might weaken the availability of skills in the surface fleet. They had seen the problems faced by the USN in producing qualified nuclear-trained officers in sufficient numbers to man the first of their SSBNs. An uncertain Wilson tried to convince his Cabinet, but in the end had to give way to his left wing and the need to cut expenditure and therefore agreed to relinquish the fifth submarine. It was a decision that was later to cost the taxpayer dearly as the Moscow ABM defences became a serious problem. On 15 February 1965, Healey duly announced:

> The Government have now completed a review of the programme, set in hand by the previous Administration, for the construction of nuclear propelled Polaris submarines. In the light of the stage now reached in the programme, they have concluded that the right course is to complete the four submarines already under construction, but not to proceed with the fifth submarine. This decision will save about £45 million in capital cost—less the cancellation charges which have still to be negotiated. We are now considering the possibility of resuming, earlier than otherwise, the nuclear-propelled hunter-killer programme, to which the Government attach great importance.[54]

The cancellation of the fifth boat meant a reduction of more than 20 per cent in the size of Britain's at-sea deterrent. One boat with sixteen missiles was still a formidable force, but as Soviet anti-ballistic missile capability increased, the effectiveness of only one submarine was to come under increasing scrutiny and in the event of some major mishap, the CASD would be threatened, potentially causing a crack in Britain's defensive shield. Furthermore, the Treasury had even wanted a reduction to three submarines which would have left the navy in the near impossible position of providing continuous deterrent cover once the refit cycle had started. Many actually believed that three submarines were possibly worse than none at all. Fortunately, as has been mentioned, only a few advance orders for components for the fifth boat had been agreed and these were all with US firms.

Cancellation of the fifth boat gave some help to Labour chancellor James Callaghan in balancing the budget, but defence was still under pressure to reduce costs. Wilson needed to visit Johnson before any firm decisions were made. The president was advised in a memo from White House economist Francis M. Bator who nudged Johnson towards better collaboration with Europe, that before further discussions on the deterrent and the MLF, 'You will wish to get David Bruce's [US Ambassador to the UK] views about how we play the British':

> This is a very hard problem for Wilson. He must cut back on defense somewhere to make his balance of payments add up without internal deflation and knows that the best way out would be to get out of the nuclear business. But selling the Queen's submarines for German money would be hard for them to swallow. I doubt if Wilson will show his hand on this issue except in a direct communication with you. He is likely to regard this as a problem for senior politicians and not for discussion with George Ball or even with Bob McNamara.[55]

The MLF gradually ceased to be an agenda item. But there were other areas of mutual interest to Britain and the US lying further to the east.

The possibility of deploying the Royal Navy's SSBNs 'East of Suez' to the Indian Ocean had apparently been first raised in a Commons debate on 23 November 1964, when Douglas-Home had replied to a question from Healey whether he considered that the five Polaris submarines would be relevant in the case of trouble in China and the Far East:

> [They] cannot be detected. I think that it would certainly be a deterrent either to the Russians or to the Chinese. But I would not wish to tie it into the N.A.T.O. Alliance absolutely and irrevocably when we might want to use it in circumstances provoked by the Chinese.[56]

It was an idea that appeared to be close to Wilson's heart.[57] In considering the Far East option, the Navy Department reported that with a fifth boat, it would theoretically be possible to deploy one SSBN to patrol the Indian or Pacific Oceans, the former not covered by US Polaris patrols. This would allow targeting of China or the Soviet Union depending on the boat's location, but lurking in the sea off the southern tip of India, the submarine could rapidly redeploy east or west depending on the target allocation. With only four boats this option rapidly receded. It was not impossible, but there were no existing facilities that could be used which would mean a costly investment in new locations and the provision of a new submarine depot ship—provisionally designated AS-01. A draft design for this ship had been completed.

The matter really came to prominence in May 1965 during a visit to the UK by Indian Prime Minister Lal Bahadur Shastri who was looking for assurance of protection against China following the latter's testing of its first nuclear device on 16 October 1964. Wilson had warmed to the idea as a way of reducing the cost of military presence in the Far East while maintaining a British role in the area, thereby continuing to play a part on the world stage. He envisaged an ANZUS alliance between the UK, Australia, New Zealand, and the US. Tenure of Singapore was increasingly unlikely and using an Australian air or naval base was being considered. Initially the US, now bogged down in the Vietnam War broadly welcomed the idea. However, on reflection, American interests in the area could potentially be compromised as a noforn (no foreign nationals) memo from Walt Rostow, counsellor of the Department of State and chairman of the Policy Planning Council to President Johnson demonstrated. It was in American interests on a short-term basis to have a British presence in Malaysia and Singapore during the conflict in Vietnam, however, on a long-term basis, Rostow believed that a continuing UK presence could be detrimental to US interests.

With Singapore looking uncertain as a long-term base, Freemantle in Australia was considered. Indian concerns were further manifested by a Chinese invasion of Indian territory high in the Himalayas where Indian and Pakistani troops were facing each other in the disputed Kutch-Sind border heightening concerns among the western powers about nuclear proliferation in India and the Far East. President

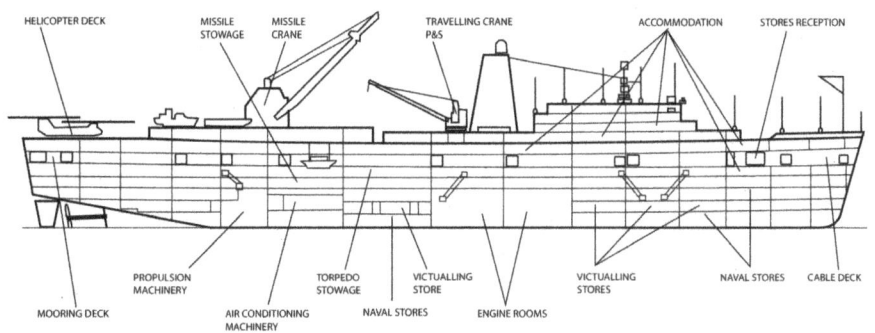

Proposed Royal Navy AS-01 Polaris depot ship for deployment east of Suez.

Johnson along with Wilson feared that without some level of assurance, India would start to develop its own nuclear programme. India further complicated matters by wanting a joint US-Soviet 'umbrella' but Zuckerman advised that this would be all but impossible to achieve. Zuckerman travelled to India in May 1965 and arranged that this would coincide with a visit by Mountbatten who was making a farewell tour of the Far East as CDS. The visit did not go particularly well. Zuckerman was first taken to the area of the Himalayas where Chinese and Indian forces were facing each other. After a visit to the Army Mountain Warfare School, the party returned to warmer climes where Zuckerman was due to resume talks with Homi Bhabha, head of India's Atomic Energy Programme. He was briefed before the meeting by General Jayanto Chaudhuri (a Sandhurst-trained officer where, owing to his moustache, he was known as 'Muchhu'.) 'Why do you want to deny us the bomb?' he asked. 'We are a nation of phallus worshippers, and we need to set up this phallus and worship it.' Bhabha, like Chaudhuri, wanted an Indian bomb. He was uninterested in any idea of non-proliferation agreement.[58, 59] The idea was effectively written off following the cancellation of the fifth submarine, but it was back in consideration by mid-1966. This time it was being considered as an alternative to operational deployment in the Atlantic. This was now seen as a way of counteracting the 1964 US proposal for a NATO Atlantic Nuclear Force which was becoming a source of embarrassment to the UK. The idea was of course not without its problems. A suitable submarine support ship would still be needed to provide something similar in concept to the US Site I on the Holy Loch. This would have to encompass a full support capability and provide accommodation for the alternative crews, along with missiles and servicing facilities. Of necessity, a major revision to the role of the planned base at Faslane would have to be undertaken.[60] Not unnaturally, the idea had much appeal among those anxious for Britain to maintain its presence in the East. There was, of course, no knowledge or even any inkling that, some eighteen months later, Secretary of Defence Denis Healey would announce Britain's withdrawal from military bases east of Suez. Realistically, however, four submarines would be severely stretched to carry out patrols in the Indian Ocean and off Southeast Asia so that nuclear protection of India and Malaysia would likewise not be possible.

While these decisions were be fought over, progress on the submarines continued. They represented a major contract, and new management processes and new department structures would be needed. One of the first problems encountered concerned the welding of the British steel used in the construction of the hull. Ultrasonic, non-destructive testing was used, but it was found difficult to obtain consistent readings and the problem was further exacerbated when hairline cracks were found in the hull of HMS *Dreadnought* during her first refit. Although easier to weld, the British steel's high silicone content gave rise to laminations in the metal's structure not present in the American steel which was conversely more difficult to weld. Despite close discussions with the trade unions, the Barrow workforce bore poor comparison with their American equivalents. Early on in the programme, Mackenzie had said that total commitment would be required to bring the project in on time. That may have been an order for the Royal Navy, but he held no sway over the labour force. They would not, for example, work three shifts and this attitude added considerably to the labour costs of the programme. Proper supervision and management were also at times lacking.[61] During the construction of *Resolution*, certain welding defects were identified during normal quality-control surveys of welding and had to be replaced. This fortunately did not hold up the completion date. Marrying the British fore and aft sections with the American centre section added additional complications. Healey calmed doubts by confirming that such defects were not unusual in the construction of complex structures.[62] That is not to say that there were not innovations in the British design that Levering Smith admired. It had been decided against using the American hovering system, preferring instead to develop a system compatible with the British design. Smith also praised the welded hull valves, their standardisation, the mounting of the propulsion machinery on a separate raft to reduce vibration and the incorporation of a 3-foot hatch in the pressure hull adjacent to the machinery spaces to facilitate removal and replacement of equipment during turn around at Faslane.[63]

Meanwhile, the Royal Navy had announced its first two SSBN command appointments: Commanders Michael Henry and Kenneth Frewer would command the port and starboard crews respectively on the *Resolution*. Fortunately, there had been active resistance to Rickover having a part in the selection process, which he, not surprisingly, had hinted at, but that was considered a step too far. On 3 August 1966, it was announced in parliament that Queen Elizabeth, the queen mother, would launch HMS *Resolution* at 12 p.m. on 15 September with the second boat HMS *Renown* planned to be launched at Birkenhead on 25 February 1967; the latter by Mrs Edna Healey, wife of Denis Healey.

The weather on the day of the *Resolution*'s launch was far from ideal. Workmen leaving in the early hours after putting finishing touches to the £76 million submarine had to cling to the rails on the superstructure. One welder commented: 'We had to go hand over hand to prevent ourselves being blown off.' Two hours before the launch, the 58-mph winds abated sufficiently to allow the launch to go ahead, but '[H]igh winds [still] buffeted [the] Barrow shipyard when the Queen Mother arrived.' Nonetheless, crowds lined the route to see the royal arrival. These included some 12,000 local schoolchildren who had been given the day off. CND supporters conducted a silent vigil and their number included Japanese rice farmer Busuke Shimoe, a survivor of the atomic bomb dropped on Hiroshima.[64] As the queen mother pulled a ship's telegraph lever and launched Britain's first Polaris submarine, the *North East Evening Mail* reported: 'Wind and broken glass showered on workmen and photographers standing beneath the Royal launching platform as thousands cheered—and a major milestone had been reached to keep Britain a deterrent power.'[65]

A week later, cracks were found in the hull. These were similar to the cracks already seen in the *Dreadnought* and were attributed to steel of an insufficiently high standard being specified. An MoD spokesman advised that such cracks were normal in heavy welded constructions of this type and involved no risk to the submarine or its 143-man crew.[66] While this would not prevent the *Resolution* from going to sea, it did mean that if the cracks got worse then remedial rewelding would have to take place during the refit cycle. This potentially added further delay to the building programme. It had been originally planned that the first two SSBNs would be launched in 1966. Nonetheless, *Resolution* was four months behind schedule and *Renown* was even further delayed. While acknowledging that the industrial disputes instigated by the fitters and welders had contributed much to the delays, it was pointed out that despite this, there was no reason to expect that the deployment schedule could not be maintained.

Once the submarine had been completed, the next step was sea trials. This allowed the submarine to be subjected to a full range of testing scenarios to ensure that it was fit for service. Trials complete, HMS *Resolution* was commissioned into the Royal Navy on 2 October 1967. To avoid offending the left wing of the party, Wilson had instructed his Cabinet to boycott the event at Barrow. The official reason given was that it conflicted with the Labour Party Conference in Scarborough, but it represented a double blow to the navy, still recovering from the decision to cancel its coveted aircraft carriers.[67] Redshaw and his wife, Joan, were guests of the Royal Navy and sat with Adm. Mackenzie and his wife at the ceremony, after which an ITN (Independent Television News) team was allowed on board and witnessed a low-key launch demonstration. Reporter Richard Dixon asked the almost inevitable question of the chances of a rogue launch. 'If you can envisage 143 people, all going mad at exactly the same time,' replied an amused Frewer, 'I suppose it is feasible.' He went on to reassure Dixon that they did have a doctor on board to keep an eye on them.[68]

In mid-November 1967, HMS *Resolution* left Barrow for her final sea trials in the Atlantic with her starboard crew before early in the new year she would head for the United States to undertake the historic British live firing of a Polaris missile. The day before she left, Frewer invited his wife and seven-year-old son, Martin, to come on board. Gillian Frewer commented that she never thought about the danger. 'I daren't,' she said, 'If I seriously thought about my husband prowling about underwater with these terrifying missiles, I think I'd go scatty.' An innovation for the crew was their wearing of name badges, almost unknown within the services but commonplace in the US Navy, prompting the *Express* journalist to comment that American influence extended not just to the rockets.[69]

The sea trials, described as 'routine service tests', consisted of a series of dives, turns, acceleration, and speed runs, undertaken by both crews, before in early January with Cdr Henry and the port crew on board she left Faslane for the United States. However, on 9 January, *The Times* reported that the previous day the *Resolution* had been seen on the surface returning to Faslane accompanied by the frigate HMS *Falmouth* (F113). The cause was established as a failed electrical generator which had to be replaced, but official sources stated that this would not prevent the submarine arriving at Cape Canaveral on time. In fact, two of the three onboard generators had failed. Minister of Defence for Equipment Roy Mason later advised parliament that, 'the fault was due to a design weakness. The affected part will be modified in all machines, including those for later nuclear submarines.'[70] Rumours that the frigate was towing the submarine were denied.[71] Repairs completed, the *Resolution* once again set sail for the US via the sound range at the Azores, where upon arrival at Charleston she had to pick up missiles before arriving at Port Canaveral on 4 February. As the submarine manoeuvred into its berth, it was to the accompaniment of bagpipes as L/Cpl David Cairns from the Royal Scots Greys played 'Scotland the Brave' and 'Highland Laddie'.[72] Cairns had won a lottery among the regiment's pipers, but although delighted to have been chosen, he was a little uncertain about his submerged transit of the Atlantic and admitted that he preferred army life where his usual job was to drive tanks. Cdrs Henry and Frewer were met by CAPT. Walter Chimiak, director of the Naval Ordnance Test Unit (NOTU) and former commanding officer of the USS *Compass Island*. The Royal Navy destroyer HMS *Aisne* (D22) was also alongside and had been tasked with accompanying the submarine on its DASO providing escort duties along with the US Navy's destroyer the USS *Fred T. Berry* (DD-858) which acted as the telemetry ship. Warned of the imminent arrival, the *Chicago Tribune* speculated that as the British submarine looked different from the American ones that were regularly seen in the area, fishermen local to Cape Canaveral 'may even drop their rods and scream "the Russians are coming".' The Royal Navy had not revealed the actual arrival date but did confirm that the *Resolution* would be undertaking test firings 'early in the new year'.[73] Reporter Dick Young did give helpful advice as to how to spot the differences between the two countries' SSBNs by pointing out that the British submarines had their diving planes on either side of the bow whereas their American equivalents were fitted halfway up the sail.[74]

It was now time to see if the marriage of American missile system and British submarine worked. This was tested by the DASO during which each crew would fire live, but unarmed, missiles. The first launch by the port crew under Henry on 15 February was a complete success. The launch was a mere 15 milliseconds late against the timeline set five years before. The DASO was vital to show that both submarine and crew were fit for operational service. *The Times* reporter Ian McDonald, who with other members of the press and naval VIPs witnessed the launch from aboard the *Berry*, wrote:

The 30ft. missile broke through the surface of the eastern test range precisely on schedule at 11.15 this morning. As the rocket engine ignited, the missile soared aloft, leaving a white trail behind. In two minutes it had vanished in the clear sky. A radio message 15 minutes later reported that the Polaris had splashed down in the target area east of the Windward Islands, some 1,500 miles away.... Vice-Admiral Sir Hugh Mackenzie ... who was onboard the *Resolution* radioed after the launch that 'the event is the culmination of a great effort on the part of the submarine commanding officer and his crew, and by the British shipyards, firms and technicians who have built the submarine and its systems'.[75]

The *Resolution* returned 'mission accomplished' to Port Canaveral, once more to the skirl of Cairns's bagpipes. Frewer, who had also watched the launch, further commented: 'It was fantastic. It was like President Kennedy said, "Once you have seen one of these fired you have never any doubt about the deterrent."'[76] After the *Resolution* had put to sea that morning, she submerged and remained just below the surface throughout the forty-five-minute countdown and the launching. Only the telemetry mast had been above the surface.

For these tests, the *Berry* sported white-painted equipment cabins mounted on the flight deck along with telescopes amidships to follow the missile after launch. For each DASO, a red-painted telemetry mast was fitted to brackets on the submarine's fin. This had the dual purpose of transferring fire control data, but also allowed the accompanying vessels to see the whereabouts of the submerged submarine. Prior to the launch, rehearsals would take place with the destroyer shadowing the submarine. It was, by then, a well-established routine with the American SSBNs, but when it came to the starboard crew's turn to launch their missiles in early March, things did not quite go to plan. On the day prior to the scheduled launch date, the sea was rough with deteriorating conditions. The *Berry*'s task was to take a parallel course to the British submarine at a distance of 500 yards. By this time, the sea was increasingly violent, and the destroyer was rolling so much that lunch was cancelled. US Navy Reserve officer LT Vergil Erwin was the officer of the deck and suddenly realised that the telemetry mast had disappeared. A short while later, the mast reappeared dead ahead of the destroyer which now seemed to be bearing down on the submarine. In fact, the *Resolution* was heading straight for the *Berry*. The resulting collision was inevitable and resulted in the telemetry mast being damaged along with a 5-foot-wide hole in the destroyer's sonar dome. The *Resolution* surfaced and both vessels returned to Port Canaveral. This was deemed an 'international incident', and Prime Minister Wilson and President Johnson were both informed, but as such, there would be no Naval Court of Inquiry and both premiers vetoed any further action and the *Berry*'s captain, CDR Charles De Armond, retained command of his ship. It seemed De Armond had suggested a change of the submarine's course to alleviate the destroyer's rolling. This was duly acknowledged by the

British vessel which responded that the request would be considered. No further response was received, but the *Resolution* turned through 180 degrees, during which manoeuvre she banked and the mast went out of sight as she turned. With minimum damage, a replacement mast was rapidly fitted and did not prevent the *Resolution* leaving port the following morning, 4 March, to successfully fire her missile. On board for this launch were, once again, Mackenzie accompanied this time by Commander of the ETR Maj.-Gen. David M. Jones. The concept was proved, and the initial challenging timeline had been achieved. Cpl Cairns was on hand to mark the submarine's arrival back at Canaveral, playing the 'Black Bear', traditionally the quickest march in the repertoire of the British Army and played on the return to barracks. He had initially been expected to wait for the second launch, but had requested passage home having experienced the, perhaps inevitable, 'disharmony' between the two crews using the same boat.[77]

Mackenzie duly wrote to Levering Smith:

> After last Monday's success the First Sea Lord made a signal of thanks to CNO and all in the USN concerned with our project and I hope this message has passed down the line to SP. I do however particularly wish to add my own sincere thanks to you and the whole of your team, service, civilian and contractors who have taught, led, inspired, encouraged and helped us during the last five years. I hope that you and SP feel as rewarded by RESOLUTION's success as we do.
>
>   The Admirals and the Captains tend of course to be in the limelight on these occasions, but my thanks, and I speak for all my team, go also to those many Americans behind the scenes, the desk officers, the finance and logistics people, the weapon system contractors and all the 'back room boys' without whose friendly and willing co-operation our target would never have been met.[78]

Britain's first SSBN had proven its operational capability. The two crews now had confidence in the design, build, and quality of their charge. Although fielding a common system with a common aim, politically the government was absolutely clear that the UK deterrent force had no US lock-keys in the onboard systems, nor did it allow USN officers or men to sail on deterrent patrols. (Similarly, there were no exchange officers on the V-force aircraft.) It was only during these DASOs that any US personnel found their way on board the UK's bombers:

> The only time we saw USN people onboard was during [these DASOs] during which time the crews went through missile system related training from loading missiles alongside all the way through to the launch procedure, at which time the system itself was given its final certification which resulted in a live missile launch and subsequent tracking of dummy warheads to target impact points to ensure within accuracy parameters. Here the process was conducted by a mix of RN and USN people nearly all of them in uniform.[79]

HMS *Renown* was the next on the slipway. The four R-class submarines were all similar, although the *Repulse* was 18 inches longer as a result of an error somewhere in reading the plans and the insertion of an extra rib behind the accommodation section. Such was their size that they could accommodate three decks running from the front of the pressure hull to the rear of the missile compartment. Still retaining the capability to launch torpedoes, the forward end consisted of the torpedo compartment which doubled as forward accommodation. Torpedoes were loaded through a hatch in the casing and slid down to the mid-deck. The compartment also included the forward escape hatch, and the space could be used to accommodate a Royal Marines boarding party should this ever, for operational reasons, be needed, leading to a maximum of 180 on board for this or for training purposes. Moving aft through the hatch in bulkhead 35, the pressure hull widened to full width and the substantial size of the submarine became apparent. In this new generation of long-patrol nuclear submarines, crew comfort and recreation facilities were prime considerations to maintain morale on board and the junior rates mess was comparatively spacious— certainly the envy of veteran submariners. Video facilities provided entertainment instead of the cine projector and screen previously required for film shows. The nearby galley seemed unusually compact for the number of meals that had to be produced, but quality and variety of food was a high priority and proved to be the envy of the surface fleet. One thing, however, remained common to the past and this was the storage space—or lack of it—for food which was crammed into every corner at the start of the patrol. A contingency supply was also added in case of a lengthened duration patrol.[80] Waste garbage was packed in sealed metal containers and ejected from the submarine via a chute located next to the galley. This precaution was to prevent the waste floating to the surface, risking revealing the submarine's position. Despite all these improvements, crew accommodation was adequate, but no more. One crew member delighted in the story of a description of the facilities being sent to the Ministry of Agriculture and Fisheries. Their reply was that whilst it was difficult to make a positive assessment without the location of the accommodation being given, on the description provided it was barely sufficient to accommodate pigs. While each crew member now had his separate bunk—unlike the 'hot bunking' previously the norm in submarines— only the commanding officer had the total privilege of his own cabin. Typically, a junior officer on a frigate would experience better accommodation than a senior officer on an SSBN. It was important that the submarine broke the patrol or surfaced only in an extreme emergency and to this end, a doctor was one of the crew. A comprehensively equipped sick bay was located near to the wardroom. Apart from routine illness and injury, anything more serious could still present problems and, whilst surgery could be undertaken *in extremis*, suppression of the condition using drugs would normally be the preferred course of action if this was considered practical. The doctor had a secondary duty monitoring the radiation levels on board and checking the atmosphere for toxic gasses. A health physics laboratory was to be found on the port side of the missile compartment. Cdre Toby Elliott, former CO of the *Resolution* and Capt. SM10, commented:

> Seventy-odd days dived was quite a long time by anyone's stretch of imagination, and actually nearly everyone had a low point at one stage or another during the patrol, perhaps at the half way point. Quite a few would draw up a countdown diary and would tick off the days, or each and every watch. I rather thought this type of approach would make time drag by, though being well aware that there would be some anxiety if it looked like the successor boat coming on to QRA was going to be delayed at all. Such bad news had to be addressed head on and the boys would respond positively and with that wonderful sense of humour best savoured when times were otherwise not good.[81]

The nerve centre of the submarine was the control room on the top deck below the fin. Functions were split by a longitudinal divide. Control of the boat was found on the port side with the sonar tracking displays on the starboard side. At the forward end, a hatch led to the conning tower with further access to the fin. The main control panel with its two control columns was very reminiscent of a multi-engined aircraft and indeed the submarine was almost 'flown' through the water. This analogy was further reinforced by the provision of an autopilot. Behind the control section were the controls for the ballast tanks and trimming controls, while further back and in its own compartment was the navigation room dominated by the two large SINS units. These were 'run side by side and the Navcentre teams monitor[ed] one against the other to assess which [was] giving the most accurate positional data'.[82] Like the US SSBNs, position could be checked either by returning to periscope depth and taking a satellite fix, or more generally receiving a LORAN signal via the towed array which extended some 400 yards behind the submarine.

The four Royal Navy 'bombers' were designed for many years of operation, so while the original systems were those extant at the time, subsequent advances in technology meant that additional or replacement components were expected to be added during refit periods. While the Type 2001 sonar—a second-generation sonar but still requiring a good deal of manual input—was still to dominate the sonar set, additional sonar suites had to be added to an already confined space. Operating these additional pieces of hardware could still be achieved without any increase to the boat's complement.

Union problems still featured all too prominently in the shipyards. Roy Mason visited Cammell Laird in January 1967, toured the *Renown*, and urged the shipyard workers to 'work themselves into a job not out of one'. The submarine, though still on a delayed schedule for a February 1967 launch, was by then some three months behind her date for operational deployment. Mason urged

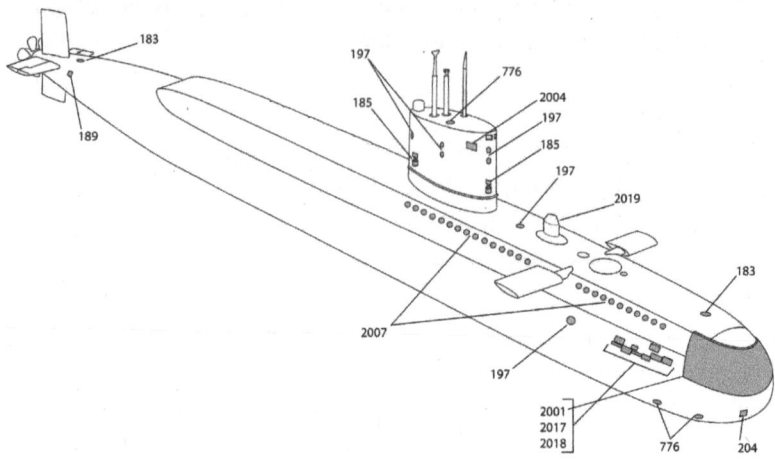

Resolution-class sonar arrays.

the work force, represented by no less than fourteen unions, and management to commit to resolving their differences and accept three-shift working to make up the delays. He further commented, 'I am not particularly happy about what I have seen on the Polaris job.'[83] Consideration was even at one stage given to towing the submarine to Barrow to be completed. Perhaps not surprisingly, there was reaction from both unions and management. Mr F. H. Turner, on behalf of the Merseyside district of the Confederation of Shipbuilding and Engineering Unions, said they were 'amazed and perturbed that Mr Mason did not seek talks with the trade union officials before arriving at hasty decisions and judgments':

> We are concerned with the fact that statements are being made that shipbuilding workers are not pulling their weight. This is the sort of statement that can do nothing but harm to the relationship built up over a number of years between the workers, shop stewards, trade union officials, and the management. [Cammell Laird's managing director, Geoffrey] Moss said twice as much work was involved in completing the submarine as had been envisaged, largely due to additional precautions since the disaster to the American nuclear submarine *Thresher*.[84]

Union confederation chairman Harry Potts added: 'We will consider some action along the lines stated by the Minister, but to talk about reducing the number of unions into two or three for the purpose of management-worker negotiations is just pie in the sky. It will mean a long process.'[85] In the somewhat chaotic world of union negotiations, later in the year work on both Cammell's submarines stopped in an action against the unions for delays in the negotiating discussions.

True to form, two weeks before the launch date, 500 fitters walked out over a two shillings-an-hour 'condition allowance', however, this was not going to delay the launch of the *Renown* which slid down the slipway on 25 February 1967 sponsored by Mrs Edna Healey, wife of the minister of defence, who launched the submarine with a bottle of apple wine. It was estimated that around 18,000 people saw the launch. However, anti-Polaris protesters were once again out in force and 'there were scuffles with the police—leave for the uniformed branch had been cancelled for the day—and seven demonstrators were arrested'.[86] The protesters were also critical of the bishop of Chester, the Right Rev. Gerald Ellison, for saying prayers at the ceremony—a long-standing naval tradition to pray for peace and the safety of the crew. Their views even reached parliament in the form of an early day motion tabled by Labour MP Tom Driberg who said that the bishop's actions 'must suggest to many people in Britain and abroad that a Christian Church officially approves of the possession and possible use of a weapon designed for the indiscriminate destruction of human life'.[87] However, for those inside the shipyard, 'it was a great day for Cammell Laird's workers and their families who crowded around the launching area. Hundreds of children occupied vantage points. Mr Robert Johnson, chairman of the shipbuilding company, said the launching of the *Renown* marked their launching as nuclear shipbuilders.'[88] In her speech, Mrs Healey gave particular recognition to navy wives, a group of women with which she had developed a particular affinity since becoming the wife of the defence secretary who was also attending his first launch. He commented that it was one of the most moving occasions at which he had been present.[89] On the same day, the USS *Triton* (SSN-586)—the world's largest attack submarine and COMSUBLANT's flagship—arrived at the Holy Loch on a routine two-day visit.

HMS *Renown* was commissioned on 15 November 1968. Mrs Healey was once again present and saw the commissioning ceremony conducted by the Rev. L. Macmamaway, a chaplain on the former battlecruiser *Renown*. Three previous captains were also there. The new *Renown*'s captains were announced as Cdr Kenneth Mills (starboard) and Cdr Robin Heath (port). Before taking command of the *Renown*, Mills had been the second-in-command of the guided missile destroyer HMS *Devonshire* (D02). During a visit to a Soviet port, Mills found that one of the Soviet officers, whom he assumed was a KGB agent, appeared to know a great deal about him. As they parted, the Russian wished Mills good luck, saying: 'I hope your next appointment is to your liking.'[90]

The *Renown*'s sea trials were not without problems. On leaving the shipyard in February 1969, the submarine's port bow hit a dock entrance, but a more serious incident occurred on the night of 13 October when the submarine surfaced in the vicinity of the Mull of Kintyre and was in collision with the MV *Moyle*, an Irish cattle boat. Damage to the fin was slight, but Capt. Martin Houston, master of the *Moyle*, said 'the full-scale air and sea search which was launched after the incident could have been avoided if the Navy had said the submarine was involved.'[91] Parliamentary Under Secretary of State for Defence for the Royal Navy Dr David Owen assured MPs that damage had been minimal and that the submarine was fully operational the following day.[92] Cdr Mills, an experienced officer, was relieved of command and replaced by Cdr Francis Ponsonby. At his subsequent court martial held in Rosyth, he persuaded the prosecutor, Capt. (later Admiral Sir) John Fieldhouse, to describe him as 'a most capable officer [whose] great personal courage and depth of integrity are much admired'.[93] To avoid a repeat of this form of embarrassment to its nuclear forces, the navy announced in January that it would review the exercise areas used by its nuclear submarines to avoid busy shipping lanes. It was also time to define the operational patrol cycle so as to keep one SSBN on patrol at all times.

Everything now completed, the *Renown* headed for Cape Canaveral, arriving on 12 July 1969 and successfully completed her DASO firings on 24 July and 11 August.

Vickers' second Polaris submarine, HMS *Repulse* was launched by the sponsor, Lady Joan Zuckerman, at Barrow on 4 November 1967. Lady Zuckerman had spent the previous night at the company's official guest house, nineteenth-century Bankfield Hall in Urswick. On the day, however, all did not go well. Firstly, Lady Zuckerman's car was delayed by ten minutes when police had to clear a way

MAJOR LAUNCH DAY EVENT		DASO LAUNCH COUNTDOWN SEQUENCE	
	Onboard C-Band and Onboard Destruct Receiver-Decoder Tests conducted 2 hours before starting countdown clock. SINS reset 1 hour before start of clock.		(Fifteen-minute tactical countdown with additional evolutions required by the Eastern Test Range)
		T-15:00	"ACTION STATIONS MISSILE." Set Condition 1SQ for DASO launch.
T-300:00	Start countdown clock. ETR Destruct Receiver-Decoder Checks.		
		T-10:00	Range provides "CLEAR TO LAUNCH."
T-255:00	SSBN underway to launch area. Commence setting Condition 2SQ. Conduct TI Calibrations, Daily Fire Control Tests, Missile Closeout Inspections, Range Destruct Checks, and Daily Missile Tests.	T-07:00	Final prediction of SSBN position at launch given to Range. Channel check of both fire control channels performed.
		T-06:00	Navigation/Fire Control Transmission Checks on master SINS completed.
T-120:00	Condition 2SQ set.		
T-90:00	SSBN arrives in launch area and submerges to launch depth. Conduct Missile Static Loop Tests.	T-03:00	Weapon System in Condition 1SQ. Instrumentation systems on missile to be launched switched to internal power.
T-45:00	SSBN commences hovering.	T-01:30	Captain gives "PERMISSION TO FIRE."
T-22:00	Preliminary prediction of SSBN position at T-0 given to ETR. Master SINS reset, if required.	T-00:45	Polaris System Officer initiates FIRE on missile to be launched.
T-15:00	"ACTION STATIONS MISSILE." (See adjoining page for more detailed sequence of events between T-15:00 and T-00:00.)	T-00:35	Missile PREPARE sequence started. Muzzle hatch opens.
T-00:00	Missile launched. After launch, SSBN surfaces and proceeds to Port Canaveral.	T-00:00	Polaris System Officer depresses tactical firing key; MISSILE AWAY.

HMS *Renown* DASO launch sequence.

through anti-nuclear protesters to reach the dockyard gate. It had been important to match the launch with the height of the tide in the Walney Channel. The delay was sufficient to cause shipbuilding manager William Parnell, company naval architect Roy Turner, and John Cameron, the MoD's principal naval overseer, to question the wisdom of continuing with the launch as they feared a late launch could be adversely affected by tidal conditions in the Channel. After a hasty inspection of a guard of honour provided by local sea cadets and the presentation of the traditional bouquet, the official party at last made its way to the platform, but even at this late stage, Parnell, Turner, and Cameron approached Redshaw to recommend cancelling the launch. Redshaw overruled them and the ceremony proceeded, Lady Zuckerman using a bottle of her homemade elderberry wine to smash across the bows of the submarine. However, the concerns expressed were justified when the current took control and the *Repulse* sped rapidly away from the accompanying tugs 'as if she was going full speed astern' towards the Jubilee Bridge, only to run aground on a sandbank. The Channel had been dredged prior to the launch, but the combination of the high tide, the resulting current, and strong winds had pushed the *Repulse* wide of the intended direction. Timber that broke away from the launching cradle floated to the surface creating a potential hazard for the tugs that went in to effect a rescue. This unfortunate drama was witnessed by the Vickers' chairman Sir Leslie Rowan and did little to enhance the shipbuilder's reputation. It took seven tugs and some twelve hours of intensive effort to pull the submarine free and tow her to the firm's Devonshire Dock for fitting out; a dockyard spokesman subsequently confirming that, fortunately, little or no damage had been done. 'Vickers workmen, marooned on the deck of the submarine, had to climb down a ladder thrown over the vessel's side to reach the small craft which clustered around waiting to take them ashore.'[94] On a more positive note, to emphasise how much work had been achieved prior to launch and to show that many systems were fully operational, before the launch ceremony Redshaw had offered a cup of tea to Rowland Baker. The tea had been made in the fully working galley aboard the submarine.

The police arrested some forty protesters and thirty-one subsequently appeared in court charged with breaching the peace or wilful obstruction of the highway. No doubt somewhat embarrassed by these events, local left-wing Labour MP Alfred Booth, a self-confessed anti-nuclear supporter, sought later in the week to distance himself from what had happened, claiming that it was not the actions of CND that had been the cause, but those of the Polaris Action Group. Booth later became secretary of state for employment in the Wilson government.

Many were surprised at Redshaw's decision against postponing the launch until the following day. Turner was later to confide:

No explanation was ever given for Redshaw's failure to ensure the sponsor stuck to the agreed and well-tried programme.... [It was] perhaps the most important mistake in his entire career, and with the Vickers Chairman, Sir Leslie Rowan on the platform, it might have led to an early end to that career had the boat been seriously damaged and the UK's deterrent programme delayed.[95]

It is perhaps a reflection on the events of the day that no state award was forthcoming for Redshaw; his knighthood in 1972 was for 'services to export'. Baker, however, received a knighthood—a most unusual honour for a civil servant of his grade. But Redshaw's 'granite like' self-confidence could have so easily have also been his downfall.

HMS *Repulse* was commissioned on 28 September 1968. Lady Zuckerman, this time accompanied by her daughter, Stella, was the guest of the commanding officers of both ship's companies. A total of around 1,000 VIPs were entertained during the subsequent reception to the musical accompaniment of the works band.

Cdr Anthony Whetstone (later to be ACNS(Ops) during the Falklands War) and the starboard crew took the submarine to sea on 6 October for her sea trials prior to her DASO. Thereafter, HMS *Repulse* arrived at the ETR on 15 March 1969 and completed two successful launch programmes by each of the crews on 27 March and 14 April under Cdrs Whetstone and John 'Phil' Wadman (port). Before leaving on their return voyage to the UK, the crews thanked the people of Brevard County Community for the generous hospitality extended to them during their visit.[96]

The last of Britain's four Polaris submarines, *Revenge*, was launched at the Cammell Laird yard on 15 March 1968. Despite clear evidence that British shipbuilding was in decline in the face of foreign competition, union activity had continued to bedevil the construction and the MoD had feared that 'last ship syndrome'—the deliberate slowing down of a contract to maintain jobs— might apply to the *Revenge*. The solution was to give an order for an SSN to the Liverpool shipyard. Their concerns were to be fully justified when the gearbox of the SSN HMS *Conqueror* (S48) was sabotaged as she neared completion, delaying completion by some months and adding £1 million to the cost. It was therefore hardly surprising that the launch of the submarine on 28 August 1969 marked the end of Cammell Laird's involvement in building nuclear submarines for the next twenty years. All further work would go to Vickers.

The launch was performed by Lady Heather Law, wife of Vice-Admiral Sir Horace Law, controller of the navy. She commented: 'I hope *Revenge* will be able to serve her purpose by not using any of her terrifying weapons, which I pray she may never do.' The inevitable anti-nuclear protesters were present and tried to interrupt proceedings. *The Times* correspondent reported:

At one point during the ceremony, a man apparently tried to throw himself in front of Lady Law as she made her way to the platform. Mr. Maurice Wyatt, a director and general manager of the shipyard. who is in charge of the Polaris project, grabbed the man and pushed him through the barrier into the arms of police. Two men in overalls shouted during the religious service, a girl ran protesting in front of the cars carrying the platform party, and a youth hurried forward brandishing an umbrella and shouting. The protesters were taken away by members of the security force. Six people were removed from the shipyard, but there were no arrests.... More than 1,400 men have been engaged on building the *Revenge*. The launching was watched by many thousands including parties of children from 11 towns in Lancashire and Cheshire. The religious service was longer than that for the last launching when the Bishop of Chester was criticized for his part. Then the prayers, as the bishop made plain, were for the men who sailed in the boat and not for the Polaris submarine. Today the Rev. M. B. Dewey, Dean of Pembroke College, Cambridge, who was chaplain in the last *Revenge*, was more embracing. His prayers were not only for the men but 'the ship in which they sail'.[97]

Also present at the launch was Under-Secretary of State for the Navy Maurice Foley who commented:

When I watched *Revenge* go down the slipway I was not thinking of deterrents—I was thinking much more of the workmanship and the skills which have gone into her design and engineering.... Every part is in the forefront of technical and scientific knowledge and expertise.[98]

The *Revenge* was one of the most famous names in Royal Navy history—the first ship of that name being the command of Sir Francis Drake. Commissioning took place on 4 December 1969. In attendance was Adm. Law who expressed pleasure in being controller of the navy from the submarine's keel laying right through to commissioning. The Royal Navy now had its full complement of four Polaris SSBNs—the 'bombers'. Then it was time for sea trials before the North Atlantic transit for the two crews to undertake the DASO programme.

HMS *Revenge* arrived some fifteen minutes ahead of schedule at Port Canaveral on 19 May 1970, the Union Flag proudly displayed on her masthead. The event still made front page news as a group of newsmen waited for the boat's CO, Cdr Basil Watson (starboard), smartly dressed in tropical whites, to emerge from the submarine. Meanwhile, the crew went about their duties, 'mooring lines were tied and retied, the forward floatation tanks were refilled, signal flags and electronic signalling devices were stored below deck, and a five-story tall 25,000-ton crane was used to lower a guard shack weighing a mere few hundred pounds onto the deck of the submarine'.[99] Also present for the arrival was Capt. Bob Garson the Royal Navy's senior Polaris UK representative on the staff of the BJSM in Washington. A fortnight later, with a group of VIPs on board, including RADM

Harold E. Shear and Adm. Sir Michael Pollock, both of whom had been closely involved with Polaris on behalf of their respective navies from the start of the programme, the *Revenge*, with her starboard crew, headed out to sea for her DASO. Sadly, not present was First Sea Lord RAdm. Le Fanu who was unable to attend through what proved to be a fatal illness. He wrote to Levering Smith:

> The doctors have told me I must thin out my engagements for a few weeks and the DASO was an obvious candidate for pruning, but oh!, how sad I am not to be with you on this climatic [*sic*] occasion.... To have been associated with Polaris from Nassau to now has been one of the big things of my life ... [and] proof of what one nation and one navy can do for another nation and another navy, is the happy end of my long honeymoon with the U.S.N. ... 'THANK YOU AND (very respectfully) WELL DONE'.[100]

After the countdown, the missile rose above the ocean and reached skywards. However, after some fifty seconds, the shore-based safety officer destroyed the missile as its telemetry showed it to be heading for New York rather than Ascension Island. Post-flight analysis showed a sequence of events not previously experienced and certain maintenance routines were duly amended. Two days later, on 1 June, the *Revenge* fired her stand-by missile which was a total success, as was the missile fired by her port crew a fortnight later.[101] The signal reporting the successful conclusion to this vital phase of proving the efficiency of this UK contribution to the NATO Defence Forces noted: 'HMS *Revenge* (Port Crew) successfully launched A3(T) missile Serial Number 2648 at 181530Z Jun following normal countdown. Predicted miss distance within acceptable limits.'[102]

Although HMS *Resolution* had sailed on patrol in 1968, it was not until April 1969 that the Royal Navy was able to maintain a continuous patrol cycle with at least one SSBN on patrol at all times. Called Operation Relentless, the UK's longest-running military operation, the CASD has been maintained unbroken since that time. Anticipating the moment when the RAF's V-force would relinquish its custody of the UK's deterrent, the Royal Navy hosted a press introduction to their forthcoming deterrent patrols when the *Renown* took a party of journalists to sea to experience a practice countdown under the watchful eye of Cdr Mills. (The party included four females which may have upset older hands who still held to the superstitions of the sea whereby females on board were believed to anger the sea gods and result in stormy sea conditions!) 'A gentle "plop" signalled that the hatch above the missile tube was open', but the submarines still had to be armed so the tube was empty.[103] Following this operation, two divers left the submarine through an escape hatch to effect imaginary repairs to the external hull.

At the stroke of midnight on 30 June 1969, the RAF handed over to the Royal Navy which had now officially subsumed the responsibility for the country's nuclear defence. However, the V-bombers were not yet redundant and maintained a nuclear capability, although no longer on 24/7 Quick Reaction Alert (QRA). Blue Steel was phased out in 1970, but the WE.177 nuclear laydown bomb was still in the inventory and no-notice exercises which involved generating and dispersing the force remained a feature of training schedules. Although this was declared to NATO in both nuclear and conventional roles, the parsimonious allocation of iron bombs saw this latter capability all but disappear by 1974, and by 1980, it was quietly withdrawn only to be resurrected in 1982 with the bombing of Port Stanley airfield during Operation Corporate, the Falklands conflict. The makeshift Vulcan tankers were withdrawn in 1984, but 55 Sqn soldiered on with Victors until 1993, including participation in Operation Desert Storm.

The Royal Navy's SSBNs on patrol were under the operational command of CTF 345 (C-in-C Western Fleet (CINC WF)) based at Northwood in Middlesex, but were assigned to NATO as part of SACEUR's nuclear forces to be used for the international defence of the Western Alliance in all circumstances. Only when 'supreme national interests were at stake' could the submarines be used independently by Britain. For this possibility, a separate set of target plans was carried on board the Royal Navy's submarines, the details of which were known to only a few people. The QRA commitment to NATO required that sixteen missiles were available at fifteen minutes' notice to fire, implying that one submarine had to be continuously on patrol. A further sixteen missiles had to either be at QRA or 'follow-on' status—at twenty-four hours' notice to fire and the SSBN at forty-seven hours' notice to put to sea. It appears that this total of thirty-two missiles was later downgraded to a total of twenty-eight, possibly a reflection on ageing missiles. The theoretical plan was: one boat on patrol, one returning from patrol, one alongside at Faslane, and one in refit. This time the cycle was tight and left little margin for unplanned delays, expected to increase as the submarines got older. To start this cycle, it was planned that the *Resolution* would go into refit at Rosyth in the summer of 1970 and use the same berth and the same technical staff that were currently employed on the refit of the *Dreadnought*. Due to a series of unfortunate circumstances, however, the refit of Britain's first SSN was considerably behind schedule, and she would still be in Rosyth when the SSBN arrived on 21 June 1970. As the Polaris boats took preference over all others, the *Dreadnought* would be pushed into the background and further delayed.[104] This first SSBN refit took just over a year, and the *Resolution* was recommissioned on 10 July 1971. The guest of honour was the queen mother who had flown up to Scotland in an aircraft of the Queen's Flight and who was to maintain a close relationship with the submarine over subsequent years, although at times the association of the royal family with the nuclear deterrent could be a sensitive matter. Her majesty was also there for the *Resolution*'s second recommissioning at Rosyth on 27 November 1977 following the submarine's second refit. She was again present on 1 October 1984 for the *Resolution*'s third commission after nearly four years in the refit dock. On arrival at Rosyth, she inspected a royal guard under the command of Lt Peter Wilkinson. Senior Royal Navy guests at the ceremony were FOSM Vice-Admiral Sir John 'Sandy' Woodward and FOSNI Vice-Admiral Nicholas Hunt. Following the ceremony, she addressed the ship's company before touring the submarine taking tea when she cut the commissioning cake, assisted by the youngest member of the crew, seventeen-year-old Ordinary Seaman Douglas Imrie. This refit cycle then came fully into play as the three other boats reached their turn to head for Rosyth.

The Clyde Bases

By April 1963, MPs were asking questions about where the UK's Polaris submarines would be based. James Stodart MP representing the Scottish Office sought to make a strong case for a Scottish base. Miss Joan Vickers MP representing Devonport pressed the case for a southern base. There were, however, overall requirements for the location; the base needed to be near to deep water, needed easy navigational access, and to be close to where the missiles would be stored. From a northern base standpoint, the regular possibility of 'scotch mist' descending over the water would also provide a useful cloak over departing submarines as the submarines operating from the Holy Loch had already discovered. Other sites had been considered. In an interview on BBC Scotland in 2014, former First Sea Lord Admiral Sir Alan West, not unknown for his straightforward views on naval matters, admitted that the navy's first choice for a Polaris base had been Falmouth, with Milford Haven in Wales also being on the short list. The latter was ruled out because introducing nuclear submarines would only have been possible if the one oil refinery in the estuary was shut down.[1]

Prior to this, in 1961 FOSM Rear-Admiral Hezlet, a highly experienced submariner and keen Polaris supporter, had envisaged protecting the submarines in an underground facility in one of three Scottish west coast tidal sea lochs: Loch Glencoul, Loch Nevis, or Loch Striven. It fell to him 'to provide authoritative opinion and formulate plans for support and training facilities in a force as yet unfamiliar with nuclear propulsion'.[2] Perhaps a little too 'James Bond' in concept and without confirmation at that time that Polaris would actually become part of the Royal Navy, his report received little support. In the end, it is perhaps a little ironic that after the effort that Macmillan had put into trying to dissuade the Americans from wanting a base for their Polaris submarines on the Clyde that that self-same stretch of water should be chosen for the Royal Navy's SSBN base. Perhaps it was hoped that the populace of Glasgow would be more accepting of a nuclear incident from British rather than American interests. In response to a request 'to ask the Civil Lord of the Admiralty how soon he will be able to announce where a base will be constructed for the British POLARIS submarines?' the reply was given on 10 April 1963: '[A]fter careful consideration of all possible sites in the United Kingdom, having regard particularly to operational and public safety considerations, we have decided to establish an operating base at Faslane on the Gare Loch.'[3] On 24 April 1963, Ian Orr-Ewing therefore duly advised parliament:

[I]t has been decided that development of existing submarine operating facilities at Faslane in the Gare Loch offers on balance the greatest advantages for a Polaris operating base. A new armament depot will be constructed at Coulport, on the eastern shore of Loch Long, about 8 miles by road and 13 miles by sea from Faslane.... Survey and similar work will start at Faslane immediately, and the base will be completed by 1968.[4]

The Times' naval correspondent reported:

The decision to utilize Faslane as a Polaris base comes as no surprise in naval circles, since its advantages for submarines have been long appreciated. With a possible cost of £25m it becomes one of the largest Government projects ever to be carried out in Scotland. The cost will be spread over five years with the peak of up to half the total cost in 1965–66. In addition to the operating base and armament depot, a weapon system training facility will be required in Britain and this is expected to cost an additional £7m. or £8m. Whether this will also be sited at Faslane is still under consideration. Coulport—where the missiles will be stored—was originally occupied for naval research purposes, and most of the land required for the new depot is already government-owned. Full-scale practice live firing of Polaris missiles will not take place in British waters nor will Polaris submarines fire practice missiles. Launching systems, however, will be tested at the operating base using inert testing vehicles which will land alongside within 100ft.[5]

The announcement was made to both Houses of Parliament, and in the Upper House, Lord Carrington as first lord of the Admiralty commented that all the Royal Navy Dockyards had failed in some respect to offer the required facilities. Nonetheless, Scotland did well out of the announcement as it not only promised new employment opportunities at Faslane where around 400 new jobs would be created of which half would be local recruitment, the construction alone requiring some 1,000 jobs. It also confirmed that Rosyth Dockyard would be undertaking the refits of the submarines. There were also many economic advantages in amalgamating the administration of fleet and Polaris submarines in the same base. Faslane had long been associated with naval activity, going back to the historic times of Scottish kings Robert the Bruce and James IV. The major downside in selecting Faslane from a current operational point of view was the Rhu Narrows at the entrance to the loch which could be mined by an enemy, thus potentially preventing the submarines' entrance or exit to and from their base. The navy, however, had a fleet of *Hunt*-class mine countermeasure vessels whose primary role was to deal with this problem. Macmillan's earlier concerns about Glasgow's vulnerability may have caused him to reflect that the area would now support the SSBNs of two navies as well as the armament depot at Coulport, the design of which was closely based on the US Navy missile facility at Bangor, Washington, with the adjacent torpedo firing range at Arrochar, a torpedo calibration range in Loch Fyne, a nearby acoustic range and the adjacent NATO armament depot in Glen Douglas, believed by many to be the storage area for the US Navy's Poseidon warheads although no credible evidence was ever presented to support this. A place of eerie silence, it held in store non-nuclear munitions for the Royal Navy, US, and Netherlands navies. There was, of course, an element of anti-nuclear protest, but for the more altruistic in the local community the local economy benefitted by £4.5 million (in 2020 prices) and provided much local employment. For the more publicity conscious, they were to discover that the royal family became regular visitors providing an opportunity for local dignitaries to feature in the local press.

Lord Carrington advised:

> Survey and similar work [would] start at Faslane immediately, and the base [would] be completed by 1968. Provisional estimates at this stage put the cost of developing the base and armament depot at between £20 million and £25 million including between £12 million and £15 million for construction work. When the base is finished it is expected that some 1,700 officers and men will be based or stationed there, together with their families.[6]

Faslane had been used by the army in the Second World War as Military Port No. 1. Luftwaffe attacks on the Atlantic-facing ports turned out to be much less than expected and usage of Faslane was likewise lower than anticipated, and after the war was over, the army showed no ongoing interest and closed the establishment on 31 March 1946. Thereafter the Gare Loch became the last resting place for surplus naval capital ships including the Royal Navy's last battleship HMS *Vanguard* when Metal Industries Ltd took over and the port became a shipbreaker's yard. In 1954, facilities were built to support the two HTP submarines discussed earlier. In September 1957, however, the navy established a submarine base at Faslane for the 3rd Submarine Squadron (SM3) supported by the depot ship HMS *Adamant* (A164) and submarines have been based there ever since. The *Adamant* was replaced on 27 May 1962 by HMS *Maidstone* (A185) which had been recently converted to support nuclear submarines. As well as supporting SM3 submarines she would in due course also briefly support the four SSBNs. The latter submarines would form the 10th Submarine Squadron (SM10) which was commissioned in March 1967. The choice of name harked back to the Royal Navy's 10th Submarine Flotilla which had served with distinction in two world wars. As well as the two RN submarine squadrons, there was a discrete Dutch naval presence usually operating two diesel submarines. Security at the base was a high priority and this was provided by Commachio Company Royal Marines (Commachio Group Royal Marines from 1983). The 'black clad Faslane SBS-trained supermen can occasionally be seen throwing themselves into the Clyde from RAF Hercules in training to repel subversives'.[7] The area of the base where the SSBN support would be developed was within the area used by Metal Industries who then considered that their continuing operations at Faslane would no longer be economic and sought compensation for loss of profits and the redundancy costs of the 250 civilians that worked at the site. Chairman Sir Charles Westlake commented: 'engineering profits almost everywhere are more difficult to achieve'. He also announced the closure of the company's loss-making salvage division, Metal Industries (Salvage) Ltd, as marine salvage was no longer considered viable.[8] In relinquishing their salvage yard to the MoD, the company did, however, agree to take on a thirty-year lease on the northern end of the Faslane complex, thus maintaining their operations in the area along with much-needed jobs. Despite the beneficial employment opportunities, left-wing trades unions were opposed to the plans. Officials of the Association of Supervisory Staffs, Executives and Technicians along with the Scottish National Union of Mineworkers said they would make speeches against it at the forthcoming Congress of the Scottish TUC, although the resolution was couched in broad anti-Polaris terms, rather than specifically mentioning Faslane.[9]

By May 1963, the Admiralty's Land Branch had started to prepare the area. Cost estimate for converting the site was £25 million, of which about half would go on construction. The Ministry of Public Building and Works was responsible for the work needed to bring the base up to standard to operate the SSBNs.[10] The most urgent need was the building of the Royal Naval Polaris School, construction of which started in December 1963. By June 1964, a contract had been signed for the development of the Coulport Armament Depot. The next phase was for a new jetty, diversion of roads, and ratings' married quarters in the nearby town of Helensburgh.[11] By early July 1965, Emrys Hughes, MP for South Ayrshire, was concerned that the recent increase in the price of cement would escalate the building costs, suggesting to Parliament Secretary for Public Building and Works James Boyden that 'we believe that this will be the most expensive white elephant which has ever been erected in Scotland?'[12] Work continued nonetheless. The Polaris School opened in June 1966 and provided the necessary training facilities thereby obviating the need to send personnel over to the US

Naval Guided Missiles School at Dam Neck, Virginia, where the USN crews were trained. Britain had already experienced having to train the RAF's Thor crews in the US, while although popular with the crews was complicated in logistic terms.

Over the hill and located on the rugged eastern shore of Loch Long was the Royal Naval Armaments Depot (RNAD) at Coulport, originally an important ferry crossing point with the land above belonging to the farm of Duchlage.[13] Nearby was Coulport House, built in 1860 by John Kibble, a mildly eccentric engineer who, adjacent to the house, built Coulport Palace, a magnificent 'greenhouse' wherein could be found, statues, plants, a pond, and a collection of model steamships. All traces of these former landmarks were to be eradicated except for the palace which was dismantled and taken to Glasgow's Botanical Gardens where it can still be seen today. Developed to store and service the Polaris missiles, the construction contract was given to Richard Costain (Civil Engineering) Ltd with a value of £3.3 million in June 1964. Many of the missile storage bunkers had to be hewn out of solid rock. In 1966, Andrew McLeod was appointed the first superintendent, but it was not, initially at least, an easy posting. On 3 April 1967, Roy Mason visited the site and admitted to journalists that water had become a problem in some of the nuclear handling buildings and modifications would have to be made. 'They have hit a lot of trouble', he admitted. 'Now they are having to establish miniature moats round the base of the buildings to deal with the water problem.'[14] He went on to confirm that five buildings had been affected and these required very stringent standards of temperature and humidity. These very unusual buildings were now dry, but the facility was not yet ready to accept the first warheads which were then in production at AWRE's Burghfield facility adjacent to Aldermaston.[15] Hurricane winds (Low Q) of exceptional strength battered central and southern Scotland in the early hours of 15 January 1968. Coulport did not escape its destructive force and the building programme suffered serious setbacks. The original plan which had called for the establishment to be capable of limited support by mid-1967 and fully operational by March 1968 was now no longer possible. In fact, by June 1968, the project was some twelve to fifteen months behind. The problems were serious enough that the US was, for a time, unwilling to grant the necessary safety certificate for the site and the first loading of HMS *Resolution* was carried out under strict American supervision.

Faslane had fared somewhat better and had been commissioned on 10 August 1967. To let families see what went on at the base, an open day was organised later in the month. Shortly afterwards, an infiltration exercise was carried out by the Royal Marines group and there was surprise and concern when 'Kilroy was here' graffiti—popular with American GIs during the Second World War—were found scrawled around secure areas of the base. Posing as civilians, the marines had joined the families and had duly cased the joint for their future clandestine visit.

The official opening ceremony took place at 11:30 a.m. on 10 May 1968. The queen mother arrived at Faslane and disembarked HM yacht *Britannia*. Escorted by Commodore Clyde, Cdre Derek Kent, she met local dignitaries and talked to navy wives and families before declaring open HMS *Neptune*, the Clyde submarine base as it was now known. Despite the rain, she signed the visitors' book under an umbrella on the casing of HMS *Resolution*, the SSBN she had launched and with which she was to maintain a close relationship. The *Resolution* had recently arrived at Faslane after her DASO firings and was then preparing for her first operational patrol. On 11 June, *The Times* reported that the SSBN was loading her missiles. On 15 June 1968, she set sail on her first patrol, but in contrast to the publicity that had followed her previous progress, this time the departure took place in secret and it was only on 21 June that *The Times* could further report that HMS *Resolution* had 'now sailed on her first operational patrol fully armed with nuclear missiles'. It was a patrol not without its teething problems. The LORAN-C navigation system failed through most of the patrol and navigation had to depend on following the charts of the seabed using a discrete echo sounder. In Czechoslovakia, the period of political liberalisation known as the Prague Spring resulted in Warsaw Pact forces being sent in to quell the uprising. For a time, it seemed that the patrol might be lengthened, something that the submarine was provisioned for but in the end was not needed. Britain's Polaris patrols had now started, although it was not until the following year that the role was fully taken over from the RAF. 'The actual departure of Polaris submarines is not announced or officially confirmed afterwards, to prevent any chance of the submarine being detectable early on in the cruise, and subsequently being tailed by potentially hostile submarines.'

The base was now ready to start preparations for the arrival of all the 'bombers', but there were to be other nuclear arrivals in the form of fleet submarines attached to SM3. The Gare Loch was becoming a busy place. Like the Holy Loch site, a floating dock was required and this had been built in Portsmouth in 1966. Admiralty Floating Dock (AFD60), designed specifically to handle Polaris submarines was then towed to Faslane where testing took place in anticipation of its first submarine customer. Crewed by a mix of navy personnel, civilian crane operators, and valve-house watchkeepers the dock became a well-known landmark at Faslane and over the next thirty years was to handle 629 'customers'—not only submarines, but a variety of other ships as well. Her first docking—of the conventional submarine HMS *Otter* (S15)—took place on 10 May 1968.

One of the penalties of living in a free society was the possibility of espionage being undertaken by Soviet ships visiting British ports. The Foreign Office and Board of Trade's view was that 'trade with the communists [was] a reality; war with them [was] only a possibility'.[16] This meant that Soviet ships had freedom of movement in the waters around the British Isles. 'Trawlers' festooned with an array of intelligence gathering equipment were already well known as they had monitored the activities of the American SSBNs. They could now add the comings and goings of the 3rd and 10th Submarine Squadrons as well. Few had any doubts that the huge Soviet fish-factory ships standing offshore also had their role to play in the intelligence war.

The missiles *sans* warheads were brought across the Atlantic in a specially converted ship, the RFA *Fort Langley* (A230). Built in Canada in 1944 as a *Fort*-class stores ship (the Canadian equivalent to the US Liberty ships), she was fitted out as an Air Stores Issuing Ship (ASIS) and saw service in the Pacific theatre, thereafter completing various different tasks until transferred to the Admiralty in February 1954. In 1967, she was converted at Chatham dockyard for her Polaris role and arrived at POMFLANT, Charlestown, on 3 November 1967 to take on her first shipload of missiles before sailing for Coulport. The ship was damaged during the January 1968 hurricane when a crane collapsed onto her superstructure. Warheads were also initially transported by sea somewhat curiously because the navy categorised them as munitions. The wisdom of this view was called to account when the armaments carrier RMAS *Throsk* (A379) disappeared for a time in the Irish Sea and the fear, fortunately unfounded, was that she had been hijacked by the Provisional IRA.[17] Warheads were also carried by road on the heavily protected 'Nuclear Convoys'. The warheads were carried in special trucks, cargo, heavy duty (TCHD). These were closely monitored by anti-nuclear groups and, perhaps inevitably, over the years suffered a quota of road traffic accidents. Although evidence of mishaps to convoys is sparse and almost certainly incomplete, the MoD did admit to eight convoy accidents between 1960 and 1991. At least three of these incidents involved vehicles at or near to Coulport.

1 April 1973: a Scottish Electricity Board Land Rover reversed into a TCHD carrying Polaris warheads.

6 August 1983: a TCHD collided with a car on the M8 near Glasgow. Two Polaris warheads on board were undamaged.

15 June 1985: near Glasgow there was brake failure on a TCHD.

Two further accidents were recorded during missile handling at Coulport. Both involved component failure on cranes, e.g.: 3 December 1987: Missile 2374 was being replaced because of a series of test failures. The replacement missile 2691 was safely in its liner. This missile collided with trailer supports because of driver error following a defect in the crane, but there was also evidence of an urgency to complete the exchange in an environment that was not conducive to a safe exchange.

The whole credibility of the Polaris deterrent depended not just on the destructive power of the missiles but also the credibility of the weapon based on the invulnerability to detection. Should the Soviets develop systems that could track the submarines, then the value of the deterrent would be significantly compromised. It was therefore presumed that considerable efforts would be made to develop such systems. Fortunately, the range of the A3 missile allowed a number of targets west of the Urals to be reached from a variety of patrol areas in the North Atlantic, Arctic, and Norwegian Seas and the Mediterranean, although the latter would require a greater transit time from the Faslane base and was therefore less attractive. Even a 1,500-mile-range missile still allowed for wide-ranging patrol areas and in fact certain targets such as Kiev (modern day Kyiv) and Leningrad would be in range as soon as the submarine had submerged. Leaving Faslane, the SSBNs would remain on the surface until they had reached areas where it was safe to dive—assumed to be around 40 fathoms. There were four exit routes: the North Channel, the strait connecting the Irish Sea with the North Atlantic, or south via the Irish Sea. The North Channel provided a variety of further exit routes: following shallow water and diving west of the Irish island of Inishtrahull, turning north through the Sound of Mull and diving west of Coll and Tiree, or continuing further north and diving in the North Minch. Clearly varying the routine should be a factor of the submarines leaving on patrol, leaving at different times of day and night, following closely behind other ships or an SSN. With both US and UK submarines using the Clyde estuary as an exit route, co-ordination of the arrivals and departures as well as anti-submarine activities was routed through the US commander-in-chief of naval forces, eastern Atlantic (a subordinate command of CINCLANTFLT), the post initially being held by ADM Harold P. Smith. Having reached the open sea, finding the SSBNs in such a vast sea area presented the Soviets with a near insurmountable problem and was uneconomical in terms of costs. Furthermore, the fact that targets were in range almost as soon as the submarine had left its base meant that it could proceed to its patrol area at slow speed making detection even more difficult. It was one thing to detect and identify a potential SSBN, but quite another to maintain contact over a prolonged period.

Whether or not RN SSBNs were deployed on the long transit to patrol areas in the Mediterranean has not been disclosed.[18]

Life on board for the Polaris crews was totally different from the traditional role of the submariner. No longer the dark secrets of the service seeking out their targets covertly and often operating on the very edges of enemy territorial waters and wary of the possible consequences of being detected. The submarines left their Faslane base, their outward passage through the Clyde estuary already prepared by other vessels to distract Soviet AGIs lurking off the coast. It was a procedure well-rehearsed from the start of the US Navy deployments from the Holy Loch. Once in the open waters of the North Atlantic, the bombers headed for their patrol areas whereupon they would reduce speed to only a few knots with only a few people knowing where they were. No communications were sent

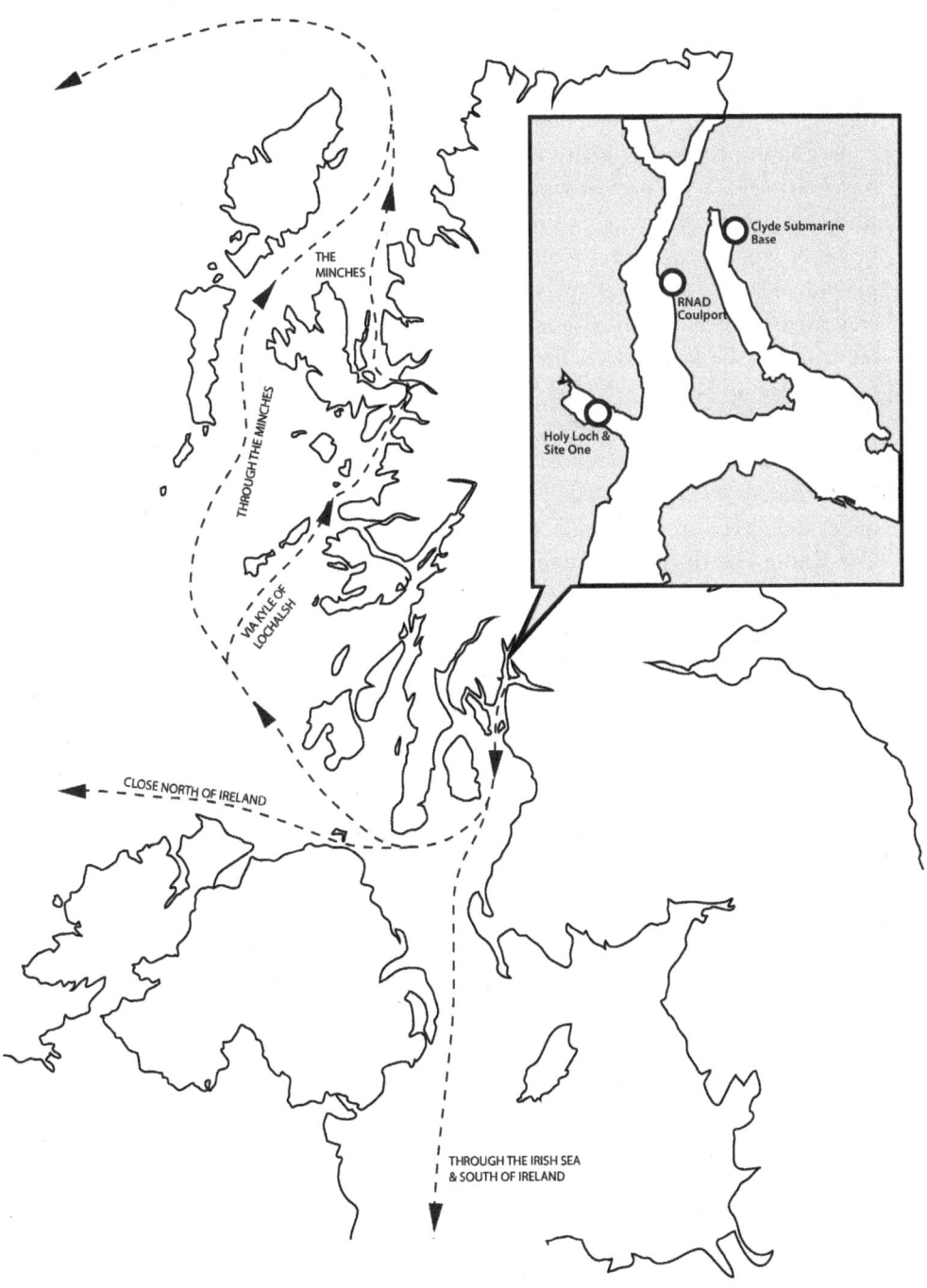

SSBN exit routes from the Clyde bases.

from the submarine which might reveal its position, but signals could be received via a trailing wire antenna and occasional ascents to periscope depth to check the SINS's accuracy by taking a satellite fix. To test crew readiness, no-notice exercises were regularly held which took the crew through the whole procedure from 'Action Stations Missile' and the subsequent verification of codes right through to just before actual launch.

Although necessarily always alert to the possible presence of unwelcome naval elements in the area, it was a monotonous routine nonetheless, which after four to six weeks was likely to reduce moral on board. Conditions for the crew, however, would have been the envy of 'old salts' who had never had the luxury of individual bunk and locker space. Intrigued by the oddities, at least by American standards, experienced on board the British SSBNs, *The Orlando Sentinel*, reporting on the *Resolution*'s first DASO, had learned something of the variety of food served on board by Royal Navy chefs trained at the Savoy Hotel and later, in the case of the *Renown*'s chef, Petty Officer Thomas Winter, from Buckingham Palace. Winter along with fellow chef George Duncan had been given permission by the palace to try out their proposed menus on none other than the queen under the direction of the palace head chef Ronald Aubrey. The *Renown*'s CO, Cdr Robin Heath (port), asked the master of the royal household, Brigadier Geoffrey Hardy-Roberts, if the two petty officers could widen their experience by studying in the royal kitchens. Each has been granted a two-month stay. 'They need experience of a larger galley', explained the *Renown*'s executive officer, Lt Cdr Hugh Thompson, '[speaking] at the Cammell Laird shipyard at Birkenhead, where *Renown* ... [was] now in final preparation for her sea trials. They have only served in small subs before. In *Renown* they will have to cater for larger numbers.'[19] Winter was later to comment that he received few complaints from the crew except when he served duck in orange sauce, a dish he had prepared at Windsor Castle for the Italian president. 'Most of them pulled a face and asked why they couldn't have roast chicken,' he said. The *Orlando Sentinel* further noted: 'Train Smash' (bacon and tomatoes) and Yellow Peril (smoked haddock) were served up alongside more traditional dishes, 'so following their successful launch of a Polaris missile [on] March 4, what better way for the crew to celebrate than with that famous British dish, chicken chow mein?' In addition, whistling on board was banned as it was believed to bring bad luck.[20]

DASO firings were an essential part of the programme towards operational readiness, but were also enjoyed by the crews as there was time to explore the many tourist attractions in the area. 'We had some very good runs ashore, getting to know quite a few of the astronauts during the heady days of moon landings and so on. We watched one night launch whilst surfaced just outside the range— an awesome spectacle.'[21] In mid-1977, the *Resolution* undertook her third DASO after her refit. Arriving on 10 June under the command of Cdr Hugh Peltor, it was in fact the starboard crew under Cdr Ian Ross that carried out a successful launch on 14 July. The crews took the opportunity to visit the various attractions at Disney World, including for some a trip on the 'other' *Nautilus* submarine from *Twenty Thousand Leagues Under the Sea*, while others were tempted by the Kennedy Space Center. It was also the opportunity to welcome some of the local Cocoa Beach population on board the British SSBN.[22]

As experience with the SSBNs led to a better understanding of the operational challenges, the operating differences between the two navies became likewise more obvious in projecting the operational lives of the RN submarines and their eight crews. Correct stock management of replacement components was a critical factor in keeping the CASD cycle unbroken. This was particularly true for the British submarines once the US Navy had moved on to Poseidon. Many of the components were refurbished for reuse and contracts existed with EB for this purpose. A chance remark by an EB employee claimed that he could always spot a component from a British submarine because it looked as though it had been maintained by agricultural engineers. British sailors seemed to have less regard for the, often considerable, value of the parts they handled.

16

Operational Problems

On 13 February 1973, HMS *Repulse* undertook a test firing. Aboard the submarine were seven admirals, but almost as soon as the missile had been launched, a first-stage malfunction saw the missile cartwheeling across the ocean until an electronic signal destroyed the missile and it plunged into the Atlantic. Vice-Admiral Terence Lewin commented: 'I'm definitely superstitious. I would have preferred the test on another day, but this was the day scheduled.'[1]

In 1977, HMS *Repulse* was undergoing her second refit when on 11 August a bomb warning was received at Rosyth dockyard. Shop stewards stopped work on the submarine when it emerged that no warning had been communicated to the work force. Work recommenced when a revised bomb warning procedure was agreed.

As already noted, credibility required at least one submarine to be at sea all the time. In 1978, union-led troubles were brewing in a variety of areas as significant wage increases were demanded for public sector workers whose wage increases has been restricted as Prime Minister James Callaghan sought to reduce inflation. From today's standpoint, the power of the unions to cause industrial disruption is somewhat difficult to fully understand. Faslane inevitably suffered when the navy was confronted by a workforce many of them brought up in the Clydeside shipyards and accustomed to a 'gloves off' approach to industrial relations. Indeed, Capt. Alec Barlow, Faslane's superintendent of base support, was quoted as saying that 50 per cent of his time was taken up in union negotiations.[2] Nor was the MoD's complex and convoluted approach to settling disputes any help in maintaining any sort of industrial harmony. In July, the unions blacklisted the three Polaris submarines not at sea. Trouble had started early in the month at Rosyth where the *Repulse* was recommissioned for the second time on 7 July after a twenty-month refit. Once again, Lady Zuckerman attended the event. The *Renown* had just arrived for her second major refit. Later in the month, strike action had hit Coulport where the *Revenge* was being prepared for the next patrol and required her missiles to be loaded. All attempts to encourage the workforce, which was nearly all civilian, to return to work to load the submarine had failed. On 25 July, Defence Secretary Frederick Mulley replied to a question from Robert Banks, MP for Harrogate:

> Attempts to persuade the work force at the Royal Naval Armament[s] Depot, Coulport, to resume normal working have not yet succeeded, although I naturally hope that an early settlement can be achieved. To ensure that our contribution to the alliance strategic deterrent is maintained, the Government must ensure that preparations for HMS *Revenge* to sail are completed very soon. We are therefore today informing the work force that naval and management personnel will complete the loading of HMS *Revenge*, starting tomorrow, and that in the interests of safety the depot will be closed temporarily to all except certain specially authorised personnel from 26th July until the loading has been completed. As regards *Repulse* and *Renown*, there is as yet no operational problem, although I shall of course keep the situation under review.[3]

Unsurprisingly, the Americans were keeping a close watch on developments. The US State Department's Sharyl P. Walter wrote in a diplomatic cable: 'In justifying its decision to use military personnel to get *Revenge* to sea, Mulley cited the need to maintain Britain's obligations to NATO. His private secretary has told us that the government is committed to doing whatever is necessary to maintain an SSBN at sea.'[4] The Americans nonetheless seemed quietly confident that Britain would resolve the problem. This they did when Mulley ordered that Coulport be closed to all civilians and RN personnel would prepare the submarine for patrol.

By the end of July, as the *Revenge* was armed and prepared for sea, industrial civil servants at the Clyde Submarine Base called for an all-out strike of 183,000 employees at naval bases throughout the country. There was not complete solidarity, however, as the 6,000 at the Rosyth Naval Base, where the *Renown* was by then starting her refit, while supporting their Faslane colleagues, nonetheless deferred their decision. On 11 August, a proposal was put to the unions by the MoD. This swiftly led to a resolution of the action as *The Times* reported:

> The Government's dispute with 183,000 industrial civil servants was drawing to a close last night as workers at key naval bases agreed to resume normal working in response to a 'final' pay offer made on Friday. Meetings representing more than 8,000 workers at the Polaris base on the Clyde and at the Rosyth naval dockyard voted in favour of a union recommendation to lift industrial action. That meant that the strike which started at the Faslane, Coulport and Arrochar bases and which had stopped work on the submarine *Resolution* ended immediately. At Rosyth work was resumed on two other Polaris submarines, the *Repulse* and the *Renown* as workers 'reluctantly' accepted the Government's offer. Mr Derek Stubbs, chairman of the local trade union advisory committee,

said that workers had accepted advice from national union officials that the offer was 'the best we could get from the Government.'[5]

In March 1981, the threat of strike action loomed once again when the civil service unions confronted the Royal Navy and the Royal Air Force, and their actions threatened to force the withdrawal of Britain from the NATO Exercise Wintex-Cimex, a biennial tri-service and civilian exercise to test response to a Soviet tactical nuclear confrontation. The strike threatened to black the *Repulse* which docked during the last week of the month and was being prepared for her next refit. The unions had already called for a half-day strike by all civil servants in reaction to naval personnel carrying out work on the *Resolution* which the unions had refused to sanction. RAF Pitreavie Castle in Fife which operated a NATO surveillance system was also threatened. Questions were now being asked about the wisdom of setting up facilities, vital to the nation's deterrent, that could so easily disrupt its effectiveness. VAdm. Mackenzie, now in retirement, commented that the Polaris Executive had felt very strongly that the navy should have kept control over the Polaris infrastructure: 'We could see a weakness of precisely the kind that has just been exemplified.'[6] Although Faslane was manned by naval staff, Coulport had a civilian workforce partly because traditionally arms depots had always been civilian manned but also because of lack of sufficient experienced naval personnel. Perhaps or because of this civil community within the depot, in July 1981 'the Royal Navy's most luxurious canteen, [b]uilt at a cost of £1,272,153' was opened: 'It has a restaurant to cater for 500, a bar seating 60. A sprung-floored dance hall, a coffee lounge, a function suite for conferences, facilities for film shows and wedding receptions, and even a badminton court.'[7] By the first week in May, the confrontation had escalated. The promise of all this, however, did not deter strike action. On 8 May, the civil service unions called out a further seventy white-collar staff at Coulport after they had been threatened with suspension for refusing to work normally. The weapons production staff attached the nuclear warheads to missiles before they were loaded onto the submarines and they joined fifty-one others already on strike along with 122 more at Faslane. The Royal Navy emphasised that the deterrent would be maintained, although a decision to move in naval personnel to work on the *Resolution* had resulted in a national half-day walkout by civil servants.[8] Matters were further complicated when workers at Laurence, Scott and Electromotors Ltd, a Manchester engineering company that manufactured and refurbished electro-motors used on board the RN's nuclear submarines, occupied the factory in protest that Mining Supplies Ltd which had recently acquired the company had announced the closure of the factory with business being transferred to Norwich. Without these motors, the submarines would be non-operational:[9]

At any one time one [of the submarines] is in dock being refurbished after a six-month tour of duty. Each time this occurs the electrical motors are taken out and sent down to LSE, Manchester to be overhauled. As each sub has only one set of spare motors, the twelve plus months delay that will occur could mean that one or more of the Polaris submarines might have to be taken out of service.

A bitter confrontation between employees, unions, and management followed. On 5 August, bailiffs attempted to take over the factory but met resistance from the workers who still voted by a significant majority to continue the occupation, but by then the AEWU had withdrawn support along with strike pay. By 18 August, time and patience had run out and fifty bailiffs armed with pickaxes and crowbars evicted the remaining strikers.[10]

On 10 October 1988, three anti-nuclear protesters managed to evade security at Faslane by cutting a hole in the perimeter fence and rushed past the security guard at the end of the gangway, managing to reach the control room of HMS *Repulse* before being arrested. Local Labour MP John McFall commented, 'not only are we talking about individuals appearing to have breached the perimeter fence, but reaching the very core of the security operation at the nuclear heart of Repulse. It is an appalling admission.'[11] Not surprisingly a full investigation immediately took place. Prime Minister Margaret Thatcher scrawled a quick note: 'I am utterly horrified. Examples of slackness in sensitive matters keep coming to light. I must have an urgent report. We could have been put in grave danger.'[12] A major review of security at the base thereafter allowed sentries to shoot on sight anyone threatening the submarines or their warheads.

The year 1982 had seen the tentative construction of the Faslane Peace Camp when a small group of anti-nuclear protesters set up a makeshift camp opposite the base. A motley collection of tents, caravans, and even a bus became a permanent fixture which exists to this day. In winter, it could become a muddy, somewhat squalid site with wisps of smoke rising from an assortment of campfires. Possibly best described as an ever-present inconvenience where a group of idealists tried to change the world to their beliefs and ways of thinking to the exclusion of others of differing opinions. Lyn, one of the protesters, wrote: 'Back at the camp—a dark, depressing feeling around—people sitting in the communal caravan looking bored. It was too wet outside to do much and the wood was so wet the fire wouldn't light.'

Chevaline

I suppose that it would have been un-British for anyone in authority to say Thank You.

R. J. Daniel

One of the most dangerous forms of human error is forgetting what one is trying to achieve.

US Defense Secretary Paul Nitze

As referred to earlier, the US Polaris A3P (Contract N00030-67-C-0085) used the Mk 58 warhead within the Mk 2 Mod 0 RV which like the proposed Antelope with the Mk 2 Mod 2 was double flared, chosen to avoid flow separation at small incidences which threatened aerodynamic stability. These RVs had a low weight to ratio drag which allowed about half a minute of subsonic terminal flight in turn permitting the use of barometric fusing. It would have seemed logical that Britain, being responsible for its own warhead package would have followed a similar route and indeed AWRE had been working on a new primary for incorporation in a UK version of the W-58, and in April 1964, Britain confirmed the decision to use the Mk 2 Mod 0. Reporting the decision to the SP Steering Task, Group CDR A. Julian commented:

> ... at least it will be a Mk 2 Mod 0 in the sense that it will look exactly like our Mk 2 system. The UK will design and fabricate the Fire Set and the nuclear system—these are items the AEC makes for us—but otherwise they will buy from us all the other parts of the system that they can. As a matter of fact, they could, if they wished, even buy the Fire Set from us, but they have decided to make it themselves.[1]

Although the US was not legally permitted to provide Britain with warheads or a complete weapon system, the exchange of information under the 1958

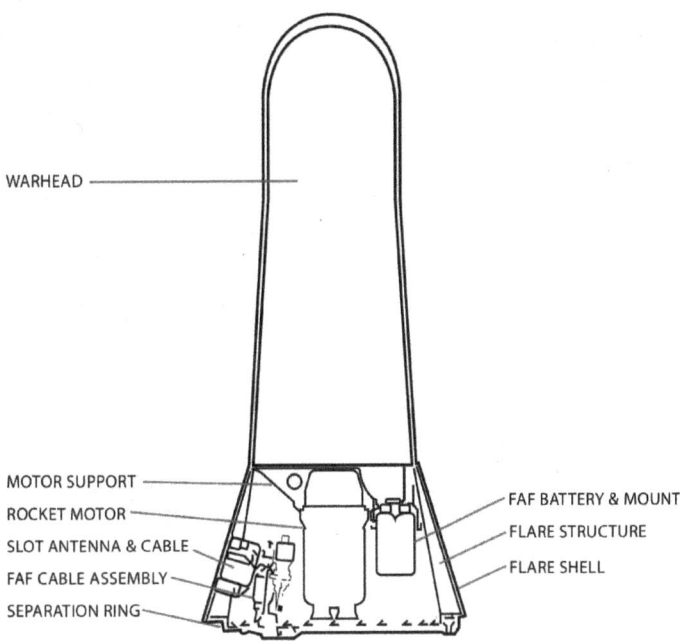

WARHEAD

MOTOR SUPPORT
ROCKET MOTOR
SLOT ANTENNA & CABLE
FAF CABLE ASSEMBLY
SEPARATION RING

FAF BATTERY & MOUNT
FLARE STRUCTURE
FLARE SHELL

Polaris A3P re-entry body—based on special projects office data, May 1963.

amendment to the MDA did allow Britain to manufacture this near copy of the Mk 58. Although it required the amendment to the agreement formally to allow the transfer of data, the US–UK link had been very intimate for some time, a factor in the equation that should not be underestimated. However, there were safety concerns raised by the Ordnance Board about the nature of the explosives used in the Mk 58. Under the designation ET.317, an alternative warhead was designed based on the US W-59 which was used on the Minuteman 1 ICBM and had been intended for Skybolt. The Mk 59 too failed British safety requirements in its primary, but work had been done under the code name RE.179 on a British warhead for the RAF's Skybolt and this had metamorphosed into ET.317, the now urgently required warhead for Polaris. The weapon was a fission-fusion-fission design with the primary code-named 'Katie', originally conceived for the Skybolt warhead, and the fusion secondary code-named 'Reggie' was identical to the Mk 59. This design complied with UK safety standards. One significant outcome of the relaxation of the MDA was that Britain could now manufacture properly engineered operational weapons, whereas Britain's weapons had previously tended to be 'scientific' in their nature.

The need for a protection against ballistic missiles was evident as soon as the first V2s began descending on their targets and the US Army had begun working on conceptual ideas of anti-ballistic missile defences immediately after the war. Any new system is a response to a need identified by intelligence, and in the case of Polaris, real concerns can be traced going back to Blue Streak which had been the subject of debate about the effectiveness of the missile against an enemy ABM system. It was realised even then that the Blue Streak warheads would need to be accompanied by penetration aids, but there was difficulty in designing penaids that would match the ReBs containing the warheads so that to enemy radar they would look the same. The Blue Streak solution was to develop low observable ReBs and this solution was carried over to the proposed Skybolt warhead. In 1961/62, the Soviet Union breached the moratorium on nuclear tests with a series of high-altitude explosions. Intelligence sources linked these to the development of an ABM system, something that the Soviets were known to have been planning since early tests took place in 1953. But a lack of more specific intelligence on Soviet developments meant that assumptions had to be made regarding the future proliferation of an ABM system which was at that stage technically undefinable. In fact, Soviet thoughts on protection against ballistic missiles go back to 1948, but by the early 1950s, the future threat of US ballistic missiles was considered such that senior Soviet military representatives were pressing for the development of a system to protect their major cities. The existing defences were based on the SA-1 SAM (NATO reporting name 'Guild') with a range of around 20 NM. Deployed in two concentric rings around Moscow, these were designed to give protection against high-flying manned bombers, but advances in technology showed the way to a future where ballistic missiles would be the threat and the SA-1s were unsuited to this new role. A further complication was that while the locations of land-based launch sites were known, thus giving the ability to compute their entry paths, it was by then also known that America was considering developing a sea-based missile system (Polaris) which would have ever-varying launch points. These concerns resulted in a protocol of 17 August 1956 whereby the Soviet council of ministers sanctioned the development of an ABM system as a high national priority:

> [The Soviets had] constantly surprised us, they kept coming up with new things that they would test and our own scientists kept postulating other things that they might do and we could have no way of knowing what they were doing, that would constantly defeat any cute tricks that we might invent for penetrating defenses.[2]

As far back as 1967, the Ministerial Committee on Nuclear Policy had noted that with three submarines on station, some thirty cities in the west of the Soviet Union could be targeted, 'and we have hitherto considered this to constitute a deterrent credible in military and political terms'.[3] But with the reality of there being only one, or possibly two available, the threat was considerably reduced. The precise need for the Polaris upgrade, however, was predicated by the subsequent development of a revised Soviet ABM system—System 'A'.

In 1962, construction had begun of the definitive A-35 Aldan ABM system to protect Moscow. The system had been tested at the Sary Shagan (Сары-Шаган) launch complex on the western edge of Lake Balkhash in Kazakhstan, construction of which had started in 1956, but it was not until four years later that the first positive indications were obtained as to the purpose of the 8,400-square-mile site. Confirmation of this was the appearance of a missile which was being developed specifically for the ABM role. On 7 November 1963, the October Revolution military parade included missiles described by the commentator as an anti-missile missile. This was given the NATO reporting name Griffon. After an integrated weapons demonstration, Marshal Vasily Kazakov, first deputy commander of Soviet artillery, commented that the Soviet Union now had 'rockets which would hit high speed aircraft and pilotless offensive devices at great altitude'. Perhaps the latter reference was generous as the missile was really a SAM aimed at manned bombers rather than ballistic missiles, although intelligence specialists believed it to be a component of the proposed Leningrad (current day St Petersburg) ABM system. This was the so called 'Tallinn' system, but it was not subsequently developed. Tallinn was based on the earlier Griffon whose booster was subsequently used on Galosh. Intelligence assessment of the Griffon suggested it was big with a large aerodynamic surface which mitigated against it operating as a high-altitude ABM missile. However, the missile first seen in public during the 1964 October Revolution Parade was a rather different matter. This was the initial variant nuclear-tipped A-350Zh ABM missile, NATO code name 'ABM-1 Galosh'. From discrete photographs taken of the two missiles (serial numbers 230618 and 241509), albeit in 70-foot containers as they passed through Red Square, much could be deduced about the missiles' capability. Galosh was a large two-stage missile. The four nozzles evident at the rear of the missile approximated to those of a known solid-fuelled booster. The weight was calculated from the number of tyres and their deflection. Using vectored thrust, the missile could be launched early in an attack and its large size suggested it had a range of around 300 NM with a high-yield nuclear warhead. The US Pen-X committee estimated that this missile would present a problem for incoming warheads which could be attacked above the atmosphere—exo-atmospherically. Although eight Galosh sites were planned, only four were built and equipped. These were at Vereya (often incorrectly transliterated as 'Bereya'), Solnechnogorsk, Klin, and Zagorsk. Each one fielded sixteen interceptor missiles together with reloads in two separate but adjacent launch complexes. The missiles, armed with a high-yield warhead of 2–3 Mt, had a range of 320 km. The large warhead required a lower level of accuracy in aim. Co-located at the sites were TRY ADD radars which fine-tuned the information from the Dunai-3U 'Dog House' (so named because it resembled a dog kennel), large phased-array battle management radar, and guided the Galosh missiles to their targets. Dog House was one of a series of early warning radars which covered a 60-degree sector aimed towards incoming missiles from the United States but with an operating back face directed at China. Originally sited to the east of Moscow, it was subsequently moved to a site between Kubinka and Naro-Fominsk, about 50 miles south-west of Moscow after the first Soviet exo-atmospheric tests. The plan was for three concentric rings at roughly 20, 35, and 50 kms from Moscow city centre. The potential existed for up to 512 launchers, although the fire control problems of such a complex system would have been significant. The system was adapted to have eight separate sites each with sixteen missiles, although, as noted, only four were completed possibly because it was realised that the full eight sites would have had fly-out trajectories that could have resulted in fratricide problems. The system protected not just the city of Moscow but extended its effect to a surrounding area very roughly the size of the UK. The Soviets were scrupulous in adhering to the letter of the ABM Treaty which referred to 'launchers'—in effect, silos—but failed to address any reload capability, a feature that had been incorporated into the design, thus increasing the number of missiles available.

The A-35 was built under the supervision of Chief Designer Grigoriy Kisunko. On 4 March 1961, the first successful test of what was known as System A (система A) took place when a V-1000 missile launched from Sary Shagan intercepted and destroyed the warhead of an R-12 IRBM target, the latter launched from the Kapustin Yar Missile Range. Detonating some 100 feet from the target, the interceptor released thousands of explosive spheres which destroyed the target warhead. This proved to the Soviets—and indeed Western intelligence—that an ABM capability could be successfully developed. Dog House was, however, not an advanced phased array. It was incoherent and scanned by sweeping frequency. The system was upgraded in the late 1970s and redesignated A350M along with an upgraded Dunai-3M 'Cat House' radar located at Chekhov which was believed to be capable of tracking up to thirty targets at one time and, it was deduced, could cover Polaris missiles launched in northern waters. Dommett commented that 'the Moscow ABM system was well balanced and achieved its purpose of making every country rework their offensive missiles at great expense'.[4] The sequence of events was later assessed by the CIA as follows:

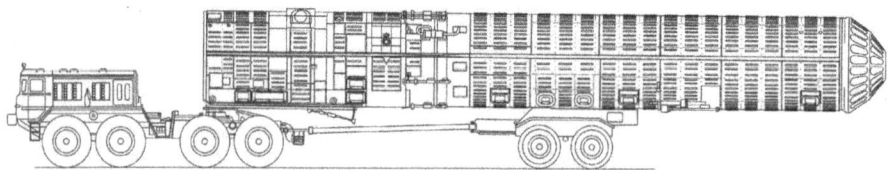

Soviet A-350 Grau SV61—NATO reporting name ABM-1 Galosh. As shown in Red Square on 7 November 1964. Drawn from CIA Photographic Interpretation Report NPIC/R-57/65.

1. Dual Hen House radars, eight sites located at various points on the edges of the Soviet Union to detect incoming missiles.
2. Dog House radar provides accurate trajectory information on a large number of targets simultaneously and served as the battle management centre for the defences.
3. Large TRY ADD radar sites provide accurate tracking of the incoming missiles.
4. Small TRY ADD radars track and guide the Galosh missiles to their targets.[5]

For the West to have credible deterrent value, the requirement was for the targeting of forty cities or second echelon military targets. Accuracy of the seaborne missiles was insufficient to make pinpoint attacks which would be left to SAC and RAF strategic bombers as long as they could penetrate Soviet air defences. This exposed a fundamental weakness for Britain in having only four boats and the adverse consequences if anything happened to reduce the number to three. Then there was the 'Moscow Criterion'; the ability to retaliate to a 'bolt from the blue' attack on the UK. One Royal Navy SSBN on patrol had to be able to achieve this otherwise the UK deterrent lost its *raison d'être*. This SSBN would always be available to launch twenty minutes after receiving the launch order and the missiles would have to be able to penetrate the Moscow ABM shield. Therein lay the credibility or otherwise of the Royal Navy's Polaris. In times of tension, a second boat could possibly be available either as it made its way to the patrol area or, given enough time, if it was alongside at Faslane it could be readied for patrol, but the high-voltage ignition inverters which were removed from the missiles as the submarine returned to the Clyde would first have to be reinserted. The US Navy had also explored launching Polaris from a surfaced submarine when the USS *Henry Clay* (SSBN-625) successfully launch an A-2 missile while at sea and on the surface on 20 April 1964.

Intelligence estimates of the Galosh capability indicated that both the Royal Navy's initial stocks of A3P and the later A3T (contract N00030-67-C-0177) were both compromised—even allowing for an estimated failure of around 15 per cent of the Galoshes that for one reason or another did not function correctly. A similar failure percentage could, arguably, be applied to Polaris. The US Navy sought to resolve the situation by deploying the next generation MIRV-equipped Poseidon C-3 missile which would be retrofitted to all of their Polaris SSBNs except the initial ten boats which were by then well through their operational lives and were too small to incorporate the required upgraded navigation and fire control systems. The US Navy also had the significant advantage of being able to launch sufficient missiles to exhaust the ABM stockpile by sheer force of numbers of incoming warheads. They were uniquely able to take this approach as there were always a number of US Navy SSBNs on patrol at any time.

Initial thoughts on the UK requirement for protection against an ABM threat originated in the spring of 1964 through a short-term but intensive study of the penetration problem. SP were informed that the committee would be chaired by the RAE with participation by the Admiralty, the Ministry of Aviation, and the MoD. Due to report on 1 August, CDR Julian commented:

> While we are not involved in this study in any way, I suspect that their report will be 'Yes, the UK does need penetration aids'. If that is their recommendation, then the penetration aids will be developed in a form that can be retrofitted to the submarines already constructed, as it does not seem possible that they can solve the PX [penetration] problem soon enough to equip their submarines sequentially.[6]

A further assessment of the overall vulnerability of Polaris was the subject of a July 1966 meeting of the 'V' (Vulnerability) Committee. Zuckerman was clearly aware of this as during a lunch at London Zoo in December with Labour Minister of Technology Tony Benn, he told the MP that 'he was keen that Denis Healey and the Defence staff should not be able to get away with further expenditure on nuclear weapons by hardening the Polaris submarine warheads'. Zuckerman added that he and philanthropist Lord Rothschild were at one over this.[7]

Official confirmation, however, came in 1967 when the United States warned Healey of the need to consider hardening UK warheads against the effects of X-rays from nearby nuclear explosions which delaminated the nylon wound heat shields on the ReBs and deposited very high amounts of energy in high-Z materials such as the gold plating in relays. The UK warheads were, by the nature of their design, believed to be particularly vulnerable because of their low weight to drag ratio (β) which resulted in a slow re-entry phase, making the warheads more susceptible to attack. The US had already started to harden all its strategic weapons and invited Zuckerman to Washington in April 1967 to be briefed on the US Navy's proposals for their Polaris missiles. The issue was originally on the agenda of the Ministerial Nuclear Committee PN(67) and to more fully understand the problem, Sir William Cook, the chief scientific adviser (CSA), set up a committee under the chairmanship of Victor Macklen (ACSA(N)) with Denis Fakley as secretary. In May, Macklen, Fred East from RAE and Ted Newley, D/AWRE, went to Washington to be given an overview of the USN's Antelope warhead upgrade. As was outlined earlier, this could be described as a 'quick fix' solution and replaced one RV with a penetration aid carrier (PAC) of similar mass but larger volume than the RV it replaced. East formed a small team in Division 6 of the Weapons Department (We.6) in the secure 'T' Area at Farnborough, which was itself within the high security Armament Research Laboratory (ARL) and suggested that an anglicised copy of Antelope could be manufactured for around £125 million.[8] The decision to follow the MIRV path for Poseidon made Antelope redundant, but it remained of interest to the UK as a concept that the UK could develop. Hardening Antelope was achieved by fitting a protective sock over the standard RV. Some indication of a UK programme to develop a new generation of warheads had maybe already surfaced late in 1967. Chapman Pincher, doyen of investigative reporters and oft scourge of No. 10, revealed in the *Daily Express* 'H-bombs small as footballs for Navy rockets'. He revealed:

Each Polaris missile to be fitted in the [Royal] Navy's atomic submarines will now carry several H-bombs instead of only one as a result of spectacular advances made by Britain's nuclear scientists. The H-bombs are little bigger than a football. They will be released when the warhead is more than 50 miles up and hurtle separately at 18,000 miles an hour to the target area. This achievement, secret until now, is the reason for the Government's insistence that the British independent deterrent will remain effective for at least eight years despite new Russian anti-missile defences. The four Polaris submarines, each carrying 16 missiles, can now deliver at least 200 nuclear bombs instead of 64.[9]

In referring to sixty-four warheads, Pincher was clearly confirming the A3 missiles. He even went as far as to reveal that the warheads would incorporate large numbers of metal strips and decoys to deceive and mislead enemy radar. Had he speculatively assumed the development path that may need to be followed to maintain an effective deterrent, or had he received some outline of what was then still an embryonic programme?

Referring to the Pincher disclosure, Neil Marten, Conservative MP for Banbury, had asked that, '[I]n the light of the Government's intention to renegotiate the Nassau Agreement can the Prime Minister say whether it is the Government's intention to fit multi-nuclear warheads to our Polaris missiles and if so, how does this fit in with election pledges?' To which Wilson replied, '[W]e have made clear that we are not embarking on a new generation of nuclear weapons or warheads in relation to our Polaris programme.'[10]

In support of Macklen, the matter was then taken up by the 'Pressgang' so-called from the acronym of the committee's title—the Polaris Re-entry System Group (PRESG). The committee received its terms of reference on 14 December 1967. Chairman was Peter Jones from AWRE and also on the committee were Don Harper, Roy Dommett from RAE and Sandy Murray from RRE as well as MoD(N) representatives. Murray was viewed as 'very gifted but uncontrollable'. This initial study was designated HR.169. Concentrating mainly on the physics rather than the engineering, PRESG reported in late 1967 that nuclear hardening was possible and that decoys would improve penetration, but the Antelope solution in itself was not sufficiently robust. However, it could possibly be used as a start point for short term Royal Navy deployment.

It was not until later that Nixon was willing to authorise the release of full Antelope data. Dommett notes that Antelope and the related Impala were the only penaid designs discussed between the two nations.[11] Now renamed the Polaris Re-entry Systems Study Group (PRESSG), the committee extended its considerations, producing a seven-volume report in June 1968. An alternative was, with some degree of logic, to seek the purchase of Poseidon C-3 missiles, ideally supplied under similar terms to the Polaris Agreement, the detail of which, it was believed, covered the purchase of a missile such as Poseidon. This reflected Zuckerman's wisdom in drafting the original agreement. This was the option that would be vigorously pursued by the Royal Navy. These would have been supplied without warheads, but with the Mk III RVs, something that would have to have congressional approval. A new smaller British warhead would have to be designed, a possibility that attracted a number of warhead designers at AWRE and would maintain jobs at the establishment. Despite Zuckerman's heterodox views, Sir Varyl Begg, who had been appointed CNS following the sudden resignation of Admiral Sir David Luce in protest at Healey's cancellation of the CVA-01, *Queen Elizabeth*-class, aircraft carrier programme, sought his support for Poseidon. He was aware that production of the A3 was shortly to finish and that the US Navy was moving on to new projects. Zuckerman remembered that Begg made no reference to ABMs and 'left with a smile on his face' when Zuckerman asked 'what difference it made what our Polaris tubes contained, provided that the Russians believed that they were nuclear missiles that could hit Moscow or Leningrad. What we believed was irrelevant.'[12]

> If a final decision is taken against Poseidon, it would be of great political and military significance. It would be, in effect, a deliberate move to break a chain of dependence on American weapons. Politically, it would represent a step to answer President de Gaulle's doubts about Britain as a market partner because of her reliance on the United States.... Mr Wilson said that Britain was not rejecting the United States in choosing Western Europe and that the Atlantic alliance had 'a great deal to gain from a stronger Europe'. But he said that Britain did not want to be 'subservient' to the United States. He told a French questioner that Britain was more effective than France in resisting American industrial domination.[13]

Wilson confirmed the decision on Poseidon in a statement to the Commons on 13 June. Mr David Winnick (MP for Croydon South) asked Wilson 'if he [would] give an assurance that the House will be informed of a Government decision to authorise the manufacture of a new generation of nuclear weapons.' Wilson replied, 'If my hon. Friend is referring to a proposal to replace the Polaris missiles by Poseidon missiles, the answer is that Her Majesty's Government have no such intention.'[14]

Nonetheless, Healey was asked for a study to be completed which addressed warhead vulnerability but requested that this be done without any civilian involvement and that the whole project should be conducted in utmost secrecy, so that it was not only unknown within the ministries but also from certain left-inclined members of the Cabinet. Zuckerman who had left the MoD in 1967 to become CSA to the Cabinet (a post that earned him the nickname 'Tsar of All Sciences') did not enjoy an easy relationship with Healey and largely dismissed the need for an upgrade to Polaris, believing that an effective Soviet ABM system was not a practical proposition and there was therefore little need to counter it. This was a position he stoically maintained, and although he eventually did not win the argument, some would hold that much time was wasted in countering his views. Any Royal Navy enthusiasm Zuckerman believed was merely a, perhaps natural, wish to keep up to date and to operate a parallel system to the Americans and was not driven by ABM considerations.

Nonetheless, a six-month study was undertaken by the PRESSG, and this explored the idea, initiated by Macklen, for an Antelope-type master dispenser which deployed ReBs in differing ways. At this stage, the idea was mainly conceptual without specifically considering the engineering criteria. The existing UK ReB was, however, too big and any modification to the shape by, for instance, cutting slices off the flare would have been aerodynamically uncertain. The problem with the existing A3T was that after separation, the three warheads were never more than 11 NM apart. At this separation, all three ReBs could theoretically be eliminated by a one-megaton warhead. The UK Antelope derivative solution therefore moved towards a separation of around twice this distance. The threat profile had to overcome the ABM defences in sufficient quantity to still leave viable warheads to present a credible deterrent. An alternative study which developed the Poseidon theme was 'Mini-Poseidon' which incorporated six Poseidon-type warheads on an A3T. Healey secretly approved continued funding for ongoing work but at a relatively low level. Taking a lead from this funding, the DoD expressed support to the MoD(N) for the Antelope option. However, the US Navy now admitted that its original estimates on Antelope were overly optimistic and effectiveness would be only around two-thirds of this projection. AWRE willingly recognised the validity of the theory behind the Antelope design, but to fulfil UK requirements, the design would have to be further hardened and be equipped to deploy more decoys, a project that became known as 'Super Antelope'. This was a development of HR.169, updating it as an exo-atmospheric system. All objects had to appear to be heading for the target city, but they had to be separated along the trajectory to avoid multiple kills. A fundamental problem existed in the relative size of the two nation's SSBN fleets which meant that a US solution relying on a barrage of missiles would not meet UK needs which would require a 'worst case scenario' solution assuming that only one SSBN with sixteen missiles was available. The chances of significant attrition of these missiles—even assuming all were launched successfully—was far more significant than the much higher number of missiles the US would be launching. The US Department of State remained aware of British interest in Antelope and the matter was considered in advance of a meeting on 8 September 1969 between Sir William Cook and John S. Foster, Jr, director, defense research and engineering. America was willing to help on three specific areas: 1. 'putting some of their samples into our test holes for experiments.... [T]his could be done without giving away any information we do not want to give them.' 2. 'Penetration aids short of some sensitive aspects to be identified. However, the British must request assistance.' 3. 'Hot X-ray effects—less information showing vulnerability of US systems.' Furthermore, 'If the British show an interest in Antelope, they would be told that if they should really decide they want it, we would think about it after receiving their request. SALT (Strategic Arms Limitation Talks) ... [is] one of the considerations.' But it was further noted that Britain considered penetrating the Moscow ABM shield as a basic premise rather than 'riding in after a US strike.... Zuckerman is pressing the opposite view and so far has prevailed.'[15]

Yet another report was produced in January 1970 and examined the relative merits of over a dozen options including Antelope, Super Antelope, and Mini-Poseidon, emphasising the implications and consequential vulnerability of the small UK force and therefore by default also its credibility. Peter Jones, principal deputy director AWRE, later commented:

> ... we were trying [to find] a sufficient solution, weighing what looked like the likely effectiveness of the Soviet System against what would be a reasonable expenditure on upgrading our system.... To do that without spending money on useless solutions or overspending meant that we were continually checking these alternative systems against the evolving pattern of the Soviet ABM.[16]

Force credibility was vital to maintaining the argument for a separate UK deterrent. Even Super Antelope, as now envisaged, may still have been vulnerable to the Soviet ABM screen. Poseidon as the second-generation weapon appeared to represent the best option and would, of course, be a parallel weapon to that used by the USN. This was an important point and was to emerge as the cornerstone of the Royal Navy's opposition to Super Antelope when they fought for the later missile choosing to turn a 'Nelson's eye' to the potential problem of Labour's left wing. But Poseidon was not without its problems as the demanding MIRV technology took time to perfect: the missile was twice recalled from service to be reworked. In September 1973, Admiral Smith reported to the Senate Armed Services Committee:

> I have seen enough to believe that it would be appropriate for us to recall essentially all of the missiles that are now deployed to disassemble and to test the various components, perhaps even to tear down some of these components and get at the basic bits and pieces.... Under this plan it is expected that the

missiles will be replaced in a routine manner without disruption of patrol cycles; however, these details are not yet firm.[17]

The UK knew of Poseidon's problems as their representatives attended the weekly SP progress meetings. There was confidence that the problems could be solved given the funds, but the USN was already working on the next missile, the ULMS, a project that became Trident C-4 and this was seen as a way of short-circuiting Poseidon's problems.

Still maintaining strictest secrecy, the various options were discussed by a sub-committee consisting of Wilson, Healey, Chancellor Roy Jenkins, and Foreign Secretary Michael Stewart and in May approval was given for yet another £1 million funding to cover a further year's work on a formal feasibility study with a view of agreeing a project definition of what was needed.

Chapman Pincher once again raised the indignation of parliament when he wrote a *Daily Express* front-page story, 'Polaris fleet "out of date" threat', claiming that 'an urgent warning by Defence Ministry chiefs that Britain's Polaris missiles may be unable to penetrate Russia's defences unless they are improved, has been rejected by the Government'.[15] Pincher revealed the broad outline of the ABM threat indicating, yet again, that he must have had some inside knowledge of the problem. A following editorial blamed the government's view on not wanting to offend the left wing of the party but also confirmed that the 'vast majority of the British people are strongly in favour of being able to look after itself'. The issue was raised in the Commons four days later and Healey replied, somewhat testily:

> The House will not expect me to comment again on a statement of that particular correspondent, whose unreliability is notorious—[shouts of: 'Oh.']— but what I can say is that the Polaris system has always been developed to carry multiple re-entry vehicles, and when first we learned that the Soviet Union might be deploying an anti-ballistic missile system we took such steps as we regarded as necessary at that time to improve its penetration capability.[18]

The general election of June 1970 surprised many with the formation of a Conservative government under Prime Minister Edward Heath with a useful thirty-seat majority. Ian MacLeod was appointed chancellor with Lord Carrington as secretary of state for defence. The new government had agreed in its manifesto to review the decision on the fifth Polaris submarine, and this may well have influenced Heath's reluctance to approve extra funds to the warhead project which really would have been unnecessary if a fifth boat had been approved. Nonetheless, in the autumn of 1970, Carrington proposed that a full Project Definition Study should indeed be completed. Heath's dilemma was that the upgrade was only needed to ensure that a successful attack on Moscow could be achieved, the Moscow Criterion being a core requirement of Britain having an independent deterrent. Otherwise, the British SSBNs could have been incorporated into NATO forces and targeted against softer targets. Six-monthly reviews would continue to take place before further funds were released and these would also consider if intelligence reports had identified any significant advances in the Soviet ABM capability. To further complicate matters, the SALT talks between America and the Soviet Union were also taking place. But America, under President Nixon, was wary of an agreement on Soviet ABMs which might require reciprocation by way of limiting MIRV development—a key element of the US nuclear arsenal and one where they were well ahead of the Soviets. Britain was hopeful that some restriction on ABM deployment linked to the talks would make achieving the Moscow Criterion a little easier while they tacitly accepted that any hope of a total ban on ABM deployment would be unrealistic. Nevertheless, the ABM Treaty (ABMT) was signed on 26 May 1972 by Nixon and General Secretary of the Communist Party of the Soviet Union Leonid Brezhnev, and ratified by the US Senate on 3 August 1972. It restricted both superpowers to 200 launchers divided equally between two cities. Two years later as neither power had embarked on a second site, this was altered to one city each: Moscow and the North Dakota Safeguard Complex. This was significant in that the number of ABM sites was now quantified. Previously, Soviet capability, actual or planned, was based on 'best guess' limited intelligence. It also demonstrated that without an upgrade, the UK deterrent could not achieve the Moscow Criterion, as even if two bombers were operational in an emergency this would account for only ninety-six warheads. In mid-1971, it was clear that American technical support would be needed with the warhead improvement. Assistance was granted by the Nixon administration, but Heath's position was complex. He had to manage an existing relationship with America as well as forging a new relationship with the EEC which Britain was to join in January 1973, fulfilling a partnership which Wilson had failed to negotiate and a partnership that remained wary of Britain's closeness to the US.

Meanwhile, the Americans were about to start a test phase on advanced hardening techniques and AWRE staff were allowed to monitor the tests, something that had always proved to be a valuable benefit.

Concurrently, CDS put forward a formal recommendation for Super Antelope, although Zuckerman's opposition still hung as a shadow over proceedings. He had 'discussed the ABM problem endlessly' with scientific advisers on both sides of the Atlantic. He enjoyed much respect and had considerable gravitas in certain influential circles and furthermore, his opinion was known to be valued by VADM Rickover.[19] A UK warhead upgrade was by this time the solution favoured by the US too as SP had indicated that the CNS was unlikely to approve Poseidon believing that Polaris was perfectly adequate for the Royal Navy's operational needs, but, recognising the desirability of an upgrade, would support co-operation on Super Antelope. Despite CNS's reservations, the Royal Navy refused to give up its aspirations for Poseidon and, in November 1971, gave clear indications of wanting the second-generation missile as the preferred solution. Knowing that the USN was upgrading to Poseidon at which point Polaris would be taken out of service, the admirals saw many advantages in operating a system in common with the US—an attitude of commonality of equipment often reflected within all the armed services. Polaris production ceased in 1968, and as the weapon system became older there may be many unforeseeable problems in the future which Britain alone would have to resolve, as indeed proved to be the case later in the missile's life. Super Antelope meant they would be fielding a missile unique to the Royal Navy, and they would not be able to fall back on the Americans for support. In addition, it was understood that certain components, particularly the second-stage motors, would have to be replaced in due course and this would mean reopening the Hercules Company's production lines in America at an estimated cost of some £30 million. But, perhaps fortuitously, the MoD refused to give cost estimates for Poseidon on the grounds of security—conveniently choosing to overlook the fact that the costs had been openly published in America.

The change of government had, if only temporarily, interrupted discussions on completion of the project definition, 'The Way Ahead', which had by then been delayed until March 1972. This recommended a five-year development programme followed by a production phase and indicated a total development cost of £175 million at 1972 prices. Carrington identified four options and called for a decision by November of that year. The choices were:

1. Super Antelope.
2. Poseidon.
3. Collaboration with the French, although it was thought that this may well affect US sensitivities towards further exchange of data.
4. The so-called 'poor man's deterrent' a hardened version of the existing A3T with increased separation but without decoys.

Despite reservations about bringing the French into play at that time, future possible collaboration with them was not completely ruled out.

Hybrid Stag also made a brief reappearance. This might have given the RN some cheer in that they would be operating the same Poseidon missile body as the USN albeit that it would de-MIRVed and have Super Antelope warheads and this seemed to be the solution favoured by Heath but was predicated on America allowing the purchase of Poseidon: a continuing uncertainty. Although a costlier option, it was likely to have a longer immunity to Soviet ABMs than Super Antelope. To keep the project going, funding would be approved in further six-month allocations. This may have been a convention convenient to the government but caused increasing uncertainty among the various contractors involved in the project. They had seen the rise and sudden fall of Blue Streak, the promises of Skybolt, and feared another such fiasco. Six-monthly tranches of funding gave them little encouragement to allocate staff of the necessary quality to the project. It also gave rise to the weak financial management that was to bedevil the earlier years of the project. Nonetheless, further evidence that the US was keen to support enhancement of the UK's Polaris force came in August 1972 when Secretary of State Henry Kissinger endorsed US willingness to assist but would not agree to the transfer of MIRV technology via Poseidon; something that the British had, in any case, cautiously anticipated. Some Americans took an ambivalent attitude to the Royal Navy's Polaris force. The American Intelligence Association reported:

FLASH ... the American people do not know how weak an ally and how helpless the BRITISH are. Make no mistake, they are about the best friends we have abroad but ... if you want the inside truth, look at this from the LONDON TIMES, May 7, 1972. LORD WIGG observes: the Polaris submarine, of which we have four armed with A3 ... is to remain equipped with a version of the A3 specifically designed to penetrate ballistic missile defences. In plain English, this implies that the Russians are almost certainly capable of destroying the original A3 missile by the use of an anti-ballistic missile. The Americans have also demonstrated by their actions new doubts about the efficacy of A3. This explains why they are going ahead with the much more expensive Poseidon which we cannot even pretend to afford.

Wigg went on to consider the effect on Britain when the Americans were now relinquishing Polaris for Poseidon: 'Ten years ago when the nation's money was being gambled on the Blue Streak project, the value of Polaris was being called into question. Although it fired its sixteen missiles while under the water the question arose: How long would it remain undetectable and invulnerable?'[20]

Undeterred, the Polaris Operations Policy Committee under the chairmanship of Rear-Admiral Sir Henry Leach embarked on a year-long study to consider both Super Antelope, now known by its Project Designation KH.793, and Poseidon.

In October 1972, a further six months' funding was approved with the hope that a decision could be reached by March 1973. By this time, CDS, Field Marshal Lord Carver, was warning that successful penetration of Moscow from the north was no longer guaranteed. Attacks from the south still presented a possibility by way of bypassing the ABM shield, but would require deployment of the British SSBNs to the Mediterranean. A UK Poseidon was therefore still in contention and was seen by some, but not all, in the USN as attractive as the overall costs of the programme would reduce with a contribution from Britain, and in any case, they argued, Britain was keen to maintain its warhead know-how—a factor that was undoubtedly true, but without a transfer of knowledge, MIRV technology remained a demanding science and also an expensive one. Realistically, it was beyond the UK's resources both financially and also in terms of staff expertise to manage the project. The Royal Navy knew that the British SSBNs could be converted to the C-3 relatively easily by removing the liners and grouting in the launch tubes, although, of course, much of the fire control systems would also have to be replaced. Poseidon's longer range would also give more sea room for the patrol areas. Commonality with the USN did arguably make sense from a British point of view, but some within the USN had many reasons for not being so enthusiastic, and in fact, most of the US defence community wanted the UK to be different as the Soviets would thus know whose missiles had been launched so there was no question of misunderstanding their origin and they would also have to develop a wider scoped defence system, a factor which would enhance the overall deterrent value for both nations.

On 13 March, Macklen went to Washington to meet with Kissinger. He was keen to assess the real nature of the ABM threat as some reports suggested that the Galosh system's capability had been overstated, a view of course shared by Zuckerman. He was also keen to reinforce the different requirements of the UK due to the small number of missiles available to it. The two options being considered around this time were Hybrid Stag and the so-called 'Option M', which utilised de-MIRVed Poseidon warheads on a Poseidon missile. Macklen discounted the latter which would be expensive (later costed at about £142 million: TNA. DEFE 13/1039) but considered Hybrid Stag worthy of taking forward. In this, he was supported by Lord Carrington. This could provide a parallel system to the USN with a missile which could counter the Soviet ABMs but which did not represent full second-generation capability and might therefore be more acceptable to a wider audience both politically and within the electorate.

Heath had already met Nixon on 1–2 February 1973. A meeting already twice postponed in the aftermath of the president authorising the Linebacker II bombing of North Vietnam and with the ominous background of the Watergate scandal. During the previous month, the US State and Defense Departments had picked up a number of indications that Heath may have been planning to ask, '[i]f the United States would be prepared to sell the POSEIDON missile system to the United Kingdom':

In his January 18 letter to Mr. Kissinger, Secretary Laird strongly urged that the US not make a commitment of any sort to the British in the event Mr. Heath made an approach at the White House level. We believe that it would not be desirable at this stage to give either an affirmative or a negative decision on the sale of POSEIDON to the UK. We believe that a sympathetic but non-committal response to the Prime Minister would best advance the interests of the US at this point.[21]

And indeed, the matters discussed included the possible supplying of Poseidon to Britain. Nixon was a great admirer of Churchill and the relationship that had existed between the two nations during the war. Heath had been advised by the Foreign Office that he should appeal to the president's desire 'to be remembered in history as a great president'.[22] Pursuing a policy of détente among the nuclear powers and increasingly influential as the president became overly preoccupied with Watergate and became distanced from Congress, Kissinger remained strongly against the transfer of MIRV technology so from his perspective it was not something that Britain was going to acquire from America, as it would also complicate the second round of SALT negotiations. Nonetheless, there were those who feared that a reluctance to help with upgrading the British deterrent might be interpreted as an effort to encourage British to relinquish its nuclear deterrent. But Kissinger was also anxious to bring France back on board in NATO:

> On the Poseidon. We want to keep Europe from developing their unity as a bloc against us. If we keep the French hoping they can get ahead of the British, this would accomplish our objective. If we gave the British MIRV while the French were so far behind, it would be bad. If we could give the British the dispensing mechanism and hold open the MIRV for the French a few years, we could keep them even.[23]

Thus, Britain's thoughts were increasingly directed towards improving the existing warheads. Chapman Pincher cast doubts on the estimated cost of Poseidon for the UK, quoting a figure of £250 million claiming that the true cost would be double that figure.[24] However, it should be noted that Levering Smith had given a figure of £280 million, and he must have been fully aware of the actual costs of Poseidon from his close management of the programme. It seems inconceivable that his cost estimate was other than reasonably accurate.

On 7 May, Heath ruled that a final decision be made by July, but only four days later, it was agreed it would be prudent to delay the decision until the government's autumn spending review. For those working on the project, it was becoming evident that it was proving much more complicated than had originally been expected and the original timelines were well beyond reach. The choice had by then crystallised to either developing Super Antelope or the more expensive option of purchasing Poseidon C-3 less the nuclear components of the Mk III warhead for which the UK would be responsible and with a dispensing system adapted to remove a MIRV capability. Release of the Mk III RV would also need congressional agreement. A further six months' funding was approved until, on 30 October 1973, no doubt weary of US vacillations, Heath finally decided on Super Antelope with responsibility transferred from Aldermaston to the procurement executive of the Ministry of Defence. On 2 January 1974, the decision was communicated to the Americans in the form of a formal request for assistance which would, by implication, include access to the Nevada test site. Even Kissinger seemed weary of the whole matter, sending the following memorandum to the secretary of defense, the chairman of the AEC, and the deputy secretary of state:

> The President has agreed to a request from the Prime Minister to extend to the UK our full cooperation in completing the Polaris improvement program (Super Antelope). You should take the actions necessary to insure that this project can go forward.... The previous restrictions limiting our participation to the project to the project definition stage are hereby rescinded.

Unimpressed, Kissinger privately termed this 'a continuing record of stupidity', to which Schlesinger added: 'It's a dumb decision. It is only a hardened warhead, and we can control their testing for the next six years.'[25] Overlooking the views that the two men held in private on the subject, a few days later, William Hyland and Jan Lodal members of Kissinger's NSC staff prepared a package for the president recommending that Nixon agree to continue support for the British project, noting that it was 'easier to accommodate the British decision on improving the Polaris than had the UK chosen to procure the Poseidon technology'. The report indicated that the British decision was mainly motivated by economic considerations:

> The Prime Minister notes that domestic problems, including the energy crisis, have forced a retrenchment in spending, but that his government is determined that this retrenchment not affect the UK's NATO commitments. Thus, he has decided on the less costly alternative of improving the existing Polaris warhead for the UK nuclear submarine fleet, rather than undergo the expense of converting to a non-MIRV version of our Poseidon missile.
>
> The Polaris improvement program involves adding to the three multiple reentry vehicles (MRV) a package of penetration aids that will ensure a British capability to overcome the existing Soviet ABM defenses. We have been cooperating with British experts on the initial experimental phase of this improvement package, but have not made a further commitment to the development, pending a British decision on whether to shift to the Poseidon.[26]

The president duly agreed to the proposal on 17 January.

American cooperation was vital to the success of the British project. Agreement was reached to accept three tests at the NTS subject to American safety criteria being fulfilled. These tests would be carried out 'below the horizon' and the presence of any British personnel for either these tests or any associated flight tests would be closely monitored.

Meanwhile, a general election had been called by Heath who was keen to obtain a mandate to confront the unrest fomented by the unions. Things did not quite go to plan when a broadly unexpected result was a hung parliament with the balance of power being held by the Liberals. After attempts for a Conservative/ Liberal pact had failed, Harold Wilson returned to 10 Downing Street as prime minister on 4 March 1974.

Although this was a secret programme, the tenth anniversary of the Nassau Agreement had caused some of the scientific media to speculate on the need to upgrade the warheads to counter Soviet ABM advances. Poseidon figured prominently in the argument. Some saw that the US missile and the progress made in ABM countermeasures were being exaggerated by the MoD to extract funds to develop new warheads. However, with no knowledge of what was actually happening, the speculation centred on the UK developing MIRV warheads to parallel the Americans. Also considered was a manoeuvrable re-entry vehicle (MARV), the type being developed by the US for the Pershing II MRBM battlefield missile. This gave the RV an autonomous capability to avoid countermeasures and home in accurately on its target.

Super Antelope/KH.793, the UK's first metric weapon, had been given the name 'Chevaline' in 1974 referring to the anglicised development programme. The origin of the name is obscure. The most common belief, prevalent in the MoD, was that Chevaline was a type of elusive mountain antelope living at high altitude. Dictionaries are, however, unable to support this definition, Chevaline being defined somewhat less prosaically as 'horseflesh'. Dommett records that the name was taken from the MoD codebook and 'did not stand for anything except our embarrassment'. The access codeword was Artificer and the US trials were code-named 'Cheval'. Nonetheless, Chevaline retained, and still retains, a certain eclectic mystique.[27]

The new weapon was, in essence, an improved front end (IFE) for the Royal Navy's A3T Polaris and, in service, was given the nomenclature A3TK. The proposed warhead was not covered under the Polaris Sales Agreement and accordingly, any transfer of data required presidential determination as it covered a possible US in-service device which would be subject to information controls. With US approval needed to release the relevant Antelope information, it took some time before drawings and other information were released, and by the time they were received, Chevaline was well underway and the data was of little practical value.

It was now clear that cost was increasingly becoming a major issue. Funding nonetheless continued in six-monthly tranches, known to only a select few. Advanced Project Definition was due to be completed by the summer of 1975. Wilson had re-inherited Chevaline, but without an overall majority, he had to be cautious. The sensitivity of the nuclear weapons issue was amply demonstrated in June when the new government was forced to admit that a British nuclear test under the code name 'Fallon' had taken place at the NTS on 23 May. This was the first underground test since the 'Charcoal' test had taken place some nine years

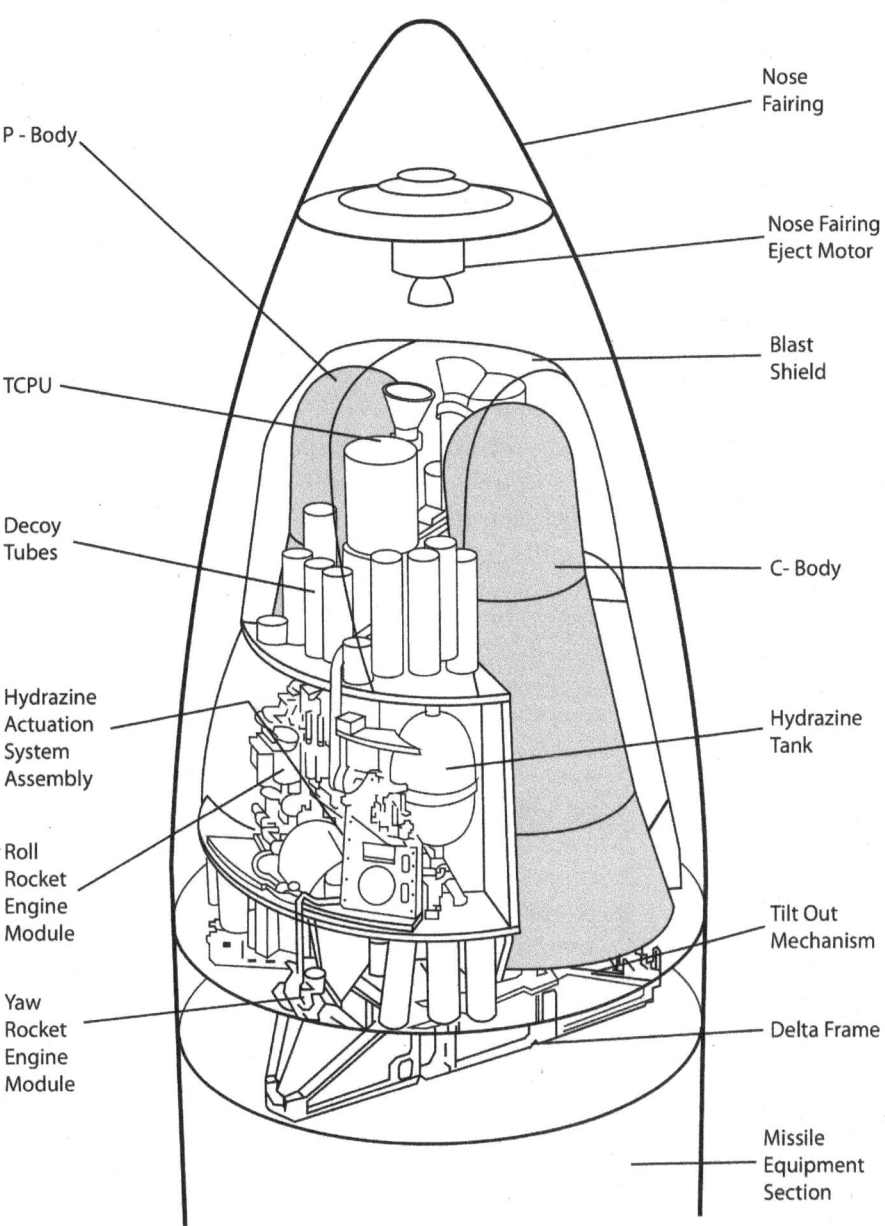

P - Body

TCPU

Decoy
Tubes

Hydrazine
Actuation
System
Assembly

Roll
Rocket
Engine
Module

Yaw
Rocket
Engine
Module

Nose
Fairing

Nose Fairing
Eject Motor

Blast
Shield

C- Body

Hydrazine
Tank

Tilt Out
Mechanism

Delta Frame

Missile
Equipment
Section

Improved front end—Chevaline A3TK.

earlier on 10 September 1965. The Charcoal test had been required to verify the primary of the UK Polaris warhead following an expensive and unsuccessful earlier test 'Courser' due to failure of the external neutron generators which were of US manufacture.[28]

Wilson was very sensitive to the whole question of nuclear testing since his government's stated aim was the removal of nuclear weapons, so he cited the previous government who 'had made arrangements for a test necessary to maintain the effectiveness of our nuclear deterrent, and the experiment took place a few weeks ago.'[29] He also advised the house that the test had been approved on the basis that 'there might be a case, purely on grounds of economy of expensive materials'.[30]

Arbor Fallon, which tested a new lightened warhead, was the first of nine Chevaline related tests in the Nevada desert and its nature was, of course, not revealed other than Wilson admitting that it had been approved by the Heath government even though the issue threatened to create a rift within the party. Criticised by the left-wing Tribune Group's Frank Allaun, Mason commented that if the government 'had purposefully taken the decision to abandon the test, we would have been prematurely taking the decision to abandon our strategic deterrent. That's not on.'[31] The same thinking was again to influence Mason on the eve of the decision to go with Chevaline. It took a very brave or a very foolish defence secretary to go down in history as having taken the decision to take Britain out of the nuclear club.

Chevaline Underground Nuclear Tests—Nevada Test Site		
Arbor Fallon	23 May 1974	Test lightened and hardened warhead
Anvil Banon	26 August 1976	Re-examine weight to range ratio
Cresset Fondutta	11 April 1978	Warhead development test
Quicksilver Quargel	18 November 1978	High speed ReB test
Quicksilver Nessel	29 November 1979	Testing trigger device
Tinderbox Colwick	26 April 1980	Warhead?
Guardian Serpa	17 December 1980	Warhead?
Praetorian Rousanne	12 November 1981	Warhead?
Praetorian Gibne	25 April 1982	Warhead?

Determined to seek an absolute majority, Wilson called another election for 10 October 1974 and obtained a marginal majority of three seats. Perhaps sensing that a decision was likely to be made soon, the simmering dislike of Chevaline within the senior ranks of the Royal Navy began to heat up, conflicting as it did with other, to many, arguably, more prestigious naval requirements which Chevaline procurement would impinge adversely on. First Sea Lord Admiral Sir Edward Ashmore (appointed CNS in March 1974) was advising the Wilson government on defence spending at a time when the services were seeing radical change. Concerned about the delays and seemingly uncontrolled cost overspend of the warhead project, he insisted that it be put under naval control and delivered safely and without further cost overruns. This, at least, appeared to appease some senior naval officers who in any case had an inherent distrust of any defence project run by scientists. Dommett points out that the naval constructors' department at Bath remained dedicated to the project.

Then a new basis for naval concern centred around the use of liquid-fuelled rocket propellants (LFRPs) in the warhead. Hydrazine was to be used in the attitude rocket system which manoeuvred the decoys. It was a highly carcinogenic substance which added to the navy's concerns over its use. They had expressed their views via the Navy Safety Committee in July 1974, but many saw these as somewhat artificial. Hydrazine was already used aboard both ships and submarines for various purposes. Both the Ordnance Board and the Magazine Safety Committee had been aware of the proposed use of hydrazine and had issued demanding guidelines for its safety. The navy cited the USN which did not use such propellants, but their systems were dissimilar from the British proposals. Undaunted, in September, a one-year further funding was approved for progress on Chevaline. It was, however, increasingly evident that a decision had to be made with urgency. Labour was in power with every expectation of a full term in office and the time was right to, once and for all, end the discussions, approve the project, and start work.

Before making the final decision, however, Mason decided that the only way to resolve the RN's dislike of the project was to visit them directly at Faslane and Coulport precisely to identify their concerns. He therefore spent a day in Scotland being briefed on the safety issues and speaking to those involved with the project. In summary, he learned that the Royal Navy was wary about operating a missile unique to themselves while the US Navy was moving onto the next generation and they did not like the thought of having hydrazine fuels within the close confines of a submarine. The RN seemed to have made a compelling case. Mason's uncharacteristically defeatist view after the day was that clearly 'the Navy doesn't want it and you can't force it on them'. Had he talked to serving submariners, rather than shore-based senior officers, about their thoughts, he would have been given a different picture. From the sailors' point of view, there was generally little concern about liquid fuels on board. Their more pragmatic concerns were that 'the reactor keeps going and chips are on the menu'.[32] But against this was the knowledge that the alternatives previously considered were, due to the delay in coming to a decision, no longer available. It was Chevaline or nothing. Nothing meant that the UK would no longer field a credible deterrent and would therefore no longer be a credible nuclear power, a reiteration of the Fallon test argument of the summer. Mason, no doubt having had time overnight to reflect on the navy's concerns, now gave a robust defence of the deterrent and, on the day following his visit to Scotland, took the decision to go ahead with Chevaline and gave management of the programme to the Royal Navy via a resurrected Polaris Steering Group, with Rear Admiral David Scott, formerly deputy controller UK Polaris Programme, appointed Chief Polaris Executive. It was, however, to be another six years until the public as a whole was aware of what was afoot. Scott was 'pathologically anti-Chevaline' which he believed was a project characterised by over-enthusiastic scientists and uncontrolled management and this created a relationship problem with Assistant Chief Scientific Adviser (Nuclear) Frank Panton who stepped down from the post to become director-general (Scientific) Establishments, Resources and Programmes (B) at the MoD. In April 1976, James Callaghan succeeded Wilson who had retired on health grounds. He felt that the programme had reached the point of no return. Huge amounts of money, undeclared to parliament, had been spent and the promise of success was ever 'just around the corner'. It was too late to cancel. In January 1975, Kissinger had briefed President Gerald Ford that Super Antelope 'Involves two specially hardened Polaris RVs and a package of penetration aids (20 replica decoys) designed to look like many incoming RVs to enemy ABM radars. The stated objective of Super Antelope is to assure British penetration of the Moscow ABM complex in an extreme "go it alone" scenario.' Kissinger added that US technical experts had found the design to be quite complex and cost estimates to be overly ambitious. He therefore cautioned that, while continuing to give support, the US should not be seen to endorse the project to avoid being implicated in what he saw as the 'inevitable problems' that would arise.[33]

Chevaline

Chevaline was developed by scientists at AWRE, the RAE at Farnborough, and Hunting Engineering Ltd (HEL). The warhead did not employ the MIRV technology of Poseidon, but the solution was nonetheless both highly sophisticated and also unique. It called upon a widespread array of different technologies which in itself no doubt added to the complexity of the system. The original Polaris A3T warhead configuration was a cluster of three warheads (A, B, and C bodies) in ReBs mounted on a bus. As MRVs, they lacked the capability of independent manoeuvrability but were dispersed over a single target giving some, albeit limited, protection to countermeasures. These warheads were a UK design 'inspired' by the US W-58 warhead, not exactly a copy but incorporating transferred US know-how. Presumably therefore, like its American sibling, the warhead fusing system was capable of either air burst or surface burst.

This meant that if only one Royal Navy SSBN was on patrol, a maximum of forty-eight warheads could be launched. Assuming that 15 per cent of these would suffer malfunction of some kind, the remaining forty-one were theoretically outnumbered by the Galosh ABM system which, of course, itself could suffer failures. Chevaline, with its origins in the Antelope programme, reversed the balance by deploying warheads and penaids—or decoys, indiscriminable to Soviet radar. While these were not independently targeted, as such, they were dispersed in a cylindrical 'threat tube' formation in space, roughly 100 miles long by 10 miles in diameter in a formation that was different for each missile. Coordination of all sixteen missiles by the time they reached the battlespace would provide a multitude of possible targets which, it was estimated, would compromise the Soviet radar. Once the various elements re-entered the atmosphere, however, the penaids rapidly deteriorated, leaving the actual warheads clearly identifiable to radar, but by this time, it was hoped that it was too late for the ABM system to initiate successful countermeasures.

The whole assembly was mounted on the penaid carrier (PAC), but space on this was at a premium. Design authority for the PAC was given to HEL who had been closely involved with the development of the RAF's WE.177 free-fall nuclear weapon. As the original centre of gravity had to be maintained, one of the three warheads had to be sacrificed—a configuration once again with its origins in the Antelope design. A number of differing configurations had been considered for the PAC—descriptively called TwinPAC, JumboPAC, or EconomyPAC—but in the end an asymmetric MonoPAC was selected.

The complete warhead assembly mounted on the PAC consisted of one warhead (the P-Body); the penaids (the D-Pack); and the second warhead (the C-Body) which was mounted directly to the missile equipment section which sat on top of the second stage. (The original design had seen the A-Body selected, but this was later changed to the C-Body.) The two warheads were mounted asymmetrically on a delta frame with the penaid assembly around and between them on a dumbbell-shaped structure made up of two forgings termed 'dogsbones' after their shape. This MonoPAC was in essence a manoeuvrable spacecraft. Both P and C bodies were identical except for their mountings and eject motors, but their positioning was carefully calculated to enable them to 'nod' under the shock of an underwater attack on the SSBN and also to avoid collisions on separation. Although they required only a small separation velocity increment, it had to be sufficient to move them far enough from the twin chamber propulsion unit (TCPU). The TII Chevaline Repositioning Motor TCPU sat on the PAC and used fuel and oxidant to fire bursts to manoeuvre the PAC in such a way that the decoys could be ejected in a predetermined sequence. This involved the unit performing multiple burns during which two types of decoys were ejected on a null range vector both forward and aft along with ejectable masking devices. The warheads had to have sufficient separation to avoid any interference from the exhaust plume of the next TCPU motor burn. Because the TCPU was firing in a near vacuum, the plume extended more than it would in the atmosphere, and this had to be taken into account for any anticipated interaction with the deployed ReBs. Over a roughly two-minute sequence of events, the first TCPU chamber repositioning burn (REP-1) separated the P-Body from the C-Body and ejected the first set of penaids. Thereafter, the second TCPU chamber fired to position the PAC in the centre of the threat cloud and eject the main body of countermeasures. This process completed, the TCPU would once again fire to randomly drive the PAC away from the centre of the threat cloud. Operationally, two burns could be performed by each chamber. The whole process was one of considerable complexity requiring a high degree of precision. The PAC had been developed at Westcott, the Rocket Propulsion Establishment (RPE) at the former RAF station of the same name in Buckinghamshire. The site had been set up in 1946 initially to examine a number of the German wartime rocket and missile programmes, but this later encompassed a number of the UK's own missile programmes particularly those using liquid fuel technology. By the 1960s, particularly since the demise of Blue Streak, there was less and less work, and the timely arrival of the Chevaline programme almost certainly saved it from closure. Filling and assembly took place at A and B sites, the thrust chambers were tested at C and D sites, subsystems gradually integrated and tested at F site, with final assembly and testing at E site where the first final test broke the site's load cells.

Considerable time had been spent on deciding whether to use solid or liquid fuels in the TCPU. Solid fuels caused problems with the unit's CG, although one considered solution was a hybrid between an initial solid burn with a subsequent liquid-fuelled burn using the empty chamber. In the end, given the severe constraints on the available space, liquid fuel was chosen as the only practical solution.

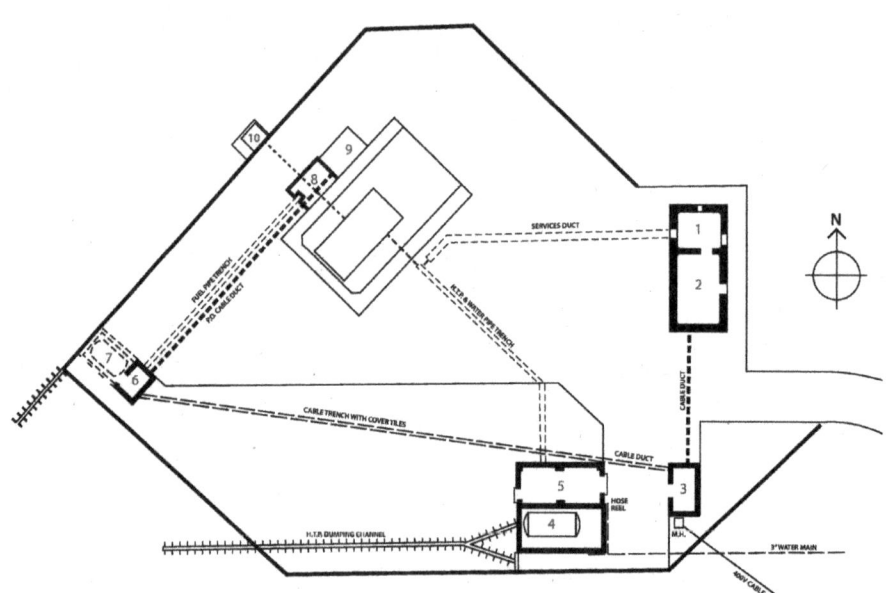

E Site (*c.* 1970). Rocket Propulsion Establishment, Westcott, Buckinghamshire. NGR: SP7102816957. Key: 1. Control room; 2. Electronics room; 3. Switch room; 4. HTP tank; 5. HTP pump house; 6. Pump house; 7. 2,000-gal. kerosene storage tank; 8. Kerosene service and sump; 9. Work shed; 10. HTP drainage sump and pump set.

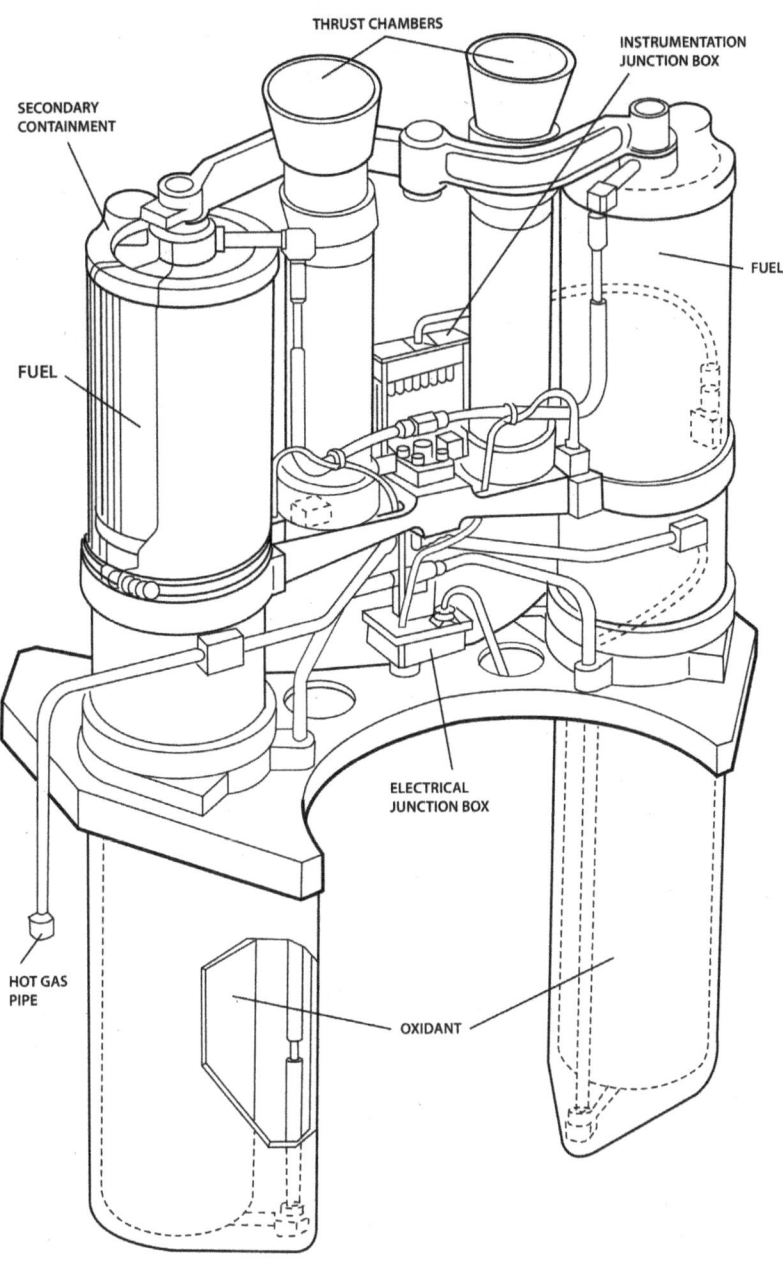

THRUST CHAMBERS

INSTRUMENTATION
JUNCTION BOX

SECONDARY
CONTAINMENT

FUEL

FUEL

ELECTRICAL
JUNCTION BOX

HOT GAS
PIPE

OXIDANT

Chevaline twin chamber propulsion unit (TCPU).

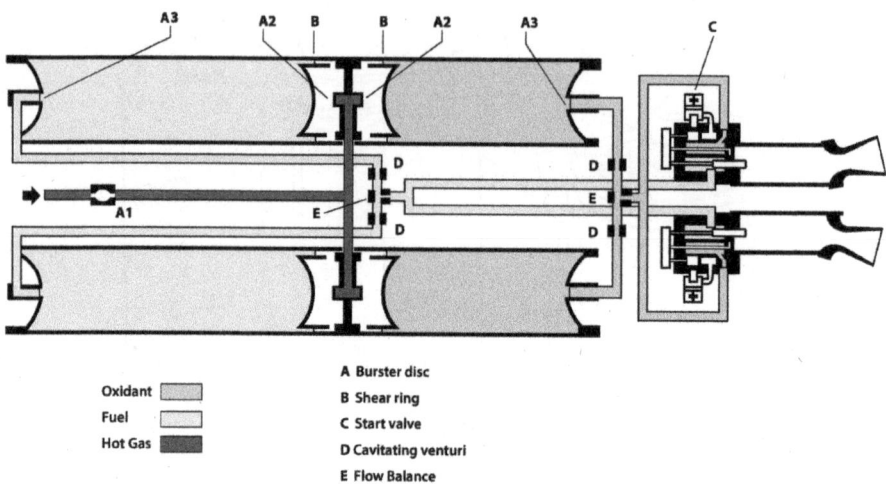

Oxidant ▭
Fuel ▭
Hot Gas ▮

A Burster disc
B Shear ring
C Start valve
D Cavitating venturi
E Flow Balance

Twin chamber propulsion unit (TCPU) schematic diagram.

The TCPU used mixed amine fuel type 1 (MAF 1) and inhibited red fuming nitric acid (IRFNA 14) with a 14 per cent nitrogen dioxide content.[34] Pressurising the tanks containing these liquids was a hot gas system generated by hydrazine using a Shell 405 catalyst licensed by Aerojet Rocketdyne. The original plan was to use a hot gas system designed by Sperry, but this proved unsatisfactory, and an alternative hydrazine actuation system (HAS) was rapidly developed by the Atlantic Research Corporation in Buffalo, New York. Naturally the RN was not happy about this inclusion of dangerous liquids and required a triple safety protection system before reluctantly accepting them on board. A liquid propellant leak detector (LPLD) was incorporated to warn of any leaks within the launch tube whereupon the tube would be flooded.

The ReBs were initially hardened by being formed from wound nylon tape, but this was found to degrade under X-ray bombardment with the surface becoming 'furry' and altering the radar profile. A proposal for the heat shield material for the ReBs was therefore to use beryllium which was a slow absorber of X-rays and would also act as a heat sink. However, Britain was behind America in dealing with the technology of this difficult and hazardous material to work with and there were a number of 'unknowns' about it, particularly what would happen to it when it reached its melting temperature. Would it ablate or sublime? The American company AVCO provided a solution in the form of three-dimensional quartz phenolic (3DQP), a pure fused silica cloth impregnated with phenolic

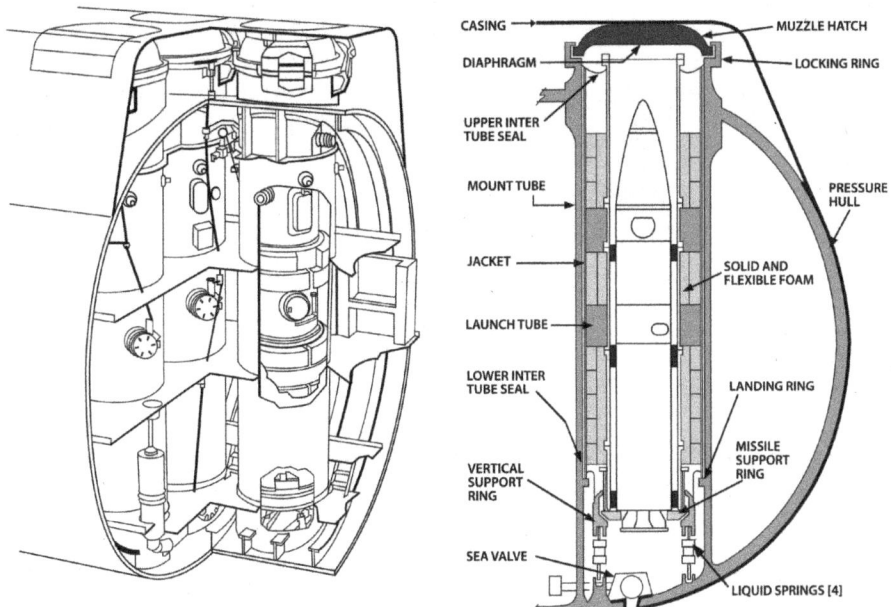

Launcher.

resin. This material hardened the ReB protecting it from high-energy neutrons, and it was the first use of the material in an ReB. Extremely hard, it could be machined like metal to the required shape. Initial production warheads came from AVCO, but subsequent ones were manufactured at the Royal Ordnance Factory at Burghfield in Berkshire. Later on, Britain was to lodge a complaint against AVCO for providing samples of the material to the French.

The warhead delivery process started with the ejection of the nosecone thus exposing the warhead assembly. Thereafter the single C-Body and the PAC were separated simultaneously. The twenty-seven penaids and decoys were ejected, both forwards and backwards, from a number of short and long carbon-fibre canisters, believed to be the first use of this material in a weapon system. Other ejectable masking devices were also deployed. These were sealed with frangible glass covers and incorporated a small rocket eject motor. This motor could only be fired if the latch holding the canister operated correctly. This was a protection against interference with the PAC deployment, however, such was the size of the latches that two decoys had to be sacrificed in the original configuration. The P-Body was also deployed during this sequence. Problems were experienced with separating the PAC from the second stage which could not be slowed down and would continue on its trajectory, thus it was essential that the PAC and the C-Body were by then sufficiently separated. Warheads were therefore ejected by gas pressure with a one third scale model being used at AWRE Foulness to test the system.

Various designs were considered for a blast shield to protect the warheads. Initially it was a circular plate over the warhead assembly, frangible glass being considered, but the final design was a fully enveloping shield made from aluminium with cork edging to dissipate the heat. During transportation and storage, the warheads were protected by a Unit 28800 sheath with the whole assembly fitting inside a TK100 reinforced container. The total weight of Chevaline was around 1,000 lb. Inevitably, perhaps, the weight increased over the original estimate, but for every increase in weight, the range was correspondingly reduced to less than 2,000 miles which in turn reduced the size of the available patrol areas thereby increasing the vulnerability of the submarines by placing them nearer to the GIUK gap which was an area of concentrated naval activity and the consequent inherent risk of detection. Eventually the Royal Navy said 'no more'.

The conceptual design—the responsibility of RAE scientist Roy Dommett who had previously worked on Blue Streak and AWRE's Peter Jones—was very clever and much of the eventual success of the overall programme lay in the emphasis placed in the early stages on systems engineering. Echoing the authority that ADM Raborn had been given when initiating the US Polaris program, Dommett could pick whom he wanted to be involved in the British programme. The systems engineering was co-ordinated by the Systems Modelling Group under the direction of Bob Ridley. The PAC had to manoeuvre rapidly below the range of Soviet radar and problems experienced in the engineering of the PAC led to many of the subsequent delays. As soon as the warheads appeared above the radar horizon the Soviets would be able to compute their launch point and prepare a counterattack. In all the discussions on the subject, there is little or no explanation of why the reduction by a third of the previously available warheads, albeit with a sophisticated array of decoys, all of this developed at considerable expense, was a preferable solution to pressing the US for Poseidon with a larger number of warheads. Nor was there then, or perhaps has ever, been a convincing argument as to under what circumstances it could be envisaged that the UK, unilaterally, would initiate a first strike against a considerably more powerful enemy.

Safety at the NTS was a major consideration and three independent safety panels had to be satisfied along with a number of other agencies who required internal safety clearances. For the flight tests at the Eastern Test Range, the US Range Safety Panel too had to be satisfied. Ultimately some 25 per cent of the costs could be attributed to safety requirements. By its very nature, the programme evoked considerable risk. A broad spectrum of tests would have to be undertaken, both functional and environmental with little previous experience to help in the process. In testing the system, Pad 29 at the ETR was refurbished, eleven launches taking place starting on 12 September 1977 with the final one on 19 May 1980. The next launches would be from a submarine. A number of minor changes to the missile were also required and these modifications were undertaken by LMSC, but the authoritative *Aviation Week* identified a weakness in that although Chevaline could expect to have a service life extending 'well into the 1990s', the hull life of the submarines meant that they 'probably [could] not be kept in service economically much beyond 1990'.[35]

During the test launches, firing to full depletion was avoided as ever-present Soviet intelligence gathering could have deduced the maximum performance of the PAC. Completed Chevalines were transported from Westcott to Coulport in a carefully choreographed operation. The convoy was accompanied by a de-tanking trailer in case of accident and care was taken to ensure the warheads were covered over when being transported around in the open. This was as a precaution against overflying photo-intelligence satellites.

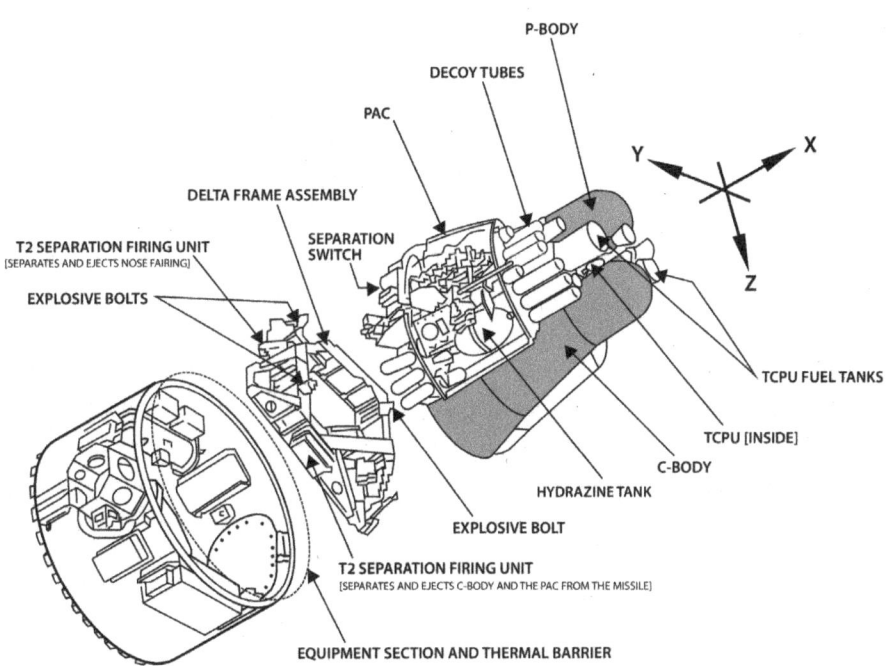

Polaris A3TK Chevaline re-entry system.

Shakespeare's Leisure Companion to the Young Prince Hal

As part of the Chevaline development, Britain also used its existing facilities at the Woomera Rocket Range in South Australia to conduct flight trials and to test various aspects of the PAC deployment. Under the direction of RAE, Skylark sounding rockets were already being launched from the site and these were adapted mainly to test the penaids. These were supplemented by Mach 4 Jabiru rockets which investigated re-entry issues and Falstaff (CQ941) rockets. The latter in particular played an important role in verifying PAC behaviour. The origin of Falstaff was a RAE proposal for a Hypersonic Research Vehicle (HRV) called Hyperion. This was to be a two/three stage rocket using a 'short burn' Royal Ordnance Stonechat motor as the first stage, a Rook or a Raven second stage, and a Cuckoo as a third stage depending on the flight profile. Stonechat was only 36 inches in diameter and large aerodynamic surfaces were added for stability in the atmosphere. Stonechat was the most powerful solid-fuelled operational rocket developed at Westcott, but the Hyperion programme, designed to test delta-winged models at speeds greater than Mach 6 at heights in excess of 100,000 feet was cancelled on the eve of the first test launch. At the same time, the RAE Weapons Department was seeking a suitable vehicle to test various components of the proposed Polaris IFE. RAE was examining beryllium for the ReBs but, as has already been noted, this was proving challenging. Sensing that there could well be problems in testing this in America, it had been decided that a test programme based at Woomera would be the best solution. With its vast, largely uninhabited land area, components, test instrumentation, camera, and film could all be recovered after the flight.

The original plan was to use a Black Arrow/Waxwing launcher which would allow a full-size PAC, but the Treasury were intent on ending that programme: 'It's cancelled and it stays cancelled.'[1] The now redundant Hyperion rocket was suggested as a viable alternative and gave rise to the Falstaff rocket. (Clearly the keen ornithologist at Westcott who had named all the other rockets after birds had either retired or missed this one.) The first flight of a Falstaff vehicle was successfully completed on 1 October 1969. This had originally been the planned Hyperion launch under the Joint HRV Programme and thus it was undertaken openly as a civilian launch which gave no indication of the future purpose of the Falstaff rockets. Designated F00, it tested both the Stonechat I motor and verified the four stabilising fins. The flight also confirmed the performance of the spin rockets and the angle of launch to satisfy programme requirements within agreed safety parameters. Launch was from WRE's new 'tandem rail' launcher which would be used for all subsequent Falstaff flights. On ignition, the rocket rapidly accelerated to 3 *g*, almost immediately lost to sight, and further accelerated up to 8 *g*. Although a useful period of time outside the sensible atmosphere (that part of the atmosphere that offers resistance to a body passing through it) of about ten minutes was achieved, this version of Falstaff was deemed too slow for useful re-entry work to be undertaken. The next Falstaff therefore used a Stonechat II motor and incorporated an adaptor section to allow a wider diameter payload bay to be used. Payload protection was a nose fairing which was a copy of the design Saunders Roe had used for Black Arrow which was almost identical in shape to the Polaris nosecone.

This adapted Falstaff could carry an early prototype PAC, but some space had to be given up to incorporate telemetry and a recoverable 70-mm camera. Although it was proposed to test a full IFE, this proved too heavy, so the payload packages were simulations of the full PAC from which experimental submunitions and decoys could be dispensed.

Although a series of ten launches—later increasing to twelve—was originally planned, the programme did not go well as a result of delays in the payloads and other competing programme needs. In the end, there were only five operational flights (F1-5), all launched from Woomera's Range E.

F1 was planned to be the first launch with active components, however, the igniter casing broke free at launch leading to a catastrophic break up and destruction of the vehicle. F2 proved more successful duplicating the flight programme of F1 but with an additional payload manoeuvre incorporating the TCPU. F3 was intended to cover the release of the P-Body, but although the Falstaff behaved according to plan, the payload failed. F4 sought to duplicate the flight programme of F3 but included further developments and was largely successful, although the attitude control failed and the payload stabilised at an incorrect angle. F5 expanded on the previous two flights and was declared a total success.[2] On completion of these flights, remaining hardware was scrapped. Although there was undoubtedly close collaboration between Britain and Australia, anything to do with nuclear weapons was extremely sensitive. In 2002, the existence of the Falstaff program was revealed and disclosed that British nuclear testing had continued for fifteen years later than the generally believed date of 1963. However, this really depended on semantics. Could the testing of components for a nuclear weapon be classed as the same as testing an actual

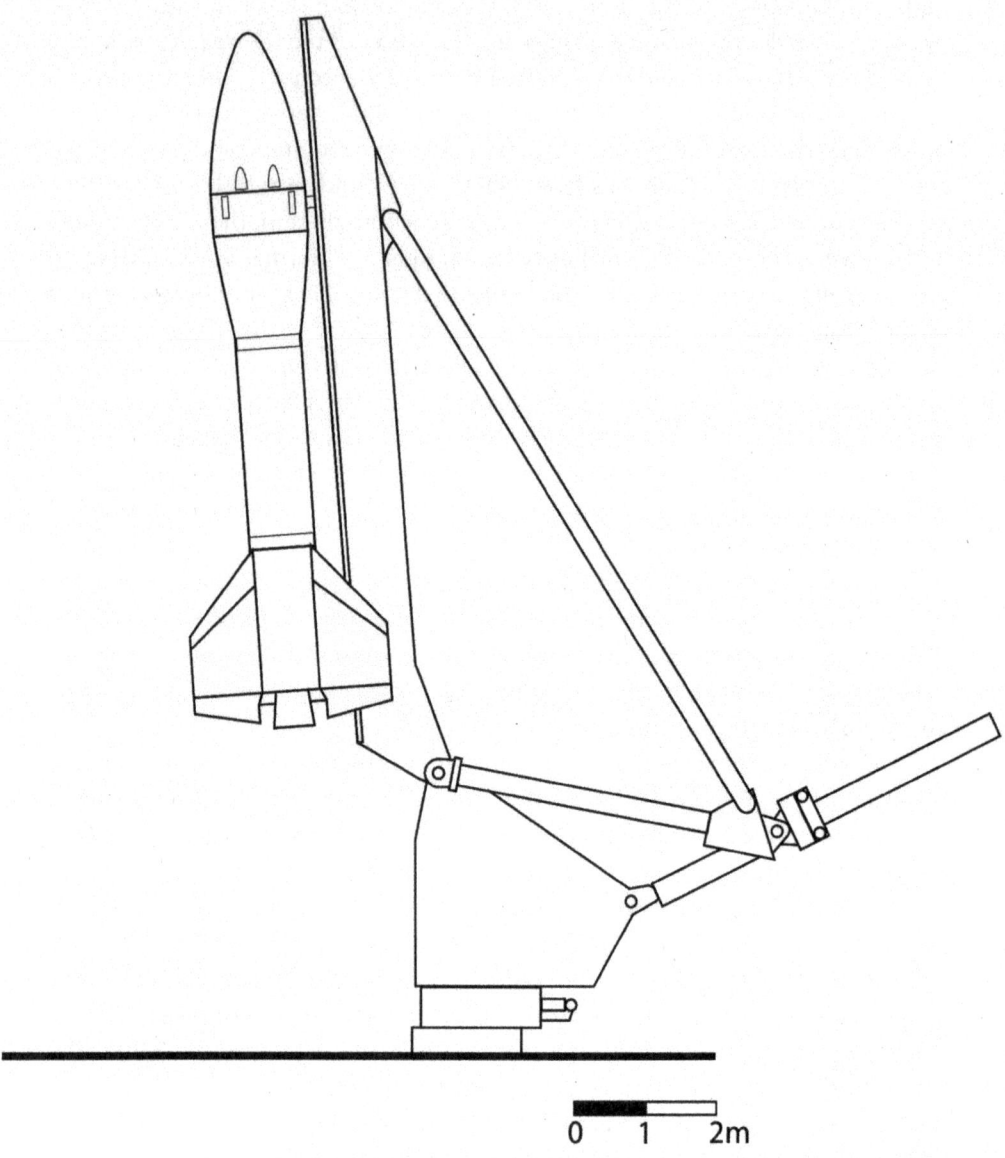

Falstaff launcher.

nuclear weapon? Full details of sounding rocket launches from Woomera still remains to be disclosed. Sadly, the films of the launches were deposited in the War Office where asbestos was subsequently identified making access (conveniently?) forbidden.

Falstaff Test Flights			
F00	1 October 1969	Stonechat I proving flight	Successful
F0	9 May 1975	Proving flight to test separation and on-board analogue telemetry	Successful
F01	19 February 1976	Full instrumentation	Successful
F1	23 May 1978	PAC penaid ejection	Failure
F2	15 September 1978	First functioning TCPU	Successful
F3	5 December 1978	As F2 plus P-Body eject	Failure
F4	14 February 1979	As F3 but no penaids	Successful
F5	4 April 1979	As F3 with full PAC	Successful

Sir Michael Quinlan, the MoD's hugely experienced deputy secretary (policy and programmes), had fervently believed that Chevaline should be kept out of the public domain in case it failed thereby inevitably putting the UK deterrent's effectiveness in doubt together with its deterrent value. But eventually it became impossible to keep the secret from a wider audience. On 24 January 1980, Defence Secretary Francis Pym announced to the House of Commons:

Without breaching the provisions of the 1972 treaty on anti-ballistic missile defence, the Soviet Union has continued to upgrade its ABM capabilities, and we have needed to respond to that upgrading so that we can maintain the deterrent assurance of our force. The previous Conservative Government therefore pressed ahead with a programme of improvements to our Polaris missiles, which our immediate predecessors continued and sustained. The House will, I am sure, understand that I cannot go deep into detail, even to correct the widely mistaken assertions which have sometimes appeared in public, but I think the programme has now reached a stage where I can properly make public more information about it.

The programme, which has the code-name Chevaline, is a very major and complex development of the missile front end, involving also changes to the fire control systems. The result will not be a MIRVed system, but it includes advanced penetration aids and the ability to manoeuvre the payload in space. The programme has been funded and managed entirely by the United Kingdom with the full co-operation of the United States Government, including the use of some of their facilities for trials and tests.

Some American firms have been employed, but most of the work in industry has gone to British firms. We have had a very successful series of flight trials and development is close to completion. Deployment will begin soon afterwards, and that will maintain the full effectiveness of our strategic deterrent into the 1990s.[3]

Aviation Week confirmed:

Britain has developed a maneuvrable [*sic*] warhead for its submarine-launched polaris [*sic*] ballistic missiles which it will deploy soon to extend the effectiveness of the missiles into the early 1990s. New warhead is codenamed Chevaline.[4]

The total estimated costs of around £1,000 million had been kept 'off budget', something that would not be allowed to happen again. The announcement was covered in a number of newspapers. 'A project to upgrade Britain's Polaris missile is nearly complete', the *Daily Express* announced giving a fairly comprehensive summary of Pym's announcement.[5] But the plan to upgrade HMS *Revenge* to become the first SSBN to accept operational Chevaline-tipped missiles when her refit was completed in 1982 was shelved as problems on test launches were still being experienced with satisfactory separation of the warheads and decoys. Meanwhile at Faslane, a Poseidon navigation system, representative of the latest Polaris sub-system, had been installed at the Polaris School and formally opened by Rear Admiral John S. Grove, chief strategic systems executive.[6]

Chevaline was by no means a wholly British program, although it eventually involved four government agencies and around fifty contractors. Co-operation from US contractors was both desirable and necessary in developing the subsystems and was provided under the US Foreign Military Sales Program. Some 45 per cent of the costs were dollar costs with the attendant risk of exchange fluctuations. A similar percentage cost was spent by or at Aldermaston with 'manpower costs completely dominating everything'. About one-third of the programme funding was for US contracted work. The urgency of the programme meant that some harsh management decisions had to be taken. Sperry UK's involvement survived only after Sperry US sent Director Mel Fader who came on the strict understanding that he had complete authority to oversee the British company's part in the programme. Even then, responsibility for the attitude control system was handed over to Bell Textron who already had substantial experience of hydrazine systems.

LC29A was once again used to undertake initial testing of the reconfigured missile. The first of eleven launches from this pad happened on 12 September 1977. This and the next launch (Chevaline PA and PB) tested just the missile, but on 26 July 1978, the first of six tests of the Development Standard IFE took place. The results of these firings gave encouragement to proceed to three launches (PT1-3) of In-service Standard IFEs. The LC29A firing programme finished on

19 May 1980 and it was now time to start a test programme with firings from submarines. The original plan, which was governed by the refit schedule, indicated that the *Revenge* would become the first Chevaline-armed SSBN. However, as the predicted in-service date of the IFE slipped, it was to be the *Renown* that was the first to be equipped with pre-production Chevaline, although her two acceptance flight trials down the ETR in November 1980 had not been a success. As a result of these failures, it was not until 30 January 1982 that a modified IFE led to four successful firings. It therefore fell to the *Renown* to undertake the first operational patrol in May 1982.

The *Revenge* was by now ready to accept Chevaline and spent May and June 1983 at the ETR where under the Chevaline DASO I programme, six operationally configured missiles were launched successfully. A year later, it was the *Resolution*'s turn during a less than fully satisfactory DASO II visit to the ETR. The second launch on 20 May 1985 saw a failure of the second stage resulting in the missile falling well short of its target. The MoD confirmed that the missile was not fitted with a Chevaline warhead on this occasion. The visit was further marred by a collision between the submarine and the fishing vessel *Proud Mary* as the submarine, commanded by Cdr M. J. Sime (port crew) prepared to submerge off the Florida coast. At around 9:25 a.m. on 10 June 1985 during preparations for the DASO, the *Resolution* collided with the 57-foot vessel. The *Resolution* and a submarine support ship, the USS *Emory S. Land* (AS-39), stopped immediately to aid the *Proud Mary* and its crew. A Coast Guard vessel from Port Canaveral hurried to the scene and provided medical aid and a portable pump for the damaged vessel:

> The sub was traveling about 15 m.p.h. and was displaying normal, internationally specified navigation lights, including two at the top of its communications mast, 80 feet above the surface. The Coast Guard reported a woman crew member on the *Proud Mary* suffered a broken kneecap, while the other three on board were treated for cuts and bruises.[7]

The *Resolution*'s diving plane caused a 15- by 6-foot gash above the waterline. Four of the fishing boat's crew received minor injuries. Blame was subsequently placed on the fishing vessel for the accident.[8] (It was not unknown for trawlers to deliberately tangle with submarines to claim damage to their nets.) No one aboard the British vessel was injured and the submarine went on to undertake a successful launch.

The *Revenge* under the command of Cdr B. R. Coward returned to the Cape in 1986 for four Polaris Evaluation Motor (PEM) DASO firings. These took place between 25 July and 2 August. As was generally the case, the launches were witnessed by a selection of VIPs. For the first two, seven naval officers and four civilians were on board. These observers were headed up by Admiral Sir Derek

Reffell, controller of the navy, and included RADM Stanley Bump, commander Submarine Group Six and a former captain of the USS *Holland*.[9]

All four SSBNs were Chevaline capable when HMS *Repulse* was recommissioned for a third time at Rosyth on 1 November 1986 following a 107-week refit. Lady Zuckerman was the guest of honour, thereby maintaining her long-standing connection with the submarine. Also present were Vice Admiral Sir John Hayes, a survivor of the sinking of the battlecruiser *Repulse* off Malaya in 1941 along with FOSNI Vice Admiral Sir George Vallings. The refit had cost £120 million and occupied a workforce of 900 personnel. It subsequently fell to the *Repulse* to conduct the final firing of a Chevaline missile which took place at the Eastern Test Range on 11 May 1987. The *Repulse* did not enjoy the happiest of careers, and on her approach to Cape Canaveral the previous month, she suffered a minor collision in the long approach channel. A repeat performance of a similar event suffered by the *Resolution* on her arrival two years before. Things improved and the submarine successfully carried out DASO III, the final launching of four A3TKE missiles giving the DGSWS team under the command of Capt. Trevor Craven the last opportunity to evaluate the missiles' performance. (See Appendix II.)

The Chevaline programme was subject to critical analysis when, in 1982, it was the subject of a parliamentary Committee of Public Accounts (Public Accounts Committee) investigation under the chairmanship of Labour MP Joel Barnett.

In the final assessment, the facts are that Chevaline was criticised from various directions. Its funding process almost certainly resulted in the project significantly exceeding budget, its complexities almost certainly determined it would be delivered late and the secrecy of the project was in itself controversial. Nonetheless, whatever view may be taken on Chevaline, it should be remembered as a very remarkable technical achievement by all those concerned. But was that enough? The Royal Navy never wanted it—for perfectly good reasons, from the start they wanted Poseidon, but politically, this showed to some people an unhealthy attachment to the United States when membership of the European Economic Community was also on the agenda. Culturally averse to the use of liquid fuels and unhappy about the restrictions that were imposed by the new warhead on their sea areas of operation, the senior service was never going to show any enthusiasm for the upgrade. Had they been more aware of the millions that had been spent, their anguish may have been even greater. One admiral, in conversation under the Chatham House Rule at a RUSI Conference in 2005, opined that he saw the possibility of the UK launching an attack on the Soviet Union without American nuclear support as 'suicidal, infinitesimal and beyond any reasonable rational comprehension. If we wanted Moscow attacked, the Americans would no doubt already be doing it. We could then deploy our missiles against other targets with no ABM shield—[the so-called "Minsk Option"]—and could have spent the money more wisely elsewhere at the time.' Victor Macklen, chief nuclear adviser to the MoD, called it a 'long and depressing story'. Or was it an ill-fated attempt to maintain expertise and employment at Aldermaston when in the end staff shortages led to the request of assistance from British Aerospace and American contractors. The PN(67) Committee in 1967 had voiced concerns that the Atomic Energy Authority had warned that Aldermaston may become unviable 'in the absence of scientifically challenging work, such as the hardening of Polaris, with the consequence that [the UK's] nuclear capability as a whole would be put at risk'.[10] Was this the price of maintaining British nuclear expertise for the future. A *Times* editorial called it 'the worst handled weapons procurements since 1945'.[11]

It had taken nearly twenty years after the ABM threat was fully recognised to develop Chevaline, and by the time it became operational in all four submarines, it would be deployed for a period much less than had been originally planned. Little publicity was given to the fact that during these twenty years, the UK deterrent had been emasculated as its ability to fulfil the Moscow Criterion was at least questionable. Surprisingly only two people were given public recognition for their part in the Chevaline programme. Admiral David Scott received a knighthood and Mel Fader an honorary OBE. Roy Dommett later received a CBE in 1991. Nonetheless, Hunting Engineering's Chevaline technology found its way to America when it was used in the Red Tigress series of launches from Cape Canaveral in the early 1990s. These used HEL designed penaids to collect data in the development of infrared and radar target discrimination technologies.

Chevaline was formally withdrawn from service on 31 October 1996. By then, the Royal Navy was patrolling with its next generation V-class Trident-armed SSBNs.

The Perils of the Sea

*Of all the branches of men in the Forces, there is none which shows more
devotion and faces grimmer perils than the submariner.*

Winston Churchill

Submarines were, and still are, not the safest places of work. Their world is a
three-dimensional one subject to many unknowns. As has often been pointed out,
more is known about the surface of the Moon than much of the ocean depths and
the broadening of capability brought about by nuclear power added a further
dimension of risk. Admiral Rickover was obsessive about safety, and although
American nuclear-powered submarines have, tragically, been lost, the reasons
have never been attributable to their reactors. The speed at which the technology
was advancing could arguably sometimes be ahead of the safety envelope in the
shipyards. To allay possible fears, Rickover would be aboard each submarine
when it first sailed for its sea trials.[1] This is in contrast to the Russian Navy which
has been characterised by a number of serious problems resulting in numerous
fatalities.

That is, of course, not to say that the US Navy was without casualties, and
although no SSBN was a casualty, the potential dangers were ever-present. On 10
April 1963, the USS *Thresher* was conducting deep diving tests some 200 miles
east of Cape Cod. The first SSN of a new class, the *Thresher* was also the first
to employ HY-80 steel in the construction of its hull and frame. Naturally there
was great interest in seeing how the submarine performed at depth. Fortuitously,
as this was not the SSN's initial trial, Rickover was not aboard. Had he been,
the story of the US nuclear submarine programme could well have been very
different.

After an indistinct message to the accompanying rescue ship, the USS *Skylark*
(ASR-20), nothing more was heard, and it was eventually accepted that the
submarine had imploded and sank in 8,400 feet of water. All 129 crew members

perished, including seventeen civilian contractors.[2] The US Navy has never fully released its findings into the cause of the sinking, and a court order issued in February 2020 to release some 600 pages of documents was postponed as a result of the COVID-19 pandemic. Various theories have been put forward, but the balance of evidence suggests a major failure of a pipe joint which allowed sea water to flood into the submarine shorting out the reactor which shut down according to plan – the standard procedure at the time. Without propulsion and with seawater coming in 'it doesn't take much to sink a submarine'.[3] Polmar suggests that the submarine was inadequately prepared for seagoing trials at the dive depth of 1,300 feet. Partly to blame he believed was the failure to fully understand that using traditional approaches to submarine construction were no longer applicable to large submarines capable of diving to considerably greater depths.[4]

The second sinking was that of the USS *Scorpion* (SSN-589). This was a replacement for the original *Scorpion* which, as we have seen, had metamorphosed to become the *George Washington*. Those of a superstitious nature believed it was wrong to resurrect the name for the next SSN as this might anger the sea-gods. Whether this was a contributory factor in the subsequent disaster is for the reader to decide, but towards the end of May 1968, the *Scorpion* was returning from a routine patrol when she sank in deep water someway south-west of the Azores, again with the loss of all ninety-nine hands. With little evidence to go on at first, but after a remote inspection of the remains, it was apparent that the submarine had been near the surface at the time. Despite persistent claims that the submarine had been sunk by a Russian SSN, the evidence presented was translated into the procedure to recharge the batteries, a routine, but less frequent, requirement even on nuclear submarines. The procedure was not without its dangers as the process involved the release of hydrogen. Diesel submarines had operated 'Condition Baker' during battery recharging on the surface. It involved closing the hatches to prevent hydrogen travelling through the boat. This was fine for diesel submarines and old habits die hard for the older crew members brought up in diesel boats. But in shutting the hatches, a dangerous build-up of hydrogen could have rapidly ensued—4 per cent was the safe level, and at twice that, spontaneous ignition with the oxygen in the air would take place. Rear Admiral Dave Oliver believes that this is what happened to the *Scorpion*.[5]

The mere geography of the oceans can also prove hazardous, as can other vessels. The USS *Seawolf* suffered a near catastrophic encounter with the seabed when she grounded off the coast of Maine on 30 January 1968, damaging her rudder, an incident that could well have led to another total loss. But it was not only underwater contours that presented as obstacle. All four of the Royal Navy's boats suffered collisions. In January 1973, the *Revenge* was being taken out of the drydock at Faslane when she collided with the *Repulse*. The latter's hydroplanes were damaged and had to be replaced. It was believed that the *Repulse* still had its full complement of missiles on board at the time. On 17 April 1974, the *Renown* struck the seabed hard while on exercise in the Firth of Clyde following her refit. Both her captain, Cdr Robin Whiteside, and the navigating officer, Lt William Pym, were subsequently court martialled for 'failing to make use of soundings to assist navigation when submerged in confined waters'. Secrecy surrounded the incident before a full assessment of the submarine had been made so that Soviet intelligence would not be alerted.[6] Rear-Admiral Sir Morgan Morgan-Giles, MP for Winchester, who on occasion had brought much mirth to the Commons proceedings, rose in defence of the officers: 'Does the Minister realise that when any commanding officer or ex-commanding officer reads of somebody hitting the putty, he immediately thinks, "There but for the grace of God ..."? Will the hon. Gentleman explain that there are good reasons for these large ships, after refit, carrying out trials in relatively shallow waters, that it is an extremely difficult job to avoid the bottom sometimes and that this was therefore a relatively trivial incident?'[7] In October 1968, HMS *Warspite* returned from patrol with the forward part of her fin covered over with a tarpaulin. It was claimed that the SSN had collided with an iceberg in the Barents Sea, but as a dockyard worker somewhat cynically pointed out, 'I've never seen paint on an iceberg.' The reality was that the SSN had been shadowing a Soviet *Echo II*-class SSGN which, apparently unaware of the British boat's presence, had unexpectedly shut down one of its engines. The *Warspite* passed under the Soviet vessel, but the forward portion of the fin was damaged by the *Echo*'s propellers. After surfacing, both submarines were able to return to their bases. Unlike the SSN role which often required close approach, such encounters for an SSBN were unlikely as their operations were to keep away from other vessels, but in the stealthy underseas arena, anything could theoretically happen. Surface vessels also presented their problems as the captain of HMS *Renown* discovered after the submarine collided with the MV *Moyle* (see page 242).[8] Operational SSBNs do not use active sonar systems for fear of revealing their locations, relying instead on passive sonar, which gives less precise information on surface vessels.

Three US SSBNs suffered potentially serious incidents. The *Simon Bolivar* (SSBN-641) was in collision with the *Betelgeuse* on 31 August 1967 some 70 miles off the US coast. The supply ship's hull was damaged and some flooding occurred. Extensive damage was also done to the submarine's fin. Fortunately, both vessels were able to make their own way back to Charleston for repairs and no casualties were recorded.

The *James Madison* was leaving the Holy Loch on 3 November 1974 *en route* to her patrol area when she collided with a Soviet SSN, the *Victor 1*-class *K-306*, trying to track her. Deputy National Security Adviser Brent Scowcroft advised Kissinger, '[h]ave just received word from the Pentagon that one of our Poseidon submarines has just collided with a Soviet submarine.'[9] Both submarines surfaced but the Soviet one subsequently submerged and disappeared. As the incident had occurred within UK territorial waters, Kissinger ordered that the matter was hushed up so as not to create a diplomatic incident and sour relations with the Soviets.[8] In fact, Russian sources were later the first to acknowledge the accident, although the submarine was incorrectly believed to be the *Nathanael Greene*.

In order to mask the sound signature of the departing submarine, stun grenades were ejected into the water, effectively blinding the sonar screens of both submarines for some time. Unfortunately, during this 'blindness', neither submarine knew they were on a collision course:

'The collision was quite strong. The Soviet boat received a small hole in the torpedo room, which was quickly dealt with. The 'American' had a badly wrinkled nose.' Captain 1st Rank Alexander Kuzmin, wrote: 'The American boat was forced to surface. We surfaced under the periscope and immediately saw her. The *Nathaniel Green* [*sic*] was in the water, listing heavily to starboard. Confused sailors climbed onto the hull, the commander from the bridge tried to understand what had happened. We had to take a photograph through the periscope, but there was no film in the navigational camera. I had to take a pencil and quickly sketch it.' *K-306* went home for two weeks at a depth of 40 meters to relieve pressure on the torpedo tube covers. An investigation into the emergency was appointed, and the commander of the submarine was severely reprimanded. The American crew were awarded Golden Dolphin badges for their courage.[10]

The third incident was on 25 April 1987 when the *Daniel Boone* was undertaking post-refit sea trials and ran aground in the James River at Newport News. To counter the current in the river, the officer of the deck (OOD) ordered the secondary propulsion system to be lowered, but this resulted in the unit being ripped off on a sandbank. Retracting the unit would have resulted in an unpluggable hole in the hull but fortunately his order was countermanded by crew in the machinery space who saw what had happened. Had the order been carried out, it would, with some certainty, have sunk the submarine.

The undersea world therefore is one where safety rules have to be scrupulously observed. The *Thresher* and *Scorpion* losses highlighted the ever-present risk of disasters, although as Rickover was wont to point out, his near obsession with safety meant that neither loss could be attributed to the nuclear presence on the SSNs. Providing the hull was still intact, deep-sea rescue was not an impossibility and to this end, the US Navy and the Royal Navy conducted joint emergency rescue procedures in June 1979. The conventional *Oberon*-class submarine HMS *Odin* (S10) played the part of the submarine in distress, lying on the seabed in some 400 feet of water off the Isle of Arran. The exercise started with a 'subsunk' distress call to the North Island Naval Air Station near San Diego. This was the base for the US Navy's two deep-submergence rescue vessels (DSRV), the *Mystic*

(DSRV-1) and the *Avalon* (DSRV-2). These two vessels with a crew of four had been built in response to the loss of the *Thresher* (although in itself this was not a survivable accident) but had focussed attention on the ever-present danger of submarine incidents. The navy had originally wanted twelve, but cost overruns had limited the eventual number to two. In response to the emergency, the *Avalon* was airlifted to Glasgow aboard a C-5A Galaxy transport of Military Airlift Command (MAC). An accompanying C-141 Starlifter brought the vessel's special equipment necessary for its task including its purpose-built road transport trailer. To avoid disruption to the normal commercial operations of Glasgow Airport, both planes landed around midnight when the airport was closed. Despite the midnight hour, a large contingent of press was present to witness the arrival and the transfer of the DSRV to its trailer for its journey to the Clyde Submarine Base. The elapsed time from the first alert to arrival at Faslane was forty-seven hours. Acting as the rescue vessel, HMS *Repulse* had the *Avalon* mounted in a cradle on her aft casing and sailed to the search area. The SSBN then released the *Avalon* which set off on a search for the *Odin* using her onboard sonar—visibility being down to a few feet in the murky waters. Having located the *Odin*, the *Avalon* attached itself exactly over the escape hatch. The *Odin*'s CO, Lt Ian Richards, opened the hatch to be greeted by the *Avalon*'s American pilot, LCDR Dick Hall. The *Odin*'s crew members were then able to enter the DSRV and were taken back to the *Repulse*. To assist in the recovery process, white paint had been added to outline *Repulse*'s fin, foreplanes, Type 2019 sonar, and the vertical rudder. This was the first time that crew members had been transferred between submerged submarines and the first time they had dived in one submarine and surfaced in another. A number of similar rescue missions were completed during the week-long exercise including 'rescues' using the smaller British Oceanics BO L-1 commercial submersible operating from its parent ship *Vickers Viking*. Faslane's escape, rescue and diving officer Cdr Brian Forbes claimed a record by being in four different submarines in one dive. Starting off in the L-1, he transferred underwater to the *Odin* before transferring to the *Avalon* and finally to the *Repulse* before surfacing. Although, in fact, neither the *Avalon* nor the *Mystic* was ever to take part in a real rescue during their operational lives, the joint exercise had proved to both navies that the capability existed to deploy the DSRV anywhere in support of a submarine in distress.

Towards the End

How can you not be prepared to go into more detail when you haven't gone into __any__ detail?

Lt Col. Michael Mates, Chairman of the Commons Defence Sub-Committee to Brian Hawtin (Assistant Under Secretary (Navy)), 28 November 1990

The *Resolution* completed the 100th patrol on 1 September 1978. The *Repulse* recorded the 200th, returning on 23 July 1990, thus also celebrating the anniversary of HMS *Victory*'s keel being laid in 1759. But the determining factor in the operational life of the Royal Navy's R-class SSBNs was the hull life of the vessels. This gradually deteriorated as a result of the pressure exerted on the hull when dived. Age can bring with it restrictions in the safe diving depth and towards the end of their operational lives, it was believed that the Royal Navy's SSBNs had difficulties passing their diving trials. The anticipated life from the start for both submarine and reactor may be taken to be around twenty years which took the submarines into the early 1990s—taking the time in commission minus the time spent in refit produced the following figures:

HMS *Resolution*	HMS *Renown*	HMS *Repulse*	HMS *Revenge*
20 years, 0 months	15 years, 11 months	18 years, 8 months	18 years, 5 months
69 patrols	44 patrols	60 patrols	56 patrols

The *Resolution*'s reactor would therefore be close to being time expired. Problems with the reactor could be anticipated and indeed had already been seen in 1976 as she underwent final power testing after her refit. A similar problem befell the *Renown*, the youngest in the fleet in terms of operational service, in 1980. While reactor faults and failures relating to them would be the most concerning, those were not the only factors involved. Noise generated as equipment became older was apparently why the *Resolution* had to return to

Rosyth in 1986/87 for remedial work to be undertaken. The *Revenge* made a number of visits to the Loch Goil acoustic range in the early 1990s and this too was thought to be because of noise problems. The *Revenge* suffered a fault in one of her missile tubes on 29 October 1978 as she prepared to go on patrol. Initial thoughts were to extend the time of the SSBN then on patrol (the *Resolution*); however, it was considered that repairs would have taken too long and the *Revenge* left on 5 November with only fifteen missiles on QRA. A monthly readiness report had to be submitted to SACEUR, but it was noted that this included the missiles at twenty-four-hour basic readiness aboard the submarine on turn-around at Faslane. Therefore, by keeping thirteen missiles onboard the *Resolution* during her inter-patrol period, a total of twenty-eight missiles could be reported to SACEUR which was in fact the normal operational requirement—sixteen at sea and thirteen on the inter-patrol boat having offloaded three at Coulport for routine servicing. There was only a minimal reduction in targeting capability. Repairs were carried out after the *Revenge* returned from patrol.[1] Despite being the oldest submarine, the *Resolution*'s crews were to bear the brunt of long duration patrols. In the twelve months from July 1990, it appears that the *Resolution* carried out two very long patrols. In August, she was at sea for 109 days, and to provide subsequent cover, the *Revenge* had to stay on patrol for seventy-nine days at the end of the year. After returning to Faslane in June 1991 from a 108-day patrol, the *Resolution* spent only five days in port before setting out for a further thirty-day patrol. Although these lengthened patrols may have seemed arduous at the time, they were totally eclipsed by a record patrol in mid-2023, when a Royal Navy *Vanguard*-class Trident SSBN returned to its Faslane base after a six-month patrol. Covered in slime and barnacles, it set an all-time record for patrol length and must have placed enormous pressure on its 130-man crew.[2]

In the spring of 1992, a seemingly unscheduled month of sea trials suggested that the *Repulse* was experiencing problems of an unspecified nature. The greatest concern, however, was finding defects in the reactors. HMS *Warspite* was in refit when, in December 1989, hairline cracks were found in the reactor. It was decided that repair was uneconomic, and it was announced in September 1990 that the SSN would be decommissioned. Falklands War veteran HMS *Valiant* was decommissioned in August 1994, possibly as a result of damage sustained when she ran aground in the North Norwegian Sea in March 1991.[3]

The ageing process also affected the Royal Navy's A3 missiles. American use of even the definitive A-series missile had never anticipated its deployment for more than a relatively short period of time as their programme was always evolving, hence the adoption of Poseidon and thereafter Trident posed no threat to the ageing process in their A-3s. For the British missiles, along with updating the warhead, there was the need to manufacture replacement first- and second-stage motors after a number of test firing failures became evident. This was because of propellant ageing and added considerable cost to maintaining the deterrent. In 1982, therefore, the US Navy's Strategic Systems Program Office (SSPO) acting on behalf of the UK, contracted with Lockheed to manufacture new first- and second-stage motors. Production of these motors by Aerojet and Hercules had finished nineteen years earlier and technology had moved on since then and this could possibly lead to problems, so the UK had requested that the new manufacture be as close as possible to the original and to at least match the reliability and performance criteria. It would appear that there was little need to replace the first-stage motors which were pretty much 'army-proof', nonetheless, the decision was made to replace these as well. Westcott put in a bid to build new second-stage motors. The K2 site was fully capable of static testing these motors and had in fact successfully fired 4-foot 6-inch-diameter motors. To their disappointment, however, their bid was unsuccessful. The project was completed satisfactorily by both manufacturers, although a complex testing programme had to be set up, including submarine launches. These new missiles were designated A3R (R for replacement). It was found that the 'same' and 'equivalent' materials were neither the same nor equivalent for a number of unknown reasons. The substitution of improved parts which on the face of it should provide an improved performance could raise new and unanticipated problems. Both types of motors were extensively tested at the Naval Weapons Center (NWC) China Lake facility. In some cases, the original materials used were no longer available, and the alternative, although meeting the original specifications, acted differently. 'A case in point was the first-stage rocket motor chamber insulator material.... Material from an alternate source was selected [which] met the original specification requirements, but when it was used in a full-scale motor, a significantly different (more rapid) erosion rate occurred.'[4] Further problems were found with the Alcoa-7075-T6 alloy used in the original production. This alloy had been superseded and the new alloy resulted in forgings with higher internal stress, resulting in fractures when the forgings were machined. 'Lockheed and the Lockheed motor subcontractor suppliers, Aerojet and Hercules, with the support of many other material suppliers and test agencies, did an admirably thorough and professional job of carrying out this successful rebuild. It is clear that they encountered many problems, even with extensive testing.'[5]

Subsequent testing of these new motors was carried out under the Polaris Evaluation Motor (PEM) programme undertaken by the *Revenge* in 1986. After Chevaline, this was the second costly upgrade to be needed to keep Britain's deterrent fit for purpose. The programme was completed by 1988 at a cost of around £300 million.

At the same time, the Soviet Union began to collapse as the Soviet President Mikhail Gorbachev instituted change. On 9 November 1989, the Berlin Wall, symbol of the divide between East and West, was broken down amid cheering crowds. Just over two years later, an event took place at Faslane which would have been unimaginable a short time before. On 4 December 1991, General Vladimir Lobov, recently appointed Russian chief of the general staff, 'was welcomed ... where no Russian had been welcomed before—in one of Britain's nuclear submarines'. The general was given a ninety-minute tour of the *Revenge* with only the map room and the missile control area out of bounds. 'A navy officer remarked: "There are a lot of people here today pinching themselves to make sure this is really happening."'[6]

By 1991, certain unease was evident about the implications of the ageing Polaris fleet on the refit programme. Junior Defence Procurement Minister Kenneth Carlisle deflected questions on the matter by saying that this was classified; however, on 9 December 1991, Carlisle announced in a written response that the *Revenge*, her scheduled refit now well overdue, would be paid off at the end of her present commission.[7] The *Guardian* had earlier reported that the submarine 'could be withdrawn from service several years ahead of schedule because long delays at Rosyth are preventing a vital refuelling programme for its reactor'. The *Renown*, then in refit, was nearly two years behind schedule as a result of cracks being detected in the pipes leading to the reactor's steam generator. The *Repulse* had not been on patrol for nearly fifteen months. The news about the *Revenge* was received badly by workers at the dockyard. The submarine was already experiencing instances of power loss having been in service some two years longer than had been intended and had been due to have a final refit lasting some three years and was expected to have the work carried out at the Scottish yard which had already been forced to pay off around 1,000 workers as the volume of work diminished. A spokesman for the yard, now under the civilian management of Babcock Marine (Rosyth) Limited, admitted that this had not come as a total surprise and had been factored into the yard's forward planning, but he admitted that 'the company is disappointed that the refit is not going ahead ... this causes a continuing shortfall in the dockyard's workload.... At this stage we have no plans further to reduce the workforce beyond these [already planned] redundancies and anticipate that by mid-1992 our workload will be broadly in balance with our capacity.'[8] The effect of the delay would mean that by the time the *Revenge* was ready to return to service, at least one Trident submarine would have joined the CASD force. The *Revenge* had been the last submarine commissioned and was now the first to be decommissioned. Meanwhile, the burden of CASD fell on the *Resolution*, the oldest submarine and the only one to be in a reasonably fit state—an MoD source confirming that no submarine would be allowed to put to sea 'if we didn't consider it safe to do so'.

The *Revenge* completed her final commission, arriving at Faslane on 13 April 1992 after completing fifty-six patrols. The same year, the *Renown* completed a five-year refit at a cost of £155 million. This refit was only scheduled to take two years, but coincided with the cracks found in the *Warspite* and this discovery extended the SSBN's refit. When the *Renown* returned for her final commission on 21 November 1992, her problems had not all been rectified and she only completed three patrols—her last one finishing on 16 June 1994—before being laid up at an annual cost of £29 million. Questioned in parliament, Minister of State for Defence Procurement James Arbuthnot replied: 'HMS *Renown* ... went out on three operational patrols. It was later decided that it was no longer needed because of the end of the cold war and because of the significant success of the Trident programme, which is under budget and on time.'[9] But the truth was that all four bombers were getting old. In June 1993, a full-scale alert took place at Faslane after radioactive liquid leaked from a pipe being used to transfer coolant to a dockside tank. Splashing onto the outer hull of the *Repulse*, three sailors were contaminated in the process. Although only a small amount of liquid was involved, the sailors underwent a washing decontamination process. A Royal Navy spokesman commented that, 'There was no danger to the public. It was discovered at an early stage and was over within an hour.' An inquiry was set up to examine why personnel at the scene had asked the emergency services and local hospitals to be on standby. A response was that it was later considered unnecessary, but it did, however, emphasise the concerns that understandably still surrounded any form of nuclear mishap.[10]

HMS *Resolution* was decommissioned on 22 October 1994 after deployments totalling 517,000 NM. On 24 February 1996, on the day before the twenty-ninth anniversary of her launch, HMS *Renown* was decommissioned at Faslane. Her last captain was Cdr Iain D. Arthur. This ceremony was followed on 13 May when HMS *Repulse* arrived at Faslane for the last time before retirement. First Sea Lord Admiral Sir Jock Slater had joined the bomber at dawn as she sailed up the Clyde for the last time. 'Aboard *Repulse* there was a mixture of pride and sadness—pride that Polaris had helped to keep world peace through the heights of the Cold [W]ar, and sadness at the end of an era. In a symbolic operation, the famous Chevaline nuclear warheads will be unloaded for the last time before the submarine is finally decommissioned.'[11] On 28 August 1966, Prime Minister John Major and Secretary of Defence Michael Portillo attended the decommissioning ceremony at Faslane and climbed down into the submarine for the last time before seeing the *Repulse*'s ensign lowered for the final time. The *Repulse* had completed the Royal Navy's 229th Polaris patrol, sixty of which were reported by ITV News to have been undertaken by the *Repulse*—all of them conducted undetected by the Russians. The SSBN's final operational journey back to Faslane had been earlier than expected and under armed guard in case of a final protest by anti-nuclear protesters. It marked the end of a near three-decade era which spanned the darkest of the Cold War years.[12] 'It was a sad day on board. Auld Lang Syne was played as CO Cdr David Phillips said: "There is a tremendous sense of occasion that after 28 years this is the last time."' It was an opportunity to reveal the nickname the submarines had acquired: 'The Greater Moscow Redevelopment Corporation', a joke understood by the Russians who were known to refer to some of the particularly ugly examples of Soviet architecture as 'targets for Polaris'.[13] The *Repulse* had travelled 630,000 NM and had seen twenty-seven commanding officers. The submarine suffered a final ignominy by grounding in the north-west Channel two months later when *en route* to her final resting place at Rosyth. By this time, the regularity of Royal Navy submarine crash rates was beginning to cause concern and was in fact to get worse in the first few years of the twenty-first century. It led to warnings that cuts in the naval budget had already left some senior officers 'frighteningly' inexperienced at commanding vessels at sea.[14]

Disposal

Nuclear submarines however present a problem of their disposal when they are de-commissioned. They remain a radiological hazard and will continue to do so for many years to come. Initially it was intended to fill them with concrete and scuttle them in the depths of the North Atlantic or the Northeast Pacific, although their deterioration over subsequent years would be nearly impossible to monitor. This fell foul of environmentalists by creating an ecological time bomb and was banned completely in 1972 by the Convention on Marine Pollution by Dumping of Wastes and Other Matter (The London Convention). Long-term storage of some sort was the only remaining option. America's practice was covered by the Ship-Submarine Recycling Program. The decommissioned submarines were taken to the Puget Sound Naval Shipyard. The hull was cut into four sections: bow, missile compartment, reactor section, and stern. The reactor compartments were separated from the rest of the hull and transported to be stored in a deep storage facility at the Hanford Nuclear Site, a decommissioned nuclear production facility on the Columbia River in Washington State. All toxic material was removed, leaving the remains of the hulls to be disposed of separately.

A decision also had to be made on how to dispose of Britain's now-redundant Polaris fleet along with the SSNs coming out of service. Unable to dump them at sea, it was therefore decided to distribute the hulks between Devonport and Rosyth. It was to the latter dockyard that the four R-class submarines were taken and tied up, still floating, in the non-tidal basin in the dockyard. There they await a decision on how to eventually dispose of them safely—a decision that successive governments have avoided taking. Along with the four Polaris boats are three SSNs: *Dreadnought*, *Churchill*, and *Swiftsure*.

All seven fortunately had their fuel rods removed, but in 2003 this practice was deemed unsafe—ten of the fourteen SSNs in Devonport had by then not had their fuel rods removed. A suitable land facility for storage of nuclear waste caused further delays. Low-level waste (LLW) is stored at Sellafield in Cumbria in concrete-lined vaults, but the submarines' reactor pressure vessels were classed as more dangerous intermediate-level waste (ILW) and are stored in temporary, but purpose-built storage above ground until a suitable final resting place can be found. However, while decisions were being postponed, there was a considerable cost in maintaining the submarines which had to be periodically taken into dry-dock for a survey and docking period (SDP) inspection every fifteen years

In 2016, the Submarine Dismantling Project (SDP) was finally started at Rosyth, some fifteen years behind schedule. The *Swiftsure* and *Resolution* were the first to have their LLW removed (Stage 1) completed in August 2018 and March 2020 respectively; this was on budget despite the process then being held up by the intervention of COVID which caused a delay in the start of the *Revenge*'s Stage 1. The removal of asbestos lagging presented a further problem. Work on the removal of ILW is scheduled to start in 2025.[15] But inevitably the hulks are deteriorating. In February 2008, a hole was discovered in the *Revenge* when the submarine was seen to be listing slightly when water had leaked into a ballast tank, but it was confirmed that there was no leak of radiation and in overall terms the submarines represent a very minimal hazard.[16]

Polaris and the Surface Fleet

As originally envisaged, consideration was given to deploying Polaris on the surface fleet and preliminary plans were put forward to modify ships of the *Baltimore* and *Albany* classes of heavy cruisers to accommodate the missiles. Regulus cruise missiles were already carried on a number of ships and were proving a meaningful addition to the USN's armoury. However, SecDef Gates was against the idea, seeing surface ships as too vulnerable to attack. Nonetheless, in January 1961, he did confirm that an exception would be made for the nuclear-powered guided missile cruiser USS *Long Beach*, at that time under construction at the Bethlehem Steel Co. in Quincy, Mass.[1] This was based on a 'split paper' report from the JCS. The intention was to fit four Polaris launch tubes, but once the success of the Polaris/submarine combination was proven, the space was redesigned to take the RUR-5 ASROC anti-submarine system. With progress in developing the submarines to carry the missiles being so positive, ship-basing fell by the wayside. However, the idea was to resurface in what may seem an unlikely quarter.

There was increasing awareness within the European countries that as the Soviet Union had achieved parity with the US in nuclear forces, the Soviet arsenal of IRBMs was not countered by equivalent missiles in the NATO arsenal now that Thor and Jupiter had been withdrawn. Polaris which, although assigned to NATO, was controlled by America, led many to think that the chance of a pre-emptive attack on Europe had increased, but would America risk involvement with ICBMs if it could keep out of such a conflict? The MLF idea never caught on, with Britain and France being the main objectors based on their decisions to add SSBNs to their respective fleets. However, a coordinating conference took place in Washington in early July 1963 to determine the operational requirements for such a force. As well as the US hosts, Britain, West Germany, Belgium, the Netherlands, Italy, Greece, and Turkey attended. These latter two countries soon lost interest, preoccupied with their conflict in Cyprus. Nonetheless, an initial outline ship design was agreed. This allowed for twenty-five ships each equipped with eight A3 missiles. Some 10,000 personnel would be needed to man them with no more than three nationalities aboard any one vessel and within that mix no more than 40 per cent from any one nation. However, an increasingly lukewarm attitude by the prospective participants as the operational complexity of the idea was fully explored meant that the idea soon withered on the vine. It was also increasingly evident that the ships would be intercepted by advances in Soviet counterforce capability, even though they would seek anonymity by sailing in defined merchant shipping lanes. They could not, by international law, masquerade as bona fide merchant vessels and would have to fly an MLF flag. In addition, Lyndon Johnson had his own ideas about the military and the MLF was not one of them and he was to become increasingly taken up with the war in Vietnam, although prior to Kennedy's assassination he had not ruled out some form of independence of nuclear sovereignty as Europe moved towards some form of unity. When Admiral Norvell Ward sought clarification from Mountbatten on the British view, the CDS replied, 'I am completed opposed to [the] multilateral force.'[2]

Kennedy had seen the MLF as a way of bringing more corporate responsibility to NATO, even going as far as determining the parameters for the operational use of the missiles. In this connection, on 16–17 January 1963, the president had talks in Washington with the Italian premier Sgr Amintore Fanfani during which he extended the offer of Polaris as a *quid pro quo* replacement for the Jupiter missiles that had been removed as part of the secret agreement to resolve the Cuban Missile Crisis. These, he indicated, would be on submarines operating in the Mediterranean, but not necessarily in Italian waters. The meeting had 'furnished a new occasion to ascertain the working solidarity of the friendship between Italy and the United States'. A week later, the Italian cabinet approved the offer, although at the same time the communist opposition led by Palmiro Togliatti was raising a vote of no confidence in the Chamber of Deputies, but had little chance of success.[3] Kennedy's cherished wish for such a NATO nuclear force received only lukewarm interest and ultimately fell by the wayside, although Italy had expressed interest in the idea provided it did not cost them anything. This perhaps caused the country to maintain its aspirations to retain the IRBM capability lost when the Jupiters were removed. On 11–12 February following, Roswell Gilpatric visited Rome where, accompanied by US Ambassador to Italy George F. Reinhardt, he met Sgr Fanfani and Minister Giulio Andreotti (who had already expressed mild disappointment that it was not McNamara that was heading the delegation). Pursuing Kennedy's offer of Polaris, from the Italian point of view, the proposal satisfied on two counts: the question of the MNF and a *quid pro quo* for the removed Jupiters. American views by then differed as they believed the idea 'was impractical and excessively costly' as well as potentially being adversely viewed by Turkey and West Germany. but accepted that it was important to keep the Italians interested in a NATO nuclear force.

In pursuit of the proposal, Italy also had long-standing ambitions in the field of nuclear submarines and discussions surrounded the provision of a *Skipjack*-type submarine with an S5W (core 2) reactor with appropriate US Navy presence during building and initial operations.[4] In the end, neither proposal ever fully materialised but, earmarked for Polaris was the cruiser *Giuseppe Garibaldi* which had been laid down in 1933 and launched three years later, being commissioned into the *Regia Marina*. Surviving the war, she was retained by the Italian Navy (*Marina Militare*). Decommissioned in 1953, she subsequently underwent two major refits. The latter one in the mid-1960s saw the addition of four Polaris launch tubes fitted on the aft superstructure along with Terrier missile launchers. Although inert rounds were tested by the Italians, no live missiles were ever supplied. However, the idea of an Italian nuclear-armed missile cruiser was resurrected in the early 1970s and a design for a missile named Alfa was drawn up. Very similar in appearance to the A3—the missile's diameter was the same as Polaris, so was clearly destined for the empty launch tubes—the missile was two-stage with the capability of carrying a 1-tonne warhead, but despite a broadly successful initial test programme, the project was abandoned in 1976.

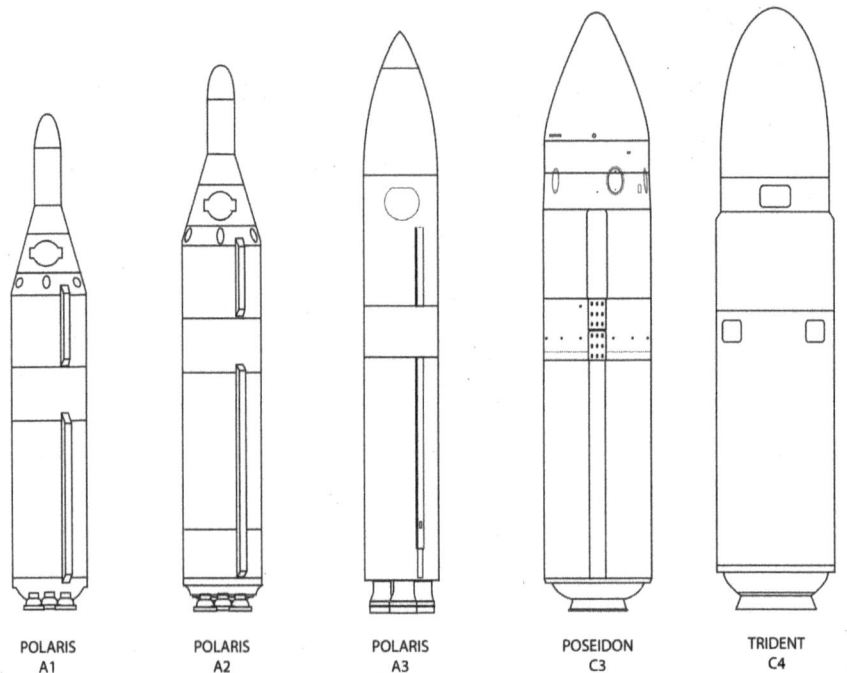

POLARIS A1 POLARIS A2 POLARIS A3 POSEIDON C3 TRIDENT C4

SLBM: evolution from Polaris to Trident.

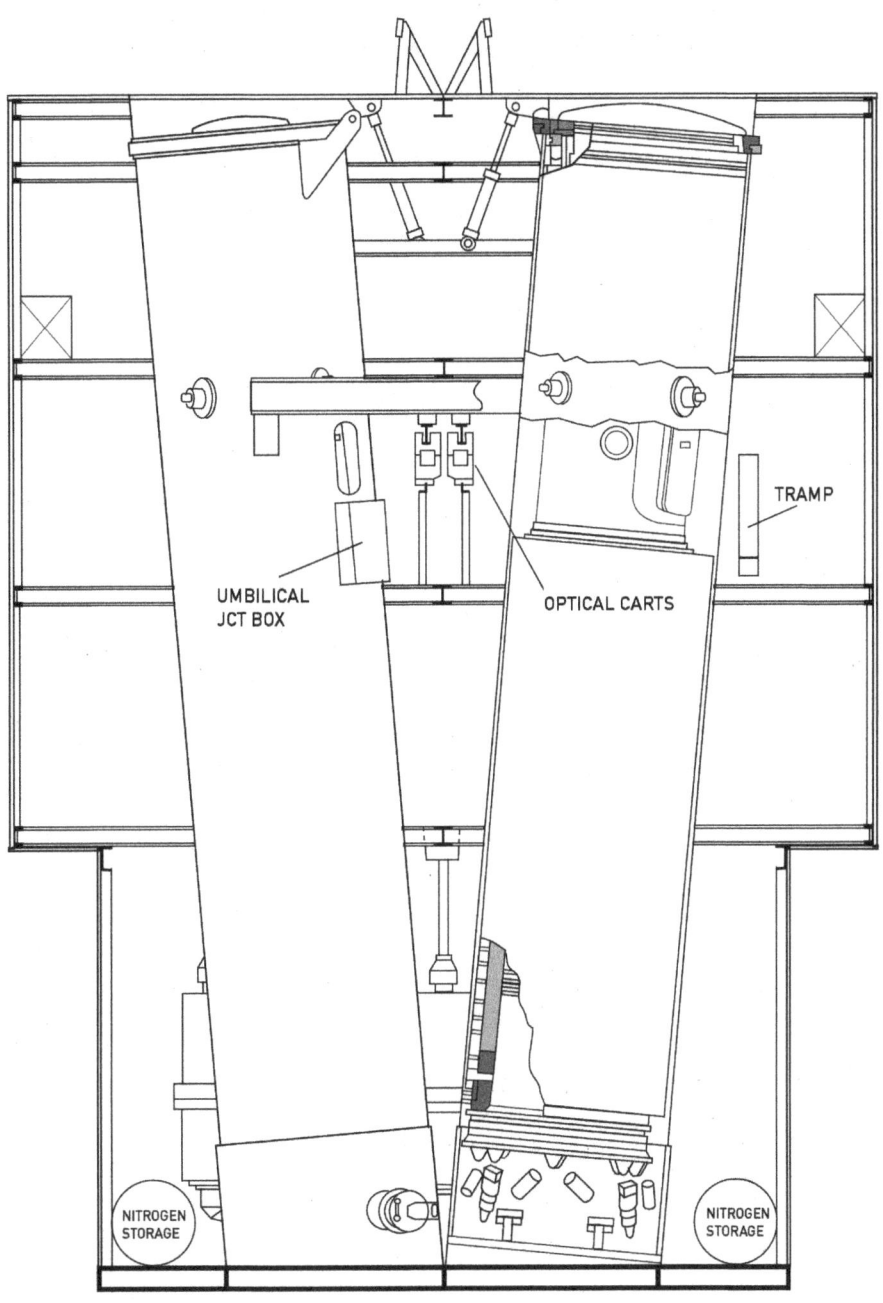

Shipborne Polaris A3 installation on Italian guided missile cruiser *Giuseppe Garibaldi*.

Epilogue

*The single most important military force for the whole free world. It's what
stands between all of us and nuclear war with the Soviet Union.*

Admiral Stansfield Turner, Former Director CIA

*At some time, we hope soon, we can work out some form of living on the same
planet without the threat of mutual destruction.*

Rear Admiral W. F. Raborn, USN

In November 1981, ADM Rickover was aboard the USS *Boston* (SSN-703)
undergoing sea trials prior to her commissioning. For the eighty-two-year-old
admiral, and unknown to him at the time, it was to be his last seagoing function.
On returning home, his wife asked if he had heard the news that President Reagan
was not going to renew his appointment. This was officially confirmed shortly
after at a meeting with Secretary of Defense Caspar Weinberger. Rickover had
survived the efforts of admirals, secretaries of the navy, and secretaries of defense
to oust him, but this had maybe led to complacency. Most of his supporters in
the Congress had died and the next generation did not accord him the same
reverence. Soon afterwards, he received a second blow. He had been pressing the
government to investigate what he believed were illegal cost overruns by General
Dynamics and other shipbuilders. However, the Justice Department informed
him by phone that there was insufficient evidence to press charges. On 8 January
1982, he was invited to the Oval Office for a farewell meeting with the president.
Standing beside the president were Weinberger and Secretary of the Navy John
F. Lehman, the latter an influential player in the politics to retire the admiral.
Rickover asked to talk to Reagan alone, and once the two secretaries had left
the room, he criticised them both for not pursuing General Dynamics for fraud.
Somewhat taken aback, the president said a few words of congratulations over

Rickover's lifetime of service to the navy and escorted him to the door. A farewell party was later organised by his friends. Attendees included three past presidents, but not Reagan. A request to the Pentagon for a military band for the occasion was brusquely turned down.[1] The admiral's career was finally and decisively over. However, few people have had such an influence over naval doctrine, and one can only speculate the course of events that US defence would have taken without him. At a dinner held on 5 October 1995, at which the fortieth anniversary of Strategic Systems Programs was celebrated, while the great and the good of the program were individually mentioned—even Britain's contribution being recorded by the inclusion of their Polaris and Trident boats in the list of all the SSBNs and the playing of the national anthems of both nations—any mention of Rickover was conspicuous by its absence. It is often the case with an authoritarian leader that, great though his/her contribution may be, it can also sometimes overrule the capacity for further development and innovation. What is true is that without the introduction of nuclear propulsion, Polaris would not have been possible.

The president had been somewhat more successful with commending Levering Smith. He wrote, however, noting that the admiral's duties were not yet over.

THE WHITE HOUSE
WASHINGTON

April 19, 1983

Dear Levering:

I want to repeat privately what I said in public this morning: we all owe you a tremendous debt of gratitude for your work on the strategic forces commission.

Your years of service in the Navy and your intimate knowledge of SLBM programs was of singular help in producing consensus where none existed before.

We appreciate all you have done, but I am counting on you to stick with your labors until the commission's recommendations are accepted by the Congress. When that happens you will have made a real contribution to our nation's security and to history.

Sincerely,

Ronald Reagan

Vice Admiral Levering Smith

On 27 August 1979, Lord Louis Mountbatten and three others were assassinated by the Provisional IRA while on his boat with members of his family off the Northern Ireland village of Mullaghmore.

Both men had been influential in bringing nuclear power into their respective navies. They shared some characteristics. Both put in very long hours. They both wanted their own way regardless of how this was to be achieved. Both disliked the whole aspect of nuclear war but believed in it as a way of maintaining peace. In other respects, they were very different. Rickover eschewed uniform unless the occasion demanded it. Mountbatten loved uniforms, none more so than when he became colonel of the Life Guards, which allowed him scarlet uniform, boots, and cuirass: 'He loved dressing up in the right uniform for any occasion.'[2] Mountbatten had at heart always hoped for a progressive move towards nuclear disarmament asking whether 'the frightening facts of the nuclear arms race, showing with appalling clarity that we are rushing headlong towards a precipice [had] been able to make any of those responsible for this disastrous course to pull themselves together and reach for the brakes?'[3] He also, unsurprisingly, had always favoured the Royal Navy's lot, and if there was to be a British deterrent, he wanted the Royal Navy to be the possessors.

By then Baron Zuckerman of Burnham Thorpe had retired from public life. The first generation, those who had seen the development of the nuclear deterrent, had handed over to the next generation.

ADM Raborn had instituted new processes and corralled the initiative and talents of US industry to put an American SSBN on station some five years ahead of the original date. Like the rapid development of the Thor by Gen. Schriever and the Jupiter by Gen. Medaris, these three men were given exceptional authority to complete their projects and bypass bureaucracy. Spurred on by Soviet successes in space launchers and the fear of the 'missile gap', these were achievements that realistically would not be possible nowadays. 'The Special Projects Office excelled at finding partners that could help achieve the program's mission and set up program offices co-located with these partners.'[4] Sapolsky wrote: 'with near unanimity, the FBM is said to be one of the most outstanding and desirable achievements in weaponry since the Second World War, and the Special Projects Office is regarded as the model of development effectiveness'.[5] In the margin of the copy of his book which he gave to ADM Levering Smith, the author added: 'thanks to LS'. SP had developed Polaris with the innovative introduction of solid propellant, had developed a submarine to carry the weapon, overcoming the problems of navigation, fire control, and the constraints of weight and space in a programme success, possibly only exceeded by NASA's Apollo program. In 1963, Raborn was a recipient of the prestigious Collier Trophy, presented to those who have made 'the greatest achievement in aeronautics or astronautics in America, with respect to improving the performance, efficiency, and safety of air or space vehicles, the value of which has been thoroughly demonstrated by actual use during the preceding year'.

Despite and regardless of the many problems that surrounded bringing the Royal Navy's Polaris submarines in on time, the project can only be described as a significant and outstanding British achievement—again, unimaginable today.

By 1974, the annual CND Aldermaston to London march had lost much of its support. Instead of the thousands that had marched in previous years, only some 200–300 arrived in Trafalgar Square to hear the traditional speeches which that year seemed to concentrate on the sale of warships to the Chilean military junta. Major nuclear protest seemed to have had its day.

Polaris is described by Norman Polmar as 'revolutionary'. It was one of the pre-eminent military achievements of the twentieth century alongside inventions such as powered flight and the atom bomb. Born during the Eisenhower administration and endorsed by a president more active in his support for innovation than is sometimes acknowledged, his strong support for Polaris following the TCP report laid the foundations for the near invulnerable weapon system. However, Raborn's contribution is often overlooked, overshadowed by the monolithic ADM Rickover.

Also to make his mark on history, this time with Apollo, was Charles Draper. But America's disastrous and widely unpopular involvement in the Vietnam War led to public demonstrations against institutions with links to the armaments industry. The Instrumentation Lab attracted these protests and forced a reassessment of its activities and its relationship with MIT. A group of 'self-appointed zealots … at MIT and other prestigious universities around the country [had] taken it upon themselves to "cleanse" the institutions of what it called war research'.[6] In response, MIT's president Howard W. Johnson appointed a committee chaired by William F. Pounds, dean of the Sloan School of Management, to review the status, nature, and sponsorship of special laboratories. Among other things, the Pounds Panel concluded that IL's involvement with the Poseidon missile contracts was incompatible with MIT sponsorship, but recognised that existing contracts should be honoured. Despite the lucrative value of military work and without any pre-discussion on the matter, Johnson announced on 24 September 1969 that on 1 January 1970, Draper would be replaced by Professor Charles L. Miller of the Urban Science Laboratory as director of the MIT Instrumentation Lab. To soften the blow, the IL would be renamed the Charles Stark Draper Laboratory. This, however, failed to appease the activists when on 29 October, members of the November Action Committee (NAC) took their fight to GE. On 5 November, the NAC arrived at the gates of the IL. As is so often the case in such matters, many of those there had little knowledge or indeed real interest in the nature of the dispute; however, signalled by Draper's dismissal, the tide was turning against the IL and the MIT executive committee voted against any further military development and furthered the matter by divesting itself of the laboratory. As professor emeritus, Draper continued his involvement with the lab, but was no longer in charge. He who had been so influential in one of the key areas of success in the FBM programme went into retirement believing that these actions had been taken largely to expiate the national guilt felt over America's defeat in Vietnam.

The British Polaris had never enjoyed full support within the MoD. Its critics came from the army, the RAF, and politicians, as well as the fragmented, but constant opposition from nuclear protesters. However, the decommissioning of the four SSBNs was not the end of the line for the Royal Navy's re-motored A3s. They were to find a use in the US Strategic Target System (STARS) program. There were a large number of Polaris boosters stored in underground sites where a constant temperature could be maintained. This saw the re-motored A3 missiles refurbished by LMSC as required and, with an additional commercially sourced ORBUS-1 third stage, were used as targets in the US Strategic Defense Initiative (SDI) programme. A total 117 first stages and 102 second stages had been acquired in support of the proposed launch schedule. Both A3P and A3R boosters were used. US Army Space and Strategic Defense Command working with Sandia National Laboratories developed two programmes, STARS 1 and 2, which used the launch vehicles to send targets and other experiments into a ballistic ICBM-type trajectory. The first launch of a STARS 1 took place from the Pacific Missile Range Naval Test Facility at Barking Sands (PMRF) in Hawaii on 26 February 1993. It was greeted with mixed blessings. To some it was seen as a boost for the local economy which had suffered as a result of destruction wrought by Hurricane Iniki the previous year, but others protested as the ground cleared for the launch facility was held sacred as an ancient burial site. This had delayed the development of the site by some three years. After the successful launch, Lt Col. Gus Manguso, product manager for STARS, commented: 'The program has come under a lot of scrutiny and a lot of public attention. I'm very pleased to prove the capabilities of the system.'[7] Later, by adding a fourth stage, the Operations and Deployment Experiments Simulator (ODES) gave the ability to deploy a manoeuvrable payload after separation from the Orbus section. Thus, elements of Chevaline had a life after the warheads came out of service under the Chevaline improved front end re-use (CIFER) programme.

To Rickover's second wife, naval nurse CDR Eleonore B. Rickover—the first, Ruth Masters Rickover, having died in June 1972—fell the honour of sponsoring the USS *Hyman G. Rickover* (SSN-709), a *Los Angeles*-class SSN, on 27 August 1983.

The phasing out of the Royal Navy's Polaris squadron coincided with the arrival of four new V-class submarines. Equipped with up to sixteen Trident II D-5 missiles which were to assume the mantle of the UK's CASD and carry it forward to the twenty-first century. At last, the Royal Navy had found commonality in weaponry with its American counterpart. Many naval strategists are now moving towards a vision of an 'empty ocean' future conflict scenario, devoid of visible, and therefore vulnerable surface ships, preferring to envisage confrontation between underwater platforms, both manned and unmanned. It seems that the submarine will embody an increasing role both strategically and tactically.

How things are changing.

Today, both the PRC and Russia have the capability to unilaterally accelerate a conflict to any level of violence, in any domain, worldwide, with any instrument of national power, and at any time.

ADM Charles Richard, CDRUSSTRATCOM: Congressional testimony,
5 April 2022

But let us leave the last word to Rickover himself:

I am not proud of the part I played in it. I did it because it was necessary for the safety of this country.

Admiral Hyman G. Rickover USN

The US Navy '41 for Freedom' and the Royal Navy SM10

GEORGE WASHINGTON CLASS			Commissioned	Decommissioned
USS *George Washington*	SSBN 598	EB	30 December 1959	24 January 1985
USS *Patrick Henry*	SSBN 599	EB	11 April 1960	25 May 1984
USS *Theodore Roosevelt*	SSBN 600	MI	13 February 1961	28 February 1981
USS *Robert E Lee*	SSBN 601	NN	16 September 1960	1 December 1983
USS *Abraham Lincoln*	SSBN 602	P	11 March 1961	28 February 1981
ETHAN ALLEN CLASS			Commissioned	Decommissioned
USS *Ethan Allen*	SSBN 608	EB	8 August 1961	31 March 1983
USS *Sam Houston*	SSBN 609	NN	6 March 1962	6 September 1991
USS *Thomas A Edison*	SSBN 610	EB	10 March 1962	1 December 1983
USS *John Marshall*	SSBN 611	NN	21 May 1962	22 July 1982
USS *Thomas Jefferson*	SSBN 618	NN	4 January 1963	24 January 1985
LAFAYETTE CLASS			Commissioned	Decommissioned
USS *Lafayette*	SSBN 616	EB	23 April 1963	12 August 1991
USS *Alexander Hamilton*	SSBN 617	EB	27 June 1963	23 February 1993
USS *Andrew Jackson*	SSBN 619	MI	3 July 1963	31 August 1989
USS *John Adams*	SSBN 620	P	12 May 1964	24 March 1989
USS *James Monroe*	SSBN 622	NN	7 December 1963	25 September 1990
USS *Nathan Hale*	SSBN 623	EB	23 November 1963	31 January 1986
USS *Woodrow Wilson*	SSBN 624	MI	27 December 1963	1 September 1994
USS *Henry Clay*	SSBN 625	NN	20 February 1964	5 November 1990
USS *Daniel Webster*	SSBN 626	EB	9 April 1964	30 August 1990
USS *James Madison*	SSBN 627	NN	28 July 1964	20 November 1992
USS *Tecumseh*	SSBN 628	EB	29 May 1964	23 July 1993
USS *Daniel Boone*	SSBN 629	MI	23 April 1964	18 February 1994

USS *John C Calhoun*	SSBN 630	NN	15 September 1964	28 March 1994
USS *Ulysses S Grant*	SSBN 631	EB	17 July 1964	12 June 1992
USS *Von Steuben*	SSBN 632	NN	30 September 1964	26 February 1994
USS *Casimir Pulaski*	SSBN 633	EB	14 August 1964	7 March 1994
USS *Stonewall Jackson*	SSBN 634	MI	26 August 1964	9 February 1995
USS *Sam Rayburn*	SSBN 635	NN	2 December 1964	31 July 1989
USS *Nathanael Greene*	SSBN 636	P	19 December 1964	15 December 1986
USS *Benjamin Franklin*	SSBN 640	EB	22 October 1965	23 November 1993
USS *Simon Bolivar*	SSBN 641	NN	29 October 1965	8 February 1995
USS *Kamehameha*	SSBN 642	MI	10 December 1965	2 April 2002
USS *George Bancroft*	SSBN 643	EB	22 January 1966	21 September 1993
USS *Lewis and Clark*	SSBN 644	NN	22 December 1995	27 June 1992
USS *James K Polk*	SSBN 645	EB	16 April 1966	8 July 1999
USS *George C Marshall*	SSBN 654	NN	29 April 1966	24 September 1992
USS *Henry L Stimson*	SSBN 655	EB	20 August 1966	5 May 1993
USS *George Washington* Carver	SSBN 656	NN	15 June 1966	18 March 1993
USS *Francis Scott Key*	SSBN 657	EB	3 December 1966	2 September 1993
USS *Mariano G Vallejo*	SSBN 658	MI	16 December 1966	9 March 1995
USS *Will Rogers*	SSBN 659	EB	1 April 1967	12 April 1993
ROYAL NAVY R-CLASS			Commissioned	Decommissioned
HMS *Resolution*	S22	V	2 October 1967	22 October 1994
HMS *Repulse*	S23	V	28 September 1968	28 August 1996
HMS *Renown*	S26	CL	15 November 1968	24 February 1996
HMS *Revenge*	S27	CL	4 December 1969	22 May 1992

Names proposed but not adopted		
Albert Einstein	Alexander Graham Bell	Andrew Carnegie
Booker T Washington	De Grasse	Enrico Fermi
Galileo	Giuseppe Garibaldi	Grover Cleveland
Leif Ericson	Douglas MacArthur	Myles Standish
Chester Nimitz	Rochambeau	Samuel F B Morse
Thomas Paine		

APPENDIX II
Chevaline Launches

12 Sept. 1977	Chevaline A3TK	PA	Launch Pad 29A
08 Nov. 1977	Chevaline A3TK	PB	Launch Pad 29A
26 Jul. 1978	Chevaline A3TK	P1	Launch Pad 29A
30 Nov. 1978	Chevaline A3TK	P2	Launch Pad 29A
04 Apr. 1979	Chevaline A3TK	P3	Launch Pad 29A
05 Jul. 1979	Chevaline A3TK	P4	Launch Pad 29A
01 Sept. 1979	Chevaline A3TK	P5	Launch Pad 29A
08 Nov. 1979	Chevaline A3TK	P6	Launch Pad 29A
21 Mar. 1980	Chevaline A3TK	PT2	Launch Pad 29A
11 Apr. 1980	Chevaline A3TK	PT1	Launch Pad 29A
19 May 1980	Chevaline A3TK	PT3	Launch Pad 29A
14 Nov. 1980	Chevaline A3TKE	PS1	*Renown*
18 Nov. 1980	Chevaline A3TKE	PS3	*Renown*
	Chevaline A3TKE	PS2	*Renown*
30 Jan. 1982	Chevaline A3TKE	PS4	*Renown*
01 Feb. 1982	Chevaline A3TKE	PS5	*Renown*
03 Feb. 1982	Chevaline A3TKE	PS6	*Renown*
08 Feb. 1982	Chevaline A3TKE	A5	*Renown*
15 May 1983	Chevaline A3TKE		*Revenge*
15 May 1983	Chevaline A3TKE		*Revenge*
09 Jun. 1983	Chevaline A3TKE		*Revenge*
09 Jun. 1983	Chevaline A3TKE		*Revenge*
11 Jun. 1983	Chevaline A3TKE		*Revenge*
11 Jun. 1983	Chevaline A3TKE		*Revenge*
19 May 1985	Chevaline A3TKE		*Resolution*
19 May 1985	Chevaline A3TKE		*Resolution*
10 Jun. 1985	Chevaline A3TKE		*Resolution*
25 Jul. 1986	Chevaline A3RTKE		*Revenge*

	Vehicle Test	Non-functioning PAC
	Vehicle Test	Missile test
	Vehicle Test	Development Standard IFE, successful flight
	Vehicle Test	Development Standard IFE, successful flight
	Vehicle Test	Development Standard IFE, PAC failed to complete mission
	Vehicle Test	Development Standard IFE, successful flight
	Vehicle Test	Development Standard IFE, booster failure
	Vehicle Test	Development Standard IFE, successful flight
	Vehicle Test	In-service Standard IFE, successful flight
	Vehicle Test	In-service Standard IFE, PAC failure
	Vehicle Test	In-service Standard IFE, successful flight
	Vehicle Test	Chevaline Acceptance Flight, two systems launched, both failed
	Vehicle Test	Chevaline Acceptance Flight, two systems launched, both failed
		Not launched, returned to RNAD for investigation
	Vehicle Test	Modified IFE, successful
	Vehicle Test	Chevaline Acceptance Flight, successful
	Vehicle Test	Chevaline Acceptance Flight, successful
	Vehicle Test	Chevaline Acceptance Flight, successful
DASO I	Vehicle Test	FD 3/D 7
	Vehicle Test	A 7/D9 NIDs
	Vehicle Test	RSOD second stage failed
	Vehicle Test	A 4/D 10
	Vehicle Test	FD 1/D 5
	Vehicle Test	A 2/D 1
DASO II	Vehicle Test	RSOD second stage failed
	Vehicle Test	Second stage upset PAC
	Vehicle Test	FD 4/D 8
PEM DASO	A3R Vehicle Test	PEM

26 Jul. 1986	Chevaline A3RTKE		*Revenge*
01 Aug. 1986	Chevaline A3RTKE		*Revenge*
02 Aug. 1986	Chevaline A3RTKE		*Revenge*
16 Apr. 1987	Chevaline A3TKE		*Repulse*
19 Apr. 1987	Chevaline A3TKE		*Repulse*
10 May 1987	Chevaline A3TKE		*Repulse*
10 May 1987	Chevaline A3TKE		*Repulse*

	A3R Vehicle Test	PEM
	A3R Vehicle Test	PEM early P-Body eject
	A3R Vehicle Test	PEM no PAC separation
DASO III	Vehicle Test	FD 91
	Vehicle Test	FD 6
	Vehicle Test	RSOD
	Vehicle Test	FD 13

APPENDIX III

Profiles

(See also: UKballisticmissiles.co.uk)

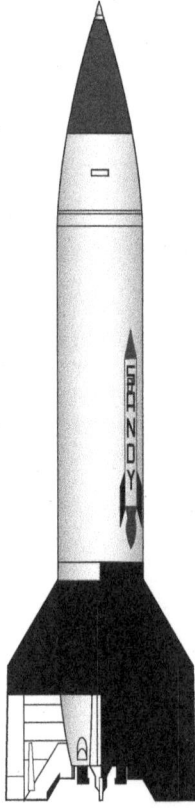 

Left: Operation Sandy, 6 September 1947. Launch of a captured A-4 (V2) missile from the deck of the USS *Midway*.

Right: Polaris A3X-1. Launched at Cape Canaveral, LC-29A, 7 August 1962.

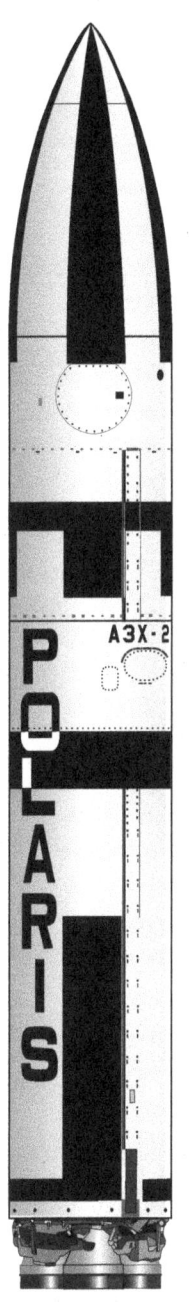
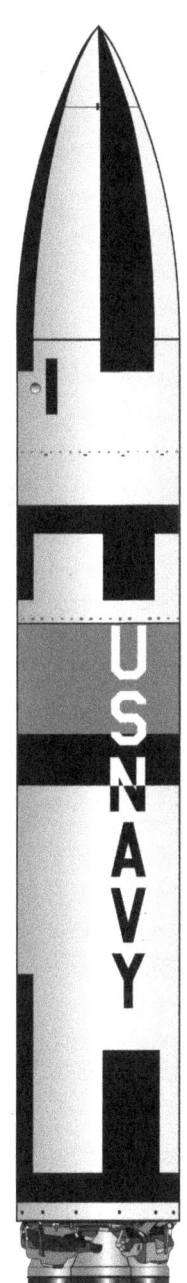
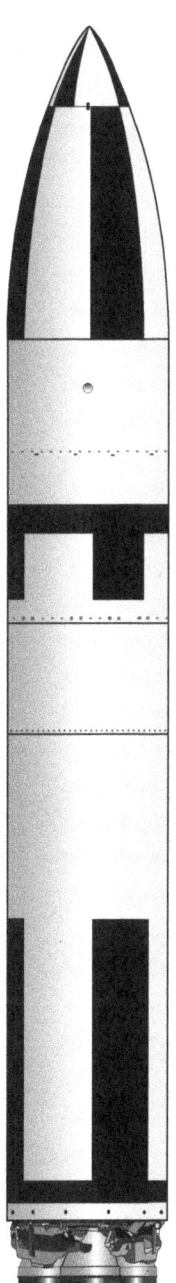

Left: Polaris A3X-27 launched from Pad 25A at Cape Canaveral, 17 July 1963.

Middle: Polaris A-3.

Right: Polaris A-3. USS *George Washington*, Cape Canaveral DASO.

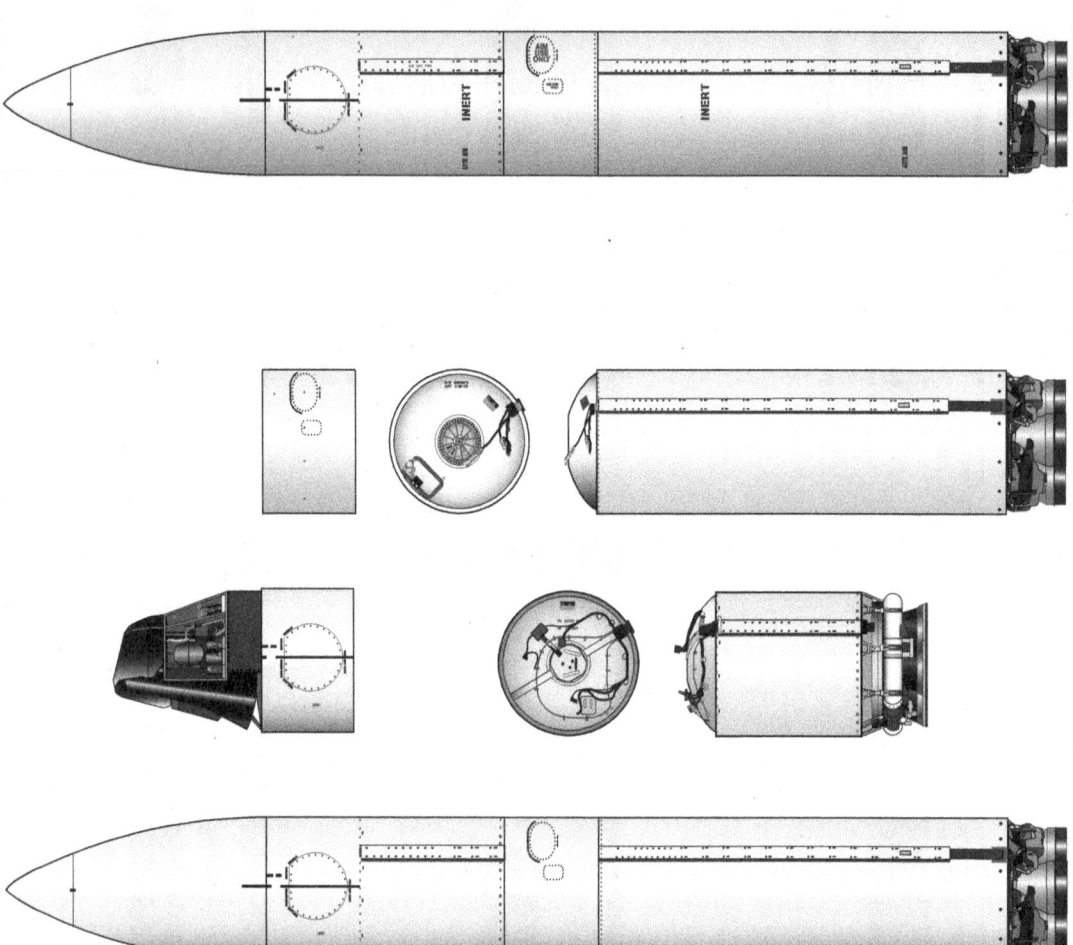

Royal Navy Polaris A3. Inert round, sectioned stages with Chevaline warhead, live round.

Left: Polaris A-3T launched by HMS *Repulse*, Cape Canaveral DASO, 13 February 1973.

Right: Polaris A-3T launched by HMS *Renown*, Cape Canaveral DASO, 16 July 1974.

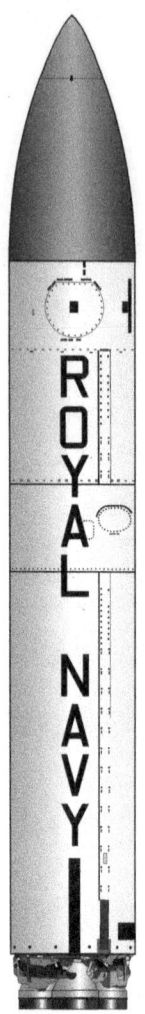
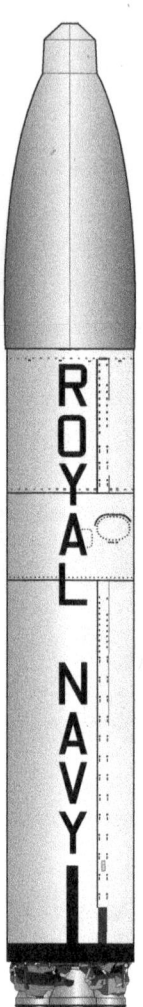

Left: Royal Navy Polaris A-3 test launch from Cape Canaveral.

Right: Polaris A-3TK. Chevaline text at Cape Canaveral.

Below: Poseidon C-3.

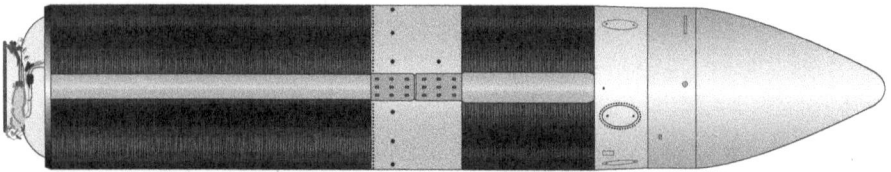

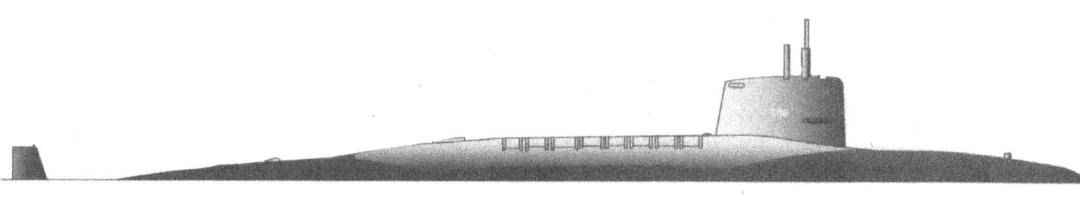

USS *George Washington* (SSBN-598) with early disruptive camouflage scheme.

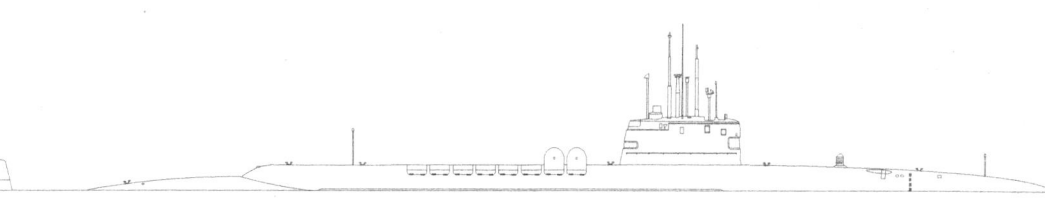

HMS *Resolution* (S22). Final commission after sixty-nine patrols, October 1994.

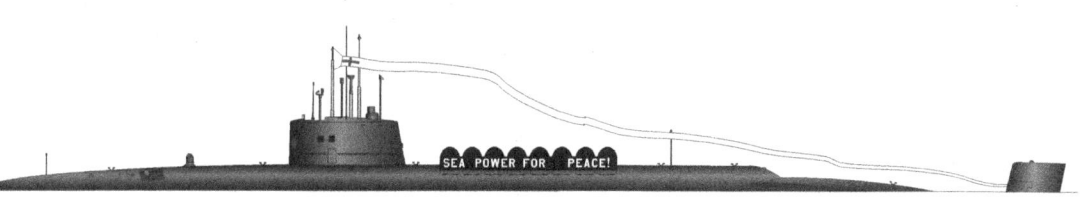

HMS *Resolution*'s paying off message to Faslane. Departing at Gare Loch *en route* to Rosyth for a two-year refit after completing thirty-nine patrols, September 1982.

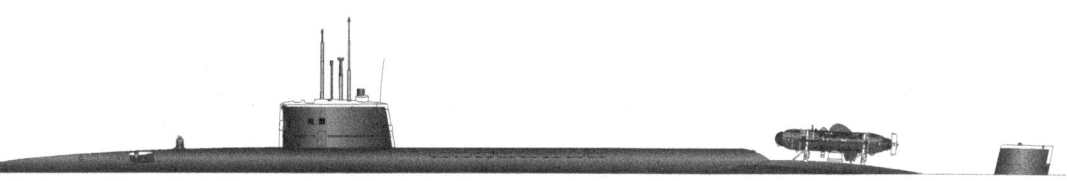

HMS *Repulse* (S-23) and DSRV-2 *Avalon*, Clyde Estuary, June 1979.

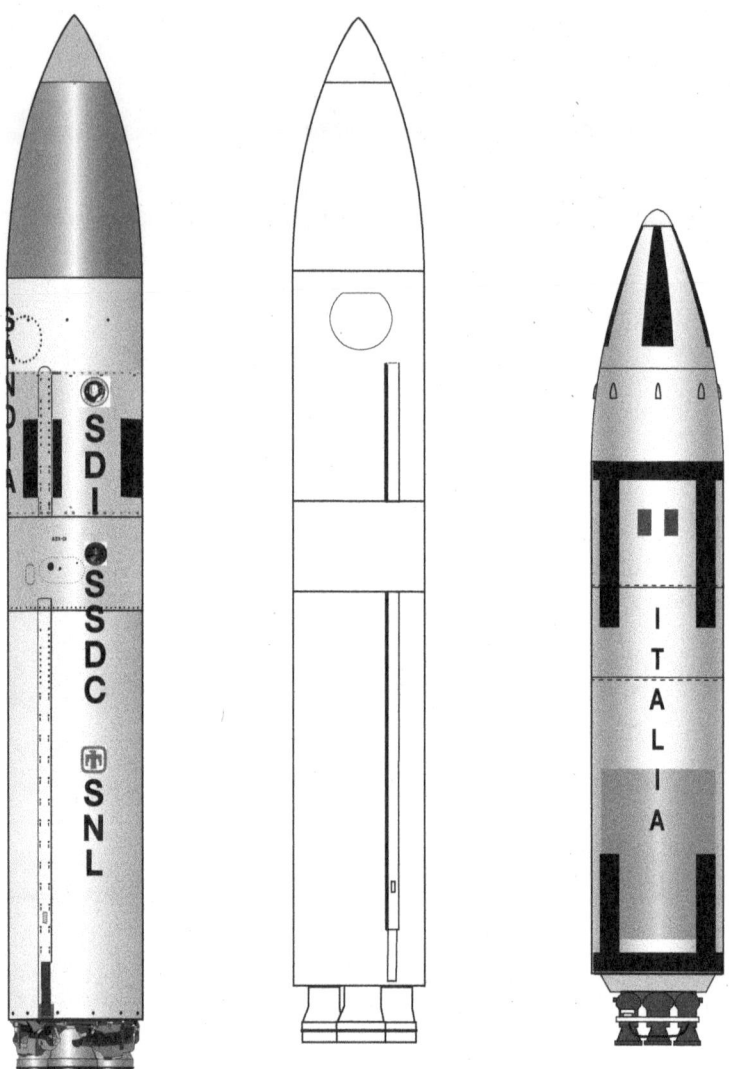

Left: Polaris STARS 1 (Strategic Target System). Refurbished A2, first and second stages. ORBUS-1, third stage.

Middle: Polaris A3.

Right: Aeritalia ALFA. Developed for the Italian Navy (*Marina Militare*).

Endnotes

Introduction

1 The Germans used the nomenclature V2 rather than the V-2 commonly used by American sources and the former will be used here.
2 Although Tibbets was made famous by his bombing of Hiroshima, on his death he had requested that his ashes be scattered not in his native Ohio lest the site might become one of pilgrimage, but rather scattered in the English Channel, an area meaningful to him from the time he spent as commanding officer of the 340th Bombardment Squadron of the 97th Bombardment Group, which was equipped with Boeing B-17s and flew bombing missions over Germany.
3 The largest previous explosion took place on 6 December 1917 when the SS *Imo* collided with the SS *Mont Blanc* in Halifax harbour, Nova Scotia. The latter vessel was carrying munitions and explosives and the resultant explosion, an estimated 2,500 tons of TNT, killed around 1,800 people and injured a further 9,000.
4 See: SECNAVINST 5030.8. *Classification of Naval Ships and Craft. US Department of The Navy.* 21 November 2006.

Chapter 1

1 The first attempt to create a separate air wing was on 11 February 1913, when Representative James Hay from Virginia introduced a bill in Congress for a separate aviation corps. The bill failed to pass.
2 Interestingly, Col. LeMay was awarded the British Distinguished Flying Cross (DFC) on 1 April 1943 along with three other commanders of US Eighth Air Force Bomb Groups, possibly as an encouragement at a time when Act ACM Sir Arthur Harris was cementing relations between the two air forces. He initially wore the ribbon the wrong way around. (Graham Pitchfork, RAF Historical Society Journal No. 75. January 2021.)
3 McCullough, *Truman* (1992), p. 968.
4 *Ibid.*, p. 543.
5 Zuckerman, *Six Men Out of the Ordinary* (1992), p. 169.
6 Rockwell, *The Rickover Effect* (1992), p. 56.
7 Kintner's experience of nuclear power later led him to take charge of the clean up after the Three-Mile Island, Pennsylvania, nuclear reactor meltdown in March 1979.

8 Rockwell, *op. cit.*, p. 143.
9 *Ibid.*, p. 366.
10 *Ibid.*, p 114.
11 www.eisenhower.archives.gov/research/online_documents/uss_nautilus/Program. pdf.
12 Oliver, *Against the Tide* (2014), p. 9.
13 Traditionally, Rickover only wore uniform when requested to do so.
14 *Naval Accidents 1945–1988.* William M. Arkin and Joshua Handler.

Chapter 2

1 Serial R7037. This aircraft failed to return from a PR flight to Cherbourg and Le Havre on 3 June 1942.
2 Dr Walter Thiel had been at Peenemünde since 1936 and was very much responsible for the advances in motor development.
3 Interrogation of German Personnel from WVA *Kochelsee*. The Glenn L. Martin Company, September 1946.
4 There were also plans to use the Arado Ar 234C jet bomber as a carrier, but these were never fulfilled.
5 Captain Eric 'Winkle' Brown RN who flew many of the captured German aircraft after the war claimed that the Messerschmitt Me 262 was the most formidable and significant aircraft produced during the war.
6 Tessmann was part of the original Project Paperclip team at White Sands. Tiesenhausen had been brought back from the *Ostfront* to assist at Peenemünde; 'von-T', as he was known, initially turned down an offer after the war to join von Braun, preferring to remain in Germany. In 1953, he changed his mind, on the promise of being allowed to bring his wife and family, and went to Huntsville. Later transferring to NASA, he assisted in the Apollo programme, but was sidelined after NASA contractors pushed to remove the Germans involved in the space programme. He died on 3 June 2018, aged 104. He was the last survivor of the German rocket team.
7 Soviet Front formations were equivalent to army groups.
8 'Survey of Development of Liquid Rockets in Germany and their Future Prospects,' *Journal of the British Interplanetary Society*, March 1951, p. 75.
9 So called, it is believed, because the chosen scientists had a paperclip attached to their file.
10 Conversation, the author with Capt. Eric Brown shortly before he died.
11 Merrill, oral history (1997), pp. 2-98.
12 *Ibid.*
13 Gates, oral history (1984), p. 3.

Chapter 3

1 This is somewhat in conflict with the views of von Braun's British interrogator, Capt. Eric 'Winkle' Brown who claimed that von Braun became reasonably conversant in English after only two weeks' tuition.
2 The five were: Dr Herman Kurzweg, Dr Richard Lehnert, Dr Gehard Eber, Ph. Wolfgang Zettler-Seidel, and Dr Peter Wegener.

3　Gallery had achieved fame during the war by capturing *U-505* on 4 June 1944—the first enemy warship captured by US forces since 1812.

4　Despite some reports to the contrary, no complete missiles were recovered from Nordhausen. Complete missiles had to be assembled from the salvaged components.

5　It is believed that this desert location gave rise to the name Sandy.

6　*The New York Times*, 3 September 1947.

7　Interestingly the official photographs of the launch issued by the US Navy were retouched to remove all details of the launch equipment.

8　US Navy Photographic Report MN6662—NPC 1947.

9　Von Braun & Ordway, *History of Rocketry and Space Travel* (1967), p. 125.

10　It was envisaged that 75,000 JB-2s, as the US version was designated, would be used for the invasion of Japan. In the event, only about 1,400 were built.

11　*Oxnard Press Courier*, 4 October 1955.

12　Many decades ago, the author built his first plastic kit. It was the Revell USS *Nautilus* which came with a Loon and its hangar on the hull casing, although again this was representative of an idea only.

13　Wertheim, oral history (1981), pp. 2–94.

14　FAS.org, *Regulus*, 25 April 2000.

Chapter 4

1　*Spaceflight*, Vol. 60, No 10. Obituary of Georg von Tiesenhausen.

2　Oberth had been awarded the *Kriegsverdienstkreuz I Klasse mit Schwertern* (War Merit Cross 1st Class, with Swords) for his courageous efforts during the bombing raid on Peenemünde. When his retirement date approached, he had been working in the US for too short a time to qualify for a pension. His earlier life in Germany, however, did qualify him for a pension there, but only if he was resident there. Despite offers of help from various American benefactors, nothing materialised and he therefore returned to German in November 1958. However, he was tempted back by an offer from Convair and worked for two years as a technical consultant on the Atlas ICBM.

3　Killian, *Sputnik, Scientists and Eisenhower* (1977), p. 67.

4　history.state.gov/historicaldocuments/frus1955-57v19/d9.

5　Also known as the 'Killian Report' or the 'TCP (Technical Capabilities Panel) Report'.

6　Killian, *op. cit.*, p. 89.

7　White and LeMay, telecom 16 July 1952 Library of Congress LeMay Diary No. 4.

8　www.thisdayinaviation.com/tag/david-madison-critchlow/.

9　Hansen, *U.S. Nuclear Weapons* (1987), p. 74.

10　Memo from Burke to Raborn and Rear Admiral John Clark, head of Guided Missiles Division.

11　*Ibid.*

12　Burke, oral history (1972), p .1.

13　*Ibid.*, p. 6.

14　Colwell, oral history (1972/3), p. 132.

15　Merrill, oral history (1997), no. 3, p. 170.

16　*Ibid.*

17　In some of the early Thor test launches, fins had become detached, but this seemed to present little compromise to the proposed trajectory.

18 Merrill, *op. cit.*, p. 169.
19 For further details, see *Naval History Magazine* (USNI), Vol. 25, No. 1, January 2011.
20 Raborn, oral history (1972), no. 1, p. 18.
21 Recent academic research attributes the major part of the idea to Power. See: Ziarnik, *To Rule the Skies* (Naval Institute Press, Annapolis, 2021).
22 An Historical View of the Polaris Fleet Ballistic Missile Program.
23 Secretary Wilson was known as 'Engine Charlie' to distinguish him from 'Washing Machine Charlie' who was head of General Electric.
24 The full title was: *Clarification of Roles and Missions to improve the Effectiveness of Operation of the Department of Defense.*
25 *FBM Chronology* (Strategic Systems Project Office, Washington), 28 November 1955.
26 McGeoch, *The British Polaris Project* (1973), p. 26.

Chapter 5

1   The presentation had been named by Raborn, the 'Dog and Pony Show' for reasons unknown.
2   Colwell, oral history (1971/72), p. 128.
3   *Ibid.*, p. 148.
4   Ward, oral history (May 1985–July 1987), no. 6, p. 363.
5   Shugg, oral history (November 1973), p. 16.
6   *Hammond Times*, Vol. 23, No. 5.
7   Lawrence Livermore National Laboratory, st.llnl.gov/news/look-back/polaris-program.
8   Freitag was later, on retirement from the navy, to join NASA, working on major US space programs.
9   Medaris, *Countdown to Decision* (1960), p. 359.
10 The first prototype Jupiter was launched on 1 March 1957. The test was only partially successful with the missile travelling just 60 miles. Not until the third test flight on 31 May did the missile achieve its full design 1,600-mile range. The rest of the test programme went relatively smoothly, which allowed the USAF to take delivery of its first Jupiters in August 1958, the missiles being deployed in bases in Turkey and Italy. Three combat training launches were conducted at Launch Pad LC-26A. Two by Italian crews and one by a Turkish one.
11 See: Defense Technical Information Center, apps.dtic.mil/sti/citations/ADA122341.
12 Medaris, *op. cit.*, p. 253.
13 Raborn, oral history (1972), no. 1, p. 22
14 *Ibid.*, p. 23.
15 *Ibid.*, p. 70.
16 Watson (ed.), *Adventure in Partnership: The Story of Polaris*, p. 6.
17 Sheenan, *A Fiery Peace in a Cold War*, (2011), p. 433.
18 Sarnoff, *Life*, 6 June 1960, p. 112.
19 Burke, oral history (1972), p. 11. Burke clarified by saying forty was not a magic number, but the maximum number that one man can handle. He later commented that he thought with the benefit of hindsight that twenty was possibly a better estimate.
20 Congressional Record—Senate 1961:15639/1963:799.

21 Raborn, *op. cit.,* p. 58. 'Merrill had a boat lying in Chesapeake and he went down there and played around on that boat for two weeks, and he decided that he was going to get out and go into civilian life. I, of course, was appalled by this and told him, "you've just queered two weeks leave for anybody else." I'll never give anybody two weeks to think about their troubles. One week, max!'

22 US Naval Institute Merrill Biography.

23 Smith had been instrumental in developing a 5-inch rocket with an anti-tank shaped charge warhead which saw operational use in Korea.

24 Raborn, *op. cit.,* p. 58.

25 Merrill, oral history (1997), no. 3, p. 177.

26 *Ibid.,* p. 176

27 Pehrson, oral history (1974), pp. 35–36.

28 Shugg, *op. cit.,* p. 17.

29 Raborn, *op. cit.,* no. 1, p. 52.

30 Sapolsky, *The Polaris System Development* (1972), pp. 94–130.

31 ADM Levering Smith meeting notes (author's collection).

32 Polmar & Allen, *Rickover: Controversy and Genius (*1982), p. 551.

33 Quoted by ADM J. B. Colwell. Pehrson, *op. cit.,* p. 50.

34 William F. Whitmore, the SP's chief scientist, was to suggest that the appointment should be 'the senior guy who will be fired if it doesn't work'.

35 Pehrson, *op. cit.,* pp. 39–40.

36 Raborn, *op. cit.,* no. 1, p. 30.

37 Draper and his team were to go on to develop the guidance units for NASA's Apollo Program.

38 Wildenberg, T., *Hot Spot of Invention* (Naval Institute Press: Annapolis, 2019*),* p. 128.

39 Duffy, R. A., 'Charles Stark Draper, 1901–1987. A Biographical Memoir', *Biographical Memoirs*, Vol. 65, Ch. 6 (National Academy of Sciences), p. 144.

40 Wildenberg, T., 'Armaments & Innovation: Inertial Navigation Made Ballistic-Missile Submarines a Reality', US *Naval History* magazine, Vol. 32–3, June 2018.

41 Wildenberg, *op. cit.,* pp. 167, 168.

42 Raborn, *op. cit.,* no. 1, p. 32.

43 The original wooden test item can be seen in the Sands Space History Center.

44 Department of the Navy, CNO Personal No. 36, 2 April 1958.

Chapter 6

1 The USN had to wait for the naming of the later Trident SSBNs to adopt this protocol.

2 *The New York Times*, 29 April 1965, p. 34 and *The Times*, 30 April 1965, p. 19.

3 JFK Library: JFKPOF/084/JFKPOF-084-013, p. 0088, and CHUR 2/509, Image 65. Kennedy to Churchill, 27 March 1962.

4 Churchill Papers, CHUR 2/509/55. Lady Churchill to Macmillan, 4 April 1962.

5 JFK Library, *op. cit.,* p. 0085.

6 Churchill Papers, CHUR 2/509/52. de Zulueta to Antony Montague Brown, 3 May 1962.

7 For more information see: Mark A. Bradley, US Naval *Proceedings*, July 1998, Vol. 124/7/1,145.

8 Shugg oral history (1973), p. 5.

9 *Ibid.,* p. 15.

10 Gates oral history (1984), p. 34.
11 Rockwell, *The Rickover Effect* (1992), p 259.
12 Ward, oral history (May 1985–July 1987), no. 6, p. 360.
13 *Ibid.*, p. 378.
14 *Missiles and Rockets*, 4 April 1960, p. 13.
15 Press release, 'Remarks by Mrs. Lyndon B. Johnson, Charleston, South Carolina, 10/7/1964', 'Mrs. Johnson—Speeches', Reference File, LBJ Presidential Library, accessed 15 August 2022, www.discoverlbj.org/item/ref-ctjspeeches-19641007-1920.

Chapter 7

1 The crane, nicknamed the 'German Crane', was originally used to lift U-boats out of the water.
2 *An investigation of the Jetevator as a means of Thrust Vector Control*, LMSC 1958.
3 Gates, oral history (1984), p. 24.
4 Raborn, 'The Polaris Missile', *Ordnance*, Vol. 44, No. 235 (July–August 1959), pp. 44–48.
5 Boyd, Capt. G. M., USNI, Proceedings, August 1962, Vol. 88/8/714. *Polaris Test Ship.*
6 *RAF Flying Review,* June 1960, p. 18.
7 *Ibid.*, and also, May 1961, p. 13.
8 *Your Washington Review*, Congressman Jerry Ford, 18 March 1960.
9 *Washington Post*, Obituaries, 16 March 2011.
10 Pehrson, oral history (USNI, 1974), p. 40.
11 Ward, oral history (1985–July 1987), p. 381.
12 Until the *Ethan Allen* was launched, the Second World War Japanese aircraft-carrying *I-400*-class submarines were the longest ever built at 400 feet. The *Ethan Allen* was 410 feet long.
13 Daniel, *The End of an Era* (2003), p. 158.
14 *Missiles and Rockets*, 21 November 1960, p. 11.
15 Ward, *op. cit.*, p. 382.
16 JFKNSF-301a-003, pp. 14–17.
17 Hansen, *U.S. Nuclear Weapons* (1988), p. 85.
18 *Orlando Sentinel*, 20 May 1961, p. 13.
19 JFKOH-KHD-01. Kurt Debus interview, 31 March 1964.
20 John F. Kennedy, 16 November 1963, *Polaris Missile Launch Photo Book.*
21 *Aviation Week*, 4 September 1961.
22 *Missiles and Rockets*, 13 August 1962, p. 15.
23 *Augmenting the Polaris System*, Aerojet General Corporation, Sacramento, California, 1964.
24 The National Academy of Sciences Tribute to Burriss.
25 *US Nuclear Tests*, p. 35, also Hansen, *op. cit.*, p. 88.
26 Countermeasures to Soviet air defences were, of course, nothing new. In 1958, the USAF had deployed the McDonnell ADM-20 Quail decoy. This was a small slab-sided missile powered by a General Electric J-85 engine which proved problematic in service. It was designed to mimic a B-52 to Soviet radar defences, thereby confusing Soviet radars and allowing the SAC bombers to get through to their targets.
27 Killian, *Sputnik, Scientists, and Eisenhower* (1977), p. 92.

28 Wertheim, oral history (1981), no. 2, p. 137.
29 *Ibid.*, no. 3, p. 188.
30 *Ibid.*, no. 2, p. 137.
31 *Ibid.*, no. 3, p. 189.
32 Letter Rickover to Bloch, 'At sea on the USS *Haddock*. 25 September 1967.'
33 The *Public Papers of the Presidents*; Eisenhower, 3 April 1958.
34 National Security Archive, *Electronic Briefing Book No. 275*, edited by William Burr.
35 In February 1943, Twining and fourteen others had survived for six days in life rafts near the New Hebrides Islands after their PBY had ditched in the sea on the way from Guadalcanal to Espiritu Santo.

Chapter 8

1 Stuart W. Symington interview, John F. Kennedy Library, JFK, no. 2, 9/4/1964.
2 Boyle was the first officer who had been trained at the RAF College founded by Lord Trenchard, the 'Father of the Royal Air Force'.
3 Menaul, *Countdown* (1980), p. 123.
4 Eisenhower Library, United Kingdom (2), Box 14.
5 Prestwick was for long believed to be the only part of the British mainland on which Sgt Elvis Presley set foot. This was to be refuted, however, when rock 'n' roll singer Tommy Steele admitted to taking the singer on a secret trip to London.
6 TNA, DEFE 19/75. Letter from Prime Minister's Secretary to Foreign Minister's Secretary, 21 June 1960.
7 TNA, PREM 11/2778.
8 *The Times*, 5 December 1960, p. 4.
9 NSA, Telegram DoS Letter Eisenhower to Macmillan, 15 July 1960.
10 *Ibid.*, October 1960.
11 TNA, ADM 205/222.
12 TNA, ADM 1/29347. FSL to BJSM, 29 July 1960.
13 These additional locations were Invergordon, where the Royal Navy had an existing facility and Loch Ewe. Neither site was considered secure enough, although Loch Ewe would largely satisfy Macmillan's concerns about a 'frightful accident'. Nor were England and Wales excluded from the survey, Falmouth and Milford Haven being the candidates. Eisenhower, however, was adamant that it was to be a base on the Clyde. The southern side of the estuary was too close to Glasgow and major conurbations. Rothesay Bay on the Isle of Bute was considered, as submarines of the Royal Navy's Third Submarine Flotilla, traditionally based in Scottish waters, had only recently vacated it and moved its (conventional) submarines and the depot ship HMS *Adamant* to Faslane on the Gare Loch. The economic effects of their departure and the developing package holiday industry were being sorely felt by the population of Bute, a traditional watering hole for Glasgow holidaymakers. This move may well have ruled out the Gare Loch as a US option as the presence of two navies would have concentrated the inevitable opposition, especially when nuclear submarines joined the Royal Navy. The base at Rothesay had associated operations at both the Holy Loch and Loch Long and the move released the Holy Loch. Close to Dunoon and nearer the open waters of the Clyde estuary this seemed to fulfil the necessary requirements.
14 TNA, ADM 1/29347, *f.* 14.
15 TNA, ADM 1/29347. Eisenhower to Macmillan, 27 October 1960.

16 *Daily Worker*, 5 November 1960.
17 TNA, ADM 205/222.
18 HoC Debate, 1 November 1960, vol. 629, c39.
19 NSA, Merchant to SoS, 9 January 1961.
20 *New York Times*, Obituary, 6 July 2009.
21 Messersmith, *The American Years: Dunoon and the US Navy* (2003), p. 19.
22 TNA, ADM 1/27201.
23 *Missiles and Rockets*, 21 November 1960, p. 11.
24 *Ibid.*, 4 April 1960, p. 13, also, *The Times*, 4 April 1961, p. 3.
25 Ward, oral history (May 1985–July 1987), p. 392.
26 *Glasgow Herald*, 15 May 1961, p. 8.
27 TNA, ADM 1/29347.
28 *The Times*, 4 April 1961, p. 3.
29 *Ibid.*, 3 November 1981, p. 4.
30 USNI, Proceedings, January 1966, Vol. 92/1/755, *Proteus—Polaris Pioneer*, Capt. L. C. McCarty.
31 www.tartanregister.gov.uk/tartanDetails?ref=3350. The tartan consisted of the following colours: the navy blue represents the naval uniform, the dark green the depth of the oceans, and the royal blue and gold overchecks represent the 'Blue' and 'Gold' crews.
32 *The New York Times*, 16 March 1963, p. 3.
33 Spaven, *Fortress Scotland* (1983), p. 33. fn. Also, *The Sunday Standard*, 29 August 1982.
34 Brochure of the Tenth Annual Polaris Trophy Weekend Regatta.
35 'The Cuban Missile Crisis and its implications for Scotland today', John Ainslie, Scottish CND, October 2012.
36 HoC Debate, 22 November 1962, vol. 667, c1402.
37 Hastings, *Abyss* (2022), p. 360.
38 Gates, oral history (1984), p. 34.
39 *The Times*, 7 March 1961, p. 6.
40 The USS *Shasta* had also been used to test various Polaris instruments using a dummy missile attached to her keel.
41 Messersmith, *op. cit.*, p. 22.
42 *All Hands*, December 1985, p. 20.
43 Neubauer, J., USNI *Proceedings*, May 1963, Vol. 89/5/723, USS *Hunley* (AS-31).
44 National Archives, Records of the Joint Chiefs of Staff, Record Group 218 (RG 218), Maxwell Taylor Files, box 36, Nassau/Jupiter/Skybolt/MLF (Folder # 1).
45 US Embassy Turkey telegram 1270 to State Department, 17 April 1963, Confidential.
46 Ellis received the Legion of Merit 'for exceptional meritorious conduct as Commanding Officer in support of forward deployed Polaris submarines'.
47 *The Scotsman*, 22 April 1988.
48 *The Times*, 2 December 1970, p. 11.
49 CIA cable. Scowcroft to Kissinger, 3 November 1974.
50 *The Times*, 15 April 1963, p. 6.
51 *The New York Times*, 7 May 1981.
52 *The Times*, 25 April 1981, p. 13.

Chapter 9

1 Proceedings of the SPO STG, 43rd Meeting, 27–28 May 1964.
2 *Aviation Week*, 30 April 1962, p. 31.
3 Hearings before the Subcommittee on International Organization and Disarmament Affairs of the Committee on Foreign Relations. US Senate. Confidential hearing held on 16 May 1969.
4 MIT/IL Press release, SIS-62, 1 April 1966.
5 Sir Frank Cooper conversation at Charterhouse Nuclear History Conference 1997.
6 Dommett correspondence.
7 Wertheim, oral history (1981), no. 4, p. 267.
8 Oral history transcript, Joseph A. Califano, interview 20 (XX), 1/28/1988, by Michael L. Gillette, LBJ Library Oral Histories, LBJ Presidential Library, accessed 13 August 2022, www.discoverlbj.org/item/oh-califanoj-19880128-20-11-74.
9 *Inside: A Public and Private Life.* Joseph A. Califano Jr. BBS Public Affairs. New York. 2004.
10 UPI Release—Levering Smith file SP-104.
11 MIT/IL, *op. cit.*
12 Wertheim, *op. cit.*, no. 2, p. 222.
13 *Ibid.*
14 *The New York Times*, 15 August 1968, p. 18.
15 *Ibid.*, 16 August 1968, p. 42.
16 Telegram US SECSTATE to US Embassy in London, 5 May 1971.
17 *The New York Times*, 4 August 1970, p. 1.
18 *Aviation Week*, 3 September 1973, p. 16.
19 Department of Defense Appropriations for Fiscal Year 1974, Part 3.

Chapter 10

1 Messersmith, *The American Years: Dunoon and the US Navy* (2003), p. 101.
2 Oliver, *Against the Tide* (2014), p. 88.
3 See: cimsec.org/chief-of-naval-operations-zumwalts-project-60-part-1/.
4 US Senate Committee on Armed Services. 25 March 1971, p. 894.
5 *Ibid.*, p. 896.
6 Zumwalt, *On Watch* (1976), p. 63.
7 Rockwell, *The Rickover Effect* (1992), p. 388.
8 *The New York Times*, 12 January 1971.
9 *Ibid.*, 11 May 1973, p. 12.
10 The Vietnam War had put ever increasing pressure on McNamara and differences with Johnson began to emerge. After resigning as secretary of defense, he went on to head the World Bank.
11 VADM Smith private correspondence, 12 November 1980 (author's collection).
12 Warner was later to become the sixth husband of actress Elizabeth Taylor.
13 Zumwalt draft copy given to VADM Smith, p. 31 (author's collection).
14 Nixon Presidential Library. Status Report on the Activities of the Office of Science and Technology, 8 December 1970.
15 Smith's handwritten notes on Zumwalt draft, p. 33 (author's collection).

16 Whitham, C., *Leverage, Leaks and Liabilities: Holy Loch and the Special Anglo-American Nuclear Relationship, 1960–65*, presentation at annual meeting of the Society for Historians of American Foreign Relations, College Park, MD, 24 June 2005.
17 *Sanity. Voice of CND*, 1977, No, 5, pp. 9 & 10.
18 *The Sunday Post*, 10 November 1991, p. 3.
19 *The Sunday Times*, 10 November 1991, pp. 1–3.
20 *The Herald*, 25 February 1998.
21 Personal Invitation Card (author's collection).
22 Letter. Nixon to Smith, 30 March 1972.
23 Personal Invitation Card (author's collection).
24 *Washington Post*, VADM Smith Obituary, 9 April 1993.

Chapter 11

1 Probert, *High Commanders of the Royal Air Force* (1991), p. 26.
2 HoC Debate, 12 May 1948, Vol. 450, c2117.
3 American physicist Robert Serber was also scheduled to be included as an observer, but forgot his parachute and was not allowed to board the aircraft. He was later to be one of the first Americans to enter both bombed cities.
4 www.churchillarchive.com/explore/page?contextId=CHUR+5%2F21A%2F1-68#image=15.
5 Gowing and Arnold, *Independence and Deterrence: Britain and Atomic Energy 1945–1952*, Vol. 1: Policy-Making (1974), p. 350.
6 *The Sunday Times*, 23 January 1983.
7 HoL Debate, 23 October 1952, vol. 178, cc933.
8 The RAF's stopgap Boeing Washington B.1s were not nuclear capable, lacking the 'Saddletree' modifications. The original 'Silverplate' code name had been compromised.
9 Aylen, J., 'First Waltz: Development and Deployment of Blue Danube, Britain's Post-War Atomic Bomb', *The International Journal for the History of Engineering & Technology*, 85:1, 31-59.
10 TNA, AIR 27/2646/1. The squadron was not so successful with their second delivery which proved to be unserviceable for some weeks.
11 TNA, AIR 27/2781.
12 The B-36 had been designed as a long-range bomber capable of return missions to Europe in the event that Germany won the war. The first B-36A (44-92004) was delivered to 7th BG at Carswell AFB on 26 June 1948.
13 The USAF announced the production of the XB-52 on 28 November 1951.
14 Zuckerman, *Nuclear Illusion and Reality* (1982), p. 84
15 Defence: Outline of Future Policy, HMSO: London. Cmnd 124.
16 NSA, Briefing Paper, Macmillan Talks, Washington, 23–25 October 1957, 'Increasing Availability of Nuclear Technology, Materials, and Weapons', MTW 1/2, 21 October 1957, Secret.
17 NSA, Memorandum for the Files, 'Macmillan Talks—U.S.-U.K. Atomic Weapons Cooperation', 24 October 1957, Top Secret.
18 Zuckerman, *Monkeys, Men and Missiles* (1988), p. 234.
19 Watkinson, *Turning Points* (1988), p. 188.
20 Mountbatten Archive. Burke to Mountbatten, 11 April 1960.
21 *Flight*, 22 July 1960, p. 115.

22 'On this day in Air Force History', Air Force Historical Foundation, 28 March 2018.
23 HoC Debate, 22 June 1960, Vol. 625, c 395.
24 Mountbatten Archive, BA J311.
25 Watkinson, *op. cit.*, p. 171.
26 Mountbatten Archive, *op. cit.* Kennon to Mountbatten 17 November 1960.
27 Baker, *Dry Ginger* (1977), p. 164.

Chapter 12

1 The first Atlas-D squadron, 576 SMS, had been activated in September 1959 to give interim capability.
2 So against Polaris was Watkinson that a plastic model of Polaris acquired by one of his staff on a visit to America was removed, on his instructions, from the MoD. Pincher, C., *Inside Story* (Sidgwick and Jackson: London, 1979), p. 299.
3 JFK Library, Zuckerman Oral History Interview—JFK, no. 1, 8/5/1966.
4 Lord Wigg commented on Macmillan's government: 'I imagine he really enjoyed turning the Cabinet Room into a slaughterhouse butchering traditional Tory monuments like Lord Chancellor Kilmuir and playing the game of Family Favourites by promoting inconsequential nonentities. He played politics rough and he was a ruthless debater.' Lord Wigg, *George Wigg* (Michael Joseph: London, 1972).
5 *The Independent*, Watkinson obituary, 23 October 2011.
6 TNA, DEFE 13/410. F.24. Ormsby Gore to Foreign Office, 12 December 1962.
7 Baker, *Dry Ginger* (1977), p. 170.
8 TNA, ADM 1/28839. Minute, 22 December 1962.
9 Zuckerman, *Six Men out of the Ordinary* (1992), p. 149.
10 JFK Library, Zuckerman Oral History Interview—JFK, no. 1, 8/5/1966.
11 Zuckerman, *Monkeys, Men and Missiles* (1988), p. 254.
12 JFKOH-HAB-06/JFKOH-HAB-06-TR.
13 Baker, *op. cit.*, p. 170.
14 NSA Memorandum of Conversation, 'Skybolt', 19 December 1962.
15 JFKPOF-042-013-p0001.
16 Eisenhower Library, United Kingdom (2), Box 14.
17 JFK Library, Thorneycroft Oral History Interview—JFK, no. 1, 6/19/1964.
18 Zuckerman, *op. cit.*, p. 265.
19 See Boyes, J., *Project Emily. Thor IRBM and the RAF* (Stroud: The History Press, 2008).
20 Pincher, *op. cit.*, p. 299.
21 ACM Sir Philip Joubert de la Ferte, *New Scientist*, 5 March 1959, p. 506.
22 *Aviation Week*, 4 February 1963, p. 37, and 11 February, p. 28.
23 HoC Debate, 9 April 2019, vol. 658, c389.
24 HoC Debate, 26 February 1964, vol. 690, cc477/8.
25 Divine, *The Broken Wing* (1966), p. 366.
26 Lord Wigg, *op. cit.*
27 *Ibid.*
28 Joint Meeting of the Foreign Defense Ministers, 5 May 1962, COSMIC Top Secret.

Chapter 13

1 JFKPOF-042-013-p0001.
2 *Missiles and Rockets,* 4 March 1963, p. 9.
3 HoC Debate, 30 January 1963, vol. 670, c965.
4 *Ibid.,* 1963, vol. 670, c984.
5 To distinguish him from 'Black' Mackenzie, another successful submarine commander.
6 McKaig had been on the navy's 'Dry List' for shore appointments but had just been given command of HMS *Manxman,* working up at Chatham for deployment to Singapore. It was a short-lived command.
7 Baker later sought permission for DPT members to wear the submariner's tie. He received a brusque reply from Flag Officer Submarines, Admiral Sir Horace Law. 'No, you're a lousy lot of b******s and I've added a bend sinister'—a heraldic device denoting illegitimacy.
8 Daniel, *The End of an Era* (2003), pp. 155–156.
9 Ward, oral history (1987), p. 364.
10 Wrongly identified by Daniel as the *Charles Adam.*
11 Daniel, *op. cit.,* p .157.
12 TNA, ADM 1/28839, f. 130/1.
13 *Ibid.,* f.133.
14 *Ibid.,* f.140.
15 *Your Washington Review,* Ford, 15 January 1958.
16 Eisenhower Library. Quarles to Eisenhower, 13 May 1959, Declassified Documents Fiscal Year 2011.
17 *Ibid.* Gates to Eisenhower, 26 June 1959.
18 TNA, ADM 1/28839. f.305/6.

Chapter 14

1 *U-1406* and *U-1407* had both been scuttled in Cuxhaven harbour by *Oberleutnant sur Zee* Gerhard Grumpfelt against the order of his senior officers. He was tried by the British Military Court at Hamburg on 12–13 May 1946 and sentenced to seven years' imprisonment, subsequently reduced to five years on appeal.
2 Evans, H., *Vickers Against the Odds 1956–1977* (Hodder & Stoughton: London, 1978), pp. 70–71.
3 Horlick, Sir T., 'Submarine Propulsion in the Royal Navy', *Proceedings of the Institution of Mechanical Engineers,* Vol. 196, No. 7, p. 67.
4 US Naval Institute, *Proceedings,* Vol. 107/3/937, March 1981, p. 16.
5 US Senate Committee on Armed Services, 25 March 1971, p. 902.
6 Ziegler, *Mountbatten* (1985). p. 559.
7 *Ibid.,* p. 558. Captain Denys Wyatt to Commander Robin Bousfield.
8 Vice-Admiral Sir Robert Hill. The Thomas Lowe Gray Memorial Lecture presented to the Institute of Mechanical Engineers, 19 April 2005.
9 *The Daily Inter Lake, Montana,* 2 October 1957, p. 6.
10 Ziegler, *op. cit.,* p. 560.
11 *The Scotsman,* 7 October 1957.
12 The designation stands for: Submarine, 3rd Generation Design, Westinghouse.

13 TNA, DEFE 19/50.
14 TNA, ADM 116/641.
15 Baker and Rydill, *The Building of the Two Dreadnoughts*, Proceedings of the Third Shipbuilding History Conference, 1983, p. 19.
16 HMS *Dreadnought* was the 295th submarine built in the Barrow shipyard. A total 264 of these were for the Royal Navy, four for the RAN, twelve for European allies, and four for the Turkish navy. The remaining eleven were for other countries prior to 1938.
17 *The Times*, 20 May 1960.
18 Shore, *Vickers' Master Shipbuilder*, (2011), p. 113.
19 Cumbria Archive Service. BDSO 15 Barrow Trades Council.
20 The narrow roads in the north of Scotland presented many problems for the large vehicles carrying equipment to the site. The steep hairpin bend at the village of Berriedale presented a particular hazard.
21 Daniel, *The End of an Era* (2003), pp. 201–202.
22 TNA, ADM 1/29347.
23 The Royal Navy used the term Fleet Submarine rather than the more evocative Hunter-Killer to emphasise the SSNs integration into the fleet rather than perhaps being seen as a separate arm of service.
24 TNA, ADM 1/29347. Admiralty to CBNS Washington, 29 November 1963.
25 Rockwell, *The Rickover Effect* (1992), p. 314.
26 Baker, *Dry Ginger* (1977), p. 170.
27 TNA, ADM 1/28839. Washington to Foreign Office, 8 January 1963
28 Menaul, *Countdown* (1980), p. 117.
29 TNA, CAB 128/36 Pt 2.
30 TNA, ADM 1/28839. f.232.
31 HoC Debate, 30 January 1963, Vol. 670, c935.
32 *Ibid.*, 4 March 1963, Vol. 673, cc107/8.
33 *Ibid.*, 27 February 1964, Vol. 690, c656
34 The Dumbarton Testing Tank was built in 1882–3 to a design by naval architect William Froude. It is believed to have been the first such facility in private hands and also the oldest such construction in the world.
35 TNA, ADM 1/28839, f. 28.
36 TNA, ADM 1/28839.
37 Nailor, *The Nassau Connection* (1988), p. 32.
38 TNA, ADM 1/28839, f. 153/3.
39 Mr Ian Orr-Ewing, civil lord to the Admiralty, HoC Debate, 30 January 1963, vol. 670, cc935.
40 TNA, ADM 1/28839, f. 155.
41 The names were put forward by Mountbatten for approval by the queen. The names were not revealed, as was the tradition, until the actual launch.
42 Shore, *op. cit.*, p. 133.
43 *Ibid.*
44 Mackenzie, *The Sword of Damocles* (1995), p. 223.
45 Shore, *op. cit.*, p. 143.
46 HoC Debate, 1 March 1955, vol. 537, c1894.
47 *Ibid.*, 12 November 1963.
48 United Kingdom, Meetings with Wilson, 03/02/1964, Country Files, NSF, Box 213, LBJ Presidential Library, accessed 19 August 2022, www.discoverlbj.org/item/nsf-cf-b213-f04.

49 *Ibid.*
50 The CO of HMS *Renown* Cdr Mike Jones told the author that *Churchill* was considered at one stage, but this would have broken the 'R' names and the name was later given to an SSN.
51 HoC Debate, 26 February 1964, vol. 480, and Zuckerman, p. 374.
52 HoC Debate, 23 November 1964, vol. 702, c923.
53 TNA, CAB 148/19.
54 HoC Debate, 15 February 1965, vol. 706, c817.
55 Memos to the President, NSF, Box 5, LBJ Presidential Library, accessed 19 August 2022, www.discoverlbj.org/item/nsf-memos-b05-f03.
56 HoC Debate, 23 November 1964, vol. 702, c929
57 *The Times,* 10 February 1965.
58 Zuckerman, *Monkeys, Men and Missiles* (1988), p. 356.
59 Bhabha, a bachelor, was interested in promoting young struggling artists. He suggested to Zuckerman that his young artist friends could produce some tiles to adorn Zuckerman's bathroom in his house at Burnham Thorpe. Zuckerman accepted the gift and invited Bhabha to inspect the tiles on his next visit to the UK. The visit, sadly, never took place. Bhabha's plane crashed into a snow-covered mountain on approach to Geneva Airport. An event that some believe was an assassination instigated by the CIA to hinder India's bomb programme.
60 *The Times,* 19 May 1966, p. 10.
61 This lack of supervision was highlighted when a skilled worker inadvertently entered the wrong submarine and opened a valve resulting in partial flooding of the submarine. Unattributable source.
62 HoC Debate, 19 October 1966, vol. 734, c44W.
63 Daniel, *op. cit.,* p. 192.
64 *The Mail* (Barrow-in-Furness), 20 June 2018.
65 NWEM, 15 September 1966.
66 *The New York Times,* 24 September 1966, p. 4.
67 Pincher, *Inside Story* (1978), p. 301.
68 www.channel4.com/news/trident-nuclear-deterrent-review-polaris-itn-archive.
69 *Daily Express,* 10 November 1967.
70 HoC Debate, 14 February 1968, vol. 758, c1330.
71 *The Times,* 9 January 1968, p. 2.
72 *The Palm Beach Post,* 5 February 1968.
73 *Chicago Tribune,* 24 December 1967.
74 *The Orlando Sentinel,* 29 October 1967.
75 *The Times,* 16 February 1968, p. 1.
76 *Ibid.*
77 Moore, *The Impact of Polaris* (1999), p. 247.
78 Letter Mckenzie to Smith, 8 March 1968 (author's collection).
79 Email, Cdre T. Elliott, 2 December 2018.
80 When HMS *Conqueror* left for the South Atlantic during the Falklands War, extra food had to be taken and tins were lined up on the decks and the crew had to walk on top of them. Gradually the deck appeared again as they ate their way through the contents.
81 Correspondence, Cdre T. Elliott, October 2022.
82 *Ibid.*
83 *Daily Express,* 31 January 1967, p. 1.
84 *The Times.,* 1 February 1967, p. 11.
85 *Daily Express,* 31 January 1967.

86 *The Times*, 27 February 1967, p. 2.

87 *Church Times*, 3 March 1967.

88 *Ibid.*

89 *Birkenhead News and Advertiser*, 1 March 1967.

90 *The Daily Telegraph*, Obituary, 19 January 2015.

91 *The Times*, 15 October 1969, p. 1.

92 HoC Debate, 3 December 1969, vol. 792, c1485.

93 *The Daily Telegraph*, Obituary, 19 January 2015.

94 NWEM, 4 November 1967.

95 Shore, *op. cit.*, p. 171.

96 *Orlando Sentinel*, 20 April 1969, p. 15.

97 *The Times*, 16 March 1968.

98 *Revenge*, booklet produced by Cammell Laird & Co.

99 *Brevard Sentinel*, 20 May 1970, p. 1.

100 Letter Le Fanu to Smith 16 June 1970. Le Fanu was nominated to be the next CDS after MRAF Sir Charles Elworthy, but he was unable to take up the post because of his illness. Promoted to admiral of the fleet in July 1970 on his retiral, he died on 28 November of the same year (author's collection).

101 Daniel, *op. cit.*, p. 194.

102 Signal from HMS *Revenge* to RUENAAA/CNO, 18 June 1970.

103 *The Times*, 28 June 1969, p. 1

104 *Ibid.*, 15 January 1970.

Chapter 15

1 BBC *Good Morning Scotland*, 9 May 2014.

2 *The Times Obituary*, 9 November 2007.

3 TNA, ADM 1/28839.

4 HoC Debate, 24 April 1963, vol. 676, c219.

5 *The Times,* 25 April 1963.

6 HoC Debate, 24 April 1963, vol. 248, cc1206.

7 Spaven, *Fortress Scotland*, (1983), p. 131.

8 *The Times*, 2 August 1961, p. 15. Metal Industries Ltd: Report and Accounts to 31 December 1960.

9 *Ibid.*, 25 April 1963, p. 12.

10 The Ministry of Works had been renamed the Ministry of Public Buildings and Works in 1962 and had taken over the Works Departments of the three services.

11 HoC Debate, 16 June 1964, vol. 696, cc172-4W.

12 *Ibid.*, 5 July 1965, vol. 715, cc1113.

13 Meaning 'dark gorge' or 'armpit' in Gaelic.

14 *The Times*, 4 April 1967.

15 HoC Debate, 24 April 1967, vol. 745, cc1134.

16 Pincher, *Inside Story* (1978), p. 58.

17 *Ibid.*, p. 305.

18 FOI 2023/03217,

19 *Daily Express*, 10 May 1968, p. 3.

20 *Orlando Sentinel*, 10 March 1968, p. 13.

21 Email, Cdre T. Elliott, 3 November 2022.

22 *Navy News*, August 1977, p. 33.

Chapter 16

1   *Star Gazette*, 14 February 1973, p. 2.
2   *Illustrated London News*, 1 October 1976, p. 73.
3   HoC Debate, 25 July 1978, vol. 954, cc1364.
4   *UK Defence Journal*, 5 April 2019.
5   *The Times*, 15 August 1978.
6   *Ibid.*, 28 April 1981.
7   *The Sunday Post*, 5 July 1981.
8   *The Times*, 9 May 1981.
9   *Ibid.*, 8 May 1981, p. 23.
10 *Lessons of a factory occupation*. Redline (Contemporary Marxist Analysis), 19
    November 2019.
11 *Daily Express*, 11 October 1988, p. 1.
12 *The Scotsman*, 30 December 2016, p. 1.
13 *Faslane: Diary of a Peace Camp* (1984), p. 53.

Chapter 17

1   SPO STG Meeting Minutes, 27–28 May 1964.
2   en.wikipedia.org/wiki/Sary_Shagan, retrieved 12 April 2023.
3   TNA, CAB 134/3120. PN(67), 1 December 1967, p. 5.
4   Dommett, various correspondence with the author.
5   CIA August 1970, *Soviet ABM Defenses: Status and Prospects*, p. 11.
6   SPO STG Meeting, *op. cit.*
7   Benn, *The Benn Diaries 1963–67* (1988), 6 December 1966, p. 99.
8   ARL was originally created in 1943 as the Airfield Radio Laboratory, changing to
    the Airfield Research Laboratory before its final change of name in 1954.
9   *Daily Express*, 7 December 1967, p. 1.
10 HoC Debate, 14 December 1967, vol. 756, c619.
11 Dommett, *op. cit.*
12 Zuckerman, *Monkeys, Men and Missiles* (1988), p. 387.
13 *The New York Times*, 9 May 1967, p. 1.
14 HoC Debate, 13 June 1967, vol. 748, c299.
15 NSA, DoS Memo: Meeting in Dr Foster's Office on US/UK Nuclear Cooperation,
    4 September 1969.
16 Ninth Report from the Committee of Public Accounts Session 1981–82, p. 11.
17 *The New York Times*, 11 September 1973, p. 19.
18 HoC Debate, 4 March 1970, vol. 797, c406.
19 Zuckerman, *op. cit.*, p. 387.
20 *Sunday Times*, 7 May 1972, Wigg, p. 34.
21 NSA, 'Forthcoming Visit of Prime Minister Heath: Possible Request for Poseidon',
    30 January 1973, Top Secret.
22 TNA, FCO 30/1744. Telegram to Palliser, 5 February 1973.
23 Memorandum of Conversation between Kissinger, Schlesinger and Scowcroft, 5
    September 1973.
24 Pincher, *Inside Story*, (1979), p. 207.
25 Memorandum of Conversation between Kissinger and Schlesinger, 8 January
    1974.

26 NSA memorandum to Kissinger, 'UK Polaris Improvement Project', 9 January 1974. NPL, NSC Files, box 731, United Kingdom, Vol. IX, October 1973.

27 Cynics thought the name was chosen to upset the navy when they took over the project. Chevaline was a broken-down old horse fit only for the knacker's yard.

28 Walker, *British Nuclear Weapons and the Test Ban 1954–1973* (2010), p. 269.

29 HoC, Debate, 24 June 1974, vol. 875, c989.

30 HoC Debate, 18 November 1965, vol. 720, cc1332.

31 newsvote.bbc.co.uk/mpapps/pagetools/email/news.bbc.co.uk/onthisday/hi/ dates/stories/june/24/newsid_2526000/2526963.stm.

32 Coker, J. Private correspondence, 2020–2022.

33 NSA, Memo, Kissinger to Ford, January 1975.

34 MAF fuels came in a variety of types. Von Braun had used MAF 4 in the Jupiter 'C' to provide the extra boost to reach orbital velocity in the launch of the Explorer satellites.

35 *Aviation Week*, 16 June 1980.

Chapter 18

1 Dommett, British Library oral history interview, pt 13.

2 Dougherty, K., & Serra, J-J., *Hypersonic Research at Woomera* (Vancouver, Canada, 2004).

3 HoC Debate, 24 January 1980, vol. 977, cc681-2.

4 *Aviation Week*, 4 February 1980.

5 *Daily Express*, 25 January 1980, p. 2.

6 *Navy News*, February 1982.

7 *Los Angeles Times*, 10 June 1985.

8 *AP News*, 10 June 1985, and *Orlando Sentinel*, 19 June 1985.

9 HMS *Revenge* PEM DASO instruction folder (author's collection).

10 TNA, CAB 134/3120, PN(67), 1 December 1967, p. 6.

11 *The Times*, 1 July 1981, p. 15.

Chapter 19

1 Rickover was meticulous in his requirements for these voyages, specifying items from a full set of khakis without insignia, a blue foul weather jacket with his name and the submarine's name attached to it, his full menu requirements, submarine's named stationery including 500 plain envelopes, and full communications facilities. On one occasion the zip on his khaki trousers would not work and thereafter an open fly would be referred to as 'admiral's prerogative'.

2 Rickover sent handwritten letters to the families of the crew. Meticulous in his approach to this, he checked and re-checked the names and addresses and gave it to someone else to check yet again. Nevertheless, a few mistakes still remained. Years later, he heard that people had said, 'You'd think he'd at least taken the trouble to do it right.' Rockwell, T., *The Rickover Effect* (USNI: Annapolis, 1992), p. 318.

3 Coker, J., Charterhouse-on-Air, July 2020.

4 For further information on the *Thresher* disaster see Polmar, N., USNI *Naval History* magazine, 'What Killed the Thresher?' April 2023 and Bryant, J., Best, F., Ricci, R., Walsh, S., and Wulfekuhle, N., USNI, *Proceedings,* 'Was the Thresher ready for Sea?' April 2023, Vol. 149/4/1/1,442.

5   Oliver, *Against the Tide* (2014), p. 44.
6   *Daily Express*, 11 June 1974, p. 2.
7   HoC Oral Answers, 2 July 1974, vol. 876.
8   HoC Debate, 3 December 1969, vol. 792, c1485
9   CIA Archive, www.cia.gov/readingroom/docs/
    CIA-RDP02-06341R000302420010-6.pdf.
10 Translated from www.ntv.ru/novosti/1751197.

Chapter 20

1   TNA, DEFE 25/335, Folio 3.
2   *Mail Online*, 12 September 2023. This lengthened patrol emphasised the problems
    placed on a four-SSBN fleet. In this case, only HMS *Vengeance* and HMS *Vigilant*
    were available as the other two SSBNs were out-of-service for maintenance and
    refits.
3   HoC Debate, 2 November 2010, vol. 693W.
4   *Report to Congress on Stockpile Reliability, Weapon Remanufacture, and the Role
    of Nuclear Testing*, October 1987, Lawrence Livermore Radiation Laboratory.
5   *Ibid.*
6   *Daily Express*, 5 December 1991, p. 10.
7   HoC Debate, vol. 2010, c349W.
8   *The Scotsman*, 11 December 1991.
9   HoC Debate, 1 February 1996, vol. 270, c1147.
10 *The Scotsman*, 21 June 1993, p. 1.
11 *Ibid.*, 14 May 1996, p. 4.
12 *Daily Express*, 29 August 1996, p. 12.
13 *Ibid.*, 14 May 1996, p. 15.
14 *Daily Telegraph*, 6 November 2010, also HoC Written Answers, 2 November
    2010, c693W
15 *Forces Net*, 24 January 2022, and *Navy Lookout*, 2 February 2022.
16 *Edinburgh Live*, 19 June 2022.

Chapter 21

1   *The New York Times*, 18 January 1961, p. 17.
2   Ward, oral history (1985–July 1987), p. 415.
3   *The New York Times*, 25 January 1963, p. 1.
4   For full details, see nsarchive.gwu.edu/document/30184-document-14-department-
    defense-briefing-book-mr-gilpatrics-visit-rome-11-12-february. Downloaded 21
    April 2023.

Epilogue

1   Rockwell, *The Rickover Effect* (1992), p. 363.
2   Watkinson, *Turning Point* (1986), p. 114.
3   'A Military Commander Surveys the Nuclear Arms Race', *International Security*,
    Vol. 4, No. 3.

4 Russell, B. C., USNI *Proceedings*, November 2018, 'Learn from the Fleet Ballistic Missile Program'.

5 Sapolsky, *The Polaris System Development* (1972), p. 233. The copy of his book given to Smith records inside the front cover: 'To Admiral Smith with my sincere appreciation and respect' (author's collection).

6 Wildenberg, *Hot Spot of Invention* (2019), pp. 217–220.

7 *Los Angeles Times*, 27 February 1993.

Bibliography

Unpublished Papers, Brochures, etc.

HMS Dreadnought, Launch brochure, Vickers-Armstrongs (Shipbuilders) Ltd
HMS Revenge, PEM DASO Booklet, July 1986
Hot Line, The American Intelligence Association, 1972
Strategic Systems Project Office Organizational Roster—September 1975
Tenth Annual Polaris Trophy Weekend Regatta, Brochure, 1971
Trajectory, Winter 1960–61, Lockheed Missiles and Space Division Office of Public
   Relations
United States Steel, Special Report, Polaris Missile—Our Newest Deterrent

Newspapers, Magazines, and Journals

All Hands, December 1985, September 1960. The Bureau of Naval Personnel
   Information Bulletin
Aviation Week
FBM ... the first forty years, Lockheed Martin
Flight Archive
Life, 3 April 1970
Proceedings, Annapolis, USNI
Prospero, Nos 1, 2, 3, & 5, British Rocket Oral History Programme, 2004–2008
Sanity, Voice of CND, 1977, No. 5
Spaceflight
Submarine Squadron Fifteen
The Daily Express
The Illustrated London News, 1 October 1976
The New York Times
The Rocket, eNewsletter of the Westcott Venture Park
The Scotsman
The Telegraph
The Times
Warship IFR, July and August 2012
Warship World, Vol. 10, No. 4, March–April 2007
The Washington Post

Articles and Published Documents

Arkin, W. M., and Handler, J., *Naval Accidents 1945–1988* (Washington D.C.: Greenpeace/Institute for Policy Studies, 1989)

Augmenting the Polaris System (Sacramento, California: Aerojet General Corporation, 1964)

Aylen, J., 'First Waltz: Development and Deployment of Blue Danube, Britain's Post-War Atomic Bomb', *The International Journal for the History of Engineering & Technology*, 2015

Baker, Sir R., and Rydill, L. J., 'The Building of the Two Dreadnoughts', *Proceedings*, Third Shipbuilding History Conference, 1983

Boyd, Capt. G. M., 'Polaris Test Ship', *Proceedings*, August 1962, Vol. 88/8/714 (Annapolis: USNI, 1962)

Burnell, B., *Polaris, PIP, Chevaline, a Different View of History* (2017)

Dictionary of American Naval Fighting Ships, Vol. 1 (1959), *Vol. 2* (1963), *Vol. 3* (1968) (Naval History Division, Washington)

Dougherty, K., and Serra, J-J., 'Hypersonic Research at Woomera: Falstaff—the Unclassified Story', Astronautical Congress 2004 (Vancouver, Canada)

Duffy, R. A., 'Charles Stark Draper', *Biographical Memoirs* (National Academy of Sciences, 1994)

Edwards, S. S., and Parker, G. H., *An Investigation of the Jetevator as a means of Thrust Vector Control* (LMSC, February 1958)

Fleet Ballistic Missile Program. Sixtieth Anniversary 2015 (Washington, DC: Strategic Systems Programs, US Navy, 2015)

Fuhrman, R. A., 'The Fleet Ballistic Missile System: Polaris to Trident', *AIAA*, Vol. 15, No. 5, 1978

Grimwood, J. M., and Strowd, F., *History of the Jupiter Missile System* (US Army Ordnance Command, 27 July 1962)

Hill, Vice-Admiral Sir R., *Admiral Hyman G. Rickover USN and the UK Nuclear Submarine Propulsion Programme* (Institution of Mechanical Engineers, 2005)

Horlick, Vice-Admiral Sir T., 'Submarine Propulsion in the Royal Navy', *Proceedings of the Institution of Mechanical Engineers*, Vol. 196, No. 7

Inactivation Ceremony, USS *George Washington Carver*, 21 October 1992.

'Interrogation of German Personnel from WVA, Kochelsee', *Engineering Report No. 2442* (The Glenn L. Martin Company, 3 September 1946)

Lavery, B., 'The British government and the Polaris Base in the Clyde', *Journal of Maritime Research*, September 2001

McCarty, Capt. L. C., *Proteus: Polaris Pioneer* (USNI, *Proceedings*, January 1966, 92/1/755)

McGeogh, I., *The British Polaris Project. A study of the British Naval Ballistic Missile System (BNBMS) Its Origins, Procurement and Effect* (Edinburgh University M. Phil Thesis, 1975)

Nims, Lt Cmdr W. E., 'Floating Dock for Polaris', *The Military Engineer*, Vol. 55, No. 363, pp. 24-25

Norris, R. S., and Cochran, T. B., *United States Nuclear Tests: July 1945 to 31 December 1992* (Washington, DC: Natural Resources Defense Council, 1994)

Nuclear Information Service, various documents

Playing with Fire. Nuclear Weapon Incidents and Accidents in the United Kingdom (Nuclear Information Service, February 2017)

Polmar, N., 'Polaris a True Revolution', USNI *Proceedings*, June 2006

Priest, A., 'In American Hands: Britain, the United States and the Polaris Nuclear Project 1962–1968', *Contemporary British History*, 19:3, 3653-376

Raborn, RADM W. F., 'The Polaris Missile', *Ordnance*, Vol. 44, No. 235 (July–August 1959), pp. 44-48; 'An Historical Review of The Interviews on the subject of Polaris' (Annapolis: USNI)

Robb, T., 'Antelope, Poseidon or a Hybrid: The Upgrading of the British Strategic Nuclear Deterrent, 1970–1974', *JSS*, Vol. 33, pp. 797–817, December 2010

Rosenberg, D. A., 'The Origins of Overkill', *International Security*, Spring 1983, Vol. 7, No. 4

Special Technology Course (Navpapers 92845) (Dam Neck, Virginia: US Naval Guided Missile School, May 1964)

Stoddart, K., 'The British Labour Government and the development of Chevaline, 1974–79', *Cold War History*, Vol. 10, 2010/3

Stuart S. M., *Polaris Fleet Ballistic Missile Program* (California: RPJ Associates, 1977)

The Fleet Ballistic Missile System (Lockheed Missiles and Space Company, Inc. Undated)

'The History of the UK Strategic Deterrent: The Chevaline Project', RAeS, *Proceedings*, 2004

Walker, J. R., 'British Nuclear Weapons Stockpiles; 1953–1977, *RUSI Journal*, Issue 4, 2021

Wright, D., 'And then there were two: The Polaris A3TK Penetration Aids Carrier (PAC)', *Contemporary British History*, 11:4, pp. 119–122

Young, K., 'The Royal Navy's Polaris Lobby 1955–62', *Journal of Strategic Studies (JSS)*, Vol. 25-3, 2002

Zuckerman, Lord S., *The Nuclear Shadow* (London: The Menard Press, 1983)

USNI Oral Histories

ADM Arleigh A. Burke
CAPT. John B. Colwell
ADM William F. Raborn
Carleton Shugg
CAPT. Grayson Merrill
Pehrson, Gordon
RADM Norvell G. Ward
RADM Robert Wertheim

Books

Arnold, L., and Smith, M., *Britain, Australia and the Bomb* (Basingstoke: Palgrave Macmillan, 2006)

Baker, R., *Dry Ginger. The Biography of Admiral of the Fleet Sir Michael Le Fanu* (Letchworth: The Garden City Press, 1977)

Betts, L., *Duncan Sandys and British Nuclear Policy-Making* (Basingstoke: Palgrave Macmillan, 2016)

Bivens, A. C., *Of Nukes and Nosecones* (Baltimore: Gateway Press, 1996)

Campbell, D., *The Unsinkable Aircraft Carrier* (London: Michael Joseph, 1984); *War Plan UK* (London: Burnett Books, 1982)

Close, F., *Trinity* (UK: Allen Lane, 2019)

Crane, J., *Submarine* (London: BBC, 1984)

Curtola, J. M., *Autumn of our Discontent: Fall 1949 and the Crises in American National Security* (Annapolis, Maryland: Naval Institute Press, 2022)

Daniel, R. J., *The End of an Era* (Penzance: Periscope Publishing, 2003)

Divine, D., *The Broken Wing* (London: Hutchison, 1966)

Dornberger, Maj.-Gen. W., *V2* (Lindon: Hurst and Blackett,1954) (Translated from the original '*Der Schuss ins Weltall*' published in Germany in 1952)

Dunion, K., (ed.) *Faslane: Diary of a Peace Camp* (Edinburgh: Polygon Books, 1984)

Evans, H., *Vickers Against the Odds 1956–1977* (London: Hodder & Stoughton, 1978)

Freedman, L., *Britain and Nuclear Weapons* (London: The Macmillan Press, 1980)

Friedman, N., *Submarine Design and Development* (London: Conway Maritime, 1984); *British Submarines in the Cold War Era* (Barnsley: Seaforth Publishing, 2021)

Goodwin, D. K., *Lyndon Johnson and the American Dream* (New York: St Martin's Griffin, 1991)

Hall, K., *The Clyde Submarine Base* (Stroud: Tempus Publishing, 1999); *Polaris* (Cheltenham: The History Press, 2018)

Hansen, C., *U.S. Nuclear Weapons: The Secret Story* (New York: Aerofax Inc., 1987)

Hastings, M., *Abyss* (London: William Collins, 2022)

Hennessey, P., *Cabinets and the Bomb* (Oxford: Oxford University Press, 2007)

Hennessey, P., and Jinks, J., *The Silent Deep: The Royal Navy Submarine Service since 1945* (Allen Lane, 2015)

Hervey, Rear-Admiral J., *Submarines Volume 7* (London: Brassey's (UK), 1994)

Hill, C. N., *A Vertical Empire*, second edition (London: Imperial College Press, 2012)

Hölsken, D., *V-Missiles of the Third Reich: The V-1 and V-2* (Sturbridge, Massachusetts: Monogram Aviation Publications, 1994)

Jones, K., and Kelley, Jnr, H., *Admiral Arleigh (31-Knot) Burke* (Annapolis, Maryland: Naval Institute Press, 2001)

Kaplan, E., *To Kill Nations* (Ithica: Cornell University, 2015)

Killian, Jnr, J. R., *Sputnik, Scientists, and Eisenhower* (Cambridge, Massachusetts, and London: The MIT Press, 1977)

Lipscomb, Cdr F. W., *The British Submarine* (Greenwich: Conway Maritime Press, 1975)

Mackenzie, Sir H., *The Sword of Damocles* (Portsmouth: RN Submarine Museum, 1955)

McCullough, D., *Truman* (Simon and Schuster, 1992)

McManus, J. P., *A History of the FBM System* (Lockheed Missiles & Space Company Inc., 1989)

Medaris, Gen. J. B., *Countdown to Decision* (London: Putnam Publishing, 1960)

Menaul, S., *Countdown. Britain's Strategic Forces* (London: Robert Hale 1980)

Messersmith, A., *The American Years: Dunoon and the US Navy* (Glendaruel: Argyll Publishing, 2003)

Moore, Dr R., *The Royal Navy and Nuclear Weapons* (London: Frank Cass Publishers, 2001); *Nuclear Illusion, Nuclear Reality* (Basingstoke: Palgrave Macmillan, 2010)

Nailor, P., *The Nassau Connection* (London, HMSO, 1988)

Navias, M. S., *Nuclear Weapons and British Strategic Planning 1955–1958* (Oxford: Clarendon Press, 2004)

Oliver, RADM D., *Against the Tide* (Annapolis, Maryland: Naval Institute Press, 2014)

Pastore, M., and Munck, P., *First Patrol: A Chronicle at the dawn of Polaris missile submarine patrols* (Independently published, 2020)

Paterson, R. H., *Britain's Strategic Nuclear Deterrent* (London: Frank Cass & Co., 1997)

Pincher, C. H., *Inside Story* (London: Sidgwick & Jackson, 1987)

Polmar, N., and Allen, T. B., *Rickover: Controversy and Genius* (New York: Simon and Schuster, 1982)

Pringle, P., and Arkin, W., *SIOP* (London: Sphere Books, 1983)

Probert, H., *High Commanders of the Royal Air Force* (London: HMSO, 1991)

Ramos, T., *From Berkeley to Berlin: How the Rad Lab helped avert Nuclear War* (Annapolis, Maryland: Naval institute Press, 2022)

Rees, E., *The Seas and the Subs* (New York: Duell, Sloan and Pearce, 1961)

Rickover, Admiral H. G., *Eminent Americans. Namesakes of the Polaris Fleet* (Washington: US Government Printing Office, 1972)

Rockwell, T., *The Rickover Effect* (Annapolis, Maryland: Naval Institute Press, 1992)

Rubel, J. H., *Reflections on Fame and Some Famous Men* (Santa Fe: Sunstone Press, 2009)

Sapolsky, H. M., *The Polaris System Development* (Cambridge, MA: Harvard University Press, 1972)

Sheenan, N., *A Fiery Peace in a Cold War* (Random House Inc., 2011)

Shepley, J., and Blair, Jnr, C., *The Hydrogen Bomb* (London: Jarrolds Publishers (London) Ltd., 1955)

Shore, L. M., *Vickers' Master Shipbuilder* (Lydney: Black Dwarf Publications, 2011)

Spaven, M., *Fortress Scotland* (London: Pluto Press, 1983)

Stoddart, K., *Losing an Empire and Finding a Role* (Basingstoke: Palgrave Macmillan, 2012)

Stumpf, D. K., *Minuteman* (Fayetteville: University of Arkansas, 2020); *Regulus: The Forgotten Weapon* (Kentucky: Turner Publishing Company, 1997)

Von Braun, W., and Ordway III, F. I., *History of Rocketry and Space Travel* (London: Thomas Nelson & Sons Ltd, 1967)

Walker, J. R., *British Nuclear Weapons and the Test Ban 1954–1973* (Farnham: Ashgate, 2010)

Watkinson, H., *Turning Points. A Record of Our Times* (Salisbury: Michael Russell, 1986)

Watson, Commander C. H., (ed.) *Adventure in Partnership: The Story of Polaris* (Connecticut: Danbury, undated)

Weir, G. E., *Forged in War* (London: Brasseys, 1998)

Wildenberg, T., *Hot Spot of Invention. Charles Stark Draper, MIT, and the Development of Inertial Guidance and Navigation* (Annapolis, Maryland: Naval Institute Press, 2019)

Wigg, Lord G., *George Wigg* (London: Michael Joseph, 1972)

Yates, R. F., and Russell, M. E., *Space Rockets and Missiles* (New York: Harper & Bros, 1960)

Ziarnik, B. D., *To Rule the Skies* (Annapolis, Maryland: Naval Institute Press, 2021)

Ziegler, P., *Mountbatten* (London: Collins, 1985)

Zuckerman, Sir S., *Monkeys, Men and Missiles* (London: Collins, 1988); *Nuclear Illusion and Reality* (London: Collins, 1982); *Six Men Out of the Ordinary* (London: Peter Owen, 1992}

Zumwalt, Jnr, E. R., *On Watch* (New York: Quadrangle Books,1976)

Index